CORE CONCEPTS

BUSINESS LAW

William H. Eldridge

Assistant Professor of
Business Law and Marketing

Kean College of New Jersey

SOUTH-WESTERN College Publishing

An International Thomson Publishing Company

Copyright © 1995
by South-Western College Publishing
Cincinnati, Ohio

ISBN: 0-538-83869-8

1 2 3 4 5 6 D1 9 8 7 6 5 4

Printed in the United States of America

Acquisitions Editor: Christopher Will
Production Editor: Robin Schuster
Cover Design: Lamson Design

I (T) P
International Thomson Publishing
South-Western is an ITP Company. The ITP trademark is used under license.

Library of Congress Cataloging-in-Publication Data

Eldridge, William, 1947–
    Core concepts of business law / William Eldridge.
        p.   cm.
    Includes index.
    ISBN 0-538-83869-8
    1. Business law—United States.   I. Title.
KF889.3.E434   1995
346.73'07—dc20
[347.3067]   94-38383
                                                         CIP

Contents

PART I

INTRODUCTION

Chapter 1

General Legal Concepts

- The American legal system is heavily influenced by the English legal system, which is built on judges' decisions about what the law is when applied to specific factual situations. This is known as common law.

- The decisions of courts are known as precedents and are followed by judges in deciding subsequent cases based on similar facts.

- Law is also derived from legislation passed by bodies such as Congress or state legislatures. These acts of legislation are known as statutes. A statute will override common law if there is a conflict.

- Business law is primarily about relationships between and among people with respect to their business dealings. Therefore, most business law falls within the classification of civil law.

- Civil law covers a broad range of topics dealing with all aspects of business relationships among people. These topics include contracts, disputes over commercial paper, organizing a business, bailments, agency, wills, creditor/debtor relationships, and other business matters.

- Contracts are legally enforceable agreements between two or more people and are the building blocks for all business relationships among people.

THE AMERICAN LEGAL SYSTEM

As most students learn in secondary school, the American legal system is built on the federal and state constitutions. These consitutions establish the foundation for the laws and regulations that govern our lives. Constitutions establish a framework for the duties of judicial and legislative bodies, which regulate the conduct of individuals and establish guidelines for commercial relationships.

However, prior to the existence of the United States, the American colonies were governed by the British system of law, a system heavily influenced by judges appointed by the crown. As these judges traveled throughout the empire, they would issue opinions deciding specific factual situations presented to them. These decisions began to be written down and distributed to lawyers and others who were interested in the areas of law discussed in the decisions.

These decisions are used to guide other judges in similar factual situations. Decisions, particularly those of higher courts, are called precedents, and allow lawyers to determine the law for their clients. This entire process of judge-made law affecting the legal system is known as the **common law.** After American independence, judges continued to be guided by previous opinions, and new opinions also became precedent for future situations.

- Ann offers Betty two dresses for $400. Betty responds that she will purchase one dress for $200. This is called a counteroffer, and according to common law, it terminates Ann's original offer. Ann does not need to respond to Betty and may cancel the original offer from her without legal liability. The court would rule in favor of Ann and make its decision public. ∎

General Legal Concepts

Once this decision is announced, it becomes part of the common law. It will be used as precedent by future courts and may be used by lawyers to guide their clients with respect to similar situations. One of the reasons why attorneys draft lengthy agreements is because they are aware of court decisions and try to protect their clients from any negative consequences that might occur in the future.

The state legislature may decide to override the court's decision in the case of Ann and Betty by passing a statute requiring that a "reasonable" counteroffer be accepted or at least be responded to in a reasonable manner. This is within the legislature's jurisdiction. Some legislatures have changed court rulings with respect to goods, which are widely marketed, tangible, movable items such as refrigerators, television sets, and other household appliances.

Laws passed by Congress or state legislatures are called statutes. If there is a conflict between a court decision and a statute, the statute will prevail. Courts, however, interpret the statutes written by legislatures.

Most statutes are written rather broadly. Courts have the responsibility for determining the actual intent of the legislature. In addition, the breadth of most statutes allows courts to interpret them with a view toward changing circumstances.

Most of the fundamental terms in our great legal documents are also rather vague. Concepts such as due process or equal protection are quite broad in scope and their meaning must be interpreted by the courts and the legislatures.

Statutes relating to business are not usually as broad, although they may still be rather ambiguous. The function of the courts is to interpret and apply these statutes to the relationships among the parties.

Criminal Law and Civil Law

Most students are familiar with the idea of criminal law, which imposes sanctions for certain acts. Indeed, most of the literature and popular entertainment about the law has been built around criminal law. Violations of criminal law include killing other human beings, stealing money or valuables, or driving while intoxicated. These are all acts for which one can be punished by fine or imprisonment.

The constitutional protections of due process, right of counsel, and trial by jury are applicable to criminal cases. But most issues involving businesses fall into the category of civil law, which governs relationships between and among people.

■ Suzy Student has a dispute with Larry Landlord about their lease. This is a civil law issue involving matters of contracts as well as real estate and rental laws. ■

■ Charlie's Chevrolet is damaged in Peter's Parking Palace. The issue of liability is another civil law question to be determined by the law of bailments, which relates to the responsibility to safeguard the property of others in one's control. ■

■ Heather endorses a check to Holly given to her by Frank. If Frank's account has no money, Heather's potential liability to Holly will be determined by the laws relating to commercial paper (checks). ■

With the exception of certain laws governing the specific conduct of business, most of this book deals with civil law, which determines how issues between and among people will be resolved. In a few areas, both criminal and civil law are involved.

■ Horatio drives a truck for XYZ Corporation. He drives while intoxicated and smashes into a car driven by Nancy. In this case, Horatio may be charged with drunken driving. In addition, XYZ may be liable under the laws relating to agency and the legal responsibility a principal has for acts of an agent. ■

Contracts: Foundation of Civil Law

Chapter 4 begins the discussion of contracts, which forms the basis for much of our system of civil law. Contracts are agreements enforceable by law. As such, contracts become a way of determining the rights and duties of people conducting business transactions.

As you shall see, a contract must be definite to be legally enforceable. A contract establishes the basis of the duties of each person who is party to the agreement. If contractual duties are not performed, the injured party may recover damages (amounts of money) from the party failing to perform his or her duties.

This remedy permits the courts to enforce the performance of contracts and their obligations. As a result, the vast majority of contracts are completed in accord with their provisions.

■ A lease is a type of contract. If there is a dispute about its terms, or about the rent, the dispute can be resolved through reference to laws relating to contracts. ■

For hundreds of years, the English-American common law governed all contracts. All agreements with respect to land, services, and tangible, movable items were covered by judge-made law.

Legal experts began to question the common law as it applied to the sale of goods (tangible, movable items) and recommended that it be changed. Most U.S. states have passed statutes changing the common law as it applied to the sale of goods. As a result, the law governing these agreements is now subject to the Uniform Commercial Code.

In this book we will review how a common law contract is formed, the elements necessary for a legal contract, and the remedies available if the contract is not performed. We will also examine the provisions relating to a contract for the sale of goods under the Uniform Commercial Code.

Other chapters in this book discuss several areas of commercial relationships among people. These include discussions of how businesses are organized, how they are regulated by governments, and how governments try to protect consumers. In addition, the book looks at the laws relating to relationships between a principal and the person who represents her (an agent).

Other topics include the laws relating to the transfer of commercial paper such as checks and promissory notes. Laws relating to property, creditor/debtor liabilities, insurance, wills, trusts, accidents, insurance, international business relationships and professional liability are also discussed.

The book also discusses bankruptcy, a topic of interest to many people in a troubled economy. Bankruptcy provides a "fresh start" for individuals and corporations. The federal Bankruptcy Code contains provisions allowing for both the liquidation of assets and the restructuring of debt. These are examined in Part 6. Other laws applicable to debtor/creditor relationships are also discussed.

Core Concepts Reviewed

- Common law is the history of court decisions which has formed much of English-American law through the centuries.

- A precedent is a court decision that will guide future courts on similar facts.

- Statutes are laws established by a legislative body.

- Criminal law consists of laws that prohibit specific types of conduct and provide penalties for their violation.

- Civil law is the body of law governing private rights and duties and remedial actions among people. Most business law falls within the classification of civil law.

- Contracts are enforceable agreements for which the law will provide remedies for lack of performance.

Questions

1. Discuss the differences between civil and criminal laws with which you are familiar.
2. Discuss any civil law type of transaction into which you have entered.
3. What types of contracts have you agreed on?
4. How is a statute different from common law?
5. Describe the provisions of any contract into which you have entered.
6. What are precedents and how do they relate to the concept of common law?
7. What are the advantages of checks? What should be the liability of each of the parties to the check? (The answer is found in Chapter 17.)

8. How do parties distribute property to future generations? (The answer is found in Chapter 13.)
9. What are the advantages of filing for bankruptcy for a debtor? (The answer is found in Chapter 20.)

A Preview of Business Law Problems

1. Sally has a contract with Sam, who does not perform the duties they had agreed on. Should Sally have any legal remedies? What should they be? (The answer is found in chapter 10.)
2. Mary parks her car in the parking garage at Don's Department Store. If her automobile is damaged, should she have a remedy against Don? What if she kept her keys? What if she gave them to a parking attendant? (The answer is found in chapter 12.)
3. Bert and Bertha enter into a partnership to sell bagels. What are their responsibilities to each other? (The answer is found in chapter 26.)
4. If Eddie wants to form a business, how could it be organized? (The answer in found in chapters 26 and 27.)
5. Sarah agrees to work for Polly. What are Polly's responsibilities for Sarah's activities? (The answer is found in chapter 23.)
6. Franklin is quite elderly and employs Mary to take care of him in his declining years. Mary convinces Franklin to leave all of his assets to her. Franklin's family is quite upset, and they wonder if they have any legal remedies. Should the family have a legal remedy? (The answer is found in Chapter 13.)

Chapter 2

Court Systems and Alternative Dispute Resolution

- A court is the location where legal disputes are normally resolved.
- Courts may grant either legal relief or equitable relief.
- Legal relief is the granting of money damages for an injury suffered by the plaintiff.
- Equitable relief compels the defendant either to perform or not perform a particular act.
- Alternative dispute resolution began in order to resolve disputes that had been delayed in the court systems. The two most common types are arbitration and mediation.

COURT SYSTEMS

The vast majority of the nation's legal disputes are resolved in this nation's state courts. Routine criminal and civil matters, for example, are resolved in state courts, which are normally divided into criminal and civil sections. In the criminal sections, the courts hear those cases relating to acts for which sanctions are imposed by society. These acts range from minor traffic violations and petty crimes to serious common law felonies such as robbery or murder. Civil sections resolve cases between and among people about private rights, disputes, and remedies. Contracts create rights and obligations between the parties. If one party does not perform his or her obligations as stated in the contract, the other party may bring a legal action.

This action may seek legal remedies like financial reimbursement, or ask for **equitable relief** like an **injunction** or a **decree of specific performance.** An injunction is a court order that states that a person may not perform a particular act. A decree of specific performance will compel the defendant to complete the duties under the contract.

Levels of Courts

State court systems are divided into different levels. Municipal courts hear petty offenses like traffic violations or minor criminal matters. In recent years, drunk driving litigation and minor drug-related offenses have also fallen within the jurisdiction of municipal courts.

The next level is often called the county or superior court. These courts hear major criminal matters such as **misdemeanors** or **felonies** for which the defendant could be sent to prison. It is at this level that defendants are entitled to trial by jury and to receive the assistance of competent counsel.

Alleged violations of local zoning ordinances or other laws by businesses are heard at the municipal level.

- Sam owns a video store in the town of East Overshoe. The local building inspector observes a neon sign in the front window. He believes the sign violates the local sign ordinance and issues a citation. If Sam is found guilty, he must pay a fine and remove the sign. ■

■ Frank does not pay unemployment or payroll taxes for a year. He is charged by the state government as a disorderly person. Frank pleads guilty, and agrees to pay the amount due over the next five years. He is placed on parole and agrees to report to his probation office regularly until the debt is paid. If he violates parole or does not pay his debt, he must appear before the municipal court. ■

More serious crimes relating to businesses will be heard in a higher-level court.

■ XYZ Corporation employees dump waste materials into the local reservoir. This is a felony under state law. The state's attorney general brings felony charges against the employees. This case will be heard in superior or county court. ■

Civil cases will also be heard in different courts. While municipal courts will hear few, if any, civil cases, minor claims against another party may be heard in small-claims courts. Larger claims will be heard in higher-level courts.

The average businessperson is likely to encounter a contractual claim brought by another. A contract is a legally enforceable agreement. If one party does not perform the contractual duties, the other party will have to seek relief.

■ Ollie has a contract with Stanley to sell his car for $15,000. Later, Ollie refuses to sell the car to Stanley. Stanley then buys a similar make and model for $17,500. Stanley may bring a legal action to place him in the same position he would have been in if Ollie had completed the sale. Stanley will be able to recover $2,500. ■

■ Gore has a contract with Hillary to buy a guitar once owned by Elvis Presley. Hillary refuses to perform the contract. Gore may bring an equitable action in state superior court to recover the guitar. Because the guitar is a unique item, the court will grant a decree of specific performance which will compel Hillary to sell the guitar to Gore. ■

A tort is an action that causes damage to property or to a person. Torts can bring about serious injuries to people, which can result in substantial monetary awards.

■ Sally drives an automobile over a curb and crashes into Herbert's house. She not only damages the house, but she also injures little Lucy, who was standing in the front door. Sally was driving on behalf of ZBX Corporation at the time and was delivering packages to its customers.

Lucy and her parents bring a legal action to recover for Lucy's injuries and for the damage to the house. They name both Sally and ZBX as defendants. Because Sally was an agent for ZBX, both she and her employer will be liable for the torts to the house.

Lucy and her parents recover $50,000 for the damage to the house and $100,000 for Lucy's injuries. Fortunately, ZBX was insured and the insurance company pays the $150,000 to Lucy's parents. Sally has no money and pays nothing. ■

■ NMO Corporation and LTX Corporation are competitors in the patio furniture business. The senior officials of NMO contact the customers of LTZ Corporation and tell them that the furniture of LTZ Corporation will warp if left out in the sun. This violates the fair competition laws of the state.

The state statute provides that any party injured by unfair competition may recover three times the damages for any injuries that may result. The statute also provides that the injured party may obtain an injunction to stop such conduct. LTZ Corporation brings an action to recover damages and for equitable relief. The Superior Court grants the injunction and awards LTZ Corporation $300,000. ■

In each state, there is an appellate court above the lower level courts. The function of the appellate court is to review the rulings of the lower courts. It is quite common for appellate courts to reverse the rulings of lower courts. Businesspeople should realize that if they lose at the lower court level, they should be prepared to appeal to a higher level.

■ Jones has an agreement for the sale of goods to Smith. There is a dispute about the agreement. Jones brings an action against Smith. The lower court rules that the agreement did not constitute an enforceable contract under common law. However, Jones's lawyer advises him that the judge should have ruled that the agreement was covered under the Uniform Commercial Code because it was for the sale of goods. Jones appeals and the appellate court rules that the agreement did consistute a legally enforceable contract. ■

■ Simmons makes a sudden stop while entering a major highway. Baxter, who was riding behind Simmons, crashes into the rear of her automobile. The lower court rules that since Simmons was partially at fault, she is barred from recovering. Simmons' lawyer argues that she should appeal. The appellate court rules that plaintiff's negligence will not bar recovery but will only serve to reduce the amount of recovery. This is known as **comparative negligence** and permits the injured partly to recover damages even if her negligence was party responsible for the accident. ■

The highest court in the state is usually called the supreme court. In New York, it is called the court of appeals. The highest state court considers questions of significance to the Constitution and questions that have been decided differently by the appellate courts.

■ LZX Corporation has been charged with a serious felony. Its senior officers refuse to testify and state that no person may be compelled to testify against himself. Because the state has a constitutional clause similar to the Fifth Amendment of the U.S. Consitution, the case reaches the state supreme court. The state supreme court hears arguments on the issue from both attorneys. The court rules that because a corporation is an "artificial person," neither the Fifth Amendment nor the state provision is applicable. ■

■ One appellate court rules that a plaintiff who was negligent may still recover from the defendant. Another appellate court rules that any negligence will bar recovery. The state supreme court takes a case on similar facts. The court listens to the arguments from both attorneys and it reviews the opinions of both appellate courts. It finally rules that the doctrine of comparative negligence will apply, and the plaintiffs may recover even if they are negligent. ■

In addition to state courts, there are also federal courts. These courts are concerned with questions involving federal law or questions pertaining to parties living in different states.

■ Behemoth Corporation has a 60 percent share of the widget market. It uses its clout with suppliers to discourage them from dealing with Williams Corporation. Williams Corporation brings an action in federal court and claims that Behemoth has violated federal antitrust laws. If it proves its case, it is entitled to three times its actual injuries and it will also be entitled to obtain injunctive relief to restrain similar conduct in the future. ■

■ Mason conducts regular business with Dixon, whose place of business is in another state. One of their contracts is for $100,000,000. Mason and Dixon have a dispute about the contract. The dispute is in excess of $100,000. This would be a case appropriate for the federal courts. ■

Allegations of actions that violate federal law are also heard in the federal courts. Some of these laws are of particular significance to businesspersons who engage in interstate commerce. A corporation that offers its shares of stock to the general public is subject to federal securities laws and the regulations of the Securities and Exchange Commission.

■ HZB Corporation offers securities to the general public. If it violates federal securities laws, it will be charged with a federal crime. If its officers are found guilty, they may spend time in a federal prison. ■

Federal prosecutors have recently made extensive use of the Racketeer Influenced and Corrupt Organization Act (RICO) to pursue organized crime and other corrupt enterprises. This has allowed the federal government to prosecute some unions and other organizations that have been influenced by corrupt practices.

A major area of prosecution for the federal government relates to antitrust matters. The Sherman and Clayton Antitrust Acts prevent conduct that may substantially lessen competition in interstate commerce. The acts permit the Justice Department to delay mergers of companies which may lessen competition and the department may also pursue a variety of remedies to prevent the merger.

■ Largo Corporation holds 60 percent of the market share of the gadget market. It wants to acquire Gongo Gadgets. This would give Largo 75 percent of the gadget market.

The Justice Department brings an action in federal court to prevent the merger. The court grants interim relief to prevent the merger. After hearing the arguments of both sides, the court grants a permanent injunction to prohibit the merger. ■

Antitrust cases can be very complicated matters involving questions relating to economics and commerce. Often, the federal court must review lengthy reports and listen to the testimony of experts.

■ Bitems Corporation has a substantial share of the dog treats market. It wants to acquire Treaties Corporation, which sells both dog and cat treats. The Justice Department brings an action to stop the merger.

Bitems defends on the grounds that, while the merger would give it a substantial share of the dog treats market, it would still have only a relatively small share of the total pet treat market. The court listens to arguments and testimony from both sides as to the differences between the dog and pet treat markets. The court then asks for detailed written reports and oral discussions on the question. Ultimately, the court renders its decision on the issue. ■

The federal courts hear other criminal issues relating to business, including laws relating to environmental and consumer protection. The Federal Trade Commission prohibits deceptive advertising or other fraudulent business practices. Other federal agencies may also order businesspersons to cease certain conduct.

Many businesspersons have been compelled to appear in federal court because of complaints brought by the Internal Revenue Service. Some complaints by the IRS have been proved groundless.

■ Jones has his corporation's tax return prepared by an accountant. The IRS charges Jones with filing a fraudulent return. He faces the possibility of going to federal prison.

At his trial, Jones's lawyer shows that Jones acted in good faith. He also demonstrates that the IRS has misinterpreted its own laws and regulations. Jones is acquitted. ■

The federal court system also has a series of appellate courts that review the decisions of lower courts. Because these courts often review the rulings of federal agencies, they assume special importance in the nation's judicial system.

■ Tom owns a local public access television station. He regularly permits local residents to put shows on the station. He begins to receive complaints about sexually related materials on these local shows. He ignores the complaints until he receives a letter from the Federal Communications Commission stating that the content of these local programs may violate its regulations.

Tom continues to ignore the complaints until he receives an order to appear at a hearing of the FCC. The commission orders that Tom's license be suspended. He appeals the decision in federal court, but the court upholds the FCC's decision. He then appeals the decision to the Court of Appeals, which reverses the decision and restores his license. ■

■ Dawson is a stockbroker who regularly trades in stocks and advises clients about securities. One day he receives a tip about a stock and purchases it for his own account. The stock rises from $10 per share to $20 per share. Dawson earns a profit of $100,000. A few weeks later, Dawson is charged with insider trading. The Securities and Exchange Commission argues that he has violated insider trading laws by being the "tippee" of nonpublic information about a company whose stock was traded on the exchanges.

Dawson is found guilty of insider trading. The case is appealed. After reading written arguments and listening to the attorneys for the commission and for Dawson, the Court of Appeals reverses the conviction. It rules that the commission had misapplied the statutes with respect to Dawson. ■

The highest court in the nation is the U.S. Supreme Court. It has the responsibility for resolving constitutional issues and other cases of significant importance. The Supreme Court also has the responsibility for supervising the activities of the lower federal courts.

The Supreme Court is not required to hear cases unless it chooses to do so. It will grant a hearing if at least four of the nine justices agree that a hearing should be granted.

■ CBT Corporation has been charged with a federal crime. One of the issues raised at the trial is whether the Fifth Amendment, which prohibits mandatory self-incrimination applies to corporations. Although the Supreme Court has previously ruled on this issue, it may want to reconsider the issue. The Court decides that because the federal prosecutors have been vigorous in pursuing corporations, it does want to review the issue. It orders a hearing on the case involving CBT. ■

Alternative Dispute Resolution

Although the federal and state courts are able to resolve the vast majority of cases, there have been a significant number of complaints about the delays in getting cases heard. As a result, some parties are pursuing other avenues for resolving disputes ordinarily heard in the courts. This method is generally known as alternative dispute resolution.

Arbitration is the process of submitting disputes between parties to an impartial person for resolution. The arbitrator then either proposes a solution or renders a decision in the matter.

Arbitration may be either binding or nonbinding. In binding arbitration, the arbitrator listens to the argument of all sides and renders a decision that will bind the parties involved.

■ Slab Boothe plays in the outfield for the New Jersey Bandits. He believes his salary for the new season should be $1,000,000. The Bandits believe his salary should be $600,000. The arbitrator considers the arguments on both sides and rules that Slab's salary should be set at $650,000. If the arbitration is binding, Slab's salary will be $650,000. ■

Nonbinding arbitration allows the parties to take action other than that recommended by the arbitrator. The parties may continue negotiations, stop negotiations, or bring actions in the courts. Binding arbitration is similar to a court judgment. Nonbinding arbitration is more similar to the concept of mediation.

Mediation consists of meetings between the parties attended by a mediator who encourages the parties to keep talking with each other. The mediator may ask the parties questions, ask for papers, or take other actions that would encourage the parties to reach an agreement.

■ Romeo Roberts and Juliet Jones have a disagreement about a contract for the purchase and sale of a parcel of land. They decide to employ a mediator to help them resolve the dispute.

The mediator brings the parties together in a room, and then examines all of the documents relating to the contract. The mediator also receives letters that the two parties have exchanged. The mediator will ask the parties if they have oral evidence to add to the documents. After listening to the parties, the mediator suggests a possible course of action. ■

Some parties, in addition to arbitration and mediation, have begun to hire private judges who may be retired court judges, to resolve disputes. This allows the parties to escape the long delays common to commercial litigation. Usually these judges and commercial arbitrators have special expertise in these areas. The parties can submit documents to the commercial arbitrator or private judge just as if they were in a governmental court.

■ Samson and Delilah have a dispute about a contract relating to a shipment of $10,000,000 of wigs made from human hair. Their lawyers advise them that it would take at least a year to resolve this case through the court system.

They decide to hire a private judge to settle the matter. Each submits the names of three candidates to the other. One name, that of a retired state superior court judge, appears on both lists. They decide to retain her, and Samson and Delilah submit the contract and related documents to her. She reviews the materials, listens to their arguments, and awards Samson $58,000 in damages. ■

Definitions Reviewed

Criminal law refers to the laws and regulations of our society which provide penalties for certain conduct.

Civil laws are the laws related to the rights and responsibilities of private parties.

Appellate courts are courts that hear appeals from the parties not satisfied with decisions and rulings of lower level courts.

An **arbitrator** is a private individual who hears disputes between parties and then issues rulings. The rulings may be either binding or nonbinding.

A **mediator** is a private individual who helps parties resolve disputes.

Supreme court is the highest court in a judicial system.

An **injunction** is a court order that compels a party to cease certain types of conduct.

Specific performance is a court decree that compels a party to complete his or her duties under the contract.

Core Concepts Reviewed

■ Courts are where criminal matters and civil law matters are resolved.

■ Courts may grant legal relief that consists of money damages to one party.

■ Courts may also grant equitable relief, like an injunction or a decree of specific performance.

■ The state courts are divided into different levels. These usually consist of municipal courts, county or superior courts, appellate courts, and a supreme court.

■ Disputing parties may also utilize alternative dispute resolution techniques such as arbitration, mediation, or the hiring of private judges.

Questions

1. Name some levels of state courts.
2. What are misdemeanors and felonies?
3. Name some cases that are heard in a state superior or county court.
4. What are appellate courts?
5. Which cases will be heard in federal court?
6. Why do federal appellate courts assume special importance in our system of justice?

7. Name some federal crimes that are applicable to businesspersons.?
8. What is arbitration?
9. What is the difference between nonbinding and binding arbitration?
10. What is mediation?

Problems

1. Donald has a dispute with Maurice about a contract. The amount of the dispute is $5,000. In which court should this dispute be brought?
2. Roger has a business in the state of New Patz. He believes that a competitor is engaging in illegal conduct that is hurting his business. He should ask the court for what type of equitable relief?
3. Hopkins has a contract to purchase a guitar pick owned by Elvis Presley. The other party refuses to sell the guitar pick to Hopkins. He should ask the court for what type of equitable relief?
4. Simpson has a contract with Bert, who lives in another state. The dispute has a monetary value of more than $100,000. In which court should Simpson bring an action?
5. Malden is contacted by federal law enforcement officials, who tell him they believe he has committed a federal crime. He comes to you for advice. What do you tell him?
6. ZBR Corporation loses a case in federal court and is found guilty of an antitrust violation. The corporation's management believes that it did not commit any violation. What should it do?
7. A federal court convicts NPX Corporation of deceptive advertising. NPX believes that its conviction raises constitutional issues of freedom of commercial speech. What should it do?
8. Benny has a contractual dispute with Bonnie. Benny would like to resolve this dispute in a way that permits them to continue their business relationship. What do you suggest he do?

Chapter 3

Ethics and Social Responsibility

- Much of the law is based on standards of ethics which have evolved through the centuries.

- However, while the law may have been built on the foundation of ethics, reference to ethics alone will not resolve complicated legal issues.

- The laws relating to business are often compromises that attempt to find a balance between private business interests and the public interest.

- Similarly, balancing the interest of private parties is an important element of business law. Laws relating to contracts and employment are an illustration of this principle. The law seeks to balance the interests of the parties to the contract and those of employees and employers.

- More recently, the law has been concerned with issues of the abuse of power and social responsibility. Laws against sexual harassment or against polluting the environment fall into these categories.

PRIVATE ETHICS AND THE LAW

Legal systems are mechanisms for bringing some order to societies of individuals. While it is useful for legal systems to be based on concepts of ethical behavior, justice, and fairness, the law must also be concerned with the need for certainty and order.

Much of American law has been based on concepts of ethical behavior and justice which were derived from religious traditions. While these traditions are appropriate for establishing criminal law, they are less useful in establishing laws governing private business relationships between parties.

However, certain concepts of fairness, good faith, and a commitment to the completion of one's obligations are the foundation of contract law. A person who is injured because the other party to the contract does not perform her obligations has both legal and equitable remedies. The ethical principle behind these remedies is that a person should be held liable for causing damage to another. But it would be unfair to allow the injured party to be placed in a better position than she would have been had the other party performed.

- Sally agrees to sell her car to Mary for $10,000. Sally later refuses to sell the car. Mary buys a similar make and model for $12,000. If she receives $2,000 in damages from Sally, she will be in the same position she would have been in if the contract had been completed. If she receives more than $2,000, she would be in a better position and this would be unfair to Sally. If Mary receives less than $2,000, it would be unfair to her because she would be in a lesser position. ■

Most people would agree that it is unethical to take advantage of a person's mistake or weakened position. On the other hand, the law wants to encourage people to exercise some degree of self-help in the conduct of their business affairs. The common law of contracts seeks to balance these two principles.

- Roger agrees to buy land from Johnson for $25,000. The land was valued at $100,000. At a subsequent trial, the evidence shows that Johnson was intoxicated when he sold the property. The evidence also showed that Johnson was heavily in debt. Roger knew both of these facts.

In this case, Roger has taken advantage of Johnson's weaknesses. The court will set aside the contract on the grounds that Roger has taken **unconscionable advantage** of Johnson. The contract will be set aside. ■

■ Bill asks for bids for a construction project. The bids he received were:
   A bid $50,000
   B bid $51,000
   C bid $49,000
   D bid $28,000
   Bill should recognize that D has made a mistake. If he enters the contract with D, it may be set aside later on the grounds that he knew or should have known of the mistake. It would be unethical for Bill to take advantage of this mistake. ■

■ Harold agrees to build a new office building for Samuels for $1,000,000. When the costs of material and labor increase, Harold argues that he will lose money on the contract and it should be set aside. He also argues it would be unethical for Samuels to take advantage of his "poor deal." The court will not set aside the contract, ruling that Harold should have anticipated a potential increase in costs. ■

In these examples, the law is attempting to balance various ethical principles as well as the interests of various people. Similar principles exist in tort law.

A tort is an act that causes damage to a person or a person's property. An enduring principle under English and American common law is that a person must pay for any injury that he causes. This is the reason that car owners must carry liability insurance on an automobile.

■ Frank runs a stoplight and crashes into Mary's car. Frank ought to pay for any injury to Mary in accordance with the ethical principle that one should pay for harm caused to others. The common law provides that Frank must restore Mary to the position she was in before the accident. Frank must pay for damage to Mary's car, her injuries, and any lost earnings. ■

■ Dr. Sawbones is a practicing surgeon. He takes out Harry's appendix, but leaves a sponge inside Harry's body. An ethical professional will pay for any damage that he causes. Dr. Sawbones is legally liable to Harry. ■

Another ethical principle is that one should not engage in conduct designed to deceive another person. Lying to another has always been regarded as unethical. The law recognizes this principle as it relates to both contracts and torts.

■ Hanson sells Swanson a new car. Hanson replaces the original engine with a much smaller one, but does not inform Swanson before the sale. Hanson's actions amount to fraud, which is the intentional deception of another. Hanson's actions give Swanson grounds to cancel the contract. ■

Fraud may also be a tort if it results in the injury to another. This may result from dishonest advertising or other promotional activities.

■ Jones advertises treated peach pits as a cure for acne. He sells these pits to Johnson for $1,000. Johnson puts these pits on his face. Unfortunately, the pits burn off some of Johnson's skin.

At trial, evidence is introduced that the treated peach pits would not cure acne. Jones is liable both for the $1,000 and for the damage to Johnson's face. Liability exists in both contract and tort law. ■

Another ethical principle relates to the proper use of one's position. Certain people — directors of corporations, agents, trustees, executors, and partners — have an ethical and **fiduciary duty** to conduct their affairs in a manner to benefit others rather than themselves.

■ Don is a director of a corporation. He has the fiduciary responsibility to act on behalf of its shareholders. If he arranges for a large loan to himself at below market rates, he is no longer acting on behalf of the shareholders. He will be liable for any benefits he has received. ■

■ Alan is an agent for Paula. He is instructed to purchase a Chippendale table for Paula for no more than $10,000. He finds a table for $9,000 and pockets the $1,000. This is an unethical action on Alan's part. He is legally liable to refund the required $1,000 to Paula. ■

■ Edward is an executor of Sam's estate. Sam died three months ago. Edward sells some of the land in the estate to himself. This is an improper action. He is not supposed to mix his personal interests with the estate. He will be compelled to return the land to the estate. ■

■ Peter is a partner in the PDZ partnership. He has the responsibility of acquiring land on behalf of the partnership.
  One day, he is offered a piece of land for the partnership. Instead, he buys the land for himself. This is an improper action. Peter is supposed to always work on behalf of the partnership. He will be compelled to return the land to the partnership. ■

ETHICS AND PUBLIC LAW

In addition to conflicts between personal interests, there may be conflicts between private interests and the public interest. This is one reason for the proliferation of governmental agencies formed during the Great Depression.

Among the causes of the stock market collapse and the subsequent depression were unethical private business practices, such as manipulation of the securities exchanges. The 1933 Securities Act and the 1934 Securities Exchange Act were designed to protect public investors from unethical conduct.

■ Dolly is one of the directors of XJT Corporation. She regularly receives information about the company which is not available to the public. If she uses this information to trade in XJT stock, she is engaging in unethical behavior. While this behavior was tolerated prior to the establishment of the Securities and Exchange Commission, it would now violate federal law.
  Insider trading is unethical and illegal because it permits people with greater knowledge to take advantage of members of the general public. These principles

have been extended to include directors, officers, and people who own a significant amount of the company's stock. ■

■ Steve owns a substantial amount of the stock in NYL Corporation. He and some other significant shareholders get together and begin buying and selling the shares in order to increase the market price.

Such manipulation of the stock on a public exchange is also unethical and unlawful. It permits insiders and substantial shareholders to gain an unfair financial advantage over outsiders and smaller shareholders. It would allow private interests to prevail over the public interest. ■

■ Sharp Company are the accountants for Fly by Night Corporation. The corporate officers and Sharp develop fraudulent financial statements, which they place in a prospectus and mail to the public as part of a stock offering. As a result of the offerings, several thousand people lost money.

Before the 1933 Securities Act, this was a common practice. It now violates the act, which requires issuers of public shares to submit financial statements to the Securities and Exchange Commission. The purpose of these statements is to provide the public with adequate information to make an informed decision about the purchase of the securities. ■

Similar laws have been passed to protect the public with respect to the use of drugs and food products. Until the passage of these laws, it was common for sellers to release products that were impure. It was also common for sellers to make exaggerated claims regarding the value of their products.

■ Donald's Drugs sells a skin cream that it states will soften the skin and eliminate fat in the body. The latter claim is false. It is unethical to falsely advertise a product's attributes. ■

This practice was common before the passage of federal and state legislation. In these instances, it was important to place the public interest above the private pursuit of profit.

Society wants people to make and sell products that will benefit consumers. The pursuit of profit is an ethical goal. However, society also wants the products to be safe. Injuries to customers are both costly to society and to the person involved.

Under tort law, a person who is injured by a defect in a product may recover for the injuries. Under strict liability law, the injured party need not show that the manufacturer or the seller was negligent. The injured party only needs to show that a defect in the product caused the injury.

■ Bob buys a new lawnmower at Larry's Lawnmowers. While he is cutting the grass, a wheel flies off and bruises his leg. It is ethical to permit Bob to recover for his injuries from the people who sold him the defective lawnmower. It is also the law. ■

Congress and the various state legislatures have also passed statutes that regulate product safety. The Federal Trade Commission and state consumer agencies are charged with protecting the public safety, meaning that they examine products to ensure that they meet public safety standards. These agencies have the power to stop sales or take other action that would benefit the public if a product is deemed to be harmful.

ETHICS AND THE ABUSE OF POWER

In American society, it is also considered unethical to use one's power in ways that are improper. The issue of **sexual harassment** is primarily one of abuse of power. The abuser is able to use his position to improperly benefit himself rather than the organization.

■ Hank is Betty's supervisor. He regularly makes obscene and lewd remarks to her. This places Betty in a very uncomfortable position. She asks him to stop, but he refuses to do so.

Because Hank's conduct interferes with Betty's work, he is guilty of sexual harassment. In addition, the organization will also be guilty of sexual harassment if it refuses to stop Hank's behavior. Because another ethical principle in our society is that a person is presumed innocent until proved guilty, Betty must bring either a civil or criminal action to stop Hank's activities. ■

A second area of unethical abuse of power relates to discrimination based gender, race, age, ethnic origin or religion. Americans want to believe that we live in a merit-based society. Our standard of ethics asks that people be judged based on merit, not on factors that are irrelevant to their performance. Both the federal and the state governments have passed laws prohibiting improper discrimination.

■ MNL Corporation decides to save money. It believes it can do so by laying off middle- to senior-level managers and workers above the age of 50. This is an unethical and unlawful action. The fired employees may bring an action in either a civil or criminal court to reverse this decision. ■

■ The town of East Overcoat has not hired a nonwhite member of its fire department in 30 years. On its face, this violates both ethical principles and the law. Members of minority groups may bring an action to compel the town to remedy past and current employment practices. ■

The federal government has passed laws outlawing discrimination. It has also attempted to remedy past practices by bringing a number of court actions to compel private and governmental organizations to hire more employees who belong to historically disadvantaged groups. While this has allowed more groups to advance economically, it has also raised new ethical issues.

Correcting past discrimination practices has come into conflict with questions of merit and seniority. All of these positions have some ethical basis.

■ Larry is a member of an ethnic group which has not been promoted in the fire department for the last 20 years. However, Larry ranks 5th in an examination for promotion and he ranks 23rd in seniority if the promotion is done on that criteria. Should he be given priority in terms of promotion? His promotion would help correct past patterns of abuse of power, but it would be "unfair" to other people. ■

Recent abuse of power by law enforcement officers has become a source of concern, because their power is sanctioned by the state. The abuse of power by law enforcement officials is worse than criminal conduct by an "ordinary" citizen because it represents an improper use of power by the "people" against the individual.

> ■ Patrolman Paul arrests a citizen, John, and falsely accuses him of drunk driving. John is found guilty and loses his license for six months and is fined $1,000. Later, it is discovered that Patrolman Paul had falsely arrested dozens of citizens in order to increase his chances for promotion.
>
> It is discovered also that Patrolmen Phil and Peter have been abusing their power by making false arrests. Later evidence indicates that Sergeant Sam had been encouraging such conduct. The superior court orders to overturn every drunk driving conviction in the town from the past five years. ■

The potential for abuse of power by those in law enforcement is one of the reasons that there are protections of individual rights. The Fourth Amendment prohibits unreasonable searches and seizures. This permits law enforcement people to conduct a search of a person's residence or business only if there is probable cause to believe a criminal act will be discovered.

Court rulings regarding this amendment have created some highly controversial ethical conflicts. On the one hand, society wants to find and punish criminals. Conversely, society wants to protect the civil rights of individuals. The courts have ruled that evidence obtained from unlawful searches may not be used at a criminal trial against the defendant.

The Fifth Amendment to the U.S. Constitution prohibits the government from compelling a defendant to testify against himself. The Miranda warnings promulgated by the Supreme Court require police to tell a suspect that he or she has the right to remain silent and to consult with an attorney.

The reasons for this ruling of the Supreme Court was to prevent police from obtaining "confessions" through physical or emotional duress. Some businesspeople have begun to complain about criminal actions brought by overzealous prosecutors who bring unnecessary actions under the Racketeer Influence and Corrupt Organization Act. Similarly, a significant number of other criminal actions brought by prosecutors have been thrown out by judges and juries based on lack of evidence. It is embarassing and expensive for businesses to defend themselves against these criminal actions.

BUSINESS ETHICS AND SOCIAL RESPONSIBILITY

Many people believe the ethical structure of American society has broken down. During the past 20 years there have been major ethical scandals at the highest levels of government, on Wall Street, among the clergy, in business, and in the sports world.

Businesspeople, particularly senior executives, have a special responsibility to society. The country allows them to earn exceptional salaries by helping their organizations to gain large profits. Ethically, it is not sufficient to simply earn profits and walk away from one's societal responsibilities. Businesspersons also need to consider the interests of society. While the law acts as a guide for one's conduct, it cannot substitute for one's own ethical standards.

■ Clyne is the president of OFX Corporation, which is located in the town of North Gaburp. His company has been located in the town for 50 years. Clyne would like to move the company to another location. There is nothing in the law to prevent him from doing so.

Clyne knows that his company is the major employer in the town. However, Clyne believes he can no longer earn an adequate profit in North Gaburp because the cost of labor is too high. Clyne has an ethical responsibility to his company's stockholders. Does he also have an ethical responsibility to the town and his employees? What should he do to meet these ethical responsibilities? ■

■ Mary works for NBG Corporation. She becomes aware that her employer is allowing toxic substances to be blown into the air. She informs the company president of the pollution, but he does nothing.

The company continues to pollute the air for several months. Every month, Mary mentions this to the president, but nothing is done to stop the pollution. What is Mary's obligation to society given these circumstances? What happens if one reports the violation to state or federal authorities? What is her ethical obligation to her family? ■

■ Joe works on the loading dock of a large liquor store. He observes his fellow employees putting bottles of liquor inside their large overcoats. This conduct occurs every time there is a large shipment of inventory. What is Joe's ethical responsibility to his employer? How might he best handle this situation? ■

The lawmakers in Congress and state legislatures have become more sensitive to some of these ethical concerns in recent years. They have passed statutes that prohibit the dismissal of employees for informing on an employer who is violating the law or committing corrupt acts. These statutes would have helped protect Mary in the second example. These are sometimes called "whistleblower" statutes because they protect employees who report wrongful acts.

■ Phillip is aware that some of his superiors are engaging in insider trading. Phillip notifies the Securities and Exchange Commission. When his boss finds out what he has done, Phillip is fired. This is an improper dismissal and Phillip must be reinstated. ■

Laws that encourage people to meet their ethical obligations and social responsibilities are likely to encourage people to engage in more ethical conduct. This is particularly important in a world where ethical lapses can cause substantial damage to the environment. These mistakes can also be financially devastating to a company.

■ Wilson is a contractor. He tries to save money by using concrete and other materials that are below local building code standards. During a severe rainstorm part of the building collapses and several tenants are injured. Wilson now faces both civil and criminal penalties. The tenants now face considerable medical expenses that taxpayers may be required to pay. Wilson's company now faces financial ruin. In this case, the law encourages proper conduct by imposing criminal and civil penalties when the law is not met. ■

It may be difficult to specify what constitutes ethical conduct. At a minimum, one should obey the law. One should also observe a law of the medical profession: "First, do no harm."

If one has doubts about the ethics of an action, ask an attorney if the act might violate the law. If it might, play it safe, and do not do it. If the act could lead to significant liability, do not do it. If the act would harm society, do not do it.

Some people use rules of thumb which can be helpful. If the act would not look good in the newspaper, do not do it. If the act might embarrass your family, do not do it. If you do not feel right about the act, do not do it.

Definitions Reviewed

Unconscionable conduct is conduct that would shock the conscience of the court because it indicates one party has taken unfair advantage of the weaker position of another.

Common law liability is the legal principle that one will be liable for any actions that cause damage to another person or that person's property.

Fiduciary duty is the duty of certain individuals to act on behalf of another person or group of persons.

Insider trading is the use of nonpublic information to trade stock. This is a violation of federal securities laws. An inside trader must surrender all profits made through the use of inside information.

Sexual harassment is the improper use of one's power to create a hostile sexual environment or to gain sexual favors.

Discrimination is the illegal treatment of people based on criteria other than merit.

Core Concepts Reviewed

■ The law is based on society's code of ethics. However, ethics alone cannot answer questions involving complicated factual situations and issues.

■ Businesspeople have ethical responsibilities to each other and to society.

■ Many people have observed that there has been a breakdown in ethics in our society. As a result, ethics is a topic that is receiving more attention in our schools and in other forums.

■ People in business have responsibilities to themselves, their employees, and their shareholders. They also have a responsibility to society as a whole.

■ Business is increasingly becoming more global in scope. Problems, opportunities, and threats are becoming more complex. The consquences of ethical lapses are becoming even greater. People in business should act in a manner that promotes social responsibility.

Questions

1. How would you define ethics?
2. Name some ethical principles.
3. Name some situations in which ethical principles come into conflict.
4. Name some instances where the law and ethical principles support each other.
5. Why can it be said that ethics alone are not adequate to resolve complicated factual questions and business issues?
6. What is a tort?
7. What is the ethical basis for holding people responsible for their torts?
8. Name some ethical scandals that have been in the news lately.
9. Name some failures of businesses, with respect to their social responsibilities, which have been in the news lately. What social responsibilities did they violate?

10. What would you say constitutes an ethical response in a given situation?
11. What are the media's ethical responsibilities to their viewers or readers?
12. How does the law protect citizens from the abuse of power by governmental officials and law enforcement officers?
13. Why is illegal discrimination a lapse of ethics?
14. How can the law encourage people to meet their ethical obligations?
15. What are the Fourth and Fifth Amendments to the U.S. Constitution? What is the purpose of each?

Problems

1. Jones works as an agent for Smith. He learns of a business opportunity while he is working for Smith. What is his ethical obligation? What is his legal obligation?
2. Johnson is the administrator of his mother's will. Johnson has what type of obligation to his mother's heirs?
3. Doyle is a police officer who responds to a chase involving an automobile traveling at high speed. After the subject vehicle is stopped, Doyle observes his fellow officers beating the driver with their batons. What is Doyle's ethical responsibility?
4. Stamber is a local prosecutor. He suspects that the town's police officers have begun to submit cases based on fraudulent evidence. What is his ethical obligation to the court? What is his obligation to society?
5. Samuels works for a contractor. He observes a series of payoffs between his boss and the local building inspector. What should he do?
6. Simpson is an employee at NYZ Corporation. He notices that his company is dumping heated water into the local reservoir. He has read a number of articles indicating that such a practice will disrupt the ecological balance of the reservoir. What should he do?
7. Mary works at LBL Corporation. She notices that her boss seems to promote female employees who are very attractive. She talks to her boss about this. Her boss says, "Sure, that's one of the perks of this job." What should she do?
8. Franklin works at Uriah's Used Car Lot. He notices that some of his co-workers are turning back the odometer before they sell the cars to unsuspecting customers. What should he do?
9. Leonard has an opportunity to acquire a rare Picasso painting from Mrs. Dotson, who is 89 years old. Mrs. Dotson is in desparate need of money. She offers the painting, valued at $1,000,000, to Leonard for $50,000. What should Leonard do?

PART II

CONTRACTS

Chapter 4

Contracts

- Contracts are legally enforceable oral or written agreements.

- A contract must contain certain elements. If they are not present, the agreement is not legally binding.

- These elements are capacity, consideration, a lawful purpose, promises to do certain acts, and execution of the contract in proper form.

- A contract is formed by the making of an offer by one party and acceptance by the other. The acceptance must be a "mirror image" of the offer. It may not change the essential terms of the offer.

- Contracts are classified in a number of ways. These classifications relate to how the offer was made, the conduct of the parties, and completion of the contractual duties by both parties.

Contracts are the foundation for all society's business and commercial relationships. In addition, contracts form the basis of a law student's first year of study. Without the certainty provided by the law of contracts, nearly all of our commercial relationships would be impossible.

Not all agreements are regarded as contracts. For example, social arrangements like dates are not regarded as contracts. The law reserves its powers of enforcement and remedies for more serious business-oriented relationships. Dates are not enforceable agreements because there is no exchange of items of value.

Parties to a contract have both rights and obligations. Either an oral or a written agreement can be a contract if the elements required by law are present. Most agreements possess the necessary elements of lawful purpose, a "meeting of the minds," legal capacity of the parties, consideration ("an exchange of things of value"), and execution in proper form.

A contract usually contains the names of the parties involved, various important terms such as price, and a description of the subject matter of the contract. A contract may be for the sale of real estate, the provision of services, or for the sale of goods. Contracts require both parties to perform their duties and obligations.

TYPES OF CONTRACTS

Contracts are classified into different types in order to help lawyers, judges, and citizens identify the type and to facilitate legal discussion. One way to classify contracts is by the method of offer and acceptance. If two parties exchange promises to do specific acts, the contract is called **bilateral.**

- Harry agrees to buy Bob's automobile for $10,000 on July 1st and Bob agrees to sell it to Harry at that price on that day. They have created a bilateral contract. Both parties are now legally bound to complete their promises and they can be held legally liable for not doing so. ▩

A second classification is a **unilateral contract,** which is formed when the offeree performs a specific act requested by the offeror. In this case, the offer may be accepted only by performing that particular act.

■ Wanda puts an advertisement in the paper stating that she will give a reward of $500 to anyone who returns her lost dog Spot. There is no contract until someone actually delivers Spot to Wanda. Even if someone finds Spot and calls Wanda, no contract exists until Spot is in Wanda's possession. ■

Business brokers are agents who sell businesses to new owners. Normally, the agent will be entitled to a commission when the agent finds a buyer who wants to buy the business and has the financial resources to do so. Finding the buyer completes this unilateral contract because it is the requested act.

The vast majority of contracts are bilateral contracts — one's promise to do something is exchanged for the other party's promise to do something else. Sales contracts clearly fall into this category. The seller has ageed to sell and the buyer has agreed to buy the subject matter of the contract. The contract is enforceable when the promises are exchanged.

In a unilateral contract, the offer has been phrased in such a way that a contract will exist only if a specific act is performed first. Often, service contracts fall into this category.

■ Betty agrees to paint Ted's portrait. The contract provides that Betty will be paid upon Ted's approval of the portrait. This is a unilateral contract. ■

Express, Implied, and Quasi Contracts

Another method of categorizing contracts is by the nature of the agreement and how it is reached. The most common of these is called an **express contract** because the terms of the agreement are explicitly spelled out either orally or in writing.

■ Mom's Diner agrees to buy 25 pies per day for $2 per pie for the next year. The pies are to be delivered every day by 7:00 A.M. This is an express contract because the terms are explicitly outlined and the agreement is clear. ■

■ The Hotel Hello chain agrees to purchase 100 beds from Beddy-Bye Bed Company for $20,000. The beds are to be delivered on July 1st. Again, the terms are expressly defined. This is an express contract. ■

■ Barry agrees to be Harold's butler for $500 per week for one year based on a 40-hour workweek. This is also an express contract because the terms are explicitly defined. ■

An **implied contract** is not explicitly defined. Rather, the contract must be inferred from the conduct of the parties involved. One or both of the parties have accepted the benefits associated with the conduct involved and the law finds that a contract has been reached.

■ Peter Painter goes to 101 Elm Street rather than 101 Maple Street and proceeds to paint the wrong house. Ellen, the owner of 101 Elm Street, watches him paint her house and says nothing to stop him. By her conduct, Ellen has implicitly agreed to have her house painted and to pay for the job. If she did not want the house painted, Ellen should not have allowed Peter to do so. She has created a contract by knowingly accepting the benefits supplied by Peter. ■

An implied contract recognizes that while the parties may not have explicitly agreed to a contract, it would be proper to find a contract based on the conduct of one or both of the parties.

A **quasi contract** is a contract that the courts will impose in order to achieve justice or to prevent someone from being unjustly enriched.

■ Jones is knocked unconscious in an accident. Dr. Smith passes the scene and administers proper medical treatment to Jones. If Dr. Smith brings an action against Jones to recover his medical fees, he will be able to recover under the theory of quasi contract. It would be unjust for Dr. Smith not to collect his fees, and Jones would be unjustly enriched by the amount of the medical services if he did not pay for them. This is true even though Jones did not request the treatment. ■

While the theory of quasi contracts allows courts to "do justice" in cases that demand it, the theory does not apply if the person's own negligence allowed the situation to occur.

■ Dr. Sawbones incorrectly diagnosed Harry's left leg as having gangrene and advised Harry that it should be removed. During the operation, Dr. Sawbones negligently removed the right leg. If Sawbones brought a quasi contract action to recover medical fees for the removal of the right leg, he would not be able to recover because it was his negligence that caused the situation. ■

Valid, Void, and Voidable Contracts

A **valid contract** is a contract in which all the elements are present and there are no legal problems associated with the agreement or the parties involved.

■ Bill, a 45-year-old man, agrees to buy a Buick from Honest Motors for $15,000. It will be delivered on June 1st. This is an example of a valid contract because there are no apparent problems with the agreement or with the parties to the contract. ■

A **void contract** is one that violates the law on its face and is not binding. Often, the agreement violates specific laws or public policy. As a result, the courts will not enforce it.

■ Bud agrees to murder Betty's business law professor for $100. This is a void contract because it violates criminal law. ■

Other contracts that would be void include those relating to gambling (an aleatory contract). These would include bets or similar arrangements.

A **voidable contract** is between a valid and a void contract. The contract is binding as long as the parties want it to be binding. However, there is something wrong with it, which allows one or both of the parties to "void" or cancel the contract. The most common reason is some problem regarding the capacity of one or more of the parties.

■ Mike, a minor, agrees to purchase an expensive automobile. If he wants to keep and pay for the automobile, he may do so. However, he may also cancel the contract because he was a minor when he agreed to it. The lesson for businesspeople is not to deal with minors. ■

Executory and Executed Contracts

Another category depends on whether the contract has been completed or is still in the process of completion.

An **executed contract** is one that has been fully completed in all material respects. There are no major tasks to be completed.

■ Rita agrees to buy Rudy's red Rover for $5,000, with a delivery date of July 1st. If, on July 1st, Rita tenders the payment and Rudy delivers the proper title, the contract has been fully executed. ■

An **executory contract** is one that is incomplete with respect to some material aspect of performance. An executed contract has been completely performed, but an executory contract has not.

■ Sherlock has a contract to perform ten investigations for Snoopie Services. Until Sherlock completes his tenth inquiry, the contract is still executory. ■

SOURCES OF CONTRACT LAW

Most contracts are still controlled by the common law of contracts, which emphasizes a precise agreement on terms. Contracts for the sale of real estate and for the provision of services are still controlled by traditional judge-made common law.

Contracts for the sale of goods, which are tangible, movable items, are now governed by the Uniform Commercial Code (UCC). The UCC has been adopted by nearly every state legislature. Generally, the UCC is much more flexible than the older common law.

The UCC was drafted with the intention of fostering the completion of contracts. It provides various gap-filling provisions that can be utilized to complete the contract if the parties do not agree on all the terms. It is important to determine which general law will prevail before attempting to apply the specific laws.

■ Jones agrees to buy a piece of real estate from Smith. As part of the agreement, Jones also agrees to purchase some household appliances in Smith's house.
   Although this is a purchase of both goods and real estate, the crux of the purchase relates to land. Therefore, the contract is governed by common law. ■

■ Larry purchases a TV set from Al's department store. The agreement provides that Larry may bring the set into the store when it needs repairs. Although the contract is for the purchase of a mix of a good and services, the main purpose is for the purchase of goods. Therefore, the contract is governed by the UCC. ■

Definitions Reviewed

A **bilateral contract** is one in which promises are exchanged between two parties.

A **unilateral contract** is when the offer can be accepted only by the performance of the act.

Express contracts are those in which the terms are explicitly defined.

Implied contracts are those in which the terms must be inferred from the conduct of the parties involved.

Quasi contracts are those that are found by the courts in order to prevent unjust enrichment and to do justice.

Executed contracts are those that have been completed.

Executory contracts are those in which the parties have not completed their obligations under the agreement.

Core Concepts Reviewed

■ If an agreement contains all the required elements, it will be a legally enforceable contract.

■ These elements are lawful purpose, capacity, consideration, promises to do certain acts, and execution in the proper form.

■ Contracts can be classified in a variety of ways depending on how the offer is made, the nature of the agreement, and whether it has been completed.

Questions

1. How is a contract formed?
2. What are the elements of a contract?
3. What is an implied contract? How is it different from an express contract?
4. What is a voidable contract? How does it differ from a valid or void contract?
5. What are executory and executed contracts?
6. To what contracts does the UCC apply?

Problems

1. Susan tells Joan that Joan needs to lose weight. Susan bets her $50 that she cannot lose ten pounds over the next month. If Joan loses the weight, is Susan's promise enforceable?
2. Irving, who is legally insane, agreed to buy an expensive fur coat. This is what type of contract?
3. Sam buys a hot dog stand from Leslie. He continues to receive mustard from Mac, who had supplied Leslie, for 30 days. Does he have a contract with Mac? If so, what type?
4. Bill agrees to sell ten grams of cocaine to Mary for $1,000. Later, Mary refuses to pay the $1,000. Is her promise enforceable? What type of contract is this?
5. Fred agrees to build a house for Alphonso. He maps out the foundation on the ground, but has done nothing else. At this stage, what type of contract is it?
6. Mabel places an advertisement in a local paper offering $25 for a cancelled first-day issue Elvis Presley stamp. What type of contract is this?
7. Mary's adult daughter, Gwen, is very ill. Gwen informs Mary that she has no money to pay her hospital bills. Mary pays them for her. Later, Mary discovers that Gwen has substantial sums of money.

   Mary sues Gwen to recover the amount paid for her medical treatment. Will Mary recover? If the answer is yes, under what theory of contracts can she prevail?

Chapter 5

Offer and Acceptance

- An offer is an indication by the offeror of a willingness to create a contract.

- An acceptance of the offer will create a contract if the acceptance is an exact replica of the offer. The acceptance may not change the offer in any way.

- A counteroffer is an attempt by the offeree to change the terms of the offer.

- A rejection of the offer by the offeree terminates the offer and is effective when received.

- An acceptance is effective when dispatched by the offeree.

- An option is an offer that gives the offeree a period of time in which to accept it.

OFFER AND ACCEPTANCE

A contract is formed by the making of an **offer** by the offeror and acceptance by the offeree. There must be an agreement on all material terms in order for there to be an enforceable contract. If there is ambiguity on a key term, the discussions of the parties will have been meaningless.

- The parties agree on every term with respect to putting each other through college except whether the schools will be state-supported or private. The "agreement" will not be an enforceable contract because of the possible difference in price.

Most contracts are bilateral in nature because the offeree *accepts* the offer by making a return promise. This results in an exchange of promises. Unilateral offers are phrased in such a way that they can be accepted only by performing the act requested by the offeror.

Defining the Offer

An offer must be phrased in such a way that it can be accepted unconditionally. It must contain all of the material ("important") terms necessary to create a contract. These terms normally include price, quantity, subject matter, names of the parties, and any other terms normally associated with similar types of agreements.

The offer must also be communicated in a reasonable manner in order to be effective. If it is not communicated reasonably, it cannot form the basis of a contract.

- Mary received a card informing her that her rent has been raised from $200 to $250 per month. On the back of the card, in small print, is a statement that all tenants will be held liable for any activities that occur anywhere on the premises. Even if Mary agrees to the rent increase, the clause on the back will not be binding because it was not effectively communicated. ■

Certain statements that may look like an offer and acceptance have been legally held to be mere preliminary negotiations. Generally, advertisements and other types of introductory suggestions fall into this category. In the past, this often led to "bait-and-switch" tactics in which merchants would advertise a product at a very low price and then have little or none of the low-priced stock available. They would substitute a higher-priced product for the advertised item. Most state legislatures have now passed statutes outlawing these practices.

The offeror may control both the nature and terms of the offer and the nature and terms of the acceptance.

■ Gerald offers to sell one of his rare coins for $1,000. He mails the offer to various coin collectors and states that any acceptance must be made by mail and by April 17th. This is permissible and is a proper way to make an offer and to define the method of acceptance. ■

Because the offeror has the legal ability to control the offer and acceptance, she also bears the responsibility for any delay or other problems in the communication with the offeree. An offer is not legally effective until received. As a result, if the offer provides a time limit for a reply, the time does not begin until the offer is actually received by the offeree. For example, a ten-day time limit would not begin until the date received.

The offeror's ability to control the terms of the offer also means that she will be responsible for any ambiguities in the offer.

■ Mona sends out an offer noting that replies must be received by June 31st. A reply received on July 1st should bind Mona because of the ambiguity in her offer. ■

This issue often arises in dealing with printed contracts such as leases or sales agreements. If the contract is vague or ambiguous, it will be interpreted against the party who drafted it.

Options

An offer that the offeror agrees to hold open for a period of time is called an **option.** At common law, an option is revocable at any time prior to acceptance unless the offeree gave the offeror something of value to keep the offer open.

■ Joey tells Amy that he will sell her his auto repair shop for $100,000 and will hold the offer open for 30 days. If Amy does not accept the offer when it is made, Joey may revoke it at any time prior to her acceptance. ■

At first glance, this may seem unfair. However, the reason for this apparent unfairness is that the offeror has given the offeree something of value (the option). In return, the offeree should give the offeror something of value if she wants to enforce the option. Almost anything given by the offeree to the offeror will be sufficient.

This is sometimes called the "common-law option rule" and it places the burden on the offeree to provide value for value. The notice of the revocation to the offeree can be given either actually or in a constructive manner.

In this example, Joey could have told Amy either orally or in writing that he was revoking the offer. He could have also communicated the revocation by selling the auto repair business to someone else in a way that would bring the sale to Amy's attention.

While this principle continues to apply to contracts still under the common law, the Uniform Commercial Code, which applies to the sale of goods, follows a somewhat different rule. The UCC states that a merchant, someone who regularly deals in goods, will be bound by an offer put into writing for a period of time not to exceed three months. This recognizes that a merchant should be held to a higher standard than an ordinary seller. It will not be necessary to give consideration to the merchant to bind him to the offer.

Other Terms in Offer

As just noted, the offeror may control the terms of the offer to include the method of reply and the length of time. The offeror may request a reply in any way she wants. If the method of reply is not specified in the offer, the offeree may reply in any reasonable manner. Unless otherwise specified, use of the mail is presumed to be a reasonable method of reply.

As noted, the offeror may determine the length of the offer as well as the other terms. If the length of the offer is not stated in the offer, it terminates after a reasonable length of time. Just what is reasonable depends on all the circumstances surrounding the offer and its subject matter.

> Jones offers to ship 1,000 cartons of eggs to Wilson, 100 miles away, for a certain price. Because of the rapid perishability of the goods, the offeree should know that a reasonable length of time is very short. If the subject matter is cement, a reasonable length of time would be longer.

As a practical matter, it is a good business practice to spell out the length of the offer in the offer itself. This helps avoid misunderstandings, which is the primary responsibility of the offeror.

Events such as the death or insanity of either the offeror or offeree will terminate the offer. The destruction of the subject matter or the intervening illegality of the offer will also terminate the offer.

Unusual Offers

An auction is an event where people make bids on an item being placed on sale. Each bid is an offer that may or may not be accepted by the person who is placing the item on sale. An auction is governed by strict rules regarding the acceptance of offers. At an auction held "without reserve," the property owner must accept the highest bid made at the auction. The owner may set a floor below which bids may not be made. This allows the owner to establish a minimum price for the property.

An auction made "with reserve" allows the owner to reject all bids. The property owner, working through the auctioneer, need not accept the highest bid. Because this may be unfair to bidders, notice that the auction is being held with reserve must be given to bidders.

Rewards

A reward is a unilateral offer that requires the offeree to perform a specific act in order to accept the offer. The reward may be directed to a specific person or to the general public.

The usual way to inform the public of a reward is to place an advertisement in a publication of general circulation.

> Jack puts an advertisement in the paper offering a $500 reward for the return of his dog, Rover. Anyone who reads the paper may accept the offer by finding and returning Rover to the owner. ■

A person who did not read about the reward is not entitled to it. This is true even if he completed the act requested. In the preceding example, a person who returns Rover without reading about the reward cannot demand it if she later hears of the advertisement. An offer must be communicated to the offeree *before* the reward can be accepted.

Revocation, Rejection, and Counteroffer

An offer may be terminated by the offeror's **revocation** prior to acceptance by the offeree. The offeror may revoke the offer unless something of value is received from the offeree.

The revocation will be effective only when the offeree receives it. The notice of revocation could be in either oral or written form. It could also be constructive when it is done in a way that will come to the offeree's attention. Upon revocation, the offer and discussion are terminated unless the offeror is willing to extend *another* offer. Although it may seem unfair, the offeree may not accept an offer after revocation by the offeror.

> Wilson offers to sell his Elvis Presley-owned Stutz Bearcat to Thompson for $50,000. Thompson asks for some time to think about it. A few days later, Wilson calls Thompson and revokes the offer. Immediately after the revocation, Thompson says, "Wait a minute, I accept your offer." It is too late. The offer has been revoked and there is no contract. ■

The same rules apply to **rejections.** A rejection is a statement by the offeree that she is not willing to accept the offer. It is effective when received. Once the rejection is received, it is too late for the offeree to change his or her mind unless the offeror is willing to revive the offer.

> ■ Again, Wilson offers to sell the Bearcat to Thompson, except that Thompson tells Wilson to forget it. Within the hour, Thompson realizes that he has made a mistake and tries to get Wilson to revive the offer. Wilson may ignore the request and there is no contract. ■

A **counteroffer** is an attempt by the offeree to change the terms of the offer. According to common law, a counteroffer is treated the same as a rejection. This means the offeror can listen to the counteroffer and accept it or walk away from it. If the offeror walks away, there is no contract.

> ■ Donna offers indecisive Irwin a Rembrandt painting for $2,000. Irwin offers $1,750. Donna may accept the counteroffer or walk away. If she walks away, there is no contract and Irwin has no remedy. ■

Acceptance

In order to create a contract, an offer must be accepted without change in the material terms. This could result from the **acceptance** of an offer by the offeree or the acceptance of a counteroffer by the original offeror. It is important to note that if the offer and acceptance do not meet the common law's standard of agreement, there is no contract and no remedy.

Unlike offers, rejections, and revocations, which are effective only once they are received, an acceptance is effective immediately upon being dispatched. The purpose behind this rule is to place the burden of responsibility on the offeror if there is a problem between the time of the making of the offer and the receipt of the acceptance. As a result, if either party attempts to revoke the offer after the dispatch of the acceptance, the revocation is ineffective.

> ■ Alan mails an offer to Barbara on June 1st. She receives it on June 3rd and immediately mails an acceptance back to Alan. On June 4th, Alan calls Barbara with a revocation of his offer. It is too late. A contract existed on June 3rd when Barbara mailed the acceptance back to Alan. There is a contract and if Alan does not perform his duties, Barbara will have a remedy for breach of contract. ■

The common law principle that an acceptance is effective upon dispatch is called the "mailbox rule." That is, a contract is legally established when the acceptance is mailed. An acceptance is also effective upon oral dispatch.

As previously noted, the acceptance must be made without material change in the offer. If the offeree attempts to make significant changes, there is no contract. According to common law, even relatively minor changes mean there are no enforceable rights by either party.

Generally, acceptance must be an affirmative act. Silence does not constitute acceptance unless silence constituted acceptance as part of an established pattern of conduct.

> ■ Bob cuts grass for Joe every two weeks and Joe says nothing but leaves him a check. After this goes on for several months, Joe need not specifically tell Bob that he accepts Bob's offer to cut the grass. ■

Definitions Reviewed

An **offer** is an invitation to create a contract. : Advertising

An **acceptance** is an indication by the person receiving the offer that she is willing to create a contract by agreeing to the offer.

A **rejection** is an indication by the offeree that she is not willing to accept the offer.

Core Concepts Reviewed

- An offer is a statement indicating a willingness to create a contract.

- An acceptance is the agreement to the offer which creates a contract. The acceptance must be a "mirror image" of the offer.

- A counteroffer is an attempt to change the offer and will not create a contract.

- A revocation immediately terminates the offer.

- A rejection immediately terminates the offer.

- An acceptance is effective when dispatched.

Questions

1. Name a contractual offer you have received.
2. Did you accept the offer? How did you make your acceptance?
3. What is a counteroffer? What is its effect on the original offer?
4. What is the "mailbox rule"?
5. When is a rejection effective? What are the consequences of a rejection?
6. When does silence constitute acceptance? When does it *not* constitute acceptance?
7. What is an option?
8. When may an option be revoked?
9. What is the difference between the rules governing options under common law and those under the UCC?
10. What are the consequences of an auction "without reserve" for the highest bidder?
11. What if the auction was "with reserve"?

Problems

1. Dabney sends a letter to Rodney offering to sell him a rare plate for $2,000. The letter further states that the offer will be held open for 30 days. Ten days after Rodney receives the offer, he learns Dabney has sold the plate to Tom. He immediately calls Dabney and "accepts" the offer. Is there a contract?
2. Richard sends a charm bracelet to Mary through the mail. The bracelet is accompanied by a letter stating that she should either return the bracelet or send Richard $50. If Mary keeps the bracelet, does she owe Richard the money?
3. Chauncey offers James $100 per day to be his driver on the days he needs chauffering services. James replies he will be Chauncey's driver for $700 per week. Is there an enforceable contract?
4. Abel offers Cain the opportunity to buy his automobile for $10,000. Cain receives the offer on April 1st. He mails his acceptance to Abel on April 4th and Abel receives it on April 6th. On April 5th, Abel mailed a revocation of the offer to Cain. Is there a contract?
5. Michelle sends an offer to Arnie to sell him her valuable antique table for $500. Michelle intended to hold the offer open for 3 days. Instead, she types in 13 days. How long does Arnie have to reply?
6. John offers Sal his 1957 Thunderbird for $20,000. Sal rejects the offer. One day later, he changes his mind and calls John to accept the offer. John refuses to listen to Sal. Does Sal have any remedy?

Chapter 6

Requirements for Writings

- The statute of frauds helps reduce the possibility of fraud in certain important contracts by requiring that they be in writing in order to be enforceable.
- The statute of frauds modifies the common law that oral contracts were as binding as written contracts.
- Because the statute is primarily a rule of evidence, the courts have modified the statute when other evidence, such as substantial performance of the agreement, indicates that a contract existed.
- The parol evidence rule states that when the contract is written, oral evidence will not be admitted to contradict the writing except under certain circumstances.
- A written contract does not need to be very extensive. It should include the subject matter, price, signatures of the parties, and any other terms normally included in such contracts.

STATUTE OF FRAUDS

Under English and American common law, oral contracts were as binding as written contracts. This was because, until the mid-nineteenth century, few people could actually read and write. As a result, if contracts had to be in writing, few agreements would have been legally enforceable.

Although written agreements are easier to understand and to enforce, most contracts may still be made orally. Proving the contract is just a question of evidence and oral evidence has value. But most state legislatures have agreed with the English Parliament that certain contracts ought to be in writing.

These include the following:

- The sale of any interest in land.
- A contract that cannot be performed within one year.
- The promise to answer for the debt or default of another.
- A contract to personally pay the debts of an estate.
- Contracts in consideration of marriage (e.g. prenuptials).
- A contract for the sale of goods of $500 or more (UCC).
- A contract for the sale of securities.

Contracts for the sale of land have always been important in English and American societies. Land is a basis of power and influence because it is the only type of property that will remain constant in size. Land can also be used to grow crops, which has always been an extremely important function. In addition, natural resources like minerals or timber can be harvested from the land.

As a result, the temptation to lie in order to acquire land used to be great. The **statute of frauds** has reduced this temptation by requiring that all contracts for the sale of land be in writing. The writing for a contract for the sale of land should include a reasonable description of the land, the names of the parties, the selling price, the date for the completion of the transaction, and the signatures of the parties. There must be writing for the sale of any interest in land. This includes life estates and other interests. An exception to the statute of frauds exists when the contract has been substantially completed.

■ Jones and Wilson orally agree that Wilson will give Jones the land in his will if Jones moves onto Wilson's land and cuts down enough trees to supply Wilson's need for timber until Wilson dies. Jones moves on the land and builds a small shack. For a period of two years he cuts down timber and delivers it to Wilson. He receives thank-you notes from Wilson every time he delivers the timber. The Statute of Frauds will not prevent this agreement from being enforceable. The evidence provided by the shack, the notes, and oral testimony will be sufficient to show a contract. If Wilson neglects to make a will, Jones can enforce the oral contract despite the statute of frauds. ■

■ Smith and Watson agree that Smith will build a road through Watson's land so that both of them can reach the highway from their homes. Smith will be allowed permanent access to the road. Smith builds the road and both he and Watson use it for five years. Watson suddenly demands that Smith stop using the road. The Statute of Frauds will not bar this contract even though it was oral. The existence of the road and its use will be evidence to show that the contract existed. ■

This exception to the statute means that it primarily applies to executory contracts. If the contract has been nearly completed, a party may not claim it is unenforceable because it is not in writing. If few of the contractual obligations have been completed, the statute applies and a writing is required.

Contracts that Cannot Be Performed within One Year

The statute of frauds also recognizes that long-term contracts are extremely important and their terms may be easily forgotten. In addition, long-term contracts may bind the parties for periods of time in excess of what they want and can prove quite costly. Therefore, the statute requires that a contract which cannot be completed within one year must be in writing.

A key term in the statute is "cannot be performed within one year." The courts have interpreted this to mean that, on its terms, the contract could not be completed within one year. If the contract could be completed within one year, a written contract is not required.

■ A "lifetime" employment contract could be completed within 1 year because the employee could die before the 12 months are over. Therefore, the contract need not be in writing. ■

But a five-year employment contract could not possibly, on its terms, be completed within one year. Therefore, it must be in writing.

The same exception of substantial performance which applies to real estate contracts also applies in this case. If enough of the contract has been completed, it will be sufficient evidence that the contract had been agreed on. For example, while a five-year employment contract would normally require a written agreement, it would still be enforceable if one year of employment had already passed. The contract would fall within the exception, and would be enforceable. Other acts related to the employment, such as pay stubs, could also be evidence of a contract and permit it to be enforced.

Contracts to Answer for Debts or for Default to Another

The drafters of the statute of frauds also recognized that it was a relatively easy matter to lie about a contract that stated that someone had agreed to pay another's debt. It is also easy to see how someone could benefit from such a lie. As a result, the statute requires such contracts be put into writing.

> ■ Glen agrees to pay Jill's debt to Martin if Jill does not. This contract must be in writing to be enforceable because of the statute of frauds. ■

The statute of frauds is the reason that a bank requires a guarantor of a loan to put this promise in writing. The substantial performance exception also applies to this type of contract. In addition, the statute will apply only if the promise is made to the creditor. It does not apply when made to the debtor.

Furthermore, some courts have ruled that the statute does not apply if the main purpose of the promise is to benefit the promisor rather than the party whose debt he agreed to pay. For example, the promisor may agree to the promise in order to assist an important employee or to get a troublesome relative out of the house. In either case, the oral promise would be enforceable because it benefits the promisor, and the statute does not apply.

Contracts in Consideration of Marriage

A marriage is essentially a contract between two people. Society is concerned because the marriage contract implicitly accepts the state's laws regarding division of the marital property and the care of any children resulting from the marriage.

Marriages have also been the source of business alliances and a means of social advancement. It used to be common practice for people to exchange money as part of the marriage contract. In addition, contracts that divide property or set aside property acquired during the marriage are still quite common.

> ■ Donald, who is a very rich man, agrees to marry Marla. He wants to protect his property. The two of them agree that she is entitled to none of the property Donald had before the marriage and to only 20 percent of any property acquired after the marriage. This would have to be in writing. ■

Given the current divorce rate in our society, the number of contracts relating to marriage is likely to increase. It is important that marriage contracts be drafted carefully with a consideration of applicable state law, the potential consequences of a divorce, and the need to protect the interests of both parties.

Personal Payment of the Debts of an Estate

An executor is someone who manages the disposition of a person's property after that person's death. It would be a relatively simple matter to claim that an executor had promised a creditor to pay the deceased's debt from his own funds. As a result, the drafters of the statute of frauds believed that promises of this type needed to be put in writing in order to be enforceable.

> ▧ Joe claims that Edward, executor of Susan's estate, had promised to pay a debt owed to him by Susan out of his own funds. The estate has insufficient assets to pay the debt. But unless Joe has the promise in writing, the promise is not enforceable. ▧

This provision also serves to protect executors from all sorts of claims from "creditors" who claim that an executor promised to personally pay the debts of a deceased person.

Other Statute of Frauds Provisions

State legislatures have also passed statutes stating which contracts must be put in writing. The UCC requires that contracts for the sale of goods over $500 must be in writing.

> ▧ Ted's TV Land sells a gigantic TV set to Big Bob's Bar for $1,000. The TV set is a good (a tangible, movable item). The UCC requires a written description of the goods, their quantity, and the names of the parties. ▧

The UCC also requires that contracts for the sale of securities (stocks and bonds) be in writing. This recognizes the importance of securities because they represent a specific interest in corporations or governments.

PAROL EVIDENCE RULE

The parol evidence rule states that if a contract has been reduced to writing, prior oral agreements between the parties will not be admissable in court to contradict the written terms except under certain circumstances. These include the following:

- ▧ If the terms of the written contract are vague or are subject to different interpretations, the court will admit oral evidence to clarify the terms. The court will admit oral evidence if the contract appears incomplete in order to fill in the missing information.
- ▧ The court will also admit oral evidence if the evidence is to show lack of genuine consent such as fraud, allegations of duress, accident, or mistake.

> ▧ Bill and Joe have a written contract for Bill to purchase a rare violin for $20,000 on July 1st. Normally, oral evidence would not be admissible to contradict the written terms, such as price or delivery date. However, oral evidence would be

admitted to show that the quality of the violin was not what the parties had believed or to show that Joe's signature was a forgery. ■

Definitions Reviewed

Oral Contracts are those not in writing.
Goods are tangible, movable items.
Securities are evidence of ownership in a corporation or evidence of debt.

Core Concepts Reviewed

- The statute of frauds requires that certain contracts be in writing in order to be enforceable.

- The writing should contain the terms of the agreement to include price, subject matter description, names of the parties, signatures, quantity, and any other essential provisions.

- The courts have altered the statute to carve out modifications such as the substantial performance exception, which show sufficient evidence of a contract. As a result, the statute applies primarily to executory contracts.

- The parol evidence rule states that, with certain exceptions, oral evidence will not be admissable to contradict a contract that has been reduced to writing.

Questions

1. What is the reason the statute of frauds was drafted?
2. To what types of contracts does the statute apply?
3. What are the major exceptions to the statute?
4. What is the parol evidence rule?
5. What are some major exceptions to the rule?
6. What is a sale of interest in land?
7. Name some interests in land.

8. Why is it accurate to say that the statute of frauds applies to executory contracts?

Problems

1. Tom orally agrees to sell his house to Diane for $100,000. Tom receives the check and Diane begins to put her personal property into Tom's house. Suddenly he stops her and says the contract is unenforceable because it is not in writing. Is he correct?
2. Phil and Renee agree to a contract calling for Renee to supply Phil with raspberry pies for three years. Before Renee sends any pies, Phil calls her and says the agreement is not enforceable because it was not put in writing. Is he correct?
3. Jones orally agrees with Stewart to pay his daughter's debt if she does not. Jones made the oral agreement in order to encourage his daughter to feel more self-sufficient and to find her own place to live. Jones later argues that his promise to Stewart is not enforceable because it was not in writing. Is he correct?
4. Randolph and Rachel agree to marry. As part of their engagement discussions, Randolph orally agrees to pay Rachel $5,000 on the day of their wedding. Is his promise enforceable?
5. Tipper and Hillary agree to a written contract regarding the sale and purchase of a vase. Unfortunately, the exact date of delivery was left out of the written agreement. Will evidence of previous oral discussions regarding the delivery date be admissable?
6. Kate is named executor of her mother's estate. She orally promises to pay the estate's debt to her sister Rose out of her own funds if the estate is unable to do so. Is her promise enforceable?

Chapter 7

Consideration

- Consideration is an element required for the creation of a valid contract.
- Consideration is the giving of something of value or the incurring of a substantial detriment.
- Both parties must give consideration for there to be a valid contract. If one party does not give something of value or incur a substantial detriment, that party cannot enforce the other party's promise.
- The consideration given must be new. Past consideration or existing obligations will not be sufficient.
- "Moral consideration" is not adequate legal consideration to form a contract.

CONSIDERATION

Consideration is a required element of a legally enforceable contract. Without consideration, an agreement that the parties thought was legally enforceable will not be. Consideration is required by the courts in order to render unenforceable those agreements that are predominantly social in nature. More important business-oriented agreements are supported by consideration.

Consideration is either the giving up of something of value or the incurring of a substantial detriment. The giving of "consideration" demonstrates that the party is serious about the agreement and intends to bind both himself and the other party.

> Cynthia agrees to buy Kelly's dining room table for $1,000 and Kelly agrees to sell the table at that price. Both parties have now given something of value and the agreement will be legally enforceable. ■

An exchange of valuable promises is regarded as satisfactory consideration. In this case, Cynthia will not need to find another seller of a dining room table and Kelly will not need to find another buyer.

The agreement is capable of being enforced from the moment that the promises are exchanged. If either party does not perform her share of the agreement, the other can bring an appropriate legal action.

> Jason fails to stop at a red light and drives his car through an intersection and crashes into Jerry's car. Jerry is injured and brings legal action against Jason because of his careless driving. The attorneys for both of them meet with Jason and Jerry. After considerable discussion, the parties agree that Jason will pay Jerry $50,000 if Jerry drops his suit. This is an enforceable agreement because each has given consideration. Jason will pay $50,000 and Jerry will incur a substantial detriment by dropping his legal action. ■

The preceding examples demonstrate the normal situations involving consideration in serious circumstances. What the courts will not enforce are mere social agreements such as dates or gratuitous promises of gifts.

- Fred agrees to pick up Jackie at 6:00 P.M. on Friday for a dinner date. At 4:00 P.M. Jackie calls Fred and cancels their date. Although the two parties had an agreement, it is not legally binding because there was no exchange of sufficient consideration. ■

- Uncle Jim promises to give his niece Nancy a watch on her birthday. Uncle Jim's promise is not enforceable because Nancy had given him nothing in return. Uncle Jim's statement is regarded as a mere gratuitous promise. ■

If the courts had to enforce promises relating to dates or gifts among relatives, the courts would have an endless number of social arrangements and potential gift cases to examine and to decide. If for no other reason than practicality, the courts would rather avoid dealing with these less serious situations.

Consideration could be found in these cases if the other party had incurred some detriment based on the promisor's promise. In the preceding example, if Nancy had purchased expensive cuff links in return for Uncle Jim's promise, his promise is more likely to be held enforceable.

Promissory Estoppel

The courts have been rather uncomfortable with the idea of detriment being consideration. Some courts have supported the idea of detriment being regarded as consideration with the doctrine of **promissory estoppel.** This doctrine states that a promise will be enforced if the promisor knew or should have known that the promisee would rely on the promise to his substantial detriment.

- Peter is told by Pets Extraordinare that if he sells his business and moves to Iraq, he will be given a Pets Extraordinaire franchise. Peter does as he is told, but is not granted the franchise. Because Pets knew that Peter would incur a substantial detriment based on its promise, it will be held liable under the doctrine of promissory estoppel and must keep the promise. ■

Promissory estoppel does not require knowledge of reliance to an exact level of certainty. Rather, the promisor should be aware of what a reasonable person would do based on the promise.

Adequacy of Consideration

As a general rule, the courts are not concerned with the amount of consideration from the parties. The courts presume that the parties are adults, who enter into agreements with adequate knowledge and capacity.

- Mary agrees to a health spa contract for ten years at $1,000 per year. Assuming that the contract was in writing and did not represent an unconscionable amount at $1,000 per year, the contract will be enforced even though the health spa seems to have acquired a particularly good deal. ■

A major exception is when the parties have substantially unequal bargaining positions. In these cases, the courts have ruled that one party may not take "unconscionable" advantage of the other party.

■ XYZ is a large department store. It agrees to a contract with Jones, an older woman of little education. The contract states that if Jones is late with any payment, all her property acquired from XYZ will be subject to repossession. Because of the unequal bargaining positions and the unconscionable nature of the contract prepared by XYZ, this provision of the contract will be ruled invalid as against public policy. ■

These examples indicate that the courts attempt to find a balance between the need to avoid opening up the courtroom to every contract, and the desire to stop unscrupulous business practices. The courts will generally not protect people from their own mistakes. This is designed to encourage a degree of self-help and independent inquiry in an imperfect world. On the other hand, the courts are unwilling to impose a contract on someone who lacks capacity, has been deceived, or has received little consideration.

Past Consideration and Preexisting Obligations

The consideration necessary for an enforceable contract must be new. It cannot be based on past acts or already existing obligations.

■ Harley sees two older women whose car is stuck in a ditch on the side of the road. He helps pull their car out of the ditch. The two women promise to give him $100 as a reward. If they do not pay him, he will not be able to enforce their promise because it was based on his past acts. If he wanted the money, he should have asked for it prior to pulling the car from the ditch. If they promised him the money before his actions, the act of pulling out their car would have supplied present consideration. ■

Similarly, a preexisting obligation cannot be the basis of consideration for a new contract. If a party is already required by contract or by law to perform specific acts, these acts cannot form the basis of a new contract.

■ Murphy, a police officer, agrees to watch Olson's house while Olson is on vacation. Olson's house is on Murphy's regular beat. Even if Olson promises to give Murphy $50 for watching the house, his promise to Murphy is not enforceable because Murphy already had a legal obligation to watch Olson's house. ■

In fact, Murphy's promise comes dangerously close to extortion and abuse of his official position. This is one of the reasons why a contract based on an existing obligation is not enforceable.

■ Peter Painter agrees to paint Hugh's house for $1,500. Halfway through the job, Painter tells Hugh that he will lose $500 on the job and asks Hugh for an additional $600. Even if Hugh agrees to pay the additional $600, he need not pay it because Painter supplied no additional consideration for the promise. If he had agreed to add a second coat, that would be sufficient consideration for the promise of $600 extra. ■

This legal doctrine often strikes people as unfair. However, it should be noted that this situation borders on economic duress. One can argue that the homeowner had little choice but to agree to the second promise. This may be one of the underlying reasons for the legal principle requiring additional consideration.

There is a major exception to the preexisting obligation rule. If the person encountered unforeseen difficulties, he can enforce a promise for additional consideration. These difficulties must not have been reasonably forseeable by the party when he agreed to the contract.

> Peter Painter agrees to paint Hugh's house for $2,000. While painting the house, Peter encounters a dark grimy substance that the average painter would not have foreseen. He asks the homeowner for an additional $1,000 to finish the job.
>
> If Hugh, the homeowner, agrees to pay the additional $1,000, he will be required to pay it. This would be regarded as an unforeseen difficulty and the painter would be entitled to the additional consideration. ▪

As this example indicates, the unforeseen difficulties must have been significant, externally caused, and not reasonably foreseeable. A mistake about the cost of paint or brushes would not be an unforeseeable event.

> A painter underestimates the cost of the job and goes to the homeowner and asks for more money. The homeowner either can agree to pay more money or not. In either case, the homeowner need not pay anything. ▪

These rulings encourage people entering contracts to accurately gauge a reasonable price for their work. In short, it encourages one to learn from one's mistakes.

Moral Consideration

If one does a good deed, one may expect to be rewarded. However, the law does not recognize "moral" acts to be a form of adequate consideration.

> Mary pulls a drowning child out of the swimming pool. She asks the child's mother for some money and claims a contract should exist for her services. Under the law, she is entitled to nothing. ▪

If the law recognized an obligation for people to have to pay when someone performs a "moral" act, the obligations would be endless. For example, a child runs out onto the street and Bill quickly slams on his brakes and saves the child's life. Do the child's parents owe Bill any money? Does society?

Contractual Exceptions

Generally, contracts will not be enforced unless both parties either give up something of value or incur substantial detriments. However, there are a few contracts that will be enforced without consideration for public policy reasons.

Voluntary pledges to charitable, religious, or educational organizations do not provide reciprocal consideration. Although the organization receives something of value, it is difficult to find the consideration to the person making the pledge. However, the courts have ruled that for public policy reasons, a charitable pledge is enforceable even though the organization has given the person making the pledge nothing of value.

> Jones gets a call from Knowledge College, his alma mater. He agrees to contribute $100. His promise is enforceable even though Knowledge College did not give him something of additional value. ▪

Some courts have based their rulings on the grounds that such pledges benefit society because they contribute to improving the general standards of educational, religious, or social welfare.

Another major exception relates to **requirements** and **outputs contracts.** A requirements contract calls for one party to buy all of the requirements of a product from a particular supplier. An outputs contract states that a party will sell everything that it makes to a particular party. In both cases, it could be argued that an outputs or requirements contract lacks consideration. In both contracts, the one party has an escape provision. Suppose the "requirements" party has no need for the other party's products or the "outputs" party produces an excessive number of products. Where is the consideration?

In fact, there may be no consideration. Outputs and requirements contracts, however, serve useful functions in our society. A requirements contract allows a person to find a supplier who will sell her all the products she needs. An outputs contract allows a person to find a customer who wants her products and is willing to buy everything she makes.

The courts have found consideration in the "good faith" requirement implicit in all contracts. While it is possible that a person wanting to take advantage of the other could claim that they have no requirements or unfairly boost output, the law imposes a reasonableness standard on each party.

> Lisa has a three-year outputs contract with Margery, who makes designer dresses. In the first year, Margery made and Lisa bought 100 dresses. In the second year, the amount is 150 dresses and Lisa takes them all. By the third year, Margery decides she has a good thing going and increases the output to 1,000 dresses. This is well beyond what is reasonable and Lisa would not have to purchase the full amount. ▪

> Elizabeth has a three-year requirements contract to purchase gadgets from Susan. In the first year Elizabeth orders 2,000 gadgets. In the second year she orders 2,500 gadgets. In year three, Susan gears up to produce at least 2,500 gadgets. However, Elizabeth has now found a new supplier and orders no gadgets from Susan. Elizabeth's failure to order any gadgets is a violation of her obligation to act in good faith. Susan has a remedy because of this failure. She can at least recover her profits based on her intended production of 2,500 gadgets. ▪

Definitions Reviewed

Outputs contract is a contract in which one party agrees to purchase all of the other party's product output.

Requirements contract is a contract in which a party agrees to buy all product requirements from the other party.

Core Concepts Reviewed

▪ Consideration is the giving of value or incurring a substantial detriment and is an essential element of the contract.

▪ The performance of preexisting obligations, past acts, or moral acts is not sufficient legal consideration.

▪ The exception to the preexisting obligation rule relates to unforeseen external difficulties.

▪ There are some exceptions to the need to provide "consideration." These include charitable pledges, requirements, and outputs contracts.

▪ Promissory estoppel is the legal principle requiring a promisor to perform his promise if he knew or should have known that a promise would incur a substantial detriment based on the promise.

Questions

1. What is "consideration"?
2. What is promissory estoppel?
3. What is an outputs contract?
4. Why is a promise in exchange for another promise sufficient consideration?
5. Why is moral consideration not legally sufficient?
6. Do you agree with the legal principle in question 5? Why or why not?

7. Explain the preexisting obligation rule. What is the major exception? Explain it.
8. What is a requirements contract?

Problems

1. Uncle Henry promises to pay $5,000 to his nephew Robert, who is 16, if Robert does not smoke, drink, or swear until he reaches age 21. Robert keeps his promise. Is he entitled to the money?
2. Whitman agrees to dig a well for Johnson for $2,000. In the middle of the digging, Whitman encounters a swampy substance. He asks Johnson for an additional $500 to complete the job. If Johnson agrees, will he be liable for the $500?
3. Mary, who had been drinking, signs a contract with Happy Health Spa for a one-year membership for $3,000. Is she bound by the contract?
4. Mike agrees to buy every lug nut made by Sam, and Sam agrees. Later, Mike argues that Sam has given no consideration and the agreement is not binding. Is he correct?
5. Cary agrees to make a $1,000 pledge to his church. Later, he changes his mind and argues that the church has given no consideration. Is he liable for his pledge?
6. Wilson agrees to supply all the widgets that Stella needs. In year one, Stella buys 1,000 widgets. Wilson gears up to produce a similar amount in year two, but Stella refuses to accept any widgets and claims there was no contract because of lack of consideration. Is she correct?

Chapter 8

Legal Capacity and Consent

■ The legal ability to consent to a contract (legal capacity) is one of the essential elements of a contract.

■ One must be age 18 in most states in order to agree to a contract. One must also be able to understand the essential terms of the contract.

■ If a party agrees to a contract without legal capacity, she can void the contract at her option.

■ Generally, contracts of minors are voidable unless they are for the necessities of life.

■ Contracts can also be voided if there was lack of true consent. This could result from insanity, mistake, fraud, or duress.

LEGAL CAPACITY

A party must have the ability to understand the essential terms of the contract. A party below the age of majority (18 in most states) is presumed not to have sufficient capacity to agree to all but the simplest of contracts. Persons above the age of consent are presumed to have capacity unless there is a specific reason why the person does not.

There may also be particular reasons why one or both of the parties may not have actually given true consent. These normally relate to inaccurate information about some material fact, insanity, or duress.

Minors

Someone below the age of consent is a minor and is presumed not to have the ability to consent to a contract. This legal principle is designed to protect minors from unfair contracts. As a result, most states will allow a minor to withdraw from a contract even if the minor has accepted benefits under the contract. In addition, most states will allow minors to return the subject matter of the contract even if it has been damaged.

■ Clem, age 16, buys a car from Massive Motors. He drives it for three months and then decides to return it. In most states he will be able to do so. Even though he has accepted the benefits, he is protected from the consequence of his actions. ■

■ Don, a minor, buys a stereo from Big Sounds. He drops the stereo while unloading it from his truck and it smashes into pieces. In most states, Don will be able to return the stereo and recover the full price. Again, the reason is to protect the minor from the consequence of his actions. ■

The lesson for business people is to avoid entering into contracts with minors unless an adult has also agreed to the contract. A major exception to this rule relates to the necessities of life. A minor must be able to purchase necessities in order to carry out daily functions. If the law did not permit them to do so, no one would provide minors with these services or goods.

- Mike, a minor, buys a train ticket to his grandmother's house, which is 30 miles away. This is an enforceable contract because it is a reasonable expenditure of funds to carry out life's daily functions. ■

- Mary, a minor, goes to Hamburger Heaven and buys two hamburgers and a soda for dinner. This will be enforceable because it is a reasonable amount to spend on food. ■

- Max, a minor, buys a compact disk. This is a reasonable expenditure for a minor to spend on entertainment. ■

- Mora, a minor, buys a round-trip ticket to Tahiti. This is not a necessity of life and is not enforceable. ■

There is no precise test to determine the difference between a necessity of life and an expenditure that will not be enforced. Generally, items such as medical expenditures and costs of finding work would be enforceable, while luxuries such as TV sets and expensive cars would not.

Ratification upon Majority

Upon reaching age 18, every minor should review all contracts agreed upon during one's minority. One still can disaffirm the contract for a reasonable time after reaching one's majority. After that, one will be legally regarded as having ratified the contract and be bound to it. A reasonable time will be determined based on all the circumstances surrounding the contract.

- Iggie reaches age 18 and immediately talks to a lawyer. As a result, he immediately disaffirms his "CD of the Day" contract with Rick's Records. He will not be held to the contract. ■

- Same facts as above except that Iggie ignores his attorney's advice and waits one year before attempting to disaffirm. Iggie will be bound by the contract. ■

If one changes the facts in these examples and places Iggie overseas in a military combat unit, six months or one year may not be an unreasonable time to disaffirm the contract.

One can also **ratify,** or affirm, the contract by explicitly stating orally or in writing that one wishes to be bound by the contract. If Iggie had contacted Rick's Records and stated that he wished to continue the contract, he would have ratified it and would be unable to disaffirm the contract in the future.

Another way to ratify a contract is to continue to accept the benefits of the contract. Had Iggie continued to accept the discounted CDs sent by Rick, he would be bound by the contract he agreed to during his minority.

In summary, a minor will be able to disaffirm all contracts, except for necessities of life, during one's minority and for a reasonable time during one's majority. Failure to disaffirm means that one is bound by the contract.

A minor may explicitly ratify a contract by stating that she wants to affirm the contract. A minor may also implicitly ratify the contract by waiting beyond a reasonable time to disaffirm it or by continuing to accept the benefits under the contract.

Persons who lack mental capacity or who were intoxicated from drugs or alcohol when the contract was made may disaffirm the agreement if they can demonstrate that they did not understand the essential terms of the agreement.

Persons already adjudicated insane obviously meet that test. Persons with other mental problems may meet the test. The tests that apply to criminal law or drunken driving do not apply. The issue is whether the person understood the contract's terms. If the contract is declared invalid, the person must pay for the value of what was received and return the subject matter of the contract.

Lack of Genuine Consent

Capacity also means the ability of the parties to give genuine consent. If there was some misunderstanding with respect to material facts, there may not have been an actual meeting of the minds. While most mistakes do not excuse the party's performance, some mistakes will. If both parties made a mistake about a material fact, either party may rescind the contract.

> Alan and Barbara agree to the sale and purchase of a rare coin bearing the stamp of a Denver mint location. Later, they discover that the Denver notation had been fraudulently placed on the coin by a third party. ■

This is a **bilateral mistake** about a material fact and the contract may be rescinded by either party. A series of cases have outlined the same rule. A bilateral (two-party) genuine mistake about a **material** (important) **fact** will be grounds for rescinding the contract.

A one-party mistake will normally not be grounds for rescinding the contract. The purpose for this rule is to promote a level of self-help by requiring people to do their own research into material facts. But, if a party makes a mistake and the other party knew or should have known about the mistake, the party making the mistake may rescind the contract.

> Alice solicits bids for the construction of a house. She receives the following the bids:
>
> | | |
> |---|---|
> | Bob | $49,000 |
> | Charlie | $48,500 |
> | Dinah | $47,000 |
> | Elizabeth | $27,000 |
>
> Alice should have recognized that Elizabeth had made a mistake and allowed Elizabeth to rescind the contract. ■

The purpose behind this rule is to prevent one party from taking advantage of a mistake by another party when they knew or should have known of the mistake. Mistakes that are just the result of poor judgment or routine changes in circumstances will not be grounds for canceling the contract.

> Cookie buys a restaurant based on his belief that the workers at the factory next door will provide a sufficient number of customers to earn a good profit. Unfortunately, the factory closes and Cookie loses his shirt.
>
> Cookie may not recover the purchase price for the restaurant. This was simply a mistake about the future and the other party is not responsible. ■

Another possible mistake relates to innocent misrepresentation about a material fact from one party to another. Because this goes to the "meeting of the minds" it will be grounds for rescinding the contract.

■ Jones misreads his deed and sells a piece of property to Cookie which is actually too far from the factory on which Cookie counted for his customers. This is an innocent misrepresentation about a material fact and Cookie may rescind the contract. ■

Fraud

Fraud is the misstatement about a material fact with either the deliberate intent to deceive or with reckless disregard as to its truth or falsity.

■ Max tells Smith that a used car has been driven 50,000 miles when he knows the odometer has been turned back from 100,000 miles. This is a deliberately wrong statement about a material fact. It is fraud and is grounds for canceling the contract. ■

■ Max tells Smith that the odometer reading of 50,000 miles is correct when he does not know whether it is correct or not. It is later discovered that the odometer had been turned back from 100,000 miles. The statement was in reckless disregard of the truth and consitutes fraud. Smith may rescind the contract. ■

The false statement must have been made about a material fact that caused the other party to enter the contract and it must have caused an injury. Not only can the injured party rescind the contract, but she can also recover three times the amount of damage.

Statements about the quality of the contract's subject matter that fall into the category of mere opinion or "sales puffery" are normally not regarded as fraud.

■ Bob buys a car from Ted, who says that it will "never give Bob any trouble." This is not fraud. Bob is expected to use his own judgment about the car and not take Ted's statements at face value. ■

Statements of opinion which are false could be regarded as fraud if they are made by an expert such an an attorney or accountant who knows that the other party is relying on the opinion. If the other party was injured as a result of the wrong opinion, he can recover damages for the loss.

Silence is not normally regarded as fraud. However, active concealment or attempts to conceal material facts about the transaction will constitute fraud. In addition, silence will be fraud if one has a special duty to disclose all material facts.

■ Charles is executor of Mary's estate. He asks the heirs for permission to purchase land owned by the estate at the current market value, but fails to tell them that a major department store wants to purchase it for an even greater amount. This would be fraud. ▪

Duress

Duress is the improper use of force to compel someone to enter into a contract. If Don Vito threatens to kill Tommy in order to get him to agree to a contract, Tommy can have the contract rescinded.

In some cases, the courts have held that the misuse of vastly superior economic power or the taking advantage of one's weakened economic position would be regarded as economic duress and grounds for rescinding the contract.

▪ J.R. knows that Cliff has a cash flow problem and if he does not receive a payment shortly, Cliff will go out of business. J.R. tells Cliff that he will pay him 30 percent of what he owes him in cash, if Cliff will cancel the remainder of the debt. This amounts to economic duress because J.R. has taken undue advantage of his position and Cliff's economic distress. ▪

Covenants Not to Compete

Buyers of new businesses or employers may want the prior owners or employees to agree not to compete with them in order to protect their businesses. Such convenants not to compete are legally permissible if they are reasonably necessary to protect the business.

''Reasonably necessary'' is defined both in terms of time and geographical scope. While legally permissible, convenants not to compete are not favored because they limit freedom of commerce. They must be part of a larger agreement as well as being reasonable.

▪ A convenant not to compete is included in an agreement to purchase a business owned by Wilson. The convenant states that Wilson may not open a competing business within a mile of the new owner's business for at least one year. This would probably be regarded as an enforceable agreement. ▪

▪ Wilson goes to work for Jones. As part of their employment contract, Wilson will be prohibited from working for anyone in a similar business anywhere in the same state for ten years. This is beyond what is reasonably necessary to protect Jones's business and will be declared invalid. ▪

Impossibility or Impactiability

Changes in circumstances may occur since the agreement was made. While a changed environment is one of the factors that should be considered by the parties, some changes go to the ability of the parties to complete their part of the agreement.

If the courts were to excuse performance simply because it had become difficult or uncertain, all contracts would be lessened in value because of their uncertainty. On the other hand, it is clear that it would be unjust to hold parties to their obligations under all circumstances.

At common law, the standard for excusing performance is impossibility. The new circumstances must be externally caused, unforeseeable, and render performance extraordinarily difficult.

- After the parties agree to the contract, a bad storm damages the subject matter of the contract. This is not unforseeable and will not excuse performance.

- The workers of one of the parties to the contract go out on strike, which makes delivery of the subject matter extremely difficult. These circumstances were not externally caused and will not excuse performance.

- The first typhoon to ever hit southern New Jersey wipes out Amanda's entire blueberry crop, which was the subject matter of her contract with Neil. Amanda's performance is excused on the grounds of impossibility.

The drafters of the Uniform Commercial Code believed that the impossibility standard was too difficult to meet. Therefore, the code substituted the phrase "commercial impracticability" for transactions involving goods. This is somewhat less difficult to meet. It still places the burden on the party claiming that performance should be excused to show that unforeseeable and externally caused changes in circumstances have made performance no longer practical.

Definitions Reviewed

To **ratify** is to confirm a contract upon reaching age 18.

A **bilateral mistake** is a mistake made by both parties to the contract.

A **material fact** is an important fact that goes to the essential nature of the contract.

Core Concepts Reviewed

- Minors, the mentally infirm, and the intoxicated will generally be excused from contracts because of lack of capacity.

- Minors will be bound by contracts for the necessities of life and will be bound by other contracts unless they disaffirm them.

- Bilateral mistakes about material facts will excuse performance. One party's mistakes will excuse performance if the other party knew or should have known of the mistake.

- Fraud, duress, or impossibility will excuse performance under common law.

- Covenants not to compete are valid if they are part of a larger agreement and are reasonable in time and scope.

Questions

1. What is a necessity of life?
2. What are the ways a minor may ratify a contract upon reaching majority?
3. Define fraud.
4. What are the remedies for fraud?
5. What are the remedies, if any, for a mistake about a material fact relating to the consent of the parties?
6. What is a convenant not to compete? When is such a covenant valid?

Problems

1. Tanya, a minor, comes from a rather affluent family. She buys a fur coat for $5,000 at age 16 and wears it for six months. She decides to return the coat at

age 17. Can she do so? Can the fur company recover any money?

2. Randolph, a minor aged 17, subscribes to the Pizza Per Day service. He continues to receive the pizza every day until he is 18 years and 4 months. He now decides to cancel the contract. Can he do so?

3. Robert and Frank agree to purchase and sell a "diamond" ring for $5,000. Neither one knows that the ring is actually rhinestone. Does Robert have a remedy? Does Frank have a remedy if the ring is actually an emerald worth $10,000?

4. Valentine agrees to buy his girlfriend a hope chest for her birthday from Hope Chest City. Before the delivery date, the designated chest is destroyed by a fire and Hope Chest City argues it is excused from performing the contract. Is it correct?

5. Toemain buys Mom's diner for $100,000. The contract of sale contains a clause prohibiting Mom from opening any similar establishment within 30 miles for ten years. Is the clause enforceable? If not, what would be enforceable?

6. Sampson tells Delilah that his car has a V-8 engine. Neither Sampson nor Delilah know much about cars. If it later turns out that the car, which was purchased by Delilah, had a V-6 engine, does Delilah have any remedy?

Chapter 9

Contractual Rights of Third Parties

- Third parties not originally party to the agreement may have rights under the contract depending on the intentions of the original parties and later actions of the parties.

- A third-party beneficiary is a person whom the original parties intended to benefit under the contract. An incidental beneficiary is a person who may benefit as a result of the contract, but whom the parties did not intend to benefit.

- A third-party beneficiary may enforce the contract. An incidental beneficiary may not.

- The original parties to the contract may also involve a third party in the contract through an assignment, delegation, or novation. An assignment transfers both a party's duties and rights. A delegation transfers one party's duties to another. A novation substitutes one party for another.

OTHER CONTRACT BENEFICIARIES

People other than the original parties may have an interest in having the contract completed. If the parties intended that the third party be able to enforce that interest, she is called a **third-party beneficiary.** If the party will benefit under the contract, but the parties did not intend to allow him to enforce that interest, he is called an **incidental beneficiary.** An incidental beneficiary may not enforce a contract.

■ Irene takes out an insurance policy with Behemoth Insurance Company and names her daughter as a beneficiary. Clearly, the two parties intended the policy to benefit her. She is a third-party beneficiary and can enforce the policy. ■

■ Smith obtains a loan from First National Bank which allows him to purchase a new house. Smith signs a loan agreement and gives the bank a mortgage on the property. A few years later, Smith sells his home to Jones. They have an agreement under which Jones agrees to pay Smith's debt to the bank. The bank is a creditor beneficiary and could enforce the agreement between Smith and Jones. ■

■ Bob has a house on Walnut Street. The city contracts with Polly Paving Company to have the street paved. The current street is in terrible condition. When it is paved, the value of all the houses on the street will go up. Even though Bob will benefit from the paving, he is merely an incidental beneficiary and has no power to enforce the contract. Neither the city nor Polly Paving intend for Bob to be able to enforce the contract. If Bob could enforce the contract, all citizens on the street could do so. ■

These examples illustrate the legal principles of common law. In the first and second examples, the parties intended that the third parties benefit from the contract and may assert their rights. In the third example, there was no intention to allow Bob to enforce the contract and he has no legal rights.

Members of the general public would rarely be regarded as third-party beneficiaries. If they were regarded as such, almost everyone could assert rights under nearly every contract. Third-party beneficiaries are normally specifically identified by the parties to the contract.

Assignment of Contracts

One of the parties may decide to transfer her rights and obligations under the contract to someone else. This is called an **assignment.** Generally, a party may assign his or her rights to the contract. This permits freedom of contract and facilitates the ability of various parties to take contracts, divide them into subsegments, and allocate responsibilities to people who will perform them satisfactorily.

The person making the transfer of the rights and obligations is called the **assignor** and the person obtaining the rights is called the **assignee.** If the parties wish to prohibit the transfer of the rights and duties under the contract, they may do so by inserting such a clause in the contract. These clauses will be respected by the courts.

A second example of when assignments are prohibited relates to personal service contracts. The reason is that such contracts are based on the special talents of the individual being employed and the individual should not be allowed to transfer the obligations to someone else who may have less ability.

> Barry agrees to be Basil's butler. Neither Basil nor Barry may assign this contract to someone else. If Barry could assign the contract, the assignee might not be as good a butler as Barry. If Basil could assign it, Barry would get a different employer than he bargained for. ■

An assignment that materially increases the burdens of the other party will also be prohibited.

> Corey has a contract to ship 1,000 cartons of tomatoes from California to Arizona. The other party assigns the contract to someone in New York. This would materially increase Corey's shipping costs and he could refuse to deliver the cartons to New York. ■

The preceding exceptions to the general rule allowing assignments do not mean that routine contracts involving some degree of individualized work or minor changes in performance cannot be assigned.

> Sam has a contract with Conway to build a house. He may assign (subcontract) portions of the contract to carpenters and plumbers unless the main contract specifically prohibits such assignments. While this may mean a somewhat different standard of performance for Conway or may slightly add to Conway's burdens, this is not sufficient for the law to prohibit assignments in this case. ■

Notice of Assignment

Because the assignee is a new party, the assignee should give notice to the other party to the contract of the existence of the assignment. This is to ensure that the other party does not render performance to the assignor, which would prevent the same performance to the assignee.

> Priscilla owes a debt of $400 to Alfred. Alfred assigns this debt to Olson. If Priscilla is not notified of the assignment, she can pay the $400 to Alfred. If Olson neglected to notify Priscilla of the assignment, he will have no remedy against her. Although Olson would have a remedy against Alfred, he might not collect his money if Alfred had spent it or left the area. ▪

Obligations of the Parties

An assignment of the contract places both the burdens and benefits on the assignee. She must now complete the obligations previously agreed to by the assignor. She is also entitled to receive what the other party promised. Unless the other party releases the assignor from liability, the assignor remains liable under the contract if the assignee does not perform.

> Desmond has a contract to deliver 100 bags of cement to Dana for $1,000. Desmond assigns this contract to Donald. If Donald delivers the 100 bags, he is entitled to receive the $1,000. If Donald fails to perform, Desmond remains liable for the delivery. If neither performs, Desmond will owe Dana damages. ▪

Assignments are found frequently in the world of commerce because they allow for the shifting of responsibilities as needs and circumstances change. They are essential in the construction industry because they permit specialization and division of responsibilities. They also tend to promote the completion of contractual obligations.

Delegation

Delegation of duties is similar to assignment. A party may delegate her duties, but retain her rights under the contract. Like an assignment, a party may not delegate her contractual duties if there is a prohibition against delegation in the contract or if the duties are for personal services. Unlike an assignment, the delegator retains rights under the contract.

> Gunther has a contract to transport Harvey's products to New York. Gunther may delegate those duties to Jackson. This is not a personal service contract. Jackson now has the obligation to transport the products. When he completes this obligation, Gunther can look to Harvey for payment and then pay Jackson. ▪

> Martha agrees to be Cindy's personal maid. Martha may not delegate these duties to someone else. The reasons are the same as those prohibiting an assignment of personal duties in a contract. ▪

The major difference between an assignment and a delegation is the retention of rights by the party delegating the duties. However, like an assignment, if the delegatee does not perform the obligations, the delegator remains liable for performing them.

Novation

Unlike an assignment or delegation, a novation totally discharges one of the two parties from the contract by substituting a third party who now takes over both the obligations and benefits of the contract. In this case, both parties agree to the substitution of the third party.

> Abel and Baker have a contract for Abel to supply Baker with a daily supply of sugar. After three months, Abel wants to relinquish his responsibilities and agrees to have Charlie take over the contract. He talks to Baker, who agrees to let Charlie take Abel's place. This is called a novation. There is now a contract between Charlie and Baker. Abel is now relieved of all of the duties and benefits under the contract. ■

A novation is much cleaner than either an assignment or a delegation because there is an agreement to replace one of the original two parties with a third. However, the party agreeing to the replacement ought to ensure that the third party is as responsibile as the original party. In the preceding example, this means that Charlie ought to be as responsible as Abel.

Accord and Satisfaction

An **accord and satisfaction** retains the same parties, but substitutes a different type of performance for the original performance in the contract.

> Sandy agrees to buy Donna's rocking chair for $100. When Sandy arrives with the check, she decides she would rather have Donna's coffee table. Sandy and Donna agree to substitute the coffee table for the rocking chair. This would be an accord and satisfaction. ■

The concept of accord and satisfaction further reinforces the common law doctrine that a contract is an agreement among the parties. They may do what they want with the contract as long as there is no violation of the law or public policy. As long as the parties agree to the different performance, the courts have no interest in the contract.

Core Concepts Reviewed

■ A third party may enforce a contract if the parties intended the third party to be a beneficiary of the contract. People who may have benefited from the contract are called incidental beneficiaries. They cannot enforce the contract.

■ An assignment is a transfer of the rights and obligations of the contract from one party to another. An assignment may be prohibited by the original parties. Personal service contracts cannot be assigned without the consent of the other party. The assignee should give proper notice to the other party to the contract.

■ A delegation is a transfer of the obligations but not the rights under the contract to another. Delegations are subject to the same restrictions as assignments.

■ A novation is the substitution of a third party based on the mutual consent of the original two parties. An accord and satisfaction is the substitution of one type of performance for another based on the mutual agreement of the parties.

Questions

1. What is a third-party beneficiary?
2. What is an incidental beneficiary?
3. Why may an incidental beneficiary not recover under the contract?
4. How does the law distinguish between the two?
5. What is an assignment? How does it differ from a delegation?
6. Why should the asignee notify the other party to the contract of the assignment?
7. Which duties to a contract may be assigned?
8. Which duties to a contract may not be assigned?
9. What is an accord and satisfaction?
10. What is a novation?

Problems

1. Ollie, an optometrist, has a contract to examine the eyes of the members of the New Mexico Hankies baseball team. May he delegate his duties to Felix, another optometrist?
2. Thiel has a contract to operate a drawbridge with the town of Long Tree. Thiel walks off the job with the bridge in the upright position. As a result, Sharon Pebbles was unable to get to work. May Ms. Pebbles bring an action against Thiel for breach of contract?
3. Shmendrake is a cook for Peter's Pizza. He has a contract for $400 per week for one year. Shmendrake goes on strike with other city pizza cooks. May the customers of Peter's Pizza enforce Shmendrake's contract and require him to make pizzas?
4. In 1992 Samantha agrees to an employment manual with her employees. It sets out the rights of both employees and management. Susan joins Samantha's happy family of employees in 1993, but Samantha claims the manual does not apply to Susan because it was written before she began employment. Is Samantha correct?
5. Big Jim has a contract to supply sausages to Frank's Furters. The parties agree to change sausages to hamburgers. Later, Big Jim tells Frank that a contract is a contract, and that he will deliver only the sausages as originally agreed upon. Does Frank have a remedy?
6. Joseph owes $450 to Jack. Jack assigns the debt to Marilyn, who neglects to notify Joseph. After Joseph pays the $450 to Jack, Marilyn brings an action against Joseph because Jack has skipped town. Will Marilyn be able to recover from Joseph? If Marilyn can find Jack, does she have any remedy against him?
7. Peter has a contract with Phil. Later, Phil would like to withdraw from the contract and substitute Lance. Peter and Phil agree to a novation that substitutes Lance for Phil. Peter becomes unhappy with Lance's performance and sues him for breach of contract. He also sues Phil and claims he is responsible for Lance's breach. Is Peter correct?
8. Conklin has a 3-year contract to drive a school bus for the Hillside School District. When Conklin dies, his executor assigns the contract to Conklin's son. When Conklin's son begins to drive the school bus, the school district objects to the assignment. Can the school prevent Conklin's son from driving the bus?

Chapter 10

Contract Termination and Remedies

Breach contract: breach contracts

TIME IS OF THE ESSENCE: Need it done by a special date.

- Most contracts are ended when the parties perform their duties and obligations as specified in the agreement.

- The level of performance required may vary based on the type of contract and terms of the agreement.

- If a party does not perform the contract's obligations, she has breached the agreement and will be held liable to the other party.

- Remedies may include money damages and equitable relief. The purpose of a legal contractual remedy is to place the party who did not breach in the same position he would have been if the contract had been completed by the other party.

CONTRACT TERMINATION

The vast majority of contracts end by satisfactory performance of the contract's obligations or by some settlement of the differences between the parties. When this occurs, the contract is discharged and the liability of the parties ends. The contract could also end through operation of law, mutual agreement of the parties to cancel the contract, or failure of one or more conditions that establish a basis for the contract's performance.

The parties may have set a date for the performance of their duties. But it is not essential that the parties perform their duties on the exact date for performance. The law recognizes human frailties with respect to time of performance. If the contract does not state that performance on the exact date is essential, peformance within a "reasonable time" will be satisfactory. A reasonable time will depend on the nature of the contract and the past dealings of the parties.

- Ross has a contract to deliver eggs to Jerry on July 1st. In this case, a reasonable time after the 1st would be very short because of the rapid perishability of eggs. ■

- Same facts as the preceding except that the contract is for bags of cement. Ross would have a longer period of time after the 1st. ■

The parties' past conduct can also be considered in determining what is a reasonable time after the date for performance.

- Rob has a contract with Laura to deliver ten lamps to Laura's store on the 1st of every month. For six months he delivers them on the 2nd, 3rd, 3rd, 2nd, 4th, and 3rd. Each time, Laura accepts the lamps without protest. If Rob delivers the lamps on the 3rd of the seventh month, it will be presumed to be within a reasonable time. ■

"Time Is of the Essence" Clause

If one of the parties wants to ensure that delivery is made on time, a "**time is of the essence**" clause should be included in the contract. This indicates that performance must be made on the exact date in the contract. If the party is late, there is a breach of contract.

In contracts for the sale of real estate, it is presumed that time is of the essence. The seller must be prepared to deliver the title and the buyer must tender the full purchase price on the closing date specified in the contract.

There are other contracts in which the parties should presume that time is of the essence.

■ Fireworks Frank has a contract to deliver his products for the Fourth of July celebration in Anytown, U.S.A. It is presumed that delivery on July 5th will be too late and will be a breach of contract. ■

Other Types of Performance

The price specified in the contract must be paid in full. It will not be sufficient to pay some percentage of the price and to argue that it is a reasonable amount. The price should be paid in U.S. currency. If payment is made by check, the obligation to pay the price is not completed until the check is paid by the financial institution against which it is drawn.

A contract's other types of performance may be judged by different standards. In some cases, the contract may state that performance must be satisfactory to some named party. This is very common in construction contracts when someone such as an architect or engineer is asked to review another's performance. In these cases, the expert must evaluate the performance in a reasonable manner. That is, she must act as a similar expert would act and not make decisions in an arbitrary manner.

■ Leon and Rowland have a contract for the construction of a new office building. The contract states that Rowland's chief engineer must approve Leon's construction progress.

Rowland's chief engineer should act in a reasonable manner and approve the construction in accordance with reasonable engineering standards. ■

Other contracts provide that a party's performance will be based on an individual's taste. Portraits, candidate photographs, or clothing would fall into this category. The person may approve or reject the performance based on individual taste, but must act in good faith.

■ Wendy buys a wedding gown from Wanda. When Wendy sees the final gown, she may approve or reject it based on her own taste. But she cannot reject it merely because she wants a different gown or has decided not to get married. ■

In a contract that does not demand approval by a specific person, a party must **substantially perform** the contractual duties in order to receive the other party's performance. Substantial performance includes the duty to act in good faith to meet the contract's obligations. It also must include a meaningful completion of the duties. Issues of substantial performance are particularly common in construction contracts where disagreements are common.

■ Fred has a contract with Melvin to build a new house on land that Melvin has recently purchased. The contract has specific requirements for the house's construction. Among these are specifications for cabinets in the den and dining room.

   After construction is completed, Melvin complains that the cabinet doors are not in alignment and refuses to pay for the house. A relatively small deviation such as this does not mean that Fred has not met his burden of substantial performance. ■

■ Jim and Jan have a contract for Jim to build a house on Jan's land. Jim builds the foundation, but has left the walls out of line. The roof is also not properly aligned. This would not be substantial performance. Until Jim corrects these problems, he is not entitled to payment. ■

Like many legal principles, it is not easy to precisely define substantial performance. There must be a good-faith effort and the level of performance must be reasonably close to 100 percent.

Operation of Law

Contracts will be terminated as a matter of law if circumstances change such that a reasonable person should believe that the contract would be ended. For example, if one were a financial advisor to another with the authority to buy and sell property, a reasonable person should expect the advisee would want the contract terminated if either party went bankrupt. Under bankruptcy law, certain contracts may be canceled when a person files for bankruptcy. As a result, if either party files for bankruptcy, the contract may be terminated as a matter of law.

   Many people have heard of the **statute of limitations** as it applies to criminal actions. Most states also have statutes of limitations as they apply to legal actions to enforce contractual rights. If a party does not enforce these rights within the statutory time limit, the rights will be lost as a matter of law.

Conditions

A **condition** is either an express or implicit basis for the completion of the parties' obligations under the contract. The condition normally relates to some event, and the parties may reference the event by a clause in the contract. Depending on how the clause is written, the condition may be a condition precedent, concurrent or subsequent, and may either relieve the party's obligations to perform or require the completion of the duties.

■ Lou wants to buy Frank's bar because it is directly across from the ABC Factory, which supplies dozens of thirsty customers. He inserts a clause in the contract that, if the factory closes within a year, the contract will be canceled and the parties will be returned to their positions before the contract. If the factory remains open, the contract will continue. If it closes, the contract will end. This would be a condition subsequent. ■

> ■ Lou wants to buy Frank's bar, but only if the ABC Corporation moves into the building across the street. Lou can insert a clause in the contract which makes the factory's opening a condition for the performance of the parties obligations. This would be a condition precedent. ■

Conditions can also be concurrent in the sense that performance of one party's promise to pay the purchase price is conditional on the other party's delivering of good title. In the real world, literal enforcement of conditions concurrent would lead to eternal gridlock with no one making the first move. For example, usually a buyer of real estate will hand over the check and then the seller will hand over the title to the land. The transaction is then completed.

Conditions could also be implied at law when they are so obviously linked with the nature of the duties. For example, if a landlord has a duty to make repairs, there is an implied condition that the tenant will allow the landlord to enter the premises in order to do so.

Rescission

Because a contract is merely a mutual agreement among the parties, they may ordinarily terminate the contract by mutual consent. Exceptions exist if there is a public interest in continuing the contract or if there is a third party with an interest in the contract.

Contracts may also be **rescinded** based on a court order. A party may receive such an order based on lack of capacity, lack of informed consent, or fraud. For example, if one of the parties was a minor or a mental incompetent, she could have the contract rescinded.

EXCUSING PERFORMANCE

A party's performance of a contract may be excused if there was a bilateral or mutual mistake. The reason is that a mutual mistake means that there was no true "meeting of the minds."

> ■ Bob agrees to sell his 1950 "D" nickel to Nate for $25. After the purchase, Nate takes the nickel to a coin expert for evaluation. The coin expert discovers that the "D" mint mark is a counterfeit and that the nickel is worth only 50 cents. Neither party knew that the mark was a counterfeit. ■

Nate may rescind the contract on the grounds of mutual mistake. Nate would have the same remedy if they had discovered the mistake before the completion of the sale.

A party's performance will normally not be excused because he made a mistake. This is designed to encourage a party to investigate the circumstances prior to entering the contract. A major exception exists when the other party knew or should have known of the mistake.

■ Handley receives the following bids for a construction project:

Wilson $50,000
Thompson $49,000
Hopkins $48,500
Witherspoon $28,500

Handley should inquire as to whether Witherspoon has made a mistake because his bid is so far below the others. If he accepts the bid without inquiring, Witherspoon would be able to rescind the contract. ■

This legal doctrine is based on the premise that one should not be able to take advantage of another's mistake. One could also argue that there was no true meeting of the minds.

Impossibility of performance is another reason for excusing performance. Routine mistakes, changes in the market, or internal difficulties will not be grounds for excusing performance. There must be an external change in circumstances such that the performance of the contract is not possible.

■ Michael Mason agrees to build a new wall for Harry Homeowner. The price of cement rises sharply and it rains for five straight days. Despite these difficulties, Michael will not be excused from performance. These were foreseeable circumstances. ■

■ Johnson agrees to deliver a new generator to Island Motors. The contract states that the generator will be delivered during the month of February when the lake surrounding Island Motors normally is frozen solid. Johnson attempts to deliver the generator, but the lake is not adequately frozen from one end to the other. The first generator falls through the ice. Johnson attempts to deliver another generator but is unsuccessful. He asks Island Motors to excuse his performance, but Island insists he perform the contract.

Johnson attempts to move the generator across the ice for a third time, but the lake is still not sufficiently frozen. Further performance by Johnson will be excused on the grounds of impossibility. ■

REMEDIES

If a party breaches a contract by not performing her obligations, the other party has a remedy. The most common remedy is the awarding of money damages. The theory of damages is to have the party who breached pay the amount of money necessary to place the injured party in the same position she would have been in if the contract had been completed. This ensures that the non-breaching party will receive what was agreed in the contract. This will include anticipated profits.

■ Kathleen agrees to buy some porcelain vases from Meredith for $10,000 but Meredith refuses to deliver them on the date promised. Kathleen then buys similar vases for $12,000 in a normal transaction in the marketplace. The amount of damages is $12,000 − $10,000 = $2,000. If Meredith pays Kathleen $2,000, it will place her in the same position as if the contract had been completed. ∎

- Robert agrees to buy Harry's automobile for $10,000 but, on the date of delivery, Robert does not have the money to pay Harry. Harry finds another buyer in a normal marketplace transaction for $8,500. If Robert pays Harry $1,500 in damages, it will place Harry in the same position as if the contract had been completed. ∎

The preceding examples also illustrate the concept of "covering." This means to find a substitute for the subject matter of the breached contract. As long as the substitute is acquired in a commercially reasonable manner, it can provide the basis for measuring damages. The difference between the cover price and the contract price will be the amount that the breaching party should pay.

If there are disputes over the level of performance, the parties can use the theory of damages to resolve the amounts due. For example, if a construction contract has not been fully completed, the landowner can pay the builder the contract price minus the amount necessary to bring the project in line with the contract's specifications.

The court may also award nominal damages that indicate that one party has breached the contract, but that there was little or no injury. For example, in a slightly uncompleted construction contract, the court could find a small breach and award $100 for a minor deviation.

Liquidated and Punitive Damages

The parties may provide for **liquidated damages** that are a predetermined amount of money or a method of measuring damages in the event of a breach of contract. **Liquidated damages** will be permissible as long as they are reasonable and do not represent a penalty.

- Tony Tenant has a contract with Larry Landlord. The contract provides that if Tony is late with his rent of $500 per month, liquidated damages of $5 per day will be added. This is reasonable and should be sustained. A late fee of $50 per day looks like a penalty and should not be sustained. ∎

Punitive damages are those additional damages above and beyond normal damages which are assessed against a defendant in order to punish him for wrongful conduct. Punitive damages are not common, but are assessed against defendants in contractual cases involving fraud or other deliberately wrongful activity.

- Uriah's Used Cars regularly turns back the odometers of the autos in his lot. Anna buys one of Uriah's cars and later brings an action for fraud. She would be entitled to recover three times the normal damages from Uriah for fraud. ∎

Equitable Remedies

An equitable remedy is one granted when money damages are inadequate to place the injured party in the same position she would have been in if the

✗ contract had been completed. A decree of specific performance is equitable relief and will be awarded when contracts concern real estate or involve unique goods.

1. ▦ Jones has a contract to buy Chilton's house. If Chilton refuses to convey the deed, Jones can bring an action for a decree of specific performance which will compel Chilton to sell the house. All land is presumed to be unique, and equitable relief is appropriate. ▦

2. ▦ Cecil has a contract to buy a guitar once owned by Elvis Presley. This is clearly a unique good and a decree of specific peformance would be an appropriate remedy. ▦

exam!

Definitions Reviewed

Liquidated damages are those damages that are specified by the parties in the contract.

A **breach of contract** is to not perform one's duties under the contract. This violates the contract's terms.

A **"time is of the essence" clause** requires the parties to complete the contract on the exact date specified.

Substantial performance is the good-faith completion of a substantial portion of the contract's terms.

Statute of limitations is the time within which a claim for breach of contract must be brought.

A **condition** is some event on which the performance of the contractual duties is based.

A **rescission** is to cancel the contract.

Punitive damages are the amounts of money awarded to punish the other party.

Core Concepts Reviewed

▦ The parties must perform their duties in order to discharge the contract. The level of performance required depends on the nature of the duties and the terms of the contract.

▦ A party who does not perform his contractual duties is in breach of contract. He will be liable for damages.

▦ Remedies for breach of contract include compensatory money damages which are designed to place the injured party in the same position she would have been if the contract had been completed.

▦ A decree of specific performance is equitable relief, which will be granted in contracts involving real estate and unique goods. It compels the other party to perform the contract.

Questions

1. To what extent must a party perform his obligations on the date specified in the contract?
2. If the contract calls for performance in accord with someone's approval, what level of performance will discharge the contract's obligations?
3. What are liquidated damages?
4. What are punitive damages?
5. What is a decree of specific performance?
6. When will it be granted?
7. What is impossibility of performance?
8. What is the criteria for determining impossibility of performance?
9. When will a mistake excuse a party's performance?

Problems

1. Smits has a contract to have a campaign portrait done by Stuart. The photo accurately reflects Smit's likeness, but he rejects it becauses it does not look sufficiently "presidential." Can Stuart recover his contractual fee?

2. Agee has a contract to have a new office building built by Kenline. The contract states all construction is to be approved by Agee's architect. The architect rejects the work without examining it. Does Kenline have a remedy?

3. Maurice has a contract to purchase a wide-screen TV set from Arne. When Arne refuses to sell the set, Maurice brings an action against Arne for specific performance of the contract. Will Maurice prevail?

4. Woody agrees to purchase Moses' Bible for $200. Later, Woody refuses to buy the Bible and Moses sells it to David for $195. Moses comes to you and asks for your advice regarding this transaction. What do you tell him?

5. Sands buys a house from Thompson on Maple Street in Springfield. When Thompson refuses to go through with the transaction, he tells Sands that he will return Sands's deposit and pay all of his expenses. Sands tells you that this is his dream house and he does not want the money. He asks for your advice. What do you tell him?

6. Hadley buys a crankshaft from Baxter. The contract provides that the delivery date is June 1st. Baxter does not deliver the crankshaft until June 3rd. Hadley brings a legal action to recover his lost profits from June 1st until June 3rd. May he recover the lost profits?

7. Novak has a dairy farm and has agreed to supply 1,000 cartons of milk to the Hilltop School District every day. One week, his cows become sick with the "bovine blues" and are unable to give milk. Novak claims that his performance is excused because it is "impossible." Is he correct?

8. Harris, in order to complete his dime collection, agrees to buy a rare dime from Waferd for $1,000. On the delivery date, Waferd refuses to convey the dime to Harris. Harris wants the coin badly, and buys one from Daly's Dimes for $1,350. He then brings an action for breach of contract against Waferd. How much should he be able to recover?

PART III

PROPERTY

Chapter 11

Property Interests

■ Personal property are items other than land. These items may be tangible or intangible.

■ Real property is land and those items that are attached to land, called fixtures.

■ Property may be held either individually or by multiple ownership. If it is held by more than one person, each must approve of its sale. There are a number of different types of multiple ownership.

■ Both real and personal property may be passed by sale, gift, or inheritance. Real property may be subject to a number of interests in addition to outright ownership.

■ Gifts of property may be made with either the intention to dispose of it for a reason relating to one's life or to make arrangements for the disposal of property because of one's inpending death.

PERSONAL PROPERTY

Personal property encompasses things other than land or items affixed to land. For example, automobiles, TV sets, yachts, and stocks and bonds are all examples of personal property. The person in possession of the personal property is presumed to be the owner unless another can prove superior rights, called good title.

■ Susan had a collection of old Falling Rocks records. The records are stolen by the family's gardener, who sells them for value to Charles. James, a mutual friend, informs Susan that the records are in Charles's possession.

Susan brings a legal action against Charles. She has friends testify that she treasured the Falling Rocks records, and that she would never sell them or give them away. Susan testifies to the same set of facts and precisely identifies the records and the album covers.

Because Charles did not acquire ownership rights from the gardener, he will lose to Susan even though he has possession of the records. Susan owned the records and did nothing to lose ownership. Susan will prevail and recover the records. ■

Large items like automobiles often have **documents of title**. Possession of these documents is extremely strong evidence of ownership of the personal property. However, in unusual cases one may prove a superior right of ownership to the personal property than the person holding the documents.

Automobile owners usually acquire title from the dealer. Normally, state laws require that the document of title be registered with the secretary of state or some similar office. The registration of the ownership at a governmental office normally provides a measure of protection against the automobile's theft as well as for creditors of the owner who have an interest in the automobile.

A warehouseman will normally give the owner of items of property stored at the warehouse a receipt. The warehouse receipt identifies the property and allows its holder to transfer the property to someone else without moving the goods.

Bills of lading are documents that a carrier issues to a shipper. The bill identifies the goods and the party who will take them at the end of the shipment. Invoices and bills of sale are other documents that indicate title to items of personal property.

Acquisition of Personal Property

A person may acquire personal property through the sale of an item from one person to another. This is probably the most common way of acquiring property, and forms the basis of our American system of commerce.

Often, a person receives some sort of evidence of title, such as a receipt or bill of sale. The seller may have acquired the property from another party, such as the manufacturer or wholesaler. In this case, it is important for the purchaser to have good title.

> ■ Terry makes TV sets. He manufactures 100 sets and sells them to Holly Wholesalers. Holly then sells them to Ricky's Retailers, who sells a set to Frank. The bill of sale will normally follow the TV set from Terry on through Frank. ■

The adoption of the Uniform Commercial Code has made it largely unnecessary to research the chain of title before purchasing property from a reputable merchant. A person who pays for the goods and acts in good faith will prevail over others with a claim to the title. But this may not apply if the seller is not a merchant. A buyer should be careful to ensure that the seller has the title to the property before buying it. A review of sales documents and a few pointed questions about the chain of custody will be helpful to the buyer.

Gifts and "Finders Keepers"

The person making the gift is called the **donor** and the person receiving the gift is called the **donee**. In order for there to be a legally completed gift, there must be a donative intent and delivery of the item. A donative intent means that the donor must intend to actually make a gift. There must be a clear intention to part with ownership of the property. This intention must be clear and must relate to the present. A future intention is not sufficient.

The delivery may be **actual** or **constructive**. A delivery of a ring, a TV set, or an automobile would be examples of actual delivery. A delivery of the keys to an automobile would be an example of a constructive delivery.

A gift made during one's life is called an **inter vivos gift**. A gift made in contemplation of one's death is called a **gift causa mortis**. This type of gift also must include a donative intent and delivery. However, there are other rules relating to its completion. The gift will be considered revoked if the donor does not die of the current illness. The term "current illness" is normally interpreted rather broadly.

■ Grandpa Wilson is dying of pneumonia. He calls his three grandchildren to his bedside and gives them each $1,000. For a few days, Grandpa gets better. He says nothing about the gifts during this period of recovery. Grandpa then has a relapse. He dies of a combination of old age and his previous illness. This would still be regarded as dying of his current illness for the purposes of the gifts. ■

A second requirement of a gift causa mortis is that the donor die before the donee. If the donee dies first, the gift from the donor is revoked. The purpose of the gift was that the donor wanted to give the donee something before he died. If the donee dies first, that purpose no longer exists, and the gift should be revoked.

■ Before Sampson dies, he wants to give his gold watch to his grandson. He calls his grandson to his bedroom and gives him the watch. The grandson is so excited that he decides to go out and celebrate at a local nightclub. On the way, he gets into an automobile accident and is killed. His grandfather hears of the news and dies of a heart attack the next day. The gold watch will revert to the grandfather's estate. ■

Another way to acquire personal property is to take it through an inheritance. People are able to give property to future generations by conveying it in their wills. Normally, this is done to show love and respect.

A person who is given property from a will is called a beneficiary. A person who receives property under a will may accept it or reject it. When a person dies, someone usually is named to administer the estate and she will distribute the property in accordance with the terms of the will or the laws of the state.

Another way to acquire property is to find it. The property could be either mislaid or abandoned. **Mislaid property** was placed at a location by an owner with the intention of retrieving it. **Abandoned property** has been placed at a location by an owner who has no intention of retrieving it. If a person finds mislaid property, it still belongs to the owner. A finder of mislaid property should report the finding to the proper authorities. There are laws that allow the finder to notify the appropriate legal entity and to claim ownership after a period of time. If personal property is mislaid, an owner is likely to return to the same location in order to find it. As a result, the property owner has a greater right to mislaid property than the finder of the property.

■ Jones sees a wallet in a hotel lobby. If he picks it up and gives it to the hotel, the hotel will have greater priority to the wallet than Jones. This is mislaid property. ■

If one finds property in the street, and reports the finding to the proper authorities, he has greater priority to it than anyone except the true owner. This will be regarded as abandoned property. When someone finds abandoned property, the finder has priority over other people to the property. It is presumed that the true owner has abandoned the property and the title to it. Factors such as the location of the property and the intention of the owner will determine if the property has been mislaid or abandoned.

Tenancy in common
L> property goes to heirs.
children.

■ Property left on counters and desks is likely to be regarded as mislaid. Property left in the street or in empty lots is likely to be regarded as abandoned. ■

Multiple Ownership

she gets property.
& joint tenancy with right of survivorship.

Real and personal property may be held by a single owner. It may also be held by more than one person. Property held by more than one person is usually held jointly. Joint ownership may be with **right of survivorship** or without the right of survivorship. Right of survivorship means that the surviving owner automatically inherits the deceased owner's share of the property upon the death of the other owner. The property may also be held without the right of suvivorship. In this case, the share of the deceased partner may be given to the deceased partner's heirs. This is called a tenancy in common.

Husbands and wives often hold real property as tenants by the entireties. A tenancy by the entireties requires a valid marriage. A tenancy by the entireties also has a right of survivorship. When one spouse dies, the other is entitled to all the property.

It has become common in recent years for spouses to hold property as joint tenants with a right of survivorship. While this facilitates transfer of property when one of the spouses dies, it can make it more difficult to sell if the spouses do not agree about the sale. It can also make tax planning more difficult.

Multiple ownership may be terminated by agreement of the parties or by a court order. If a joint tenancy with right of survivorship is terminated, it becomes a tenancy in common. Tenants in common may sell their individual interest without the consent of the other.

Intangible Personal Property

Copyright!

Personal property also includes intangible items like stocks, bonds, patents, and copyrights. **Intangible property,** like stocks, represent ownership interests in something else. These interests cannot be seen or touched. However, they are important to our society. Intangible property may be held singly or jointly. It may be sold, given away, or inherited by another.

A patent is the right to gain exclusive use of an invention or a scientific process. Patent law is a very complex area that requires knowledge of both science and the law. A patent relates to some scientific invention or process that is unique. A person may acquire an exclusive use of the invention or process for 17 years. She may also sell licenses that authorize other people to use the process.

■ Susan invents a process for turning lead into gold. She may use the process herself or she may sell licenses to use the process to someone else. This could obviously be a very lucrative venture. ■

A copyright gives a person the exclusive use to an artistic or literary work. Songs may be the subject of a copyright. Articles and books may be the subject of a copyright. A copyright lasts for the life of a person plus 50 years. Copyrights, like patents, may be bought and sold.

- Michael Baxton is a well-known singer. He purchases the copyrights to every song recorded by the Neetos, a well-known recording group who performed during the 1960s. Michael may now record the songs and use them in his own act. In addition, he can prevent others from recording them. ▪

An account receivable is the right to be paid based on a debt that is owed. Accounts receivable are common to large retail stores that sell goods based on credit. Each credit customer will have an account receivable with the store. These accounts receivable are intangibles because they cannot be touched. They do have value to the creditor. One of the chief values of an account receivable is that it can be borrowed against and can serve as collateral for the loan.

- Sam's General Store and Novelty Shop has 500 accounts receivable from its customers totaling $50,000. Sam's borrows $20,000 from the Ninth National Bank. It also gives its accounts receivable as collateral for the loan.

  In the event that Sam does not repay the loan, the bank can take over the accounts receivable and collect the accounts from Sam's customers to pay off the loan. Often, banks have a very good idea as to the percentage of accounts receivable which they will be able to collect and can make their loans in accordance with collection schedules. ▪

Accounts receivable may also be sold from one party to another. Financial institutions regularly buy accounts receivable and collect the amounts themselves. Other intangibles, like stocks, bonds, patents, and copyrights, may also be used as collateral. These intangibles may also be sold to other parties. This type of transaction may become very complicated and appropriate advice should be obtained from qualified counsel.

REAL PROPERTY

land

Real property consists of land and items that are affixed to land. An item that is attached to land is known as a **fixture.** A fixture is an item of personal property that has become a permanent part of the real estate.

- Jones owns land known as Blackacre. He puts concrete posts on the property and drives them deep into the land. The posts were personal property before being driven into the land, but then became part of the realty. These posts have become fixtures. ▪

Sometimes, it is unclear if an item of personal property has become a fixture. The law has developed several tests to decide the issue. The first is to look at how permanently the item is attached to the land. If it would be very difficult to remove the personal property without harming the realty, it is likely that it has become a fixture.

Another test is the intention of the parties. Although it is often difficult to determine what is in the mind of an individual, one may discern the intention from court testimony and from the person's actions. If it is clear that a person intended that the personal property become a fixture, the law is more likely to regard it as a fixture.

A third test is the nature of the personal property. If the personal property has been specially designed for the real property, it is likely to be regarded as a fixture. If the personal property is rather common and could be used in other real property, it is less likely to be regarded as a fixture.

■ Ruggles Rugs designs a special carpet to be installed in Harry's store. The rug exactly matches Harry's decor and fits precisely into Harry's odd-shaped showroom. When Harry sells his store to Marvin, Harry wants to take the rug, but Marvin objects. Given the specialized nature of the rug, it would be regarded as a fixture and Harry could not remove it. It has become part of the real estate and belongs to the new owner. ■

■ Jones puts down a new carpet. He nails the carpet on the floor with large nails. It would be impossible to remove the carpet without damaging the floor. The carpet would be regarded as a fixture because it is permanently attached to the real property. ■

Interests in Land (Realty)

One of the unique characteristics of land is that it is subject to a number of interests other than outright ownership. Land has always been divided into interests in order to satisfy specific needs of different parties.

A **life estate** is the right to use realty for the remainder of one's life. A life estate is an interest in realty which was commonly given to a surviving spouse. A life estate is still a valuable interest to give a child because it allows the child to remain in the family home.

■ John and Mary Wilson own a large home in the country. They have a daughter, Jane, who has some physical problems that make it difficult for her to work. John and Mary give Jane a life estate. This will permit her to stay in the house after her parents are dead. ■

A life estate may be sold to another. The length of the life estate will still be measured by the life of the seller. While less common than in prior years, use of a life estate is still a valuable tool. It can be used to safeguard the family home and, in some cases, giving a life estate can result in estate tax savings.

Another type of interest in real estate is an **easement.** An easement gives a person the right to cross land or use the land for a very specific purpose. This is an interest frequently given to a utility company.

■ Jones owns Blackacre, on which his family's eight-room house is located. Jones needs to have gas in his house in order to heat it.

The gas company needs to run a line through the land from the street to the house. Jones gives the gas company an easement to run the line through his property. ■

An easement may be private or public. The easement in the preceding example is a private arrangement between Jones and the gas company. The easement could also be public. For example, if a landowner allows pedestrians to use the land as a shortcut between two streets, the easement is public and the land-owner may be barred from closing the shortcut in the future.

Although a life estate ends when the person dies, an easement runs with the land. That is, the easement will continue after the ownership of the land has been transferred to someone else.

■ If Jones sells his land to Cochran, the gas company's easement will continue. ■

Another interest in land is a **license,** which gives a person the right to use the land for some period of time. A license to use land could be express. When a person goes to a ball game, she is usually granted a license to sit at the stadium for the length of the game. The terms of that license can usually be found on the back of the ticket to the game.

The license could also be implied. A homeowner grants an implied license to allow a postal carrier to deliver the mail by crossing the property to reach the mailbox. Implied licenses are also granted to other people who deliver items to one's home or come to check meters or perform other functions.

Leases

A **lease** grants a person — the tenant — the right to use land for some period of time. The owner of the land is the landlord and the person occupying the land is the tenant. A lease may be for a period of years, months, or at-will. A lease is sometimes called a tenancy.

A lease for a period of more than one year would normally fall under the statute of frauds and should be put into writing. The lease should include the names of the parties, a description of the premises, the length of the lease, the amount of the rent, the method and time for payment, and any provisions for renewal. Other terms might include information about deposits, the rate of interest on the deposit, liquidated damages for late payment of the rent, the right of the landlord to inspect, and any other provisions that would be of importance to the parties. The parties should include provisions regarding the legal ability of the tenant to sublease the property to another party.

The state legislatures have passed a number of statutes that regulate leases. In many states, the lease must be written in "plain English" so that it can be understood by an average person. This eliminates many clauses which were found in some leases.

Other statutes require the landlord to keep the tenant's deposit in an account that earns interest on the tenant's behalf. A series of other statutes have made it difficult to remove the tenant in the event of a dispute over the rent or other matters.

The common law tended to favor the landlord in disputes with the tenant. Courts began with the premise that a landowner had the right to control his property. It was presumed that the landowner had the right to establish the provisions of the lease with a tenant, but growth of large apartment buildings altered this situation. Direct contact between tenants and landlords tended to diminish, making form contracts more important. At the same time, the proximity and larger numbers of tenants gave them added political influence.

These factors resulted in state legislatures passing a number of laws to give tenants additional bargaining power. Furthermore, many local governments now have the authority to regulate local rental markets. As a result of these factors, many jurisdictions passed laws that set maximum rents or otherwise affect landlord-tenant relations.

■ Jones has a lease with Smith in the town of Daisy, New Sweater. A local ordinance provides that Jones may not raise Smith's rent more than the area-wide rate of inflation. If Jones wants a higher increase, he must petition the local rent-control board, which will listen to both sides and then rule on the request. ■

■ Holmes owns an apartment building in the town of Daisy Park. His standard lease states that tenants may not sublease the apartment to anyone else. Watson, one of Holmes's tenants, gets the other tenants to join an association and petition the local city council to pass an ordinance requiring landlords to allow tenants to sublet their apartments. The council debates the matter and passes an ordinance stating that a landlord's decision on subleasing must be based on "reasonable" criteria. It creates a local board to determine what is "reasonable" and to develop a rental code. ■

Other Conditions and Terms   The tenant, absent terms to the contrary, is entitled to the exclusive possession of the premises during the period of the lease. The tenant must make ordinary repairs to the premises. She may be held liable for injuries that occur within the premises and are the result of her negligence. She may also be held liable for failure to notify the landlord of the need for any major repairs within the premises.

■ Roz rents an apartment from Large Landlord, Inc. She has been living in it for six months when she notices a medium-size hole in the living room floor. She places a throw rug over the hole but does nothing else. A few months later the hole has gotten bigger. Roz still does nothing. One night, she has Robert to dinner. He steps on the throw rug and falls through the hole into the apartment below. Roz will be held liable for her negligence in not having the floor repaired. ■

The landlord is responsible for maintaining the common areas of the tenant's building. The landlord must take reasonable care of the premises and will be liable for failing to maintain them in that condition if a tenant or another person is injured as a result of the failure.

■ Sarah is a tenant in Amazing Apartments. She invites Stuart to dinner. He walks down the hallway to her apartment and slips on some water, which was left on the hallway by the landlord's custodian. The landlord's liability extends to people, such as Stuart, who a landlord could expect to be on the premises. ■

A landlord may not attempt to exclude her liability for negligence in not maintaining the premises. Clauses in the lease which attempt to do so will be ruled invalid as a matter of public policy. If a tenant is injured as a result of the landlord's negligence, a clause in the lease stating that the tenant may not sue will not protect the landlord.

At common law, a landlord would not be held liable for crimes committed on the premises. However, some recent court decisions have held landlords liable for failure to take adequate precautions to prevent crime. In a society characterized by a high crime rate, these court decisions provide added protection to tenants.

Rent and Warranty of Habitability   The primary responsibility of the tenant is to pay the rent when it is due. At common law, a tenant was required to pay the rent regardless of the condition of the premises or the completion of the landlord's other duties. Recent court decisions and legislation have substantially modified the previous common law. The legal concept of **constructive eviction** states that a tenant may withhold rent if the building's conditions are so bad that the dwelling becomes not livable. This concept has been bolstered by court decisions and legislation that establishes a **warranty of habitability.** This means the premises must be fit to live in. If they are not, the tenant need not pay the rent. There are no precise criteria for establishing if the premises are habitable. Small defects would not make the premises uninhabitable, but major defects would.

■ Hopkins lives in an apartment owned by Regency Apartments, Inc. There are small leaks in the plumbing. The leaks cause some minor and annoying drips. Hopkins decides not to pay his rent and cites a violation of the warranty of habitability. These relatively small problems would not be sufficient to excuse Hopkins of his responsibility to pay the rent. ■

■ Susan lives in Aardvaark Apartments. There are major plumbing problems, which cause large leaks and leave substantial puddles throughout the apartment. This makes it impossible for Susan to live a normal life or to have guests in her apartment. This would be a breach of the warranty of habitability and Susan may withhold her rent. ■

The tenant may be liable if she is late with the rent payment. The parties may set damages for the late payment of rent by the tenant. The amount is called liquidated damages. These damages will be upheld as long as they are reasonable. But if the damages are unreasonably high, they will not be upheld.

The landlord may evict the tenant if he fails to pay the rent or if he damages the property. The landlord must notify the tenant in accordance with the lease's provisions. If the tenant refuses to leave after being notified, the landlord may bring court action to have the tenant evicted.

At common law, the mere failure to pay the rent would have been sufficient to remove the tenant. In recent years, it has become more difficult to evict the tenant. Court delays and statutory provisions supporting tenants rights have limited the power of landlords.

A tenant will be liable if he causes damages to the premises. The tenant will be liable for triple damages if the tenant commits or permits deliberate damages to be done to the premises.

■ Coleman and his friend decide to have a Fourth of July party in Coleman's apartment. They buy some sparklers and fireworks and set them off in the apartment. This causes severe damage to the floor and to the walls. Coleman will be liable for three times the damage to the walls and the floor. Coleman may also be evicted from the apartment. If Coleman has given the landlord a security deposit, the landlord may take the damages out of the deposit. ■

If the landlord evicts the tenant, the landlord has a duty to act in good faith to try to minimize the tenant's damages. The landlord may complete this duty by renting the premises to another tenant. The landlord is expected to make a reasonable effort to find a new tenant. If the landlord places an advertisement in a paper of general circulation, it will be presumed that this duty has been satisfied.

■ Terry, a tenant in Larry's house, signed a one-year lease for $3,000 in annual rent. Terry stops paying rent after six months and leaves the house. Larry finds a new tenant after a three-month search and leases Terry's room for the same rent. Terry will owe three months' rent or $750. ■

Conveying Ownership

Ownership of real property is called a fee simple title. Real property may be owned by one person or by more than one person. Ownership in realty may be conveyed by inheritance or by operation of law.

Because of the historic importance of real estate ownership, special requirements are imposed on the transfer. All contracts for the sale of real estate must be in writing in order to satisfy the statute of frauds. There is normally more than one written document associated with the sale of real estate.

A seller may either employ a real estate agent to help him sell the realty or may sell it himself. The seller will reach an agreement with the purchasers of the realty. This agreement must be put into writing. The contract should contain the names of the parties, a reasonable description of the property, the consideration (price), the date for closing, a description of any fixtures subject to the sale, and any other information that is material to the sale. These added terms might include a description of any interests of people other than the owner on the property, the method and times of payment, and the amount of the initial deposit. All of the parties should sign the contract.

Another method of conveying title is by inheritance. A person may bequeath realty just like any other property. The executor or administrator will settle the estate and then convey the land. This will require the issuance of letters testamentary by the court, which will allow the executor to convey the property.

Owners of real property may convey it as a gift just as they may give personal property. The usual rules relating to gifts apply to a gift of real property. There must be a donor and donee, an intent to make a gift and a delivery of the property. Delivery of real property is accomplished by giving the deed to the property.

Real property may also be acquired through adverse possession. If a person openly occupies land without the permission of the owner for a period of time in excess of what the state statute requires, she will become the land's owner.

■ For 23 years, Angie has lived on land belonging to Gregory, without his permission. She makes no attempt to hide her possession. On the contrary, she has built a small dwelling and lives in it. Angie has acquired ownership of the property. ■

Transfer of realty by sale, gift, or inheritance requires the delivery of a deed. A **deed** is a document indicating the ownership of real estate. A deed contains the legal description of the property, its location, the names of the grantor and grantee, language indicating a desire to transfer the property, signatures of witnesses, and signatures of the grantor and grantee.

A deed is normally witnessed by a legal official such as a notary public. It is also usually recorded in the county where the property is located. This confirms the ownership of the property and places others on notice as to who owns the property.

Types of Deeds   A deed is evidence of ownership. However, there are different types of deeds and some have different provisions than others. Although a deed indicates ownership, others may still contest the grantee's right to the realty. If there is a contest, the provisions of the deed may give the grantee a remedy against the grantor.

In a **general warranty deed,** the grantor warrants that she has good title to the property, that there are no encumbrances on the property other than those listed on the deed, and that she will defend the grantee's title to the property. In a **special warranty deed,** the grantor warrants only that she has done nothing to impair the grantee's title.

A **quitclaim deed** has the least value of all. It states, in essence, that the grantor is conveying only whatever title she has. The grantor gives no warranty at all.

■ Mary gives Herbert a quitclaim deed on Blackacre. If Mary has good title to Blackacre, Herbert now has good title. If Joe can prove he had better title to Blackacre than Mary, he will prevail in a contest with Herbert. In addition, if Joe defeats Herbert in a contest over the title, Herbert will have no remedy against Mary. If Mary had given Herbert a general warranty deed, he would have had a remedy against Mary. ■

Because of the uncertainties regarding title and the value of deeds, title insurance is a method of protecting the grantee. Title insurance allows the grantee to pay a premium to the title insurance company and receive a lump-sum payment if the claim to the property's title is lost because of some defect. The grantee may not recover the property, but is compensated for the loss. Banks that lend money to new homeowners normally require that the borrower purchase title insurance.

Mortgages

A financial institution that lends money to someone for the purpose of purchasing real estate will want to have some security for the loan. A **mortgage** and the other agreements between the borrower and the lender set forth the terms for the repayment of the loan. They also allow the lender to foreclose on the realty and sell it to pay off the loan if the borrower does not make the payments.

The owner of the property is the mortgagor and the lender is the mortgagee. The mortgagor usually promises to keep the property in good repair, pay all local taxes, and do nothing which would hurt the interests of the mortgagee. The mortgagee also normally requires the mortgagor to obtain insurance on the property. This insurance will cover damage to the property from fire and other hazards.

The mortgagee should record his interest in the property to place other potential creditors on notice. The landowner may use the land for security on other loans. This will create secondary interests that are subordinate to that of the primary mortgagee.

The mortgagee may assign its interest in the mortgage to other financial insitutions. This is a rather common practice among banks, mortgage companies, and other financial institutions. The consent of the mortgagor is usually not necessary for the assignment.

A mortgagor may sell the property and allow the buyer to take responsibility for making the payments. This is called an assumption of the mortgage. Some agreements prohibit an assumption of the mortgage without the consent of the mortgagee. Because this may make it burdensome for a homeowner to sell the house, some states have made it more difficult for a financial institution to enforce this provision.

Default by Owner   The landowner's major obligation is to make the payments to the mortgagee when they are due. If the mortgagor defaults on the payments of either the principal or the interest, the mortgagee may foreclose on the property.

Despite the impression of some, financial institutions do not want to foreclose on property. They want to lend money and have it paid back without problems. If the mortgagee must foreclose, it is entitled to any attorney's fees necessary to enforce its rights.

If the mortgagee must foreclose, it should sell the property in a commercially reasonable manner with the objective of gaining as high a price as possible. The sale may be public or private. If it is commercially reasonable, it will be permissible. A sale to the mortgagee's employee would not be permissible.

If the mortgagee receives a price sufficient to pay off the loan, the mortgagor will be relieved of any further financial obligation. If it receives less than the amount due, it may recover the difference from the mortgagor. If it receives more than the amount owed, it must give the landowner the difference.

■ Jones owns a house, on which he still owes $100,000, when he loses his job. He is unable to continue his payments on his mortgage to the Twenty-third National Bank. The bank has no choice but to foreclose on his house. The bank holds a public auction and accepts the highest bid of $90,000. Jones will still owe $10,000 to the bank. ■

If there are secondary mortgages, these must also be paid from the amount that is obtained from the foreclosure action.

■ Wilson owns a house on which there is still a primary mortgage of $120,000 and a secondary mortgage of $50,000. He defaults on both mortgages and the primary mortgagee is forced to foreclose on his home. The primary mortgagee finds a buyer after a series of advertisements for $150,000. The primary mortgage of $120,000 will be paid. The secondary mortgagee will be paid $30,000 and Wilson still owes $20,000 to the secondary mortgagee. ■

Other Interests and Eminent Domain

If a landowner owes money to others, they may obtain liens on the land. This places the owner in the position of satisfying the lien before she is able to convey the property to someone else.

One possible lien includes that by a judgment creditor. For example, a person may win a breach of contract or liability suit. A method of enforcing the judgment is to place a lien on a landowner's property.

A person who does work on the landowner's property, such as a mason, painter, or other worker, expects to be paid. If they are not paid, they may place a lien on the property for the amount they are owed.

Local, state, and federal governments may also place liens on a landowner's property if taxes are not paid. Federal and state governments levy income taxes, which must be paid. Local governments will levy taxes on the landowner's property. If these taxes are not paid, the government will place a lien on the property owner's land.

The right of the government to "buy" realty for a public purpose is called **eminent domain.**

While a fee simple owner has greater rights than anyone else to the land, the government may take the land in order to carry out a public purpose. The government must pay fair value for the land. The government will usually propose one value and the landowner will propose another value. The parties may be able to reach an agreement between themselves. If not, the government and the landowner may let the court decide on the true value.

■ Hatcher owns Blackacre. The state government wants to put a highway through the land. The state government places a value of $100,000 on the land. Hatcher hires his own expert to value the land. She states the land is worth $250,000. The two parties cannot reach an agreement. They go to court and the judge values the land at $165,000. This is what Hatcher will receive. ■

Definitions Reviewed

A **documents of title** is written evidence of ownership of goods.
A **donor** is a person making a gift.
A **donee** is a person receiving a gift.
Mislaid property is property that the true owner wants to reaquire.

Abandoned property is property the owner has no intention of retrieving.
The **right of survivorship** gives a joint tenant ownership of property if the other joint tenant dies.
Intangible property is personal property one cannot touch. Stocks represent ownership rights in a cor-

poration and are an example of intangible property.

Real property is land and items affixed to the land.

A **fixture** is an item of personal property which has become permanently attached to real property.

Life estate is the right to live on land for one's life.

Easement is the right to use land for a specific purpose.

License is the right to use land for a particular purpose. It is normally of shorter duration than an easement.

A **lease** is a written contract from a landlord allowing a tenant to reside on land for some period of time.

Constructive eviction is the right of a tenant to withhold rent if the premises are not habitable.

A **warranty of habitability** is the landlord's guarantee that the premises are fit for normal living.

A **deed** is a document that indicates the ownership of real estate.

A **general warranty deed** warrants that the seller of land has good title.

A **special warranty deed** warrants that the seller of land has done nothing to impair the buyer's title.

A **quitclaim deed**—seller conveys to buyer whatever rights he has in the land.

A **mortgage** is a security interest in land given by the owner to a creditor.

Core Concepts Reviewed

■ Real property (realty) is land and those items that are affixed to the land.

■ Personal property consists of everything other than real property. Personal property can be tangible or intangible property.

■ There are two types of gifts. A lifetime or inter vivos gift is made with a motive to benefit someone during one's life. A gift causa mortis is made by a person in contemplation of death.

■ Both real and personal property may be transferred by sale, gift, or inheritance.

■ Both real and personal property may be owned singly or by more than one person. Multiple owners may hold the property with a right of survivorship, which means that the surviving owner receives the property when the other owner dies.

■ Land may be divided into different ownership interests. A fee simple interest represents the largest share of rights in land. A life estate is the right to occupy land during one's life.

Questions

1. What is personal property?
2. What is real property?
3. What is a fixture?
4. What are the tests for determining if an item is a fixture?
5. What is an inter vivos gift? What are the requirements for the completion of the gift?
6. What is a gift causa mortis? What are the added requirements for a completed gift causa mortis?
7. What is a life estate?
8. What is the difference between lost and mislaid property? What are the consequences for a finder?
9. What is a right of survivorship? What are the consequences to the surviving owner?
10. Give some examples of intangible property.
11. What is an easement?
12. What is a tenant's liability for its premises?
13. What is the liability of the landlord?
14. What is the warranty of habitability?
15. How does the warranty affect the concept of constructive eviction?
16. What is a quitclaim deed?
17. What is a mortgage?
18. What is eminent domain?

Problems

1. Tom owns a tavern in the town of Liquor City. He has a special countertop installed in the tavern. When he sells the real property he wants to take the counter with him, but the new owner argues that it is a fixture and must remain with the tavern. Who will prevail?

2. Donna has a ring that belonged to her mother. She tells her daughter, Barbara, that she will give her the ring before she dies. Donna never gives Barbara the ring. When Donna dies, Barbara demands the ring from Donna's executor. Should Barbara receive the ring?

3. Bob has a serious heart condition. He decides to give his grandson, Joe, the watch that belonged to his father. He gives the watch to Joe. Bob does better for about a month, but then dies of a heart attack. Bob's executor demands that Joe give the watch back to the estate. He argues that Bob had not completed the gift. Who will prevail and why?

4. Frank sees a wallet in a hotel lobby. While he wants to find the true owner, he wants to keep the wallet's contents if he cannot find the true owner. What should he do?

5. Sam and Sally are married. They own Blackacre as joint tenants with the right of survivorship. Sam decides he wants to sell his half of the property, but Sally will not give her permission to sell. If Sam tries to sell the property, will he be successful?

6. Sam and Sally continue to fight about the real estate. When Sam dies, his will states that his share of the property will belong to their daughter, Susan. Will Susan or Sally prevail in a contest over the land?

7. Lucy lives in the Lucky Landlord's apartments. She invites her boyfriend, Lou, to dinner. Lou steps on a piece of soap in the kitchen and falls down. No one knows how the soap got onto the kitchen floor. Lou's lower-left leg is injured. Lou sues both Lucy and Lucky Landlord. Who will be liable for Lou's lower-left leg injury?

8. After Lou finishes his dinner, he steps out into the hallway and trips over a mop left on the hallway floor by Lucky Landlord's custodian. This time he injures his lower back. He sues both Lucy and Lucky Landlord. Who will be liable for the injury to Lou's lower back?

9. Grandmom Gertrude lives in a high-crime area apartment. She has regularly complained to Frank, her landlord, that the front door is left unlocked, but he does nothing about it. One night a mugger breaks into Grandmom Gertrude's apartment. He takes a TV set and then hits Grandmom Gertrude over the head with a baseball bat. The evidence shows that the mugger just walked in the front door.

Grandmom Gertrude sues Frank. He argues that he cannot be held responsible for crimes committed in the neighborhood. Who will prevail?

10. Wendy lives in an apartment in a big city. One day she sees a cockroach on the kitchen floor. It is the first insect she has ever seen on the premises. Wendy stops paying her rent and claims that she has been constructively evicted. Is she correct?

11. Joan lives in a different apartment building in a different part of town. One day she looks down and sees that her white kitchen floor looks black. She then notices that the floor appears to be moving. Upon a further glance, she sees that the floor is actually covered with thousands of little black insects. She refuses to pay her rent and argues that she has been contructively evicted. Will she prevail?

12. Tom Turbo lives on the old family homestead of Greenacre. The state needs the land for a new jughandle it will construct to connect the road in front of Greenacre to the state highway. Turbo says Greenacre has been in his family for over a century and he won't sell. He further says, "This is America and I don't have to give up my land." Will Turbo prevail? Why or why not?

Chapter 12

Bailments and Property Rental

- A bailment is the temporary relinquishment of personal property by the owner to another. A bailment is not a sale. The owner intends to get the property back. The owner of the property is called the bailor and the person receiving the property is called the bailee.

- A bailment may be for the primary benefit of the bailor or for the primary benefit of the bailee. The bailment may also be for the mutual benefit of both the bailor and the bailee.

- The explosion of the rental business has created new interest in the law of bailments. A person who rents an automobile has created a bailment. A person who rents a videocassette also creates a bailment. A person who leaves an automobile in a parking lot creates a bailment if the key is left with an attendant.

- The test as to whether a bailment has been created is whether the bailor has given up control to the bailee.

- Both the bailor and the bailee have certain duties with respect to the bailment. The bailee's major duty is to safeguard the property subject to the bailment. The bailor's duty is to ensure that the bailed property is not dangerous or likely to injure the bailee.

BAILMENTS

Bailment is one of those strange legal terms that confuses people. A bailment has nothing to do with going to jail or getting out of jail. A **bailment** is the temporary relinquishing of property by the owner to another. The owner has the intent of retrieving the property at a later date. The crucial test of whether one has created a bailment relates to control of the property. If the owner keeps control, it is a license. If the owner gives up control, it is a bailment.

- A car owner parks her car in a parking lot. If she keeps the keys, the lot's owner has given the car's owner a license to park the car in his lot. ▦

- A car owner parks her car in a parking lot and hands her keys to the parking lot attendant. She has now created a bailment. ▦

- A person eating at a restaurant leaves her coat on a coat hook near the front of the restaurant. This is not a bailment. ▦

- A person leaves her coat with the coat-check person and takes a ticket. This does create a bailment. ▦

The crucial test is the extent to which the owner of the property has relinquished control to the other party. The owner of the property is the **bailor** and the person to whom it is given is called the **bailee.** When a bailment has been created, both the bailor and the bailee have certain duties.

Bailee's Duty of Reasonable Care

When a bailment is created, a bailee has a duty of reasonable care with respect to the property. Reasonable care means that the bailee must use that degree of care which a reasonably prudent person would use under the same circumstances. If the property is damaged while it is in the control of the bailee, a rebuttable presumption is created that the bailee failed to use reasonable care.

■ Frank parks his car at Joe's car lot and hands the keys to Joe. When he returns, Frank notices that his car has a huge dent in the hood.

When Frank gave his keys to Joe, a bailment was created. It is presumed that Joe's negligence caused the damage to the hood. Joe may rebut the presumption only by showing that the damage was caused by some other reason over which he had no control. ■

■ Lucy leaves her typewriter to be repaired at Tom's Typewriter Shop. When she returns with her ticket one month later, the typewriter is missing. Since this is a bailment it is presumed that Tom's negligence resulted in the loss of the typewriter. Unless Tom can explain the loss of the typewriter, he will be held liable to Lucy. ■

The **presumption of negligence** could be overcome by a showing that the loss of the bailed property was caused by some unforeseeable, external factors. These might include an act of war, an unexpected governmental action, or unusual weather conditions.

As indicated by the preceding examples, the delivery of the item could be actual or constructive. Handing over the keys to a car would be an example of a constructive delivery. The delivery of a coat would be actual delivery. The owner has created a bailment with the establishment that received it.

The presumption of negligence is one of the key differences between a bailment and a license. In a license agreement, the licensor is simply giving the licensee permission to use the space. The licensor does not take control of the personal property and cannot be held liable for its loss.

Types of Bailments

A **mutual benefit bailment** is one in which both the bailor and the bailee receive something of value from the bailment. The vast majority of bailments fall into this category. Nearly all rental agreements fall into this category.

In a mutual bailment case, the bailee is expected to exercise the same degree of care as would be exercised over personal property. The bailee may not be required to exercise extraordinary care, but must not be careless with the bailor's property.

A bailment for the primary benefit of the bailee would occur if the bailor lent the bailee property for use without charge. In this case, the bailee must exercise a high degree of care over the property. The degree of care should reflect the free use of the property.

■ Bob lends Joe his lawnmower for the weekend. Because Joe is getting free use of the mower, he should take extraordinary care of it. While he might not protect his own mower from the rain, he should do so with Bob's mower. He should also take additional steps to protect it from other hazards. ■

At the other extreme, a bailment might be for the primary benefit of the bailor. In this case, the required care demanded of the bailee would be less since he is doing the bailor a favor.

■ Bob asks Joe to warm up his car over the weekend while he is on vacation. If Joe accepts the assignment, he must make certain that the car is not stolen and he must warm it up as agreed. This does not mean that Joe must take every possible precaution to make certain that the car is safe. ■

Commercial Bailees

If the bailee is a **commercial bailee** such as a warehouseman, she must exercise a degree of care suitable for people in that occupation. Because commercial bailees charge a fee, they are expected to be professionals, and they must exercise the degree of care associated with professionals.

■ A warehouseman is expected to store items in a manner that will keep them dry and safe from the elements. While the average bailee may not take such precautions, a warehouseman should place items on wooden pallets to keep them away from water that might flow into the building. ■

In addition, a professional bailee must take care to examine all the documents associated with transferring the items to another. If the bailee gives the items to the wrong person, she can be held liable for negligence. An ordinary bailee will be held liable for intentionally giving the items to the wrong person.

A commercial bailee may limit his liability to the bailor with respect to assuming the risk for certain bailed goods. He may not attempt to limit liability for his negligence in the future.

Hotels are a type of commercial bailee. They may hold items of value for guests or patrons may place valuable items in their rooms. At common law, innkeepers or hotel owners had unlimited liability for items that were lost or stolen. Now, most states have passed laws that allow hotel owners to limit their liability if they place notices in the rooms advising their guests of the limitation.

■ Donald checks into a hotel room with some valuable items in his luggage. On the door to the hotel is a notice that limits the hotel's liability to $500 unless the valuables are stored in the hotel safe. If Donald leaves valuable items above that amount in his room, the hotel will not be liable if they are lost or stolen. ■

Another type of commercial bailee would include parking lots. As previously noted, attempts to limit the commercial bailees liability for their own negligence will be void as being against public policy. For example, Don parks his car in the hotel parking lot and an attendant takes his key. When he returns, the car has been stolen. The attendant points to a sign that states, "This parking lot is not responsible for the theft of vehicles or their contents." This sign has no legal significance. It is void against public policy and will not protect the parking lot against liability resulting from its own negligence. Most businesses are aware of these court decisions, but they leave these signs in place to intimidate people who are not aware of the law.

■ Sally brings her clothes to Larry's Laundromat. She puts them in the machine and they are torn to bits. Larry points at a sign that reads, "If your clothes are damaged by our machines, it's your tough luck." If Sally does not know the law, she is likely to do nothing. ■

Liability of Carriers

A **common carrier** is a very special type of bailee. A carrier's responsibility is to take goods and deliver them from one location to another. A carrier has the responsibility of delivering the goods safely and without damage. A carrier will be liable if the goods are lost or damaged during the shipment unless the loss was caused by an act of God, an act of a public enemy, an act caused by the shipper, an act of public authority, or the inherent nature of the goods.

■ Wilson gives his goods to Tom's Trucking for transport down the Atlantic coast. A heavy rainstorm pelts some of the trucks. Water flows in and damages the goods.
     While this rainstorm was caused by nature, it is not an act of God which will excuse Tom's Trucking from liability. The firm will be liable for the damage to Wilson's property. ■

■ When Jackson is delivering a truckload of textbooks, the truck is stopped and hijacked by a group of young people wearing college and high school sweatshirts. The truck is recovered, but the books are gone.
     Although Jackson may regard this as an act by a public enemy, these students are not a declared public enemy, and Jackson will still be liable. ■

■ Hopkins is delivering a truckload of fireworks when they begin to explode. He pulls over the truck and yanks open the door in time to see a rocket fly past his ear. Later it is discovered that the fireworks were inherently unstable and should not have been delivered by truck. In this case, Hopkins will not be liable. ■

Bailee Rights

Previously, the law was primarily concerned with the bailee's duties. After all, the major obligation of the bailee was to safeguard the bailed property and to deliver it back to the bailor in good condition.

However, the bailee does have the right to make reasonable use of the property except when it is obvious that she should not use it. For example, a parking lot attendant should not decide to use one of its customer's cars. A coatroom attendant should not decide to wear a person's coat and walk around the block wearing it.

If the bailee rents the property, it is clear that she has the right to use it for the purposes intended. It would be impermissible to use it for improper purposes.

■ Joe Bob rents a car from Smertz Rent-a-Car. He immediately enters it in the local stock race and crashes into the vehicle ahead of him. This would be an improper use and Joe Bob would be liable for the damage. ■

■ Robin rents a videocassette from Ralph's Rent-a-Movie. She uses it to hammer a small nail into her wall. This would be an improper use. ■

If the bailee is holding the property for the benefit of the bailor, the bailee is entitled to a fee for her services. If the bailee is a commercial bailee, she is entitled to the fee specified in the agreement. In addition, most states allow commercial bailees to place a lien on the property if the fee is not paid. This may compel the bailor to sell the property in order to pay the bailee.

Rights and Duties of Bailors   *paid fee!*

The bailor is entitled to receive her property in the same condition as it was delivered. If she is a **commercial bailor,** she is entitled to the fee specified in the agreement. This is becoming a more important issue as more items are being rented for periodic use.

At common law, a bailor had the duty to warn the bailee of any hidden defects of which the bailor was aware.

■ Joe lends Tom his lawnmower for the weekend. Joe knows that the blade is loose. This is not a defect that Tom would discover based on a reasonable inspection. Joe has an obligation to warn him about the blade. If he does not and Tom is injured as a result, Joe will be liable for the injury. ■

A bailor would also have an obligation to inform the bailee if others will be asked to use or purchase the property.

■ Howard lends Daniel his automobile. He neglects to tell Daniel that Bob has a key to the car and may use it over the weekend. Daniel parks the automobile in front of his house. Bob comes to the car and opens the car door. Daniel rushes out of the house because he believes Howard's automobile is about to be stolen. Daniel and Bob get into a fistfight about the automobile. Howard will be liable for any injuries that result. ■

Rental of Property

While people have been renting property to others for years, there has been an explosion in the rental market over the past several decades. This has significantly changed the law of bailments and made it more important to society.

The mass rental of items has also significantly changed the duties of the parties. This is particularly true regarding the duties of the bailor. While the bailor has always had the obligation to provide safe products and to warn the bailee of potential defects, the obligation has been strengthened by the growth of commercial bailors.

People who rent products have less opportunity to inspect them and must rely on the capabilities of the bailor. As a result, if the product does not work for the purposes intended, the bailor should bear the responsibility. This is particularly true if someone has been injured as a result of a product defect.

If the product does not work as intended, the bailee has a remedy for breach of contract. There is an implied warranty that the property will be suitable for the purpose for which it was rented.

■ Bill rents a videocassette at Val's Videos. The tape malfunctions and Bill is unable to watch the cassette. He would be entitled to have his rental fee returned. ■

A breach of warranty that the bailed item will work as intended also raises all the usual issues that prevail with respect to a breach of contract. These issues would include any consequential damages that flow from the breach.

■ Ralph rents a hole digger from Tools Unlimited. He needs the digger to complete a series of wells related to one of his construction projects. The hole digger does not work correctly and Ralph cannot finish the job. As a result, he hurts his relationship with the customer and loses a major contract for the next job. May he recover damages related to the current job and the one he lost? Under contract law, the answer is in the negative because Tools Unlimited could not have known about the extent of the possible loss unless Ralph had told them. ■

The same issue would occur with respect to time. If time is of the essence and an unexpectedly large loss would result from a delay, the person renting the property should inform the bailor. If the bailee does not inform the bailor, the bailor should not be held liable because of the subsequent delay.

Other contractual matters in a rental agreement between bailor and bailee might include issues relating to a lack of true consent and lack of capacity.

■ Mike, a minor, rents a 100-inch super-high-intensity TV set from Terry's TV Land for one year. The price for this rental is $1,000. Because Mike is a minor and this is not a contract for a necessity of life, it is voidable. ■

Rental agreements are a type of bailment. The laws relating to both contracts and bailments are applicable. It will be interesting to observe the evolution of bailment law as the rental market continues to grow.

Tort Liability of Bailor

Normally, damages relating to a contractual breach are relatively small, but the damages can be very substantial if an injury results from a product defect. Determining whether the bailor is liable may depend on whether the bailor enters bailment agreements for compensation. Commercial bailors will be held to a higher standard of care than bailors who are not compensated.

■ Jones lends his lawnmower to Frank. Hawkins rents a lawnmower from Larry's Lawnmowers. Larry will be held to a higher standard of care than Jones. Jones must warn Frank of any latent defects in the mower. Larry must provide a safe lawnmower. ■

At common law, a bailor could be held liable for negligently giving the bailee an unsafe product. This is still true and gains added significance for commercial bailors.

■ Lou rents a hair dryer from Hair City. When he uses the dryer, it malfunctions and burns his head. It is discovered later that the dryer had also burned the last two people who had rented it. Hair City will be liable for its negligence, and for the amount to compensate Lou for his burned head. ■

In addition to being held liable under general principles of negligence, some courts have also begun to apply a warranty of merchantability to commercial bailors. The premise is that a commercial bailor is similar to a merchant and should be held to the same standard. As a result, someone who rents items commercially will be held liable if a defect in the product causes an injury to the user or someone else. The bailor will be held liable regardless of the bailor's negligence.

■ Alan rents a tent from Tent City and puts it up in the middle of his backyard. In the middle of the night, the tent poles break and the tent falls on Alan. He is badly injured. Based on the warranty of merchantability, Tent City will be liable if a defect in the poles or the tent caused Alan's injury. Tent City will be liable even if Alan cannot show any specific act of negligence. ■

■ Pat rents a hammer from Hammer City, which is on the main highway near his home. Pat uses the hammer to drive in a nail. Unfortunately, the head of the hammer flies off the handle and hits him on the head. Pat will be able to recover from Hammer City because there was a defect in the product that caused his injury. Pat need not show negligence. ■

The preceding examples illustrate the **doctrine of strict liability.** The defendant will be held liable if a defect in a product rented by a bailee caused injury. The bailor will still be liable even if he can demonstrate that he used reasonable care. Courts have held that this liability will also extend to any person the bailor could have reasonably foreseen would be injured by the defect.

■ Susan rents an automobile from Cathy's Car Rental. She is driving on her vacation to Rizzy World with her friend Norma. The brakes on the car fail and Susan crashes into a tree. Susan is not hurt, but Norma is badly injured.

At the trial, Cathy's Car Rental demonstrates that it checks the brakes every day and produces records to that effect. Cathy will be held liable under the doctrine of strict liability for Norma's injuries. Cathy could have reasonably foreseen that Susan would have a passenger in the car. ■

These legal doctrines of strict liability for a commercial bailor who rents defective products were designed to permit recovery for an injured party and to promote product safety. While they have accomplished these goals, they have also led to an increase in lawsuits and an increase in the cost of products for both buyers and renters.

The bailor will have a defense if the bailee used the product improperly. But this is not easy to show. Bailors have to expect some degree of different use. The legal test is whether the use was one that the bailor could have reasonably expected.

■ Lloyd rents a portable hair dryer from Hair City, a commercial bailor. He washes his cat and uses the dryer on the cat's fur. Unfortunately, the dryer is set on "hot," and the cat's fur catches on fire. The cat is injured. This is a use that Hair City might have reasonably expected. It may be a bit unusual, but it is within the scope of the product. ■

■ John rents a hedge trimmer from Hank's Hedgies. He decides to cut down some of his trees after he finishes the hedges. The clipper grabs into the trees and breaks apart. One of the pieces flies out and cuts John's face. Although John was injured, he should not be able to recover from Hank's. This is not a use that Hedgies could have expected. ■

Because of the possibility of product misuse, commercial bailors should place notices on rental items. They should indicate not only the purposes of the product, but also which uses are not appropriate. This should help prevent injuries and could also provide a degree of protection to the bailor.

An issue closely related to product misuse is the bailee's use of required or recommended safety equipment. If the bailee did not use safety equipment, should he be able to recover?

■ Jones rents a welding iron from Weldon's Welders. When he got the welding irons, Walt Weldon handed him a pamphlet that described how the iron should be used. It stated in bold print that the operator should always wear safety goggles. Despite the warning, Jones used the welding iron without the goggles. A spark flew up and injured his eye. Even in strict liability jurisdictions, Jones will probably not be able to recover. He used the product in disregard of the instructions and his own safety. Absent some showing of a product defect that would have caused the injury regardless of the use of goggles, Weldon's will not be liable. ■

In states that require some showing of negligence by the defendant, Jones's conduct would either reduce or preclude his recovery. In some states, Jones's failure to use the goggles would be viewed as at least comparative negligence and would reduce any recovery. In others, it would be regarded as contributory negligence and would bar any recovery.

A flagrant disregard of the safety instructions will bar recovery by a bailee.

■ Harry rents a snowblower from Snow City. Despite written instructions not to dismantle any part of the snowblower and to use it only for driveways and sidewalks, Harry removes the safety guard. He takes the snowblower into the mountains and starts to clear ski trails for Ski Paradise.

Halfway through the sixth ski trail, the blower falls apart. One of the pieces cuts Harry's leg. Harry will not be able to recover because of his misuse of the product. ■

Definitions Reviewed

Presumption of negligence: if a bailment is created, the bailee is presumed to be negligent if the property is damaged while in his control.

A **commercial bailee** is someone who is paid for holding the property of another.

A **common carrier** is someone who transports property from one location to another for a fee.

A **commercial bailor** is someone who rents property to bailees.

Doctrine of strict liability is the legal doctrine that a commercial bailor will be held liable if a defect in the product causes injury.

Core Concepts Reviewed

■ A bailment is the temporary relinquishment of property from the owner to another. The property owner, called the bailor, expects to receive the property back in the same condition as it was in when given to the the bailee.

■ A bailment is not a sale because the owner does not part with the title to the property.

■ A bailment is different from a license because the bailee takes physical control of the property. A license merely gives a person the right to use property.

■ When a bailment is established, it creates certain responsibilities for both parties. The bailee's major responsibility is to protect the property until it is returned to the bailor.

■ If the property is damaged while it is in the possession of the bailee, it is presumed that the bailee was negligent and was responsible for the loss.

■ Commercial bailees are those who take care of property for a fee. They are held to an even higher standard of care than an ordinary bailee. Warehousemen, innkeepers, and common carriers are held to a higher standard of care than an ordinary bailee.

■ The rapid growth of the personal property rental market has resulted in a new group of commercial bailors who are held to higher standards than ordinary bailors. They receive a fee for renting their products and are expected to supply safe products to their customers.

■ Some courts have applied a warranty of merchantability to commercial bailors. This means that they will be held liable if a defect in the product causes an injury to either the bailee or to another.

■ The bailor will have defenses against liability if the bailee misused the product or disregarded instructions as to its use. In some states, the misuse of the product will preclude recovery or will reduce the level of damages.

Questions

1. Distinguish bailments from licenses.
2. What is the presumption of negligence? To whom does it apply? When does it apply?
3. Name some different types of bailments. How do the responsibilities of bailors and bailees differ in these bailments?
4. What is a commercial bailee?
5. Name some types of commercial bailees.
6. What is a common carrier?
7. What are the liabilities of a common carrier?
8. When will a common carrier not be liable?
9. What provisions limiting a commercial bailee's liability will be valid?
10. What type of provisions to limit liability will not be valid?
11. What are the rights of the bailor in a mutually beneficial bailment?
12. What are the rights of the bailee in a mutual-benefit bailment?
13. What is a commercial bailor?
14. What are the duties of a commercial bailor?
15. How do the duties of a commercial bailor differ from the duties of an ordinary bailor?
16. What is the warranty of merchantability?
17. How does the misuse of the product by the bailee affect the liability of a commercial bailor?

Problems

1. Mary goes to a soccer game at Kick Stadium. She parks her car at a lot outside of the stadium after being directed into the lot by a uniformed parking attendant. She takes her key and other valuables into the stadium. After the game, Mary returns to the lot and discovers that she has dents on the hood and the side doors. Does Mary have a claim against either the stadium or its parking facilities?

2. Suzie goes to a high-quality restaurant that features valet parking and white-linen service. She leaves her coat with an attendant at the cloak room. There is a sign next to the room which reads, "not responsible for lost or damaged coats." When Suzie returns from dinner, she discovers that her coat is missing. Suzie complains, but the attendant points to the sign and says, "Too bad." Does Suzie have a claim against the restaurant?

3. Phil puts his products in a railroad car in the Reliable Railway Line to be shipped from New York to Chicago. He pays Reliable Railway their fare and receives a receipt. In the middle of the trip, the Reliable Railway train is held up by a group of unknown terrorists. Phil's products, and those of every other shipper, are stolen. Reliable Railways defends against Phil's claim by arguing that this was an act of a public enemy. Can Phil recover?

4. Danny rents a paint sprayer from Penny's Paint Palace. In the accompanying brochure it states that the paint sprayer is for home use only. Despite this warning, Danny uses the sprayer to paint a large commercial building in the neighborhood. The sprayer has been worn out by the large amount of spraying. Does Penny's Paint Palace have any remedy?

5. Norman asks Larry if he can borrow his hatchet. Larry tells him, "OK, I'll let you have it over the weekend for 20 bucks." Norman gives Larry the 20 bucks and takes the hatchet. Larry forgets to tell Norman that the handle has a tendency to come off with use. Norman uses the hatchet over the weekend. In mid-swing, the hatchet's head flies off and hits Norman in the head. Does Norman have a remedy against Larry?

6. Gilbert rents a word processor from Words'R'Us in order to type a term paper for his class in business law at Knowledge College. Unfortunately, the word processor does not work and Gilbert cannot type his term paper. Gilbert fails business law and does not graduate from Knowledge College. May Gilbert recover lost earnings from Words'R'Us?

7. Lewis rents a television set from Tom's TV Land in order to have a Super Bowl party at his house. In the middle of the fourth quarter, Randy, one of Lewis's guests, bends down to adjust the volume switch, and the picture tube blows up in his face. When Randy sues Tom's TV Land, it defends on the grounds that it did not rent the TV to Randy and is not liable for his injures. What is the result?

8. Joe rents a butcher knife from Kyle's Knives. Joe brings it home and cuts some meat with the knife. He then decides to use it to trim some of his hair next to his ears. Joe cuts off one of his ears, and brings suit against Kyle's to recover for his injuries. Will he be able to recover?

9. Sam rents a sledgehammer from Hank's Hammers and brings it home. He uses the sledgehammer to drive some large nails into his concrete patio. Hank's wife, Harriet, then asks him to put in a nail for a picture frame in their living room. Hank takes the sledgehammer and hits the nail. He hits it so hard that the plaster cracks and the wall is ruined. In addition, one of the pieces of plaster flies off and cuts Sam's face. When Sam brings an action to recover for the damage to his wall and his face, Hank's Hammers defends on the grounds of product misuse. Can Sam recover?

10. Debbie goes to Beaver Beach where she rents a beach umbrella from Ursula's Umbrellas. Debbie is told that the umbrella should be set up by a beach boy. Ursula's beach boy is away putting up another customer's umbrella.

Debbie says that she wants to get to the beach, and that she will set it up herself. She pays for the umbrella and sets it up. One hour later, the umbrella falls down and injures Debbie. Debbie sues Ursula's for her injuries. At the trial, evidence is introduced showing that the umbrella will fall down if the wind is blowing and the umbrella is not set up properly. Will Debbie be able to recover for her injuries?

NOT!

Chapter 13

Trusts, Wills, and Estates

Wife or husband
got 1/3 if not in will!

- A trust is a legal mechanism that allows a creator of the trust to give assets to a trustee to manage them on behalf of a beneficiary. The creator can protect others through a trust.

- A trust established to take effect during one's lifetime is called a living or inter vivos trust. A trust established in one's will to take effect upon one's death is called a testamentary trust.

- A will is a document that disposes of a person's property upon one's death. Because of the nature of a will, there are special requirements that must be satisfied in order for the will to be valid.

- A person who dies with a will is said to die testate. A person who dies without a will is said to die intestate. In either event, the deceased's estate must go through the process of probate before assets are distributed to the heirs.

- Both the trustee and anyone who adminsters an estate have fiduciary responsibilities to manage the account competently and in the best interests of the parties involved.

TRUSTS

Trusts are one of the law's most interesting concepts. A trust is a legal document that establishes a vehicle for allowing a person to give assets to another to manage on her behalf or on behalf of another.

The person who establishes the trust is called the settlor, trustor, or creator. The person who receives the property and manages it is called the trustee. The person on whose behalf the trust is administered is called the beneficiary. The property in the trust is called the **corpus.** The document establishing the trust is called the instrument, trust document, or trust declaration.

> Bert Bigbucks has his attorney draft a living-trust document that names the local trust company as the trustee. The document names his retarded granddaughter as a beneficiary. He places $1,000,000 of stock in the trust. The trust company has the legal title to the stock. It must manage the corpus for the benefit of the granddaughter, who has the equitable title. ■

As noted in the preceding example, the trustee has the legal title to the trust property. This allows the trustee to hold, buy, and sell assets in the trust. The beneficiary has the equitable title to the **corpus.** While the beneficiary may not buy and sell assets in the trust, she has the right to expect that the trust assets will be managed for her benefit.

A trustee must always act in the best interests of the beneficiary. The trustee, as a fiduciary, must also exercise sound business judgment. At the least, the trustee chosen by Bert Bigbucks should diversify the stock porfolio so that the holdings are spread out over many companies. The beneficiary may bring legal action if the trustee fails to act in accordance with its fiduciary duty and the beneficiary is damaged as a result of such a failure.

Types of Trusts

An inter vivos or living trust is a trust document that creates a trust during the lifetime of the settlor. It takes effect immediately on the delivery of the assets and the signature of the creator. In a living trust, the settlor parts with the assets while alive. She may make the trust irrevocable or revocable. If the trust is irrevocable, the assets may not be returned to the creator. If the trust is irrevocable, certain tax advantages may also ensue.

If the trust is revocable, the settlor may have the assets returned. While this is a safer course for the settlor, it can undermine the purposes of the trust. It will also eliminate any tax advantages sought by the settlor.

Trusts may be utilized for a variety of lifetime purposes. A trust could be established to benefit a minor, an elderly adult, a pet, or the settlor herself.

- Mary is an elderly, rather sickly woman. She places her assets into a trust account and names Nineteenth National Bank as trustee. She names herself as beneficiary. As a result of this trust, she protects her assets, receives professional management, and can arrange to receive a monthly check representing income from the trust. ■

- Bob has an elderly father who needs financial assistance. He knows his father hates to ask him for money. Bob establishes a trust, naming a bank as trustee and his father as beneficiary. The bank sends his father a monthly check from the trust income. In this way, his father is helped, and need not ask Bob for money. ■

Another type of trust is called a testamentary trust. This trust takes effect upon the death of the settlor. It is usually placed in the will of the settlor but it could also be done with another document. Because a testamentary trust does not take effect until death, the settlor is able to keep the assets while she is alive.

A testamentary trust may be established to assist spouses, children, pets, or charities. The use of testamentary trusts is particularly helpful because it can save estate taxes, help the beneficiaries, and permit the settlor to retain his assets.

- Alice owns two cats that she loves very much. She lives alone and has no close relatives. In her will, she establishes a testamentary trust and names her cats as beneficiaries. She appoints her attorney, Frederick Conley, as trustee. Frederick will then manage the trust for the benefit of the cats. ■

- Debra belongs to the local "Good Times Are Happening" church. She has become part of their big happy family. Debra does not have much money and needs what she does have for living expenses. She sets up a testamentary trust in her will. She names the Thirty-first National Bank as trustee and designates the GTAH church as the beneficiary. It will receive the income from the trust. ■

Trusts may be established for a variety of charitable purposes. Many charities are funded by trust income. One could use a trust to benefit the elderly, colleges, students, houses of worship, people with special problems, or anyone else.

If the purpose of the trust is left vague, circumstances change, or if the designated charity ceases to function, it may be unclear whether the trust should continue. In these cases, the court may exercise the **cy pres doctrine**.

This doctrine states that a court will try to find another charitable purpose rather than have the trust fail.

> In 1900, Franklin established a trust to provide scholarships for children of buggy-whip manufacturers in the city of Detroit. By 1940, there were no more buggy-whip manufacturers in the city. It would be appropriate for a court to award the scholarships to children of automobile manufacturers under the cy pres doctrine. ■

Application of the cy pres doctrine will allow charitable trusts to come as close as possible to satisfying the settlor's original purpose.

Special Trust Situations

A **spendthrift trust** contains provisions that attempt to restrict the beneficiary's right to assign his interest in the trust to creditors or others. This type of trust is designed to protect beneficiaries from their own reckless spending.

These provisions would restrict a creditor's right to have his debts paid. As a result, some states have sharply restricted the ability of beneficiaries to cite these provisions in order to avoid the attachment of their trust income. This has usually been done by statute.

The provisions in a spendthrift trust may be binding if drawn in good faith. They will have no effect if there was an attempt to commit fraud.

> Howard owes his creditors over $300,000. He takes his assets of $400,000 and puts it in a trust. He names himself as beneficiary and appoints his son as trustee. The trust states that the income from the trust may not be assigned to anyone or attached by creditors. This is an attempt to defraud Howard's creditors and the provisions will be invalid. ■

An **implied trust or constructive trust** is a trust imposed by the courts when it is clear that the parties intended to create a trust to prevent fraud or to do justice.

> Bob and Fred agree to buy a car once owned by Elvis Presley. They plan to take the car around the country and charge people to take rides in it. Bob buys the automobile without Fred and begins the tour. Fred could bring a legal action to have the car held in trust for the benefit of both Bob and Fred. The evidence would indicate that an implied trust would exist. ■

> Willie the Weasel sold toasters door-to-door. He collected over $1,000, but did not deliver the toasters to the customers. If they bring a legal action, the court can require that the money be held in a constructive trust for the benefit of the customers. This concept of a constructive trust could be used to prevent the defrauding of Willie's customers. ■

Administration of the Trust

A trust is a legal instrument that allows property to be administered by the trustee on behalf of the beneficiary. There is usually a person who will receive the trust proceeds upon the death of the beneficiary or some other event. This person is called a **remainderman.** If there is a remainderman, the trustee must balance the interests of the beneficiary and the remainderman. This can often be a difficult task.

> ▪ Bill is a trust officer at Thirty-ninth National Bank. It is his responsibility to invest $1,000,000 left in trust for the benefit of Susan. Sally is the remainderperson of the trust.
>
> If Bill places all of the assets in bonds, he will maximize the income flow on behalf of Susan. However, this would be unfair to Sally because it would not allow capital to grow. Therefore, Bill could place the money in a mixed portfolio of stocks and bonds. The income from stock dividends and bond interest payments would generate sufficient income for Susan. The potential for capital growth from the stock would make the investment fair to Sally. ▪

The trustee must exercise sound business judgment when managing the assets of the trust. It would not be prudent to take the assets and place all the investments in extremely risky investments. It would be proper to find some balance between safe investments that produce income and those that offer potential for capital growth.

Some trusts permit the trustee to invade the trust corpus on behalf of the beneficiary. While this can assist the beneficiary if she has specific needs, it also reduces the amount of trust corpus which will be available for the benefit of the remainderperson. This would be another instance when the trustee would need to exercise good judgment when performing her duties.

Because the trustee has the duty to exercise both good legal and financial judgment, it is advisable to name someone as trustee who has a solid business background. Trustees usually employ experts such as financial consultants, attorneys, and accountants to help them with their duties.

Although family members may be named as trustees, this can create unnecessary friction within the family. It is usually a good idea to name a professional trustee such as a bank, attorney, or accountant. If the trustee and the beneficiary are the same person, there is no purpose to the trust, and the trust will fail.

Trust Termination

The trust agreement normally provides for the change or termination of the trust based on some event. These provisions usually relate to either the death or coming of the age of the initial beneficiary. The trust may provide that the income will go to another beneficiary after the first.

> ▪ Sam became a very wealthy man while running his own business. He establishes a testamentary trust. He names his wife as beneficiary and provides that when she dies, his daughter will become the new beneficiary. ▪

> ▪ Joan sets up a trust and names her cat as the beneficiary. The trust further provides that when the cat dies, the ASPCA becomes the new beneficiary. By these provisions, the cat is cared for and then the income will go to the society. ▪

Although the trust provisions may be innovative, the trust may not go on forever. The common-law rule against perpetuities provides that for private trusts, a future interest must vest within a period of time of current lives plus 21 years.

While the rule has been declared so complicated that even the average attorney cannot understand it, it does limit the ability of settlors to provide for the trust to continue forever. The trust must come to an end at some point. If it did not, a settlor would have too much control over future generations. In addition, the trust could be used to tie up wealth and avoid taxation.

When the trust terminates, the trustee has additional responsibilities. The trustee should distribute the assets of the trust in accordance with the provisions of the trust. Usually, this means distributing the assets to the remainderman. In addition, the trustee often files an accounting that sets forth the activities of the trustee during her administration of the trust.

> ■ The Bob Bigbucks trust has come to an end. During its life the trustee acquired income from stocks and bonds that were placed into the trust. The trustee also sold some of the old stocks and bought new ones. In addition, the trustee received fees for managing the trust. ■

In some states, the courts that regulate trusts will require a detailed written accounting of every transaction from the trust's beginning to its end. If minors are involved, the court will appoint guardians. Only after the court and everyone else approves the written accounting will the court grant permission to terminate the trust, relieve the trustee from further liability, and distribute the assets.

A court-approved accounting is probably desirable for larger trusts. An agreement signed by all the parties which approves the actions of the trustee will probably be adequate for smaller trusts.

WILLS AND ESTATES

A will is the document a person uses to dispose of the assets she acquired during her life to her beneficiaries. Because of the nature of the document, there are special requirements for it to be valid. There is likely to be a substantial amount of money involved, the maker is dead and can not testify regarding the will's provisions or its validity. Therefore, the will must be signed by the maker and witnessed by at least two people to establish its validity.

A person who writes a will is called a **testator,** and is said to die testate. Persons who receive property under the will are referred to as beneficiaries. The process of approving a will and distributing the assets is called **probate.** Normally, the process and the distribution of the assets must be approved by the county surrogate's court. A person appointed to administer the estate in the will is called an **executor.** A person appointed by the court is called an **administrator.** A person's legal ability to draft a will is called testamentary capacity.

A person must be of legal age to draft a will. She must also have the requisite mental capacity to understand the nature of a will, its essential provisions, and the people who would normally be beneficiaries. A will may be contested on grounds of fraud, lack of mental capacity, duress, or **undue influence.**

■ Jones drafts his will because he is told almost every day by his son that he must leave everything to his oldest male child. Jones is an immigrant from a country where this is the tradition, and he does not know American customs. He does not consult an attorney.

　　When Jones wrote his will, his son was staring over his shoulder to make certain that all property was given to him. His three sisters bring an action to set aside the will after Jones's death. They would probably succeed on the grounds of duress. ■

Undue influence is a milder form of duress. It is the use of superior position of power to exert excessive influence over the testator. This is common when the will's drafter is quite elderly and may be easily persuaded by another.

■ Smith is an elderly man. He is persuaded by his young female housekeeper to leave all of his assets to her. Because of his age and his dependency on her for care, he does what she asks. Smith's children may bring an action to set the will aside on the grounds of undue influence. The housekeeper has taken unfair advantage of her position of power. ■

Signing the Will

It is a good idea to have a will drafted by an attorney. The testator will announce in the presence of the witnesses (it is good practice to have three witnesses) that this is his last will and testament and that he understands its provisions. The testator should then sign the will. The witnesses should watch him sign the will.

The witnesses should then sign the will in the presence of each other and of those who are present. It is a good idea to have witnesses who are younger than the testator. If there is a contest over the will's validity, younger witnesses are more likely to be able to testify.

The will should contain a clause stating that the testator has testamentary capacity and that he understands he is disposing of his property in his will. The will should also contain a clause revoking any and all prior wills. The will should be dated so it is clear that it was the last one made.

Modifying and Revoking the Will

A will may be modified by the testator at any time prior to his death. Normally, the best way to modify a previous will is to write an entirely new will. In most cases, this would eliminate any doubts about which will was the most recent.

But there may be some cases in which one wants to retain the major portions of the existing will. It may be easier to add some new minor provisions than to renew old feuds about the will's provisions. In addition, some laws ''grand-father'' certain requirements, meaning that they exempt provisions written before a certain date. In these cases, it may be preferable to write a codicil, which is a minor revision to a will.

Grandfather Harris wrote a will many years ago in which he set up trusts for his children and grandchildren. Since that time, the tax laws have changed and now provide for higher taxes on similar types of trusts. However, the law was written to exclude trusts created before a certain date. Grandfather Harris's will was written before that date. In this case, it would be wise to draft a codicil to add any new provisions and to leave the original will intact. ■

Some people believe they can modify a will by making written changes on an existing will. This is not a good practice. In some cases, this will be regarded as the destruction of the existing will and can render it invalid.

A person may revoke a will by writing a new one. She should indicate in the most recent version that all previous wills are being revoked. A person may also revoke a will by mutilating the old one. Broad cross outs, lines through the paper, or tearing the will into pieces would be examples of revocation.

In some states, the birth of a new child, divorce, or the murder of the testator by a beneficiary will result either in modification or revocation of the will. One should check the laws of a state or with competent counsel if one's life situation changes significantly.

UNUSUAL WILLS

It is better practice to have the will drafted formally. Historically, since many people did not have access to attorneys, less formal wills have been recognized as valid through the years.

Holographic wills are those drafted in the handwriting of the testator. Some states recognize them as valid even though there are no witnesses. However, this type of will is not recommended. The potential for fraud is high and many states will not recognize them.

Oral wills may be valid provided that they are taken by a person who has nothing to gain from the will. They are used in the military when people are about to enter dangerous conditions.

Private Wayne is about to go off to battle. He asks permission to tell someone how he wants to dispose of his property if he dies. One of the legal officers rushes out to his foxhole. Private Wayne tells Captain Lawyer how he wants to dispose of his personal property. Captain Lawyer jots down Private Wayne's last wishes. If he should die in battle, his instructions to Captain Lawyer may be admissible as his last will and testament. ■

RIGHTS OF SPOUSES AND OTHERS

A will is only one way of disposing of property. A person could die without a will and allow the property to be passed in accordance with state laws dealing with these matters.

Of special concern to state lawmakers has been the position of the spouse, which usually meant the financial situation of the wife. In many states, a spouse has the right to "take against the will." The spouse may elect to take a specific percentage of the estate's assets rather than accept what she would have received under the will.

If the deceased dies without a will, the property will be distributed according to the laws of **intestacy** in that state. These laws do not cover property that passes to a survivor through a **joint tenancy with the right of survivorship.** The laws of intestacy generally provide for the distribution of the deceased's property to spouses, children, grandchildren, and parents.

A will or the laws of intestacy may provide that the property will pass to future generations either per capita or per stirpes. One way of illustrating these concepts is by example.

■ Grandpa Logan, a widower, had two children who died before he did. His son, Tom, had two children. His daughter, Sarah, had one child. If either the will or the laws of intestacy require a per capita distribution to future generations, each of the three grandchildren would receive a one-third interest of the estate. ■

■ Same facts as the preceding, except that either the will or the laws of intestacy require a per stirpes distribution. In this case, Sarah's child will receive one-half of the estate. Each of Tom's two children will receive one-quarter ($\frac{1}{2} \times \frac{1}{2} = \frac{1}{4}$) of the estate. ■

SETTLING THE ESTATE

The responsibility of either the executor or the administrator is to distribute the estate in accord with either the will or the law. During the period of administration, the estate may earn income from its investments. This income belongs to the estate and becomes part of the distribution. In addition, the estate must pay taxes on the income.

The estate must pay the debts of the deceased. These debts often include medical expenses related to the last illness as well as funeral costs. This is a reason that people should have some insurance.

Each creditor must submit proof of the claim to the executor. The estate remains responsible for the contracts of the deceased. If the estate has little cash, some assets may have to be sold. There may also be federal and state estate taxes that must be paid. Although the federal marital estate tax deduction reduces the liklihood of tax obligations for many estates, an executor can expect that there will be some taxes to pay. Cash from insurance payable to the estate can be used to pay these taxes.

After all obligations have been paid, the executor can begin to distribute the assets as stated in the will. Many **decedents** want certain personal property to go to particular family members. It is a good idea to specify these matters in the will. One should not expect that each family member will do what the deceased would have wanted. For similar reasons, it is a good idea to name someone other than a family member as the executor.

■ Agnes, a widow, has three daughters. She names the eldest as executor. This angers the other two daughters, who wanted to be the executor. Agnes's will provides that her jewelry "should be divided equally among the three daughters." This places the eldest daughter in an extremely difficult position. She will need to balance her own interest with those of her two sisters. The possibility for friction, feuds, and legal action could be endless. ■

The executor or administrator must always act on behalf of the estate. As a fiduciary, the executor may not act in his own interest. In order to protect herself from even the appearance of a conflict of interest, the executor should not acquire estate property without the consent of all the beneficiaries.

■ Frank is the executor for Mabel's estate. The estate has a piece of land that Frank has determined could be part of a new shopping center along a major highway. If Frank buys the land, he will have a conflict of interest. He will want to acquire the land at the lowest possible price, but the estate should receive the highest possible price. Frank should not buy the land unless he has the written permission of all the estate's beneficiaries. He must disclose all the facts to the beneficiaries. ■

After the executor has paid the debts and taxes and distributed the assets, the executor may apply for a court order approving his actions. The executor will prepare a statement outlining each transaction, purchase, and sale of the assets, and the distribution of the estate's assets to the beneficiaries.

If the beneficiaries do not object, the court will approve the actions of the executor. The executor is entitled to fees for services rendered. A professional executor will submit a request to be paid in accord with a fee schedule. Banks, trust companies, attorneys, accountants, and financial consultants will often administer estates for a fee.

■ American Trust Company professionally administers estates and trusts. It is named as executor of Mora Morehead's estates, which consists of stocks and bonds. It keeps the portfolio the same and receives income from stock dividends and bonds. It pays the deceased's debts and estate taxes. It then distributes the stocks and bonds in accordance with the provisions in the will. It puts together a detailed accounting of its activities and submits it to the local surrogate supervising the estate. The judge frowns when he observes the rather mediocre investment performance, but detects no major errors. The judge approves its request for executor fees in the amount of ¼ of 1 percent of the estate's assets. ■

Because a large number of husbands and wives hold property as joint tenants with the right of survivorship, many assets pass to the surviving spouse without going through probate. Books have been written about methods of avoiding the necessity of probate. This does not mean, however, that people should avoid making wills. A will adds clarity to the disposition of one's assets. It can also help the court decide who should have custody of any minor children. In addition, proper use of trusts and wills can reduce taxes and provide for any special needs of future generations. Living trusts and joint ownership with right of survivorship may reduce probate costs, but they can also limit the parties' ability to perform sound estate and tax planning.

Definitions Reviewed

Corpus is the amount of property placed in a trust and held by the trustee.

Cy pres doctrine states that if the purpose for a charitable trust no longer exists, the courts will try to find another charitable purpose rather than have the trust end.

A **spendthrift trust** contains provisions that attempt to restrict the ability of another to gain access to the income or the principal.

An **implied or constructive trust** is one established by the courts in order to safeguard assets for others.

A **remainderman** is the person receiving the trust proceeds after the beneficiary.

A **testator** is a person who draws a will.

Probate is the process of settling a person's estate.

An **executor** is a person appointed by a testator to administer an estate.

An **administrator** is a person appointed by the court to administer an estate.

Undue influence is the improper use of one's position of power to benefit oneself at the expense of the remainder of the estate.

A **holographic will** is personally handwritten by the testator.

Intestacy are laws that control the distribution of a deceased's estate if she did not draft a will.

Joint tenancy with right of survivorship means two people own property. The surviving joint tenant will own the property after the death of the other joint tenant.

Heirs are persons who survive someone who has died and will receive that person's assets.

Core Concepts Reviewed

■ A trust is a legal mechanism that provides for a person to give assets to a trustee to manage on behalf of a beneficiary. A trust is a legal entity in which the trustee owns the legal title and the beneficiary owns the equitable title.

■ An inter vivos or living trust is established during the settlor's lifetime. It is effective immediately. A testamentary trust is written in a person's will and takes effect upon her death.

■ A will is the legal document that disposes of a person's property upon her death. The will must be written by someone with testamentary capacity. It is generally witnessed by three witnesses who have no interest in the property under the will.

■ An executor is the person named in the will who is responsible for carrying out its provisions. The court will appoint an administrator for managing the estate if there is no executor. Executors and administrators are fiduciaries who must always act in the best interests of the estate.

■ A will may be set aside on the grounds of lack of testamentary capacity, fraud, duress, or undue influence. A person who improperly utilizes his power to benefit from a testator's weakness is guilty of undue influence.

Questions

1. Define a trust.
2. Who are the major parties to a trust?
3. Name two types of trust.
4. What is the difference between a trust and a will?
5. What are some of the benefits of trusts?
6. What is a constructive trust?
7. Define testamentary capacity.
8. Define undue influence.
9. How does one modify a will?
10. How does one revoke a will?
11. What is a holographic will?
12. What is the right of the spouse to take against the will?
13. What is probate?
14. What are the laws of intestacy? When are they applicable?
15. How does an executor settle an estate?

Problems

1. Hanson is an elderly man with health problems. He has no close relatives, but does have substantial assets. He is worried about his future and has come to you for advice. What do you suggest?

2. Frances is an elderly woman who has three parakeets and no relatives. She wants to ensure that the birds are cared for after her death. She also wants to remember the pleasure her birds have given her after they die. She has come to you for advice. What do you suggest?

3. The Gottrocks Trust was drafted to benefit the three Gottrocks children. When the last child dies, the corpus is to be divided among the six Gottrocks grandchildren. There is $1,500,000 in the corpus. The youngest Gottrocks child is age 18. How should the money in the corpus be invested?

4. The Pinbreak Trust is a trust created by Percy Pinbreak in 1880 to benefit "young men who are attending Old Ivy University." Since the trust was established, Old Ivy has become coeducational. A local group at the university has challenged this provision of the trust on the grounds that Old Ivy receives federal funding and the trust provision is discriminatory. If you were the judge hearing this case, how would you rule?

5. Duncan is the trustee of the Bonkins Trust. The trust contains several oriental rugs of substantial value. Duncan sells the rugs to his daughter for $300. The beneficiaries believe the price is extremely low. They bring an action against Duncan. He defends on the grounds that he holds the legal title to the property and can do what he wants with the trust property. Who should prevail?

6. Barney is a father with three children and a wife. As he gets older he begins to go out with younger women. Before he dies, he begins to date Boom Boom LaVerne, age 21. When he dies, he leaves all of the assets in his will to Boom Boom. Do his wife and children have any remedies?

7. Munson is the executor of his father's estate. His mother is still alive and he has one sister. His father's will states that his personal property shall be divided equally among his wife and children. Munson takes all of his father's watches, rings, and other jewelry. He tells his mother that a father would want his son to have his jewelry. He tells his sister that she can have their mother's jewelry when she dies. Do Munson's mother and sister have a remedy?

8. Warren had two daughters, Edie and Wendy. Edie had one son, Ralph. Wendy had two sons, Herbert and Harold. Edie and Wendy were killed in a bungee-jumping accident. Warren's will provided that his property would be transferred per stirpes to the next generation. When Warren dies, how much of the estate does each grandson receive?

9. Helen is an elderly woman aged 91. Her grandson, an attorney, drafted her most recent will about a year ago. However, Helen has gotten angry at her daughter and decides to take her out of her will. She takes the will drafted by her grandson and crosses out her daughter's name whenever it appears. Has Helen succeeded in accomplishing her objective?

10. Lucy and Ethel conduct a raffle for a television set. They pretend to be representing a reputable charity in order to convince people to buy the tickets. They give away the TV set, but keep the money. If the ticket buyers bring a legal action against Lucy and Ethel, what would be an appropriate remedy?

PART IV

SALE OF GOODS

Chapter 14

Uniform Commercial Code: Sale of Goods

A firm offer made by non-merchant: can take back the offer!

if merchant: can't take back offer!

- The Uniform Commercial Code (UCC) changes the common law with respect to the sale of goods. The UCC creates gap-filling provisions that fill in terms the parties may have left out.

- Goods are tangible, moveable items commonly sold in the marketplace. The UCC does not apply to contracts for the sale of real estate or services.

- A merchant is someone who regularly deals in goods. A merchant is treated differently than an occasional seller.

- UCC contracts must be in writing if they are for the sale of goods of $500 or more.

SALES OF GOODS

The purchase and sale of goods are normally conducted by businesspeople in a manner different from the contractual arrangements of occasional buyers and sellers. Legal scholars believed that the common law did not adequately address the needs of people who regularly trade in goods. As a result, the drafters of the UCC changed the common law to meet these needs.

Of particular concern to the drafters was the high degree of specificity with respect to the agreement's terms required by the common law to sustain a contract. Parties often had substantial discussions only to discover they had no contract. If one key term was missing, the parties had no contract. They also had no remedies.

This seemed clearly unfair. It was particularly unproductive when the parties conducted business on a continuing basis. The drafters of the UCC included provisions that fill many of the gaps in order to make the discussions an enforceable contract.

Terms

UCC Article 2 applies to the sale of **goods.** The term goods applies to tangible, movable items. It does not apply to real estate or services. These continue to be governed by the common law of contracts. UCC Article 2 also does not apply to intangible property.

The issue of whether the UCC or common law of contracts applies is important because of the differences between the two. Discussions that may create an enforceable contract under the UCC may not create an enforceable contract at common law.

If the contract is a mixture between the sale of goods and services, the issue of which law applies may not be an easy one to resolve. The issue is decided by looking at the contract and determining if it is more of a sale of goods or more of a service contract.

- Bill buys an automobile from Joe's Used Car lot for $15,000. The contract has clauses that outline the service provisions relating to the maintenance of the car. ■

Although this contract has some service requirements, it is clearly more of a sale of goods. As a result, the UCC will apply rather than the common law of contracts.

Price is the consideration agreed upon by the parties for the purchase and sale of the goods subject to the contract. If the price has been left out of the contract, the parties can refer to the market price. Goods are commonly sold in the market, so the market price is a relatively easy figure to obtain. One can also look at previous exchanges of the parties if the marketplace does not provide the price. Another way to determine price is to look at individual trades among the parties to the contract or among other persons.

Existing goods are those already made and owned by the seller. In order to make a sale, the goods must be in existence. If there are no existing goods, the parties can make a contract only to sell goods in the future. **Identified goods** are existing goods that have been designated to be delivered to the buyer. A buyer may obtain insurance on goods that have already been identified as going to him. **Future goods** are those yet to be made but which the seller expects to make in the future. These can be the subject of a contract to sell the goods when they are made.

A **bill of sale** is written evidence of title to tangible, movable property (goods). Many transactions are made without a transfer of a bill of sale, but it is desirable to use for a transaction involving larger or more expensive items. A bill of sale does not have to be in any particular form, but should include a description of the goods, the names of the parties, the price, and the quantity.

DIFFERENCES BETWEEN THE UCC AND COMMON LAW

As noted in the previous chapters, the common law of contracts requires a high degree of agreement regarding all of the key terms. If these terms are not included, there is no contract. The UCC was designed to keep the "agreement" going rather than having it brought to a premature end.

A major difference between the two is the rules relating to offers that are kept open. At common law, the offer is revocable at will unless the offeree gave the offeror some consideration. Under the UCC, if a **merchant** puts an offer in writing, it will be binding for a period up to three months even without consideration. This recognizes the greater duty a merchant has to a prospective customer. This is known as a firm offer.

At common law, the terms of the offer had to be very precise. Under the UCC, there are provisions that fill gaps the parties may have left in the agreement. If the price was not included, the UCC provides that the market price may be utilized. If the place for delivery is not included, the place is the seller's place of business. If the seller has no place of business, the place is the seller's residence.

If the precise terms of payment are not identified, payment is due at the time and place the buyer is to receive the goods. If the goods are to be shipped but the shipping obligations were not specified, it is the seller's obligation to make the shipping arrangements. These arrangements are to be made within the bounds of what is commercially reasonable.

If the time for performance is not specified, the time of performance is a reasonable time. Reasonableness may be determined from market practices, previous dealings of the parties, and similar transactions among other parties in the same area.

The one term that the UCC cannot supply relates to the quantity of goods in the transaction. While other terms can be derived from the code, the marketplace, or from prior transactions, there is no source for determining quantity other than from the parties themselves. Therefore, if the parties have not reached an agreement on quantity, there is no enforceable contract.

Requirements for Writing

Contracts for the sale of goods under $500 may be done without any writing. However, the UCC requires that contracts for the sale of goods of $500 or more must be evidenced by some writing. The writing must contain the quantity of goods, a description of the contract's subject matter, and the signature of the party who is denying the existence of the contract.

If the contract is between merchants, the requirement for writing may be satisfied when two conditions are met. A written confirmation was sent by one merchant to the other, and the other merchant did not send a written notice of objection within ten days.

The UCC recognizes the common law exception of partial performance to the requirements for writing. If the buyer has made partial payment or accepted all or some of the goods, the contract will be binding.

> Ralson and Jeremy have discussions about the sale and purchase of 100 shoes for $1,500. Jeremy sends a payment for $750 after Ralson sends him 50 shoes. Ralson prepares for the second delivery, but Jeremy calls Ralson and states they do not have a contract because it is over $500 and they have nothing in writing. Ralson would be able to enforce the contract because of the UCC's partial payment and acceptance exceptions. ∎

Another exception relates to specially manufactured goods that could not be resold by the seller. If the buyer orders goods for the buyer's special needs, an oral contract will be enforceable if two conditions are met: the goods are not suitable for use by others in the ordinary course of business, and the seller has made substantial progress in the manufacture of the goods.

If the parties admit to the existance of a contract, the contract will be enforceable to the extent it was admitted. For example, if the parties had a contract for two shipments, a party may admit to the existence of a contract for one shipment, and the contract will be enforceable with respect to that shipment.

In all of these exceptions, substantial evidence of a contract exists despite the lack of one in writing. This is similar to the substantial performance exception at common law and fulfills the essential purposes of the statute of frauds provisions.

Offer and Acceptance

At common law, the acceptance of an offer must be a mirror image of the offer. If the offeree attempts to change the offer in a material way (counteroffer), the offer is treated as being rejected. The UCC handles this matter differently.

In the busy world of commerce, both the offeror and offeree may have their own forms that they use to create a contract. These forms are likely to contain different terms. Under the UCC, different terms in a form indicating acceptance will not prevent a binding acceptance unless the acceptance is expressly conditioned on these different terms.

If one or more of the parties are nonmerchants, an additional term is treated as a proposed addition. If accepted by the offeror, if becomes part of the contract. If not, the contract is based on the original offer.

The matter is resolved differently if both parties are merchants. In an exchange of forms between merchants, the additional terms become part of the agreement unless the offer expressly limits acceptance to its terms, or the additional terms would materially alter the offer's terms, or the offeror objects to these terms within a reasonable time.

> Bruce and Kathy are merchants. Bruce sends Kathy an offer to sell 5,000 bracelets. His form contains the phrase "all sales are final." Kathy wants to resell the bracelets to her store's customers, but she wants to be able to return those bracelets not sold. She "accepts" Bruce's offer on one of her forms, which notes that she may return any bracelets that remain unsold. This would be a material change, and would not constitute an acceptance under UCC provisions. It is also the type of material change to which Bruce should object in order to ensure that there is no contract. Of course, Bruce could also accept the additional term and create a contract. ■

These rules are another example of how the UCC attempts to give the parties opportunities to keep the agreement going. At common law, relatively minor differences between the offer and acceptance would doom the contract.

At common law, an acceptance could be made through any reasonable medium. The use of the mails, phone, or telegraph would be acceptable. The same rule applies to sales transactions covered by the UCC. The UCC also retains the "mailbox rule," which states that an acceptance is effective when placed in the mailbox. After an acceptance is dispatched, it is too late to change the terms of the offer or to revoke it. A contract has been created which will bind both parties.

An offer to purchase goods may also be accepted by the prompt promise to ship the goods or by the prompt shipment of the goods. If the goods conform to the specifications in the offer, there is a binding and performed contract. If the goods shipped are nonconforming, the offer has been accepted and there is a breach of the contract.

It could still be worthwhile for the seller to ship nonconforming goods if the breach was minor. The loss of the minor amount of damages could be outweighed by obtaining the purchase price in the contract minus the deduction.

A seller may also send nonconforming goods to the buyer and notify the buyer that it is being done as an accommodation. This is a counteroffer that the buyer may accept or reject. This is neither an acceptance nor a breach.

> Hodkins needs a certain Big Bulk motor oil and asks Boris if he can supply it. Boris believes that his own Big Boy motor oil will meet Hodkins's needs and sends him a crate. Hodkins can examine the oil and either accept or reject it.

Contract Modification

At common law, modifications of contracts had to be supported by new consideration because the existing contract consititutes a preexisting obligation. The UCC does not require additional consideration to modify a contract. This more accurately reflects the practices of merchants.

Modifications to sales contracts may be made orally unless the parties have agreed otherwise. If the modifications relate to contracts that must be in writing, the modifications must also be in writing. If the modification would bring a contract not requiring a writing above the amount that would require writing, the modification must be in writing.

Definitions Reviewed

Goods are tangible, movable items regulated by the Uniform Commercial Code.

Existing goods are those goods made and owned by the seller.

Identified goods are those existing goods that have been designated as going to the buyer.

Future goods are those goods that will be made in the future.

A **bill of sale** is evidence of the transfer of ownership to goods.

A **merchant** is someone who regularly deals in goods.

Core Concepts Reviewed

■ The Uniform Commercial Code covers the sale of tangible, movable items. The UCC departs from the common law in several major areas.

■ The UCC provides gap-filling provisions in order to help the parties reach an agreement that will be enforceable.

■ Offer and acceptance are resolved differently than common law in some significant aspects. Most important is that an acceptance does not have to be an exact mirror image of the offer. The UCC provides provisions for handling different terms in the offer and acceptance.

Questions

1. What are goods?
2. Who is a merchant?
3. What is a bill of sale?
4. What is a "firm offer"?
5. Name some differences between the common law and the UCC relating to the sale of goods.
6. When must a contract for the sale of goods be in writing?
7. What terms must be included in the writing?
8. How does the UCC modify the preexisting obligation rule?
9. Must a contract for the sale of goods state a price?
10. Name some differences between the UCC and the common law with respect to an offer and acceptance.

Problems

1. Jones buys a computer from Burger for $1,500. The contract calls for Burger to service the computer quarterly and to advise Jones. Is this contract covered by the UCC or common law?

2. Wilson and Pickett discuss the sale and purchase of five porcelain plates for $3,000. They reach agreement on the major terms in their letters, but fail to include a delivery date. Pickett later argues that they do not have a contract because of the lack of a formal agreement and of a specific delivery date. Is he correct?

3. Cooper buys an automobile from Farrell for $3,000. After it is delivered and accepted, he changes his mind and claims there was no contract because it was not in writing. Is he correct?

4. Reed makes workbenches and sells them to his friends every two months. Is he a merchant?

5. Mary asks Susan to design and make a particular set of cabinets for her dining room. The purchase price is $2,000. Susan makes the cabinets. Their agreement was not put in writing and Mary later claims there was no binding contract. Is she correct?

6. Watkins and Higginbottom have a contract under which Watkins is to supply Higginbottom with 100 cans of grade B motor oil every month for one year. The agreement is in writing.

   After three months, Higginbottom requests that Watkins supply grade A motor oil at the same price. Watkins wants to continue the contract and agrees to the written modification. Later, Watkins wants to switch back to grade B oil, and claims that the modification is not binding because it was not supported by additional consideration. Is he correct?

7. Claudette has a contract for the sale of goods to Susan. The contract neglected to state a place for delivery. What is the proper place for delivery under the UCC?

Chapter 15

Title to Goods and Warranties

- Title is evidence of ownership of property. Determination of passage of title can be significant regarding questions of loss, damage, and insurance.

- Acceptance is the buyer's acknowledgment that he is willing to take the goods as the new owner. This helps determine breach of contract issues.

- A warranty is a guarantee which the seller gives to the buyer. Warranties can be either express or implied.

- Under the Uniform Commercial Code (UCC), every merchant gives a buyer an implied warranty of merchantability that the goods sold are fit for normal purposes.

TRANSFERRING TITLE

Although issues regarding the transfer of title are less important than previously, the transfer of title still is significant in determining who bears the risk of loss and damage to the goods. The terms of the agreement are the first place to determine when title has passed. The risk of loss of goods generally passes from the seller to the buyer when the seller completes the shipping obligations under the contract.

A **shipment contract** is one in which the seller's obligation is to deliver the goods to a carrier for shipment to the buyer. The seller's duty is completed when this is accomplished, and the risk of loss then passes to the buyer. The buyer should arrange for payment of the carrier and for any insurance.

A **destination contract** requires the seller to arrange for delivery to the buyer's place of business. In this contract, the seller's obligations are not completed until the goods are delivered. The seller will bear any loss until the goods reach the buyer, and should arrange for both transportation and needed insurance.

Free-on-Board Terms

"Free on board" (FOB) means that someone has paid to ship goods by a carrier to a certain point.

> Greg's place of business is in New York and the buyer's place of business is in Los Angeles. The shipping term in the contract indicates that the seller's responsibility is FOB New York. On the other hand, the contract may state the seller's (Greg's) duty is FOB Los Angeles. This would be a destination contract and the seller pays for the goods to be shipped to Los Angeles. ■

Problems with Title

At common law, one could transfer only the title one possessed. This meant that if there was some problem in the chain of title from owner to owner, the most current owner might not have a secure title.

Stolen goods

This has been changed under the UCC. The new owner cannot obtain good title if the previous owner had no title at all (void title). However, the new owner can acquire good title if the previous owner had at least some claim to good title (voidable title).

One cannot acquire any title if one obtains goods through theft. A person who possesses the goods through theft has void title and cannot pass good title to future owners even if they pay full value. The original owner retains good title to the goods as opposed to the thief or future owners.

> Hawkins has a TV set stolen by Baird, who sells it for reasonable value to Watkins. Hawkins later discovers this fact and brings an action to recover the set from Watkins. Hawkins will prevail in the lawsuit because Watkins cannot acquire good title from a thief. Watkins will have an action against Baird if he can locate him.

A buyer can obtain voidable title if he acquires the goods through fraud or through an improper payment such as a bad check. In these cases, the buyer can pass good title to a future purchaser for reasonable value.

> Dill acquires goods from Robinson by paying him with a bad check. Dill immediately sells these goods to Lucas for reasonable value and then leaves the country. Robinson brings an action against Lucas to recover the goods. He will not prevail. Although Dill had only a voidable title, Lucas can acquire good title by paying him reasonable value without knowledge that there was anything wrong with Dill's title.

If an owner entrusts goods to a merchant and the merchant improperly sells them for reasonable value to a purchaser acting in good faith, the original owner will not be able to reacquire the goods from the new owner.

> Maude brings her bicycle to Bryan's Bicycle Shop for repair. Bryan sells it to Max, who paid reasonable value and knew nothing of Maude's ownership of the bicycle. Max has good title and Maude cannot recover the bike from Max. Maude could bring an action against Bryan if Bryan can be found.

The last two examples often strike people as unfair, but one of the purposes of the UCC is to promote the flow of commerce and to reduce the necessity of examining one's title to goods. A bona fide purchaser should prevail over the original owner who placed the goods into the stream of commerce. Otherwise, people would be required to research every title before making a purchase.

Acceptance

The buyer can complete the contract by indicating that she is willing to become the owner of the goods. This is known as **acceptance.** This word has a different meaning than accepting an offer.

The goods may be accepted when the buyer explicitly states that she is willing to become the owner of the goods. A second method is to wait beyond a reasonable time to reject the goods. A third method of accepting goods is for the buyer to treat the goods in a way that indicates she is willing to be their owner.

■ Bobby has a contract with Julian to sell him ten drums. When the goods are delivered, Julian says nothing. He takes the drums and lets them be played by his band on three consecutive weekends. Julian has accepted the goods by treating them as if he were the owner. ■

■ Morton has a contract to sell Eleanor 10,000 coffee mugs. He delivers the mugs on time. Eleanor says nothing, and resells them to her customers. Because Eleanor has treated the goods as if she were the owner by selling them, this will be regarded as an acceptance. ■

A buyer who accepts the goods, either explicitly or implicitly, has taken on the risk of loss. He is also liable for breach of contract if he fails to pay for them. Taking the goods is not necessarily acceptance. For example, a COD (cash on delivery) contract states that the buyer must pay cash *before* taking the goods. The UCC allows the buyer to take the goods without accepting them. The buyer has an additional reasonable period of time to inspect the goods before this will be regarded as acceptance.

A **sale on approval** is a sale that allows the buyer to have a trial period before acceptance. The seller is taking the responsibility of giving the buyer this trial period and bears the risk of loss while the goods are held by the buyer. The seller also bears the risk of loss if the goods are shipped back to the seller.

A **sale or return** is an arrangement in which the buyer intends to resell the goods. The buyer takes responsibility for this arrangement and bears the risk of loss while she holds the goods. The buyer also bears the risk of loss if they are shipped back to the seller for any reason.

A **consignment** is essentially an agency agreement. This risk of loss between the consignor and consignee can be negotiated between the two. If the agreement does not specify the risk of loss, the UCC treats a consignment along the same lines as a sale or return.

WARRANTIES

A **warranty** is a guarantee that a product will work in a particular manner. A warranty may be expressly given by the seller, implied by law, or implied by the factual conditions. If the product does not comply with the warranty, the seller will be liable for the difference between the actual and the guaranteed performance. The seller can also be liable for personal injury if the product fails to work in accord with the warranty and this failure causes the injury.

The warranty need not specifically state that it is a guarantee. The warranty may outline specifications or it may state that the product will conform to a certain model or standard that will form the basis of the bargain. A warranty is a statement about a fact. It is not an opinion.

■ A statement that a television set will receive all local channels is a warranty. A statement that, "it is the best on the market" is not a warranty. ■

The warranty could also be a promise that the product will conform to a model, sample, or standard. It is no longer legal to show the buyer a model of the product and then to supply the buyer with goods of inferior quality.

> George shows Aaron a particular piece of furniture with a walnut finish, and they reach a contract on that basis. George later delivers Aaron a similar piece of furniture with a simulated walnut finish. This is a breach of the express warranty George gave Aaron when he showed him the original furniture. ▩

There are some warranties that are implied as a matter of law. Every seller warrants that he is conveying good title to the buyer. The seller also warrants that the title is free of all encumbrances and security interests that are not already known to the buyer.

All contracts for the sale of goods contain an implied warranty of good faith in the parties' performance of the contract. Each party gives the other an **implied warranty** that she will comply with the contract's provisions and act in good faith to make the agreement work.

Warranty of Merchantability

The UCC states that every merchant grants an implied warranty of merchantability to buyers of the goods. This warranty is a guarantee that the goods will be fit for the normal purposes for which they are sold. If the warranty is breached, the buyer can recover the difference between how the goods worked and how they were supposed to work. More important, it provides a remedy for recovering losses caused by a product defect.

Under common law, a person injured by a product had to show some negligence on the part of the manufacturer or seller. The negligence could have been in the design or manufacture of the product. The injured party can now recover if she shows that the warranty of merchantability was breached and the breach resulted in the injury.

> Heather buys a car made by Tiger Motors. On her second day of driving, the brakes fail and the auto crashes into a brick wall. Heather can recover money damages from Tiger Motors because of the breach of the warranty of merchantability. It is not necessary for Heather to show specific acts of negligence. She needs to show only that the warranty of merchantability was breached and she was injured as a result. ▩

Many states have also extended the warranty of merchantability beyond the buyer to other people who the manufacturer could have reasonably foreseen would use or be injured by the product.

> Morty buys a hedge clipper made by Hudson Hedgies. When clipping his hedges, the blade jumps out from the trimmer and injures Morty's son, who was playing in the yard.
>
> Morty's son will be able to recover from Hudson Hedgies for his injuries resulting from the breach of warranty. Hudson could have reasonably foreseen that someone nearby would be injured if the blade came out of the trimmer. ▩

Despite the wide-ranging nature of the seller's liability, it still must be shown that the buyer used the product appropriately and that this use caused the injury.

■ Careless Charlie buys a screwdriver made by Townsend Tools. While driving in a screw, Charlie becomes frustrated. He attempts to hammer it in with the plastic end of the screwdriver.

The plastic breaks and shatters into little pieces. One of the pieces cuts Charlie's face. This was not a proper use of the tool, and Charlie will not be able to recover because he misused the screwdriver. ■

Some courts have been rather liberal in construing proper use. They have held that manufacturers will be liable if they could have reasonably foreseen that the buyer would use the product in such a way. This allows injured parties to recover even if the use was somewhat inappropriate but foreseeable.

Juries have often been left to decide whether the failure to use manufacturer's suggested safety equipment would be a bar to recovery. In some states any negligence (failure to use due care) by the injured party would bar any recovery. The development of comparative negligence and strict liability principles have made this less likely.

The plaintiff must still demonstrate that the product defect was the **proximate cause** of the injury. Proximate cause means that the defect was a direct cause of the injury.

■ Conrad buys a TV set from ACR Televisions. When he bends down to turn the dial, the set explodes in his face, injuring Conrad. This would be proximate cause. ■

■ Conrad is watching the television set. It blows up at the same time a large jet flies very low over the house. The blast from the jet and the set cause a trophy to fall off the mantlepiece and hit Conrad on his head. It would be more difficult to show proximate cause in this case. ■

The warranty of merchantability also applies when one orders food at a restaurant. Interesting problems arise when one bites down on an object one did not expect, and is injured. If the object is completely foreign to the food, one should be able to recover.

■ Zeke orders a glass of his favorite soft drink, Blast Cola. While drinking the soda, he swallows a nut that had fallen into the glass. By the time he coughs out the nut, Zeke has injured his throat. This is clearly a foreign object, and Zeke should be able to recover for his injuries. ■

A more complicated question arises when one is injured by a "natural" object in the food. In these cases, the courts have generally relied on the "reasonable expectation" test. That is, would one reasonably expect to find the object in the food.

■ Luke buys a chicken from Frank's Chicks. While eating a piece of chicken, Luke bites down on a chicken bone and hurts a tooth. Luke could have reasonably expected to find a chicken bone in a chicken and will not be able to recover. ■

■ Luke orders chicken soup in a restaurant. He swallows a piece of bone in the soup. In this case, one can argue that it is not reasonable to find such a bone in soup. ■

The implied warranty of merchantability has resulted in a growth of the number and success of product liability actions. On the one hand, it has led to an increase in product and insurance costs. Conversely, it has probably served to promote safety measures and reduce the number of product-related injuries.

Additional Warranties

A **warranty of fitness** for a particular purpose is created when the seller is aware that the buyer is relying on the seller's product for a particular use or purpose. For example, a runner may want a particular pair of shoes to run a marathon. If he informs the seller of the intended use, the seller will be held to the standard of providing shoes fit for a marathon rather than normal running.

In these cases, it will not be sufficient for the merchant to show that he merely satisfied the implied warranty of merchantability. The merchant must demonstrate that the goods met the standard of being fit for the particular use.

A merchant will be relieved of liability if the buyer was the one who supplied the specifications to the seller. In this case, the buyer warrants that the seller will not be held liable in the event the goods do not work. If they are made in accordance with the buyer's specifications, the buyer bears the responsibility.

A merchant who regularly deals in goods warrants to the buyer that the goods are not violating any patents or copyrights. The buyer makes the same warranty if he supplies specifications to the seller for making the goods. Both parties have the obligation to notify the other if an action is brought against them for patent or copyright infringement.

Disclaimers

The seller may state that no warranties exist (disclaim) in the transaction. However, a **disclaimer** of warranties is generally regarded as an admission that the seller is not willing to stand behind the goods. As a result, a disclaimer tends to diminish the value of the goods.

The warranty of merchantability is such an essential part of a sales transaction that it can only be disclaimed in conspicuous language. The disclaimer must be put in either different color ink or in larger print than the rest of the agreement. Disclaimers are normally phrased in ways noted in the examples below:

- "THIS CONTRACT HAS NO WARRANTIES OTHER THAN THOSE STATED SPECIFICALLY HEREIN."

- These goods are sold "AS IS." (This is common language to disclaim the warranty of merchantability.)

A disclaimer of the warranty of merchantability is a statement that there is no guarantee that the goods will work as promised. It would be quite unusual to see such a disclaimer associated with new goods. A disclaimer of the warranty of merchantability is often associated with the sale of used or damaged goods.

Definitions Reviewed

A **shipment contract** specifies that the buyer pays for the shipment of goods after the seller delivers to the carrier.

A **destination contract** specifies that the seller has the obligation to ship the goods to the buyer.

Acceptance is the indication to become the owner of the goods subject to the contract.

A **sale on approval** specifies the buyer will have a trial period before being required to accept the goods.

A **sale or return** gives the buyer a period of time in which to resell the goods.

In a **consignment,** the risk of loss is negotiated by the consignor and consignee.

A **warranty** is a guarantee that a product will work in particular manner.

An **implied warranty** is the guarantee created either by the law or by the facts.

Proximate cause means the product defect is a direct cause of the injury.

A **warranty of fitness** is a guarantee that the goods are fit for a specific purpose.

A **disclaimer** is a statement that there is no warranty.

Core Concepts Reviewed

evidence of ownership!

■ Title is evidence of ownership of goods. Transfer depends on the seller's completion of her obligations under the contract with respect to shipment of the goods.

■ Acceptance is the agreement of the buyer to take the goods subject to the contract. Acceptance can be either express or implied. Acceptance under the UCC allows the buyer an opportunity to inspect the goods after delivery.

■ A warranty is a guarantee that goods will perform in accord with certain standards. Under the UCC, every merchant warrants that the goods will be fit for the purposes sold. This is called the warranty of merchantability.

■ A warranty can only be disclaimed by clear and conspicuous language in the agreement.

Questions

1. What is title?
2. What is the difference between shipment and destination contracts?
3. What is the difference between a sale on approval and a sale or return?
4. What is the warranty of merchantability?
5. What is a warranty of fitness for a particular purpose?
6. How does one disclaim the warranty of merchantability?
7. What is acceptance?
8. Name the three ways one may accept goods.
9. What is "proximate cause"?
10. How does the misuse of a product affect an injured party's chances for recovery?

Problems

1. Jones takes her violin to Violet Violins to have it repaired. Violet sells the violin for reasonable value to Joshua, and then leaves the country. If Jones brings an action to recover the violin from Joshua, who will prevail?
2. Smith has a rare cello that Harry steals from his house. Harry sells it to Wilson, who paid reasonable value for the cello. Wilson knew nothing about the theft until he learned that Harry had left the country. If Smith brings an action against Wilson to recover the cello, will he be successful?
3. Mary sells her pearl necklace to Joan, who pays for it with a bad check. Joan sells it to Zelda, who knew nothing of the check and paid reasonable value. If Mary brings an action against Zelda, will she be successful?
4. O'Reilly orders a bowl of New England fish chowder at a restaurant in Boston. She bites down on a fish bone in the soup and breaks a tooth. Can she recover from the restaurant for her injuries?
5. Sampson buys a fertilizer spreader from Manure Land. When he operates it, a wheel flies off and hits Little Billy, who was playing next door. Can Billy recover from Manure Land?

6. Dotson has a destination contract with Velez. While the goods are being shipped, they are damaged. Who bears the risk of loss?

7. Mary orders a special gown for a local dance contest from Gwen's Gowns. When she gets the gown, Mary discovers that while it is fit for normal use, it is too uncomfortable for a dance contest. She refuses to pay Gwen, who brings an action to recover the price. Will Gwen prevail?

8. Sally has a contract with Barbara which allows her to examine specially made collector plates before purchasing them. While the plates are in Sally's possession, one of them falls and is broken. Who is responsible for the loss?

9. Muriel and Dee Dee have a contract that allows Dee Dee to sell special rings made by Muriel. One of the rings is cracked while in Dee Dee's possession. Who is responsible for the loss?

10. Mary gets a COD shipment of new books from Books'R'Us. She pays for them with cash. However, when she opens the crate, she finds the wrong books have been shipped. She contacts Books'R'Us and is told that she has accepted the books and they will not refund her money. Are they correct?

Chapter 16

Performance and Remedies

- Every party to a sales contract has the obligation to act in a manner that will result in a fair and equitable performance of the agreement. This includes the obligation to act in good faith.

- Each party must perform her obligations under the contract to receive the performance of the other party. If the party does not, he has breached the contract, and the other party has a remedy.

- The UCC has relaxed the impossibility standard of common law, and now allows a standard of "commercial impracticability" as a reason for not performing the contract.

- A bulk transfer is the sale of all or a substantial portion of the seller's inventory. The buyer and seller must give notice to the seller's creditors that the sale is about to occur.

PERFORMANCE OF CONTRACTS

The seller's main obligation under a sales contract is to deliver conforming goods and the buyer's main obligation is to pay for them. If both parties perform their obligations, the contract has been completed and the parties are discharged.

When the seller is prepared to deliver the goods, she must keep them available for the period of time reasonably necessary to enable the buyer to take possession. The amount of time which is reasonable will depend on the subject matter. If the goods are perishable, the period of time is shorter because the buyer should take the goods quickly in order to avoid spoilage. Conversely, if the goods will not spoil, the seller must wait for a longer period of time.

Past dealings under the current contract, or under previous contracts, is evidence of what would be reasonable. The parties or the courts could also refer to the prevailing practices in the marketplace.

The seller's obligation to **tender** conforming goods should also be made at a reasonable hour and at the location specified by the contract. If no location is stated in the contract, the UCC provides that the place of tender should be the seller's place of business. If the seller has no place of business, the location is the seller's residence.

The contract could provide for the seller to have the goods sent to the buyer. The contract might state that the seller make the goods available, and the buyer is responsible for either picking up the goods or arranging for their delivery.

A third option is to notify the buyer that the goods are in the hands of a bailee. A bailee is a person or organization that has temporary possession of items of property owned by someone else. It is quite common to have goods located at a warehouse or a similar facility and to have a new owner obtain them from the bailee.

The seller must provide a **negotiable document of title** as part of the obligation to tender the goods in proper form. A negotiable document of title allows the buyer to obtain the goods without inquiring into the chain of title.

A nonnegotiable document of title will not be proper delivery unless the buyer does not object to the failure to provide a negotiable document. A nonnegotiable document of title requires a bailee to determine the identity of the titleholder and is not as easy to transfer to another party. A nonnegotiable title places additional burdens on the buyer which would not exist if the seller had provided a negotiable document.

Perfect Tender

At common law, every aspect of the contractual provisions had to be perfectly followed in order for tender by the seller to be regarded as legally sufficient.

■ A common-law contract states that the subject matter will be shipped by boat, but the seller uses land transportation instead. Some courts would rule that this was not **perfect tender,** and that the contract had been breached. ■

Under the UCC, the seller must still deliver conforming goods in order to fulfill his obligations under the contract. The buyer may accept the entire shipment of goods, reject the entire shipment if they are nonconforming, or accept part of the shipment and reject the portion that is not conforming.

But, the UCC retains the perfect tender rule because the buyer may reject the entire shipment even if there are only minor defects.

■ Sam sends Frank a shipment of 500 ashtrays. Two of the 500 are broken. Under the UCC perfect tender rule, Frank could reject the entire shipment. ■

The buyer must state her reasons for rejecting the goods. The reasons must be those that can be determined by a reasonable inspection of the goods. If the buyer does not disclose the reason for rejection, he may not rely on the unstated reason to justify rejection or to establish a breach of contract if the seller could have cured, or corrected, the defect.

The right of the seller to cure a nonconformity does not exist under common law, but does exist under the UCC. It gives the seller another opportunity to conform with the contract's terms. A seller may cure the defect by notifying the buyer of his intention to correct the nonconformity before the time for performance has passed, and then actually doing so.

Another case when the seller has the right to cure is when the seller delivers nonconforming goods on the delivery date but had reasonable grounds to believe they still would be acceptable. If he notifies the buyer, he still has a reasonable time in which to cure the defect.

■ Don must deliver 1,000 ashtrays to Harry by December 1. He delivers them on November 15th. He receives a call from Harry that 50 of them are broken. He tells Harry that he will take care of the problem and delivers 50 new ashtrays to Harry by December 1. Don has cured and there is no breach of contract. ■

■ Joe has a contract to deliver 100 wooden picture frames to Bruce on November 1st. He delivers 100 simulated wooden frames on that date. Bruce had accepted simulated wood in the past.

This time, Bruce informs Joe that he needs the real wood frames because he is decorating a hotel with an all-wood motif. Joe has a reasonable time in which to deliver 100 real wood frames. If he makes the delivery, he will not have breached the contract. ∎

The provisions allowing the seller to cure a nonconforming delivery is another indication of the UCC's attempts to keep the agreement of the parties moving forward. At common law, a nonconforming delivery would have resulted in a breach of contract.

An installment contract requires the seller to deliver the goods in separate shipments at different times. A buyer may reject an installment if the defect materially impairs the value of that installment and cannot be cured. The buyer may reject the entire contract only if the defect in the installment substantially impairs the value of the entire contract.

The buyer may refuse to accept the goods if the seller fails to make proper shipping arrangements or if the shipment results in a material delay or loss to the buyer. The seller may use a commercially reasonable substitute if the form of delivery stated in the contract is unavailable. Both of these provisions are departures from the **perfect tender rule.**

Buyer's Rights and Duties

The buyer must accept and pay for the goods if they conform to the contract. The buyer has the right to make a reasonable inspection of the goods and to reject them if they do not conform to the contract. Because of the perfect tender rule, the buyer may reject the goods for any nonconformity.

The buyer may revoke her acceptance if she later finds a nonconformity that materially lessens the value of the goods. The key term is "materially lessens." This is a higher standard than that required to reject the goods upon their initial delivery.

As noted in the previous chapter, the buyer may accept the goods by expressly stating that she will accept the goods. She may also accept the goods by waiting beyond a reasonable time to notify the seller that she is rejecting the goods. A third way of accepting the goods is to treat them in a way that would indicate the desire to be the owner. If the buyer resells the goods, this would be implied acceptance.

Unless otherwise agreed, the buyer must pay for the goods when delivered. The buyer may pay for the goods in any commercially reasonable manner. This would include payment by check. However, the seller may ask for payment in cash or by any other specific means of payment. If the seller asks for money, she must give the buyer a reasonable time to produce the cash.

Performance

Circumstances may occur which raise doubts about whether a party will perform his obligations under the contract. The other party may demand adequate assurance that the contract will not be breached. The party may demand that this be put in writing. The party may suspend his own performance until he receives the assurance. Failure to provide it within a reasonable time is a repudiation of the contract.

If a party believes she will have difficulty performing the contract, she may notify the other party that performance will not be forthcoming. This is called an **anticipatory repudiation.** Such notice is a good business practice because it allows the other party an opportunity to seek similar performance from someone else.

Although anticipatory repudiation may help maintain the business relationship, it does not excuse performance. The party repudiating the contract is liable for any damages resulting from the failure to perform.

The injured party may wait for performance by the repudiating party for a commercially reasonable time. If the repudiating party does not perform the duties, the injured party may seek legal remedies. The injured party could also regard the contract as breached and pursue remedies immediately.

The repudiating party may retract the repudiation before the time of performance has passed. She may not do so if the other party has already indicated that he regards the repudiation as final, that he has materially altered his position, or that he has cancelled the contract.

Bulk Transfers

A **bulk transfer** is the sale of all or a substantial portion of the seller's equipment, inventory, or other assets. It does not include sales in the ordinary course of business.

Hudson sells ashtrays and other tobacco-related items. Wilson buys 50 of Hudson's 100 ashtray-inventory to place on tables in Wilson's new restaurant. This is not a bulk transfer. ■

A bulk transfer has the potential of placing the seller's creditors at a severe disadvantage because many creditors rely on being able to gain access to the assets of the seller. If they are sold to the buyer, they are lost to the seller's creditors.

As a result, the UCC imposes certain requirements on both the seller and buyer. The seller must provide the buyer with the names and addresses of his creditors. The seller and buyer must make a list of the property being sold. The buyer must file the list in a public office specified by law. The buyer must also notify the seller's creditors, by mail, of the sale ten days before paying for the goods or taking possession.

The UCC provides that the buyer will not be liable to unpaid creditors if he has complied with the notice requirements. On the other hand, the creditors will be able to reach assets in the buyer's possession if the buyer did not comply with the requirements. The seller is liable for any errors or omissions made during this process which damage either the buyer or the seller's creditors.

Excusing Performance

The parties' performance may be excused under the contract if the subject matter is destroyed, or there are other unforeseen changes in circumstances which are not the fault of the parties. While common law requires that performance be impossible to be excused, the UCC standard is one of **commercial impracticability.**

In order to meet the test of commercial impracticability under the UCC, the change in circumstances must be reasonably unforeseeable by the parties and externally caused. Routine changes are not grounds for excusing performances. If relatively minor changes excused performance, the certainty of all contracts would be lost.

- Ferdie and Felix have a contract for the sale and purchase of cartons of milk. Some of Ferdie's workers get sick, and Ferdie does not want to deliver the milk. Labor problems are regular events and are reasonably forseeable. Felix may enforce the contract. ■

- Because of an increase in the price of milk, Ferdie would lose money on the contract. This would not meet the standard of commercial impracticability because increases in prices are reasonably foreseeable. Felix may enforce the contract. ■

Unusual natural disasters such as hurricanes, typhoons, or earthquakes are more likely to make the contract commercially impractical and excuse performance. Government regulations or acts of war might also be grounds to excuse the contract based on commercial impracticability. The UCC standard is somewhat easier to meet than the common-law standard of impossibility, but the causes must still be externally caused and not foreseeable by the parties.

If contracts become commercially impractical, the seller of the goods must notify each buyer of the difficulties. She should also attempt to allocate available goods among buyers in accordance with contractual requirements of reasonableness and good faith.

A buyer who is notified that the seller will not perform the contract or who must allocate the sale of goods because of commercial impracticability may terminate the contract. The termination notice must be in writing. The notice will end the parties' obligations under the contract.

Seller's Remedies

If the buyer accepts the goods but does not pay for them, the seller's remedy is to recover the contract price. If the buyer rejects goods that conform to the contract's specifications, the seller's remedy is to recover the amount necessary to place him in the same position he would have been if the contract had been completed.

The buyer might reject goods that conform to the contract. The seller can sell the goods to another buyer. If the sale is done in a commercially reasonable manner, the measure of damages is the difference between the contract price and the resale price.

- Victoria delivers 100 wicker chairs to Marilyn which conform to the contract. Marilyn, who no longer needs the chairs, ships them back to Victoria. The contract price was $10,000.

Buyer breaches contract!

Victoria resells the chairs to Charlotte's Chairs for $7,500. The measure of damages is $10,000 − $7,500 = $2,500. Victoria is also entitled to any incidental damages such as additional shipping costs resulting from her resale to Charlotte. ■

The seller is also entitled to the same remedy if the buyer notifies her that he will not perform the contract. The seller is entitled to the difference between the contract price and the resale price.

■ Lee has a contract with Stewart to deliver 10,000 light bulbs for $15,000. Stewart repudiates the contract before delivery. Lee resells the bulbs to Luke's Lighting for $11,500. Lee would be entitled to $15,000 − $11,500 = $3,500 plus incidental damages. ■

If the buyer repudiates before the seller completes manufacture, the seller has a number of remedies. He may cancel the contract and cease manufacture. He could resell for scrap or salvage value. The seller may stop delivery if the goods have been sent but not yet received by the buyer. As previously noted, the seller may continue manufacture and resell the goods.

If the seller has doubts about the buyer's ability to make the payment, the seller has certain remedies. The seller may refuse to deliver the goods unless she is paid in cash. In addition, the seller may demand cash for goods previously delivered.

Buyer's Remedies

The buyer's remedies under the UCC are similar to those at common law. They also place the buyer in the same position she would have been if the contract had been completed.

The buyer may recover advance payments and cancel the contract if the seller does not deliver the goods. The buyer can also purchase the goods elsewhere. This is described as a cover. If the buyer "covers," the buyer will recover as damages the difference between the cover and contract price.

■ Daniel enters a contract to buy a big-screen television set from Dawkins for $1,000. When Dawkins does not deliver, Daniel buys a similar set from Tom's Televisions for $1,250. Daniel is entitled to $250 in damages plus any incidental costs. ■

The UCC maintains the equitable relief of a decree of specific performance. This compels the seller to sell the goods to the buyer. Equitable relief will be granted only if the goods are unique or the buyer is unable to cover.

■ Nora has a contract to buy a guitar once owned by Elvis Presley from Nancy's Guitars for $9,999. Nancy later refuses to transfer the guitar to Nora. Nora will be able to obtain a decree of specific performance which will compel Nancy to sell her the guitar. ■

If the seller delivers goods that do not conform to the contract, the buyer may recover any advance payments and rescind the contract. The buyer may also obtain similar goods and bring an action to recover the difference between the cover price and contract price.

In the world of business, sellers often deliver goods with minor nonconformities. The buyer normally accepts the goods, and then works out an appropriate reduction in the price. The proper reduction would be the amount necessary to correct the defects in the goods. This would also be the appropriate amount of damages if the matter went to court.

Under the UCC, a buyer may revoke an acceptance if she later discovers a defect that would "substantially impair" the value of the goods.

> A slightly cracked wheel cover would not substantially impair the value of a new automobile, but a cracked transmission would. ■

A proper revocation of an acceptance places the parties in the same position as if the buyer had rejected nonconforming goods, and the remedies are the same. If the defect is minor, the parties can negotiate the difference in value between the goods without the defect and with the defect.

The parties could also agree in advance to calculate the amount of damages if there are defects in the goods. These are known as liquidated damages and will be valid as long as they are reasonable. If they appear to be a penalty, they will not be upheld.

Definitions Reviewed

tender = offer of acceptance [handwritten]

A **tender** is an offer for acceptance.

A **negotiable document of title** allows the holder to take delivery of goods from a bailee. The bailee need not specifically determine the identity of the holder.

According to the **perfect tender rule,** the seller must deliver the goods in accord with all the contractual provisions related to delivery.

Anticipatory repudiation is notice by one of the parties that he will not perform his obligations under the contract.

A **bulk transfer** refers to the sale of all or a substantial portion of a seller's equipment, inventory, or other assets.

Commercial impracticability refers to externally caused, not foreseeable changes in circumstances that will excuse the parties from performing the contract.

Core Concepts Reviewed

■ A seller's obligation is to deliver goods that conform to the specifications in the contract. If the seller does not perform these obligations, the buyer has remedies that range from recovering money damages to requiring the seller to sell the goods.

■ The buyer's obligation is to pay for conforming goods. If the buyer does not pay, the seller has remedies ranging from recovering the purchase price or other damages based on the resale of the goods.

■ The UCC allows commercial impracticability to be used as a reason for not performing the contract.

■ Bulk transfers are sales of a major portion of the sellers' inventory to a buyer. Because of the potential for harm to the seller's creditors, additional notice requirements to these creditors are imposed on both the buyer and seller.

Questions

1. What is the general measure of compensatory money damages for a breach of contract?
2. What is a decree of specific performance?
3. When will a decree of specific performance be granted?

4. What is a bulk transfer?
5. What is commercial impracticability?
6. What is an anticipatory repudiation?
7. What is the perfect tender rule?
8. When may a buyer revoke an acceptance?

Problems

1. Smith has a contract to deliver 100 guns to Wesson for $10,000. Wesson makes a reasonable inspection on delivery and accepts the guns. Later, he discovers 50 of them have broken firing pins. Smith tells Wesson that he has to keep the guns because he accepted them. Does Wesson have a remedy?
2. Sally pays cash for a COD shipment and takes the goods. Later, she discovers major defects in them. The seller says she must keep them because she already paid for them. Does Sally have any remedy?
3. Olson has a contract with White to deliver ten typewriters. Olson discovers he will be unable to deliver them and notifies White. White buys ten identical machines and sends Olson a bill for the difference between the cover price and the contract price. Olson refuses to pay and claims White should have waited until the time for performance had passed. Is he correct?

4. Hotchkiss has a contract to deliver 100 pods to Sullivan for $20,000. Sullivan calls Hotchkiss ten days before the delivery date and refuses to take the shipment. Hotchkiss sells the pods to Peters Pods for $15,000. What is his remedy?
5. Jenkins has a contract to supply Holland with bricks for making a tunnel. Holland calls Jenkins a few days before delivery and says because the cost of plaster has risen rapidly, the tunnel's construction has been postponed, and he no longer needs the bricks. Holland later argues he is excused from the contract on the grounds of commercial impracticability. Is he correct?
6. Cathy has a contract to deliver 100 cartons of pizzas to Susan. Her truck was hijacked on the way to Susan's place of business with the pizzas. Cathy claims this excuses her performance. Is she correct?
7. Harold has a contract to deliver a Ming vase to Howard. When Harold refuses to deliver the vase, he tells Howard that his only remedy is to buy another vase and sue him for the difference. Is Harold correct?
8. Franklin has a contract to sell Sampson more than 60 percent of his inventory. They complete the sale without informing Franklin's creditors. When Franklin is unable to pay his creditors, they sue both Franklin and Sampson. What are the creditors' remedies against each of them?

PART V

COMMERCIAL PAPER

Chapter 17

Commercial Paper and Negotiability

- Commercial paper is a writing that can be easily transferred from one person to another. Commercial paper acts as a substitute for money or as an instrument of credit.

- The concept of negotiability is key to commercial paper. Negotiation is the transfer of commercial paper from one person to another. People who write commercial paper or transfer it will be liable to people who become holders of the paper.

- Indorsement is the transfer of commercial paper from one person to another. An indorsement of commercial paper means that the indorser will accept certain liabilities.

- There are different types of commercial paper. The best known commercial paper is a check, which allows the drawer to make payments based on the money in a checking account. Other types of commercial paper include notes, bonds, debentures, and other evidence of debt.

- Commercial paper must be presented for payment. If payment is not made, the party may pursue payment from the other parties to the paper.

- Acceptance is the agreement to assume liability for the payment of the paper.

COMMERCIAL PAPER

Commercial papers are writings that may be easily transferred from person to person. When negotiable, commercial paper acts as a substitute for money. There are different types of commercial paper. The best known are checks, but others include notes, debentures, certificates of deposit, and other evidence of indebtedness.

Terms Defined

Draft—a written order by one person to a financial institution, such as a bank, which requires the institution to pay a sum certain to the holder of the draft or to the order of a named person. A check is a draft.

Drawer—the person who draws a draft (the person who signs the check).

Drawee—the institution on which the draft is drawn. It has the obligation to pay the amount on the check if there are sufficient funds in the drawer's account.

Maker—the person who executes (makes) a promissory note.

Promissory note—a signed writing that contains an unconditional promise from one person to another agreeing to pay a sum certain at a particular time.

Payee—the person to whom a negotiable instrument is payable.

Holder—the person who holds a draft or note. The person who is in possession of commercial paper.

Holder in Due Course—a person who purchases commercial paper for value with no knowledge that there are any defenses to the obligation to make payment.

Indorser—a holder of commercial paper who transfers it to someone else by placing a signature on the back of the instrument.

Indorsement—the writing on the back of commercial paper which permits its transfer from one person to another.

Check—a draft drawn on a bank and payable on demand.

Certified check—a check certified as being good by the bank on which it is drawn and which bears the word "certified" on its face.

Bad or "rubber" check—a check drawn without sufficient funds in the bank account to cover the amount of the check. In many states, the issuance of bad checks is a disorderly persons offense for which there are criminal penalities.

Cashier's check—a check drawn on a bank's own funds. This is a useful instrument to utilize if payment by a buyer to a seller is uncertain. The seller may demand payment by a cashier's check.

Negotiation of Commercial Paper

Negotiable paper may be easily transferred from one party to another. The purpose of negotiable paper is to permit it to be treated as nearly equal to cash as possible.

Because the parties to negotiable paper can be liable for the full amount on the instrument, the requirements for negotiation are very strict. Every element must be present for the paper to be negotiable.

The negotiable instrument must be in writing. While checks and other negotiable paper are usually printed on standardized forms in order to facilitate their use, a negotiable instrument need not fit such a format. For example, a person could write a check on an envelope as long as the other requirements were met.

A negotiable instrument must be signed by the maker or drawer. This is the reason that checks have a place for the drawer's signature. This element would not be satisfied by a signature on a different piece of paper which is attached to the instrument.

A negotiable instrument must contain an **unconditional promise** or order to pay. The promise may not be conditioned on a future event or on the terms of any other document.

■ An instrument contains a promise to pay $5,000, but only when the Beatles are reunited for a concert in Peoria, Illinois. This would not be an unconditional promise. ■

■ An instrument contains a promise to pay $6,000, but only if the profits of the ABC Corporation increase by at least 10 percent. This would not be an unconditional promise, and the instrument would not be negotiable. ■

A negotiable instrument must be payable in a definite sum of money. This could be in U.S. currency or in a currency convertible to U.S. currency. It would not be sufficient if the amount is payable at the option of the maker or was subject to a condition. For example, this element would not be satisfied if the sum was expressed as a percentage of future revenues or profits.

A negotiable instrument must be payable on demand or at a definite time. This will not be satisfied if the instrument is payable at some future event. The time for payment must be found in the body of the instrument.

■ Sam issues an instrument payable 30 days after Elvis Presley gives a concert in New York City. This would not be negotiable. ■

The instrument must be payable to the "bearer" or "to the order of." These specific words are important to the concept of negotiability. If the instrument is payable to the bearer, it may be presented or negotiated by anyone holding it. If it is payable "to the order of," it may be presented by the named person or to anyone to whom she negotiates the instrument.

■ Checks are usually printed with the words "to the order of" immediately in front of the blank where the drawer fills in the payee's name. Ed has a checking account with the Twenty-third National Bank. He draws a check to Edna. Because the check is payable to the order of Edna, she may present the check to Twenty-third or negotiate the check by signing the back. ■

■ Jones makes a check payable to "bearer." All of the other elements of negotiability are satisfied. He hands the check to Smith. Smith may present the check for payment. He may also negotiate it by handing it to another bearer. ■

The value of negotiability is that instruments may be treated as cash. There is no need to check the title of the parties to the instruments. Neither is there a need to research the legitimacy of the instrument. While a nonnegotiable instrument is not as easily transferrable, it is binding on the parties involved.

Types of Instruments

A draft is a document signed by the drawer which instructs the drawee, who holds an account for the drawer, to pay to the order of the payee a certain sum of money. Usually, the drawee is a bank. The financial institution has an obligation to pay drafts (checks) if there are sufficient funds in the account.

The drawee has no obligation to pay drafts unless there are adequate funds in the account. A check written without sufficient funds is called a **bad** or **rubber check.** When the bank rejects a bad check, it is said to be dishonored. When a bank dishonors a check, the payee may pursue payment directly from the drawer. The bank has a duty to make certain that the signature on the check belongs to the drawer. It will be held liable if it pays a check with a signature other than the drawer's.

A draft may be a sight draft or a time draft. A sight draft is payable on demand. A time draft is not payable on demand. It gives the drawee some time to pay the amount on the draft. A check is a sight draft.

A negotiable promissory note is a promise to pay a sum certain either on demand or at a definite time in the future to either the bearer or to a specific person. The person who executes the note is called a maker. Unlike a draft, there is no drawee who will pay the instrument. The maker must pay the instrument.

■ Hudson executes a promissory note payable to Heston for $10,000 on June 30th. When Heston presents the note on June 30th, Hudson must pay the $10,000 to him on that date. If he does not, Hudson will be in default. ■

Bonds are promissory notes issued by corporations or by local, state, or national governments. They promise to pay the holder the face amount at a certain time and at a stated rate of interest. Bonds may be nonnegotiable or negotiable. The current trend is to make all bonds negotiable bearer instruments for easy transfer.

■ XYZ Corporation issues bonds to investors. The face amount of these bonds is $10,000. The due date is June 30, 2001. The interest rate is 8 percent.

If Simms buys one of these bonds, he will receive $800 per year. He will be paid that amount until June 30, 2001, at which time he will turn in the bond and receive $10,000.

If the bond is nonnegotiable, it represents a debt from XYZ Corporation to Simms. If the bond is negotiable, Simms may sell it in the marketplace to someone else. Depending on the level of interest rates at the time, Simms may have either a net gain or loss. If market interest rates exceed 8 percent, the bond will be worth less than face value. If interest rates are less than 8 percent, the bond will be worth more than face value. ■

Certificates of deposit (CDs) are negotiable instruments issued by banks. They promise the holder that she will earn a stated rate of interest on her principal amount until the principal can be withdrawn. Certificates of deposit (CDs) are very useful investments for affluent individuals or large corporations. They earn a higher rate of interest than normal savings accounts for individuals and provide large corporations with a convenient place to put excess cash. CDs also allow banks to attract additional deposits from investors and to compete with other investment vehicles such as bonds.

Transfer of Commercial Paper

If commercial paper is transferred by negotiation, the holder may have greater rights than the immediate transferor. Negotiation is the transfer of commercial paper from a transferor to a transferee such that the transferee becomes a holder. A holder has at least the rights of the transferor. If the transferee takes the paper as a holder in due course (HDC), she acquires even greater rights than the transferor. A holder is a person who has possession of a negotiable instrument. A holder who acquired the instrument for value and without knowledge of any defenses to its payment is a holder in due course.

Negotiation is accomplished by indorsement by the proper party and delivery to another. If the paper was made payable to a specific payee, the payee may endorse the paper by placing his signature on the back of the instrument. He then completes negotiation by delivering the paper to the transferee.

■ Brendan receives a check made payable to his order. He can indorse the check by writing his name on the back. He completes negotiation by delivering the check to a transferee. ■

If the instrument is made payable to the bearer, negotiation may be accomplished by delivery. An indorsement by the bearer is not necessary to complete negotiation.

■ Morton writes a check for $1,000, and makes it out to "cash." This is a bearer instrument. Morton hands the check to Agnes. She may negotiate the check by delivering it to another person. ■

Order paper can become bearer paper if the indorser simply signs the back of the paper without making it payable to a specific person. Similarly, the holder of bearer paper can make it order paper by making the indorsement to a specific person.

■ Hilton receives commercial paper made out to bearer. He indorses the paper "to Frank Fondue." He has converted bearer paper to order paper. Frank may negotiate it only by placing his name on the back of the paper. ■

■ Buzzy receives commercial paper made payable to "Buzzy." If he indorses the paper by signing "Buzzy" on the back but not making it payable to a specific person, he has converted the paper to bearer paper. The holder may simply deliver it to another transferor (holder) to complete negotiation. ■

TYPES OF INDORSEMENTS

There are different types of indorsements by holders of negotiable instruments. Each of the indorsements accomplishes a different result and has different consequences for the future negotiability of the instrument.

A **blank indorsement** is simply the signature of the holder on the back of the instrument. The indorsement does not identify any specific party. A blank indorsement converts all negotiable paper into bearer paper. The paper may then be negotiated by mere delivery.

■ Thomas writes a check to Raymond Raybar. Raymond takes the check and simply signs his name on the back. This is a blank indorsement and converts the check to a bearer instrument. The check may then be transferred without further indorsement to a new transferee. ■

A **special indorsement** specifically identifies the name of the transferee and contains the signature of the indorser. The instrument now becomes order paper and can be negotiated only if the new holder indorses it.

■ Thomas writes a check to Raymond except that, this time, Raymond Raybar indorses the instrument "payable to Joe Jones," and places his signature on the back. This instrument may now be transferred only if Joe Jones signs it. ■

Most indorsements are unqualified because they do not attempt to restrict the liability of the indorser. An indorser may be held liable for the face amount of the instrument unless she restricts the indorsement. A blank or special indorsement without any additional language is an unqualified indorsement. If the drawer or maker defaults on the instrument, the indorser may be held liable.

A **qualified indorsement** attempts to limit the liability of the indorser on the instrument. In the case of a qualified indorsement, words such as "without recourse" are used. These words mean that the indorser will not guarantee payment of the instrument.

■ Franklin holds a check made payable to him. The drawer of the check is Johnson. Franklin wants to indorse the instrument to Ralph Detweiler. But, he has some doubts about Johnson's check being good and he does not want to be held liable for it. Franklin indorses the check as follows: "Pay to Ralph Detweiler, without recourse, Franklin F. Franklin." This will limit his liability to Detweiler. ■

An instrument with a qualified indorsement may still be negotiated to someone else. A special qualified indorsement is still order paper, and an instrument with a blank qualified indorsement is still bearer paper.

A **restrictive indorsement** contains language that restricts the use of the paper. The most common is an indorsement that reads "for deposit only." This puts others on notice that nothing should be done with the instrument except to deposit it in an account.

Banks use this type of indorsement as part of the collection process. In addition, use of the restrictive indorsement is good practice when one is taking a significant number of checks to the bank. It prevents someone who finds the checks from cashing them. A bank will be liable for doing anything other than depositing a check with a restrictive indorsement.

A **conditional indorsement** states that the indorsement is subject to some event. It is similar to a condition in a contract. Depending on how it is phrased, the condition may be either the occurrence or nonoccurrence of some particular event. Liability will occur only if that condition is met.

■ Brown indorses a check to Dobbs. But, the language of the indorsement states, "pay to Dobbs if the profits of the Brown Company increase by 10 percent in 1995." Brown has limited his liability by placing the condition on the check. He will have no liability unless the condition is met. ■

■ Jones wants to buy a restaurant from Mom. However, he wants the restaurant only if the ZBT factory next door reopens. This would supply the customers he needs. Jones is also the payee of a check. He indorses the check "Pay to Mom if ZBT factory opens within 20 days, Johnny J. Jones." This is a conditional indorsement. If the factory does not open in 20 days, Jones has no liability to Mom. ■

An indorsement in trust is often used by a professional who maintains fiduciary accounts for clients. An attorney will take a check or other negotiable paper and indorse it payable to his trust account on behalf of his client.

■ Alan B. Attorney receives a check from the buyer of a house. His client, Owen Owner, is the seller of the house. Alan indorses the check, "pay in trust to Owen Owner Fiduciary Account, Alan B. Attorney." ■

Wrongful Indorsements

One of the issues associated with commercial paper is the possibility that the signature of a payee or another holder might be forged. If an instrument is forged, the forger will bear the responsibility for any loss.

But, if the forger cannot be found, someone will bear the loss. The general rule is that the party who first receives the forged instrument will bear the loss.

■ Priscilla draws a check to Parker. Paul steals the check from Parker, forges Parker's signature, and gives it to George. If Paul cannot be located, George will bear the loss. ■

There are some exceptions to this rule. The first of these is the imposter rule. If an imposter induces a drawer to draw a check to him, the drawer will bear the loss as opposed to any future holders. The same rule applies to makers of notes.

■ Schmidt is an excellent make-up artist and a fine impersonator. He imitates Logan, to whom Jenson owes a debt. Jenson draws Schmidt/Logan a check for $5,000. Schmidt immediately indorses the check for value to Margaret. He then skips the country.

When Margaret presents the check to Jenson, he will be liable on the instrument. Jensen was the one who placed the check into the stream of commerce. He also issued the check and took the chance that Schmidt was Logan. He should bear the loss because he had the best chance to prevent it. ■

A second example of holding the maker liable is when an agent of the drawer/maker takes part in the invention of either an imposter or a fictitious payee.

■ Dr. Nick works at Grace Hospital. Dr. Nick is responsible for ordering drugs at the hospital. He sends phony invoices to the treasurer of the hospital which indicate that King's Drugs has supplied the hospital with $10,000 worth of pills. The treasurer draws a check to King's Drugs, which is actually a front for Dr. Nick. He indorses the check and transfers it for value to George. Grace Hospital should bear the loss rather than George because it was in a better position to supervise its agents and to prevent the fraud commited by Dr. Nick. ■

HOLDERS IN DUE COURSE

The purpose of commercial paper is to facilitate easy transfer and allow it to act as a substitute for money. While an assignee takes only the rights of the assignor, a holder of commercial paper who takes the paper in accord with certain requirements will have greater rights than the transferor.

A holder in due course (HDC) will hold the instrument free from many defenses that the drawer of a check or maker of a note could have asserted against others. To qualify as an HDC, a person must first qualify as a holder. A holder is in possession of a negotiable instrument indorsed to his order, to bearer, or in blank.

An HDC must take the instrument for value. This means that the holder cannot have received the paper as a gift. While it is permissible for the holder to take the instrument at a discount, an excessive discount may indicate the taking was not in good faith. The holder should pay reasonable value for the instrument.

An HDC must also take the instrument in good faith. The HDC must have taken the instrument without notice of defenses or adverse claims to the instrument. If someone takes the instrument who knew or should have known of a defense to its payment, that person is not an HDC.

A holder will not have taken the instrument in good faith if he knows that the instrument has been dishonored, is overdue, has a defense attached to it, or that another person has a claim to it. A person will have notice of a defect if he has actual notice of the defect, has been given notice of the defect, or should have known from all the circumstances that a defect exists.

Instruments that are due on a certain date are considered overdue on the next business day.

■ Notes are usually due at a definite time. If a note is due on June 30, 1995, it will be overdue on July 1, 1995. Someone who acquires the note after that date is merely a holder and not an HDC. ■

A check is due on demand. It will be overdue after demand or after a reasonable time. A reasonable time for a check is presumed to be 30 days after it is dated. A check acquired after this period would be overdue and a transferee who acquires the instrument cannot be an HDC.

A person cannot become an HDC if she knows that the instrument has been dishonored. An instrument has been dishonored if it has been presented for payment and payment has been refused.

■ Jennifer is the payee of a check drawn on Harvey's account. When the check is presented, it is dishonored because Harvey's account has insufficient funds. The bank has stamped "insufficient funds" on the check. Jennifer gives the check for value to Sam. He cannot be an HDC. ■

If there is no notice on the check reflecting a dishonor, a person could still be an HDC. In the previous example, Smith could still have been an HDC if nothing had been stamped on the check.

A person may not be an HDC if she has notice of any defense to the instrument. In this case, a defense is something that would permit the drawer or maker to deny liability.

If the instrument is incomplete in any material respect when received, the transferee can not be an HDC. For example, a check would be incomplete if the amount was left blank. If the place for the amount was blank when received, the transferee cannot be an HDC. On the other hand, if the blank had been completed without authorization, a person could still become an HDC if she acquired the instrument without knowledge of the unauthorized completion.

Obvious irregularities in the instrument such as crossed out words, figures, or signatures should put the transferee on notice of problems. A blatant forgery should also put the holder on notice. However, very clever forgeries, alterations, or minor irregularities that are undetected will not by themselves prevent a transferee from becoming an HDC.

A transferee cannot be an HDC if he knows that the instrument is voidable. An instrument is voidable if was acquired through fraud, duress, or misrepresentation. Similarly, a transferee cannot be an HDC if he was aware that the instrument was discharged. For example, if a transferee knew a check had already been paid, she cannot be an HDC.

Definitions Reviewed

Unconditional promise is a promise to pay a negotiable instrument. It is not based on a future condition.

Certificate of deposit is a negotiable instrument issued by a bank.

Blank indorsement is an indorsement not made to a specific person.

Special indorsement specifically identifies the name of the transferee.

Qualified indorsement attempts to limit the liability of the indorser.

Restrictive indorsement restricts future transfers of the instrument.

Conditional indorsement states the indorsement is conditioned on some event.

Core Concepts Reviewed

■ Commercial paper is easily transferable and acts as a substitute for money.

■ Commercial paper consists of such instruments as checks, notes, bonds, and certificates of deposits. They play a major role in forming the capital structure of our free enterprise system.

■ Commercial paper may be either negotiable or nonnegotiable. Negotiable paper is easily transferable.

■ Because negotiable commercial paper is easily transferable, it must strictly comply with certain elements. The instrument must contain an unconditional promise to pay a sum certain, must be payable on demand or at a definite time, and must be payable to the bearer or to "the order of" a named person.

■ The most common negotiable instrument is the check. A check is payable on demand. The person who executes a check is a drawer. The institution on which it is drawn is called the drawee. It has the obligation to pay all checks on which the drawer has sufficient funds. The drawee has the obligation to check the signature to ensure that it is the drawer's. It will be liable for paying checks on forged signatures. A "rubber check" is one drawn without sufficient funds. A person can be held civilly and criminally liable for writing rubber checks.

■ A note is an instrument that promises to pay someone a certain amount at a certain time. Normally, the note also pays a certain rate of interest. Bonds are similar to notes. Both notes and bonds are commonly issued by corporations and governments.

■ Commercial paper may be transferred by assignment or by negotiation. While an assignee receives only the rights of the assignor, a holder who takes by negotiation may receive greater rights and benefits than the immediate transferor.

■ Negotiation is accomplished by indorsement and delivery. There are a variety of indorsements. Some make the instrument bearer paper while others will require further indorsement by the holder. Other indorsements will restrict certain uses of the instrument.

■ Future transferees are on notice of the nature of the indorsement and are bound to honor it.

■ The transferee with the greatest rights to a negotiable instrument is a holder in due course. In order to be an HDC, one must take the instrument for value, in good faith, and without knowledge of any defense or defect or without knowledge that it has been dishonored. An HDC will take the instrument free of many defenses that would prevail over an ordinary transferee.

Questions

1. What is commercial paper?
2. What is its purpose?
3. Name some types of commercial paper.
4. What is a check?
5. Name the parties to a check.
6. When can one demand payment on a check?
7. When is a negotiation complete?
8. What are the requirements of negotiability?
9. Define an unconditional promise.
10. What is a "rubber check"?
11. What are the liabilities of a drawee?
12. What is a blank indorsement?
13. What is a restrictive indorsement?
14. What is a "fictitious payee"?

15. Who is responsible for the actions of a "fictitious payee"?
16. What is an "imposter payee"?
17. Who is responsible for the actions of an "imposter payee"?
18. What is a "holder in due course"?
19. What is taking in "good faith"?
20. What is a "reasonable" time for payment of a check?

Problems

1. Chuck owes Arnold $2,000. He takes a plain white piece of paper and writes on it. "I owe Arnold $2,000 payable on May 1, 1995. I will also pay 8 percent per year interest until that date." Chuck places his signature on the bottom of the piece of paper. Is this document enforceable? Is it negotiable by Arnold?

2. Larry has an account at Thirty-seventh National Bank. He takes an unused envelope and writes on it, "payable to the order of Peter Davidson $1,000 from my account at Thirty-seventh National Bank." He signs the envelope at the bottom.

   If his account has sufficient assets to pay the amount, should the bank pay the amount on the envelope? Can Peter negotiate the envelope to someone else?

3. Terry has a checking account with Forty-third National Bank. Harold, a burglar, sneaks into Terry's house, and steals Terry's TV set and checkbook. The burglar then writes out three checks for $500 each, signs Terry's name, and cashes them at Terry's bank. Terry claims that she should not be liable on the checks. Is she correct?

4. Bob writes a note payable to "the order of Harry the Horse" for $2,000, payable on the date when "a filly from Dunroven Farms wins the Triple Crown." Is the note negotiable?

5. Sally writes a note to Eric on April 1, 1995. She lists the amount as 6 percent of the next fiscal year's profits of the Underwire Foundation Company of New York and Cleveland. Is this note negotiable?

6. Stewart is the treasurer of the local Strong Backs and Helping Hands Association of Westrock. The association conducts its annual charity ball and raises $2,000. Almost all of it is in small checks. Stewart writes "for deposit only" on each check before taking them to the bank.

   On his way to the bank, Stewart is mugged and all his checks are stolen. The thief rushes to the bank and cashes the checks. The association demands that the bank reimburse it for the full amount. Is it entitled to reimbursement?

7. Howard draws a check to Jennifer. She wants to use the check to buy a beauty shop in the city of Cleveland. However, she wants the shop only if the local bowling alley, Lucky Lanes, which is next to the shop, remains open.

   Jennifer figures that she will draw many of her customers from the bowling alley. She indorses Howard's check with her name and the sentence, "Only if Lucky Lanes remains open for the next 28 days," and gives it to Mona, the owner of the shop. Lucky Lanes closes the next week. Mona presents the check to Howard, who refuses to pay it. She then demands payment from Jennifer, who also refuses. Mona sues both Howard and Jennifer. Are either or both of them liable for the check?

8. The ABC Company has a new purchasing agent named Ralph. He submits vouchers for a company of which he is the principal owner. The treasurer of ABC issues checks based on the vouchers, which later prove to be false.

   ABC later demands that its drawee bank reimburse it for the amount distributed. Will it prevail?

9. Jones indorses a check for $10,000 to Hopkins and receives $1,000 in return. Later, it is determined that the check had been lost by Harris and written by Jones.

   The evidence indicates that Jones and Hopkins had previously conducted similar transactions. However, there was no specific evidence that Hopkins knew of Jones' activities. Is Hopkins an HDC and entitled to recover from Harris?

10. Bowe writes a check to Pike, dated May 1st, for $10,000. On June 6th, Pike negotiates the check to Trout for $6,000. Is Trout a holder in due course?

11. Jones is the payee of a check drawn by Stokes. When he presents the check for payment, Stokes tells him to forget it. Jones decides that since Stokes will not pay it, he can give it to his daughter Mary as a present. Is she a holder in due course if she did not know the check had been dishonored?

Chapter 18

Liability on Commercial Paper

- A drawer has liability for a check if there are not sufficient funds in her account with the drawee. Subsequent indorsers of a check will be secondarily liable on the instrument.

- A maker is primarily liable on a note. Indorsers will be secondarily liable on a note if the maker does not pay.

- Holders of an instrument expect to be paid. They may proceed on the theories of warranty liability, contract liability, and negligence. They may proceed against all the persons who signed the instrument.

- A holder will generally be able to prevail on the instrument, although certain defenses to the instrument will prevail over the holder.

- A holder in due course (HDC) is a special type of holder. An HDC is protected from nearly every defense of the drawer, maker, or indorser. The HDC will prevail over personal defenses but will not prevail over universal defenses, which go to the legitimacy of the instrument.

- The parties to the instrument may be discharged from liability in a number of ways. These include discharge by payment, discharge by cancellation of the instrument, and discharge by impairment of collateral or other interests.

LIABILITY ON NEGOTIABLE INSTRUMENTS

The first theory of liability is that of warranty liability. Every person who transfers negotiable paper for value warrants to the transferee that:

- The transferor has good title to the instrument or acts on behalf of someone who has good title.
- All signatures on the instrument are genuine or authorized.
- The instrument has not been materially altered.
- No defenses of any party are good against the person who is making the transfer.
- The person making the transfer has no knowledge of the insolvency of the maker, acceptor, or drawee of an unaccepted instrument.

If the instrument is transferred by indorsement, the indorser makes these transfer warranties to the immediate transferee and to subsequent holders who take the instrument in good faith. If the transfer is made without an indorsement, the warranties are made only to the immediate transferee and not to future holders.

- Smith draws a check to Green who indorses it with the words "Payable to Frank Brown, Ronald J. Green." Brown then indorses the check with the words "payable to Margaret Black, Frank Brown." Green will be liable for the transfer warranties to Brown and Black. Brown will be liable to Black. Black could bring an action against either Brown or Green if the drawer, Smith, does not pay the check. ▦

▦ Sanders executes a note in bearer form and gives it to Hopkins who transfers it to Franklin without indorsement. Franklin then transfers it without indorsement to Simpson. The indorsers' liability extends only to the immediate transferees. ▦

▦ Kelly writes a check to Steve Donaldson. He alters the amount on the check from $10 to $10,000. He indorses the instrument for value to Godkin with the words, "Payable to Albert Godkin, Steve Donaldson." Godkin then indorses the check for value to Roger Dash with the words, "Payable to Roger Dash, Albert Godkin."

Donaldson will be liable to both Godkin and Dash for his alteration. Godkin will be liable to Dash for Donaldson's alteration. If Godkin is held liable by Dash, he has a claim against Donaldson. ▦

Contractual Liability

If a person signs a negotiable instrument, she is creating a contract with future holders. In the case of bearer paper, usually the only person whose signature is on the paper is the maker or drawer. If the paper is order paper, one can expect to have the signatures of indorsers as well as the drawer or maker.

The maker of a note has primary liability on the note. Acceptors of checks and drafts have primary liability for the instrument as originally written. Drawers of checks and drafts and indorsers of negotiable paper have secondary liability. The reason an acceptor is primarily liable on a check is because the purpose of a checking account is to have the drawee accept the instrument and pay for it. Therefore, when the drawee bank agrees to pay a check, it should have primary responsibility for doing so.

Secondary liability allows a holder to recover from another party if the parties with primary liability will not or cannot pay the amount on the instrument. Secondary parties will be liable if the negotiable instrument is properly presented for payment, the instrument is dishonored, payment is refused, and notice is given to the party secondarily liable on the instrument.

Presentment is the demand for payment or acceptance of an instrument. An instrument is dishonored when payment or acceptance is refused by the party with primary liability. Timely notice should be given of the dishonor to parties with secondary liability to hold them liable. Unless notice of the dishonor is given within a reasonable time to the secondary party, that party cannot be held liable.

Notice should be given to parties with secondary liability by the party who wants to hold them liable. The notice should be given in a reasonable manner and in a timely fashion. Banks must give notice before midnight of the next banking day. Others must give notice before midnight of the third business day.

Specified Liabilities

A maker of a note is primarily liable on the instrument. The maker's liability stems from her unconditional promise to pay a specified amount at a certain time. Holders of the note need do nothing to enforce this obligation.

A drawee is the repository of the funds of the drawer. A check or other draft is an order to pay. While the drawee is not liable to the holder of the instrument for failing to pay, the drawee is expected to pay if there are sufficient funds in the drawer's account. The drawee will be liable to the drawer for any damages for its wrongful refusal to pay on the instrument.

■ Henry has a checking account at Forty-ninth National Bank. He writes a check to Frank for $3,000 to pay for an old debt. Henry and Frank are about to enter some major business deals. When Frank presents the check at Forty-ninth National Bank, an inexperienced teller mixes up the account numbers and informs Frank that Henry's account does not have sufficient funds. He stamps the check "Payment Refused for Insufficient Funds." ■

Frank becomes angry and tells Henry that their deals are off until the old debt is settled. He demands that he receive an additional $500 to settle the debt. Henry can bring an action against Forty-ninth National to recover the additional $500.

An **acceptor** is a drawee who states that there are sufficient funds to pay for a check by writing the words "accepted" or "certified" on the check. Requests for certified checks are common in business. They are useful when the drawer is unknown, long distances are involved, or business is being done through the mail.

When the drawee accepts an instrument, it discharges the drawer and indorsers from liability. Certification of checks is a service that most banks are willing to provide for a fee.

■ Rupert wants to purchase some large equipment. Rupert is located in New York and the seller is located in Los Angeles. The seller has had no previous business dealings with Rupert. It has also had various banks return some bad checks sent by buyers.

Rupert has an account at Thirteenth National Bank and has a check certified by the bank. He sends the certified check to the seller with his order form. The seller may now hold the bank liable on the check. ■

If the drawee refuses to pay the check for any reason (the reason is usually lack of funds), the drawer remains liable for the check. Issuing bad checks may expose a drawer to both criminal and civil liability.

■ Donald has an account with Twenty-fifth National Bank. He has only $3 left in the account. Despite this, he goes to Brewski City Liquor Store and purchases $59 worth of liquor. Donald's check is not honored by Twenty-fifth National Bank.

Donald still owes Brewski City Liquor Store $59. In addition, criminal charges may be brought against Donald for issuing the bad check. ■

Liability of Indorsers

An indorser may be liable on a negotiable instrument if the party with primary liability does not pay. A person who places an unqualified indorsement on an instrument will be liable to the current and subsequent holders. Indorsers will be liable to each other in the order they indorsed the instrument.

Indorsers will not be liable if they put a restriction on it. The words "without recourse" mean that an indorser is not accepting liability for the instrument.

A party who wishes to hold an indorser liable on the instrument must comply with the same rules relating to notice of the dishonor as apply to other parties. Generally, a party must notify the indorser by midnight of the third business day following the dishonor of the instrument.

Previous sections discussed the theories of liability of the indorser. An indorser may be held liable on theories of contract, warranty or negligence. An unqualified indorser is liable on both the contract and warranty theories. A qualified indorser does not have contractual liability but retains warranty liability.

> ▨ Max draws a check to Steve, who unqualifiedly indorses the check to Mary. When she presents the check for payment, it is dishonored by the bank. ▪

Mary attempts to collect from Max to no avail. She notifies Steve of the dishonor within the appropriate time. If Steve has the resources, he must pay Mary the face amount of the check.

A person who signs a note either as a maker or as an indorser in order to guarantee payment may also be held liable on the instrument. This is common practice when one of the parties to a loan is a minor or someone with a bad credit rating.

> ▨ Mary's sister Rhoda wants to purchase an automobile, but she earns little money and has no credit history. The bank refuses to extend her a loan unless someone else agrees to co-sign. ▪

Mary co-signs both the note to the bank and the underlying loan agreement. Although the bank, Mary, and Rhoda all presume that Rhoda will pay the loan, Mary will also be liable to the bank if Rhoda does not pay.

LIABILITY TO HOLDERS IN DUE COURSE

The concept of a holder in due course (HDC) was previously discussed. An HDC is someone who takes a negotiable instrument in good faith and for reasonable value. An HDC has the greatest protection from defenses that can be raised by the other parties to the instruments.

Those defenses that will not prevail against an HDC are called **personal defenses.** Those few defenses that go directly to the making of the instrument will prevail over an HDC. These are called **universal defenses.** Both personal and universal defenses may be raised against a mere holder of a negotiable instrument.

Universal (real) defenses will prevail over both a holder and an HDC. If a universal defense is proved, the HDC will not recover. The first universal defense is lack of mental capacity.

A minor is presumed to lack mental capacity, and a minor may disaffirm a contract. A minor is someone below the age of majority (age 18 in most states).

A negotiable instrument is a type of contract. Unless the minor deliberately misrepresented her age, she will be able to deny liability for the instrument.

A person who has already been judged mentally incompetent also will be able to deny liability. A mental incompetency proceeding is one held by a court with all parties represented. A party who merely asserts lack of mental capacity has only a personal defense. A person who has been judged mentally incompetent may disaffirm all of his contracts. A negotiable instrument is another contract that may be denied. A person asserting lack of mental capacity must demonstrate that he was unable to understand the essential terms of the contract. In this case, he must show that he did not understand the terms of the negotiable instrument.

Duress may be a personal or a universal defense. Duress may be pressure or excessive influence. This would be "ordinary duress" and would be a personal defense, whereas extreme duress is a universal defense. To prove extreme duress requires evidence of force or violence.

> Michael Moreleon requires people who owe him gambling debts to sign negotiable instruments with extremely high interest rates. If they do not sign, he puts a gun to their head until they do. This would be an example of extreme duress and a universal defense against an HDC.

A contract for illegal purposes is void from its inception. Because a negotiable instrument is a type of contract, a negotiable instrument supporting an unlawful transaction will be void.

> Herb sells cocaine to Jay for $10,000. Jay pays him with a note with an interest rate of 30 percent per annum. This is an unlawful transaction. Both the contract between Herb and Jay and the negotiable instrument are void.

An **aleatory contract** is one that relates to gambling. If a negotiable instrument is related to gambling contracts, it would be void from its inception except in a few American jurisdictions.

> Sean agrees to purchase gambling equipment from Frank for $10,000. Sean signs a promissory note to support the transaction for $10,000.

Because the note is based on an unlawful transaction, it would be void. Negotiable instruments based on other unlawful activities such as contracts to commit crimes would also be void.

People could be persuaded by a misstatement of fact to sign a negotiable instrument. If the facts are stated with the intention of deceiving the maker, this is fraud. This is called fraud in the inducement. It constitutes a personal defense and is available against a holder. It would not, however, be available against an HDC.

Fraud in the execution or fraud in the inception occurs when one person deceives another person about the nature of the instrument. This type of fraud would be a real defense and available against an HDC.

> Rose is a woman who is 103 years old. Her family regularly has her sign documents related to her substantial wealth. One day, her niece Caroline brings

her a large number of documents to sign. Caroline inserts a note payable to herself for $10,000.

Rose has always trusted Caroline and signs all the documents, including the note. This is fraud in the making. This is a universal defense and Rose will prevail over an HDC. Both Rose and all future holders will have a remedy against Caroline for her fraudulent actions. ■

Persons who execute negotiable instruments are expected to exercise reasonable care over these instruments. If they are negligent, the real defense against an HDC may be denied to them. In the preceding example, Rose's advanced age and her previous experiences with Caroline would likely be considered in her favor.

But, a younger person or one with more business experience might not be able to assert the defense.

■ Myron is a successful businessperson who works for a large bank. His financial advisor gives him a number of documents to sign. Among them is a negotiable instrument. Myron signs the document without looking at it. ■

In this case, Myron should have looked at the document. His negligence will probably prevent him from asserting the defense of fraud in the execution against a future HDC.

A similar universal defense is that of forgery. If someone wrongfully places a signature on a negotiable instrument, the "maker" or "drawer" will have a defense. This defense would normally be good against both holders and HDCs.

Again, the negligence of the "drawer" or "maker" would be a factor in the success of the defense.

■ Monroe is a successful businessperson who handles the finances of other businesspeople. One day he is writing out some personal checks in the backseat of a taxicab.

When he departs the cab, he leaves his checkbook on the back seat. The next person in the cab, Harry, takes Monroe's checkbook. He pulls several checks, writes them to himself as payee and signs Monroe's name. He indorses these checks for value to an HDC. ■

Monroe would not be able to assert the universal defense of fraud in the instrument's making. He is an adult businessperson with financial skills and should have known the potential consequences of leaving his checkbook in a taxicab. His negligence will preclude him from prevailing with this defense.

An alteration that is material will be a defense against holders. A material alteration is one that is important. Minor alterations that have no impact on the existence or amount of liability are not material. If the alteration is material, it will be a defense against holders. If the alteration relates to the amount payable, an HDC will be able to recover the original amount in the instrument.

■ Victor writes a check to Douglas, who alters the amount from $5,000 to $50,000. While the alteration is a defense against holders, an HDC could enforce the check up to $5,000. ■

If the alteration was obvious, it would prevent the holder from becoming an HDC. An obvious alteration would raise questions about a person's good faith. If the maker or drawer's negligence contributed to the alteration, it will prevent the drawer or maker from prevailing over an HDC.

> ■ Victor regularly signs checks and leaves the space for writing the amount in words blank. This could contribute to alterations in the instrument. Victor would be liable for any alterations and must pay the HDC. ■

Another universal defense is a discharge in bankruptcy. The purpose of a bankruptcy proceeding is to give people a "fresh start." When the proceedings are concluded, the bankrupt is discharged from previous debts. A negotiable instrument is a previous debt. A court-ordered discharge in bankruptcy is a defense against both a holder and an HDC.

Personal Defenses

Personal defenses will prevail over a mere holder, but will not prevail over an HDC. Personal defenses are those that would be defenses to a breach-of-contract suit. A negotiable instrument is a type of contract. Both the holder and the maker are parties to this contract. A defense that would prevail in an action related to a contract will prevail in this action. The reason that an HDC will still win is the law's intention that negotiable instruments be treated as money. A good method of promoting this objective is to allow HDCs to prevail against all but the most serious defenses.

One personal defense is that of lack of consideration. The party may use this defense against the payee or against holders. In this defense, the maker or drawer is asserting that he did not receive anything in return for his issuance of the instrument or did not receive the bargained exchange of values.

> ■ Kevin gives his nephew, David, a promissory note as a gift. He received nothing in exchange. Kevin may use lack of consideration as a defense against an action by David to enforce the instrument. ■

> ■ Betsy buys a car from Frank's Used Car Lot. Betsy gives a promissory note in exchange for the vehicle. Frank indorses the note to Charlotte. She has taken these notes from Frank many times previously and is aware that some customers have had problems with their vehicles. Betsy's car proves to be no exception. The moment that she drives the vehicle out of the lot, it breaks down. Despite her best efforts, she is unable to make it run. ■

Betsy will have a defense against the note. She may defend against Frank because the auto does not work. Charlotte is only a holder because she was aware that a defense to the note might exist.

As indicated earlier in this chapter, fraud will be a universal defense to the instrument if the fraud relates to the making of the instrument. However, fraud will be a personal defense if it relates to the reasons that the instrument was made.

> ■ Barbara buys a 1981 Hupmobile on the salesperson's assurances that the car has been driven only 25,000 miles. She writes a promissory note to pay for the automobile to Hup's Hot Cars. It negotiates the note for value to Jones.

Later, it is determined that the odometer was actually turned back from 100,000 to 25,000 miles. This is fraud. While fraud is a defense that would be admissible against the car dealer and mere holders, it would not be available against an HDC. Jones would prevail against Barbara. ▨

Extreme duress, such as the use of physical force or violence, would be a universal defense available against an HDC. But, duress that amounts to threats or undue influence is only a personal defense and will not prevail over an HDC.

▨ Millie is a bedridden elderly woman who receives nursing care from Maggie. Millie is entirely dependent on Maggie's assistance. One day Maggie comes to Millie and tells her that if she does not sign a $5,000 promissory note payable to Maggie, she will not receive good care in the future.

When Millie refuses to sign, Maggie reminds Millie just how vulnerable she would be if there was a fire or if she fell to the floor. Maggie tells Millie that if she cried out, "Help me, I've fallen and I can't get up," no one would help her. Millie then signs the note.

While this would constitute duress or undue influence, it would not be the type of duress that would prevail against an HDC. Millie could prevail against Maggie and a mere holder, but not an HDC to the note. ▨

Normally, there will be no liability on an instrument unless it has been lawfully delivered. An improper or unlawful delivery will be a defense against a mere holder, but not an HDC.

A person who honors (pays) a negotiable instrument should take the instrument when it has been paid. If he forgets to take the instrument, he need not pay it again to the person he paid. However, if the instrument should come into the hands of an HDC, the defense of prior payment will not defeat the claim of an HDC.

▨ Palmer was the maker of a note to Hopkins. The two of them have not been on good terms, and when Hopkins presents the note, Palmer throws an envelope of cash in his direction.

Palmer walks out, and forgets to take the note. Hopkins takes the note and the envelope, and negotiates the note to Johnson, who is an HDC. If Hopkins had presented the note, Palmer would have prevailed. If Johnson presents the note, he will prevail over the defense of the payment to Hopkins. ▨

A person who owes payment on a note may offset the face amount owed against ordinary holders by any counterclaim owed to him. This is not permissible against an HDC.

▨ Rivera draws a check to Smathers for $1,000. Later, Smathers incurs a debt of $300 to Rivera. If Smathers presents the check for payment, Rivera may deduct the $300 debt. If Smathers had negotiated the check to an HDC, Rivera could not make the same deduction. ▨

Limitations on Holders in Due Course

As noted in this chapter, a holder in due course will be protected from most defenses that would prevail in an ordinary contract case. The purpose of this shield against contractual defenses was to allow negotiable paper to be treated like money. Individuals who took the paper in good faith would not be required to examine the history behind the paper.

But the HDC shield may result in some injustice. It has been common practice for sellers of major items to transfer the contract of sale and related promissory notes to banks or finance companies. These financial institutions could lend money to a seller based on the accounts receivable. In addition, they took the negotiable instruments as HDCs.

This meant that a consumer would not be able to assert the same defenses against the financial institution as could be asserted against the original seller. This placed consumers at a severe and unfair disadvantage.

The Federal Trade Commission has issued regulations stating that consumers will be able to assert the same claims and defenses against holders of consumer credit contracts as could have been asserted against the seller. In addition, some state legislatures have adopted laws further restricting the protections afforded to holders or holders in due course in consumer-related transactions. As a result, the rights of consumers have been strengthened and those of holders have been reduced. This does not fundamentally reduce the protections afforded to an HDC and does not weaken the essential purpose of negotiable paper.

DISCHARGE OF LIABILITY

The first method of **discharging** a negotiable instrument is for the party with primary liability to pay the amount due on the instrument. If the instrument is a note, the maker should make the payment.

If the instrument is a check, liability will be discharged upon payment by the drawee. If there are not sufficient funds in the account, discharge may be accomplished upon payment by the drawer.

If payment is made by an indorser, the payment discharges all subsequent parties on the instrument. The indorser then has a claim against the party with primary liability and all prior indorsers.

Liability on the instrument will also be discharged if it is cancelled. An instrument may be cancelled by tearing it up, by writing "paid" across it, or by striking out the signatures of the maker or indorsers. If one party is discharged, all subsequent parties are also discharged.

Any other acts that might threaten the interests of the parties will discharge their liability on the instrument. For example, if one party releases the collateral supporting a negotiable instrument, other parties, such as indorsers, will be also discharged.

Gratuitous acts like the destruction or mutilation of the instrument by a party with prior liability will discharge subsequent parties. A party with primary liability has an obligation to protect the other parties to the instrument.

Definitions Reviewed

Presentment is the demand for payment or acceptance of a negotiable instrument.

An **acceptor** certifies sufficient funds exist to pay for a check by writing "accepted" or "certified" on the check.

Personal defenses tend to relate to contractual liability and will not defeat an HDC.

Real defenses are defenses tending to go to the making of the instrument and will defeat an HDC (also called universal defenses).

Duress is the use of excessive economic or physical pressure.

Aleatory contract is a contract related to gambling.

Discharge ends liability on a negotiable instrument.

Core Concepts Reviewed

■ Parties to a negotiable instrument have various rights and liabilities. The parties with primary liability have the obligation to pay the face amount when the instrument is presented or when due. Parties with secondary liability must pay if the primary parties do not. Indorsers have secondary liability to subsequent parties on the instrument.

■ Holders of the instrument generally take it subject to the same defenses available against a party to a contract. However, an HDC is protected against contractual defenses but is subject to those defenses that go to the actual making of the instrument.

■ Defenses that will not prevail against an HDC are called personal defenses. Those defenses that will prevail against an HDC are called real or universal defenses.

■ Liability to holders is primarily based on the concepts of contract and warranty. Signatories to the instrument create a contract with future holders of the instrument. They also give warranties to future holders and may be held liable on them.

■ All of the parties to the negotiable instrument have the obligation not to jeopardize the interests of the other parties. A discharge of liability by one party will discharge the liability of others.

Questions

1. What is a holder?
2. What is a holder in due course?
3. What is the difference between the two?
4. Who is primarily liable on a note?
5. Who is primarily liable on a check?
6. What is an indorser's liability on a negotiable instrument?
7. What are personal defenses?
8. Name some personal defenses.
9. What are universal (real) defenses?
10. Name some universal (real) defenses.
11. What is the difference between fraud in the execution and fraud in the inducement?
12. What is the difference between undue influence and extreme duress?
13. Name some warranties that signatories of a negotiable instrument give to holders.
14. What are some limitations on the holders in due course doctrine?
15. How may a negotiable instrument be discharged?

Problems

1. NYL Corporation purchases a generator from Big Generators, Inc., for $100,000. NYL gives Big Generators a promissory note for that amount. The note also provides for payment of 10 percent in interest per year.

Generators negotiates the note for value to ABC Corporation. Later, the generator begins to have difficulties and NYL stops both principal and interest payments. ABC argues it is an HDC and the nonperformance is not its problem. Generators cites a state statute that declares that in "consumer transactions" an HDC is subject to the same defenses as all other parties to the transaction. Who will prevail?

2. Mary buys a wedding dress at Wendy's Wild Weddings. She pays for the gown with a check for $1,500. She writes on the front of the check, "Payment for a wedding gown that fits properly."

Wendy quickly negotiates the check for value to Priscilla. When Mary gets home, she discovers that the gown does not fit properly and immediately calls the bank to stop payment on the check. The bank does stop payment. Priscilla is unable to cash the check as a result of the stop-payment order.

Priscilla brings an action against Mary. She claims that she is an HDC and should receive payment whether the gown fits or not. Will she prevail?

3. Blackwell was the holder of a note made by Whitehorse. The note is in bearer form. Blackwell transferred the note without indorsement to Green, who transferred the note to Baker.

When Whitehorse does not pay the amount due on the note, Baker brings an action against both Blackwell and Green. Blackwell claims that he cannot be held liable to Baker. Is he correct?

4. Blackwell was also the payee of a check drawn by Whitehorse. Blackwell indorsed the check to Green, who indorsed it to Baker. Both signed the check.

When the drawee bank refused to honor the check because of lack of funds, Baker brings an action on the check against both Blackwell and Green. Blackwell claims that only Green, as the immediate indorser, is liable to Baker and that he cannot be held liable. Is he correct?

5. Sanderson writes a check to Maplethorpe, who cleverly alters the amount due on the check from $5 to $5,000. Maplethorpe indorses the check to Hawkins, who indorses the check to Sweeney, who is an HDC.

Sanderson's bank refuses to honor the check for lack of sufficient funds. Maplethorpe has skipped the country and cannot be found. Hawkins claims that he did not know anything about the alteration. Does Sweeney have any remedies? On what could they be based?

6. Ken has a checking account at Forty-ninth National Bank. He has $1,000 in the account when he writes a check to Doug for $200. When Doug presents the check, the teller misreads the $1,000 figure for $100 and refuses to pay it.

She stamps the words "payment refused, insufficient funds," on the check. She hands the check back to Doug. He then takes the check and shows it to almost everyone he knows. As a result, Ken's reputation and credit position are damaged. Does Ken have any remedies?

7. Larry draws a check for $30,000 to pay for a new sports car he purchased from Ralph. He takes the automobile, and Ralph negotiates the check for value to Noreen, who is an HDC.

Larry puts a stop payment order on the check the next day, and the drawee bank refuses to pay Noreen. Larry also returns the sports car to Ralph. When Noreen brings an action on the note, Larry argues that he was "feeling very depressed" when he purchased the car and should not have to pay Noreen on the check. Who will prevail in a lawsuit between Larry and Noreen?

8. Renee buys a sketch, purported to be by Picasso, for $8,000. She writes a check for the sketch to Vinnie's Art Gallery. Vinnie indorses the check for value to Sam, who pays Vinnie $6,000.

Before Sam can cash the check, Renee discovers that the sketch is not by Picasso. She places a stop order on the check and the bank refuses to honor it. Sam brings an action against Renee. She defends on the grounds of fraud. Will she be successful?

9. Harold works for a boss who imposes a hiring fee on all new employees. He demands that they sign promissory notes for $1,000 when they start work.

Harold signs a note to Ross the Boss for the $1,000. Harold protests, but Ross insists. Ross then negotiates the note to Bennie for $800. When Bennie presents the note for payment, Harold defends on the grounds of duress. Will he be succesful with this defense?

PART VI

DEBTOR/ CREDITOR RELATIONS AND RISK MANAGEMENT

Chapter 19

Secured Transactions

■ A creditor is someone owed money by a debtor. The parties to such a relationship normally evidence this debt by a written agreement that outlines all its terms. These terms usually include the amount, repayment date, repayment schedule, interest rate and finance charges, and procedures with respect to default.

■ Debts may be incurred either for personal or business reasons. Creditors may rely on the debtor's income or general assets for repayment. They may also rely on specific property for repayment.

■ The creditor may obtain a specific interest in the debtor's property to secure repayment of the debt. This is called a security interest.

■ The creditor must perform certain activities in order to obtain a security interest. The first of these is to obtain a security agreement from the debtor, and to give that person value in the form of a loan or credit. If the debtor has rights in the collateral, the attachment of the security agreement will be complete.

■ The creditor must give notice to other potential creditors of the security interest in the property. This process is called perfection. One may perfect a security interest in 3 ways. Automatic perfection which requires no further action is applicable to consumer goods. The other two methods are by filing a financing statement or by taking possession of the property.

■ If a creditor perfects a security interest, the interest will be protected from other creditors. If the debtor defaults on repayment, the creditor may take the collateral and sell it to repay the debt.

CREDITOR/DEBTOR RELATIONS

A **debtor** is someone who owes money to another person. A **creditor** is the person to whom the debt is owed. A debt may result from a loan to the debtor by the creditor. A loan is usually accompanied by a written agreement between the creditor and the debtor.

The agreement should contain the names of the creditor and the debtor, the amount of the loan, the repayment schedule, the interest rate, and any other material terms related to the loan. The debtor may be a person or a business. Similarly, the creditor may be a business or a person.

A person may also become a creditor by allowing someone to purchase property without paying the full purchase price. This is called an extension of credit. If the amount is large, the parties should put the agreement into writing. If the parties involved are business organizations, this agreement is likely to be quite extensive.

Common loans or sales on credit include purchases of big-ticket items like automobiles or boats. Few people have sufficient assets or income to pay the full purchase price.

■ Hubert wants to purchase a new luxury Burpmobile for $30,000, but he does not have the full purchase price. He puts $15,000 down. Benny's Burpmobiles allows him to take the automobile after Hubert gives Benny's a note for the remaining $15,000.

The note provides that the principal amount will be paid in two years. It also provides for an interest rate of 12 percent. Hubert earns a substantial income and Benny's Burpmobile expects that he will pay the loan from his income. It allows him to take the title to the automobile without any restrictions on the title. ■

■ ZAK Industries wants to buy a generator from Gene's Generators for $25,000. ZAK signs an agreement that provides for it to pay the $25,000 over the next year. It also provides for a 10 percent interest rate. ZAK generates substantial income per year and is a regular customer of Gene's. As a result, Gene's lets ZAK have the title to the generator without taking any specific interest in the generator. The agreement also provides for liquidated damages of $300 a month if the full $25,000 has not been paid by the due date. ■

Many debts and extensions of credit are handled in similar ways. The creditor will rely on the income flow of the debtor to pay the debt. But the creditor may also want another method of paying off the debt.

Many financial institutions train lending officers to look for "two ways out." This means that the creditor should find a way of being paid other than from the debtor's income. This allows the creditor to be repaid even if something should happen to reduce the debtor's income flow.

In a poor economy, when large corporations are laying off workers and various levels of management, it is not unusual for incomes to be sharply reduced. An alternative form of repayment is to obtain access to the debtor's assets. The debtor may give the creditor the right to seize either a specific asset or the debtor's general assets if the debt is not repaid.

The creditor should place this **security agreement** into writing. This is common practice in large retail stores that extend credit to customers for TV sets, refrigerators, or other durables. It also is a regular practice in transactions between businesses.

■ NCB Industries wants to purchase a very large motor to run a machine that it uses to make its products. NCB buys the motor from Mammoth Motors for $50,000. It puts $20,000 down and agrees to pay the remaining $30,000 over the next two years.

As part of the agreement, NCB agrees to pay an interest rate of 10 percent. It also agrees to allow Mammoth Motors to take the motor back if NCB does not repay its loan. ■

■ Kate buys a clothes washer and dryer on credit at Fink's Department Store. Her agreement with Fink's provides that the store may seize the product if she does not repay the amount due. ■

Creditors may simply obtain the right to take back the item that was purchased with the loan or extension of credit. It may also obtain from the debtor the right to seize other assets the debtor may own. While this will help protect the creditor, it will not protect the creditor from other creditors. This includes general creditors who may pursue the debtor's assets to repay the loan and creditors with a specific interest in the debtor's property.

If the creditor wants to protect himself from other creditors, he will need to do more than gain the power to seize the debtor's assets. He should be required to give some notice to other potential creditors not to rely on taking the debtor's assets in order to be repaid. This is the premise underlying secured transactions.

Secured Transactions

A creditor may take an interest in a debtor's property that is protected from the claims of other creditors. Article 9 of the Uniform Commercial Code provides that a creditor may have a **security interest** in the debtor's property. This gives the creditor the right to seize the property. But the **secured creditor** must take certain steps in order to create this security interest. This is called the process of **attachment.** In addition, the secured creditor must give adequate notice to other potential creditors of the debtor. This is called the process of perfection.

CREATION OF A SECURITY INTEREST

Under the Uniform Commercial Code, a creditor may take a security interest in personal property. A creditor's interests in real property are not covered. They are governed by different state laws. The UCC divides personal property into different categories and somewhat different laws apply to each.

The first category is goods. These are movable, tangible items of personal property. Goods are divided into additional subcategories. Consumer goods are those purchased by a person either for personal or household use. These constitute the vast majority of items sold by the nation's large retail stores.

> Sally Smuthers goes to Skevey's Department Store and buys a TV set and a refrigerator. Both of these items are consumer goods. If she buys them on credit, Skevey's may wish to obtain a security interest from Sally in the goods. ▪

Inventory consists of tangible movable items. However, these goods are bought by the buyer for resale to the ultimate consumer. One characteristic of inventory is its constant turnover. The buyer purchases a certain amount of goods, and then sells them to consumers. He then obtains more goods, and sells them to consumers.

Equipment is items that are used for business purposes such as making products. Machinery or related items would be examples of equipment.

> Lamps Unlimited purchases a lathe from Lathes, Inc., for $37,500. Lamps agrees to give Lathes a security interest in the lathe. This would be an example of a security interest in equipment because the lathe will be used to make the lamps. The debtor will have a special incentive to pay the loan. If he does not, he will lose a piece of equipment he needs in his business. ▪

Another category of personal property is paper that is evidence of ownership of other property. These might include documents such as a warehouse receipts. A warehouse receipt is evidence that the holder has a right to take property held in a warehouse. This property might include goods of substantial value.

> ▧ Toby's Toasters borrows $50,000 from the Twenty-ninth National Bank. It gives the bank a security interest in its warehouse receipt. The receipt enables the holder to take possession of 1,000 toasters held in a warehouse in the Bronx. ▧

Another form of paper which evidences ownership is a negotiable instrument. Common examples include stocks and bonds, which indicate either ownership in an organization or a debt from an organization to the holder. Chattel paper is a note containing a promise from one person to pay money to another.

These documents are a good form of property in which to have a security interest because they are relatively easy to hold and to transfer for cash. The costs of safeguarding these assets is relatively small.

> ▧ Bert Bigbucks has a substantial amount of stock that he purchased for a relatively inexpensive price. He does not want to sell the stock because he would be required to pay substantial capital gains tax. Bert wants to borrow $100,000 to pay for an addition to his house. He obtains the loan from Forty-third National Bank. The bank takes a security interest in the stock. In this way, Bert is not required to sell the stock. He may obtain the loan and the bank can be repaid from Bert's income. If the loan is not repaid, the bank may sell the stock. ▧

Another category is that of general intangibles. These could include accounts receivable, copyrights, and patents. Accounts receivable represent amounts owed from one person to another. These are commonly found between retailers and their customers. For example, a consumer may purchase goods from a store and promise to pay for them at a future date. The store is likely to accumulate a significant number of these accounts during the course of months or years.

It may take these accounts and ask a bank to use them as security for a loan. This is a practice that allows a store to receive cash that it will use to purchase inventory or to conduct other business activities.

The financial institution will then be repaid by collecting from the debtor. The debtor can pay the creditor from the profits generated by the business. If the debtor is unable to pay, the creditor can collect the amounts due from the debtor's customers.

The debtor could also give the creditor a security interest in copyrights or patents. This could be very helpful to an artist or inventor who needs financing.

> ▧ Stuart invents a new toilet cleanser. His friend, Felix, writes a new song about love and toilet cleansers. Stuart patents the toilet cleanser and Felix copyrights the song. They join together to market the toilet cleanser.
>
> But they do not have enough capital to launch their venture. They go to Thirty-seventh National Bank and obtain a loan of $25,000. The loan agreement provides that Felix and Stuart will repay the loan from the earnings of the business. The bank also takes a security interest in the patent and the copyright.

The bank may sell the rights to the song and the toilet cleanser to repay the loan. ▪

Attachment

A creditor may obtain the right to seize property of the debtor and have this right protected from other creditors. However, the creditor must follow certain procedures to have this right created and protected.

Attachment is the process of creating a security interest. In order to have an attachment of the security interest, three steps must be completed.

First, there must be a security agreement between the creditor and the debtor. The security agreement must adequately describe the property (collateral) in which the security interest is taken. Although the creditor may have lent the debtor the money to purchase the property, the ownership rights remain with the debtor. As a result, the debtor must sign the security agreement unless she gives possession of the collateral (**pledge**) to the secured party.

The security agreement should describe the collateral and set forth the debtor's obligation to repay the creditor. It should state the time of repayment, interest rate, and other material terms. The security agreement should also describe the creditor's rights to obtain the collateral if the debtor should default.

The second step is for the secured party (creditor) to give something of value to the debtor. This satisfies the requirement for consideration that exists for all contracts. The creditor could give the debtor a loan or extend credit to the debtor. In this case, a prior claim of the creditor will satisfy the requirement for value.

The debtor must also have rights in the collateral. These could be present or future rights. The debtor may give a security interest in property currently in his possession or to be acquired in the future.

▪ Jones purchases a wide-screen TV set for $1,000 from Big Tippy's Big Sets. He signs a security agreement which states that he will pay the $1,000 within one year from the date of purchase. The security agreement also provides that he will pay an interest rate of 12 percent during the year. It gives Big Tippy's the right to take possession of the set if Jones defaults on either principal or interest payments. ▪

In this case, all three elements of a proper attachment have been met. Jones received rights in the collateral when he bought the set, he has received value from the creditor in the form of the extension of credit, and he has signed a security agreement. The security interest states the material terms of the agreement between Big Tippy's and Jones. It also describes the specifics of the set in sufficient detail so that it may be indentified by other persons.

Floating Liens

As noted above, all three elements must exist to create a security interest. The debtor must have ownership rights in the property, the creditor must give value, and a security agreement must exist which adequately describes the property. In the case of business inventory, these three elements present some problems.

Business inventory is in a constant state of flux. Old inventory is sold and new inventory is delivered to replace it. It would be difficult to describe the collateral adequately because it keeps changing. The debtor's ownership rights would be difficult to establish because much of the inventory had not been made when the agreement was signed. Finally, the creditor's value was given for the old inventory and not the new inventory. If the three elements were strictly construed, none of them would be present and no security interest could exist.

However, the UCC permits the creditor to take a security interest in after-acquired property. The security interest will be valid if it adequately describes the property. This is called a **floating lien.**

> Massive Motors wants a loan to purchase more inventory for its showroom. It borrows $30,000 from the Twenty-third National Bank. Massive and the bank sign a security agreement that gives the bank a security interest in the current and after-acquired inventory of automobiles. The agreement also provides for Massive to pay the loan within one year, at which time the bank will consider additional financing. The agreement provides for a 10 percent interest rate.

The agreement also provides that Massive will keep a certain level of inventory of automobiles on its premises at all times. It further provides that a representative from the bank will check the inventory every month. This helps protect the bank's security interest.

"Floating lien" security interests could also be obtained on future property of the debtor. This is a common arrangement when the creditor grants a revolving credit loan. This type of lending arrangement provides that the debtor may draw down more of the loan as it acquires additional property. The new property then becomes part of the security interest.

The debtor and creditor may also provide for the creditor to receive the proceeds from the sale of the collateral. This allows the debtor to sell the property to customers and have the proceeds automatically remitted to the creditor to repay the loan. Use of floating liens can be a highly profitable activity for financial institutions because they can lend money to retailers, permit them to conduct their business, and protect their security interest.

Perfection

The secured party must place other creditors on notice of his security interest in order to have it protected from the claims of others. This process is called perfection. Perfection may be accomplished in three ways: by taking possession of the collateral, by filing a **financing statement,** and, in the case of consumer goods, through automatic possession.

Possession is the type of perfection that most obviously places other creditors on notice of the security interest. If the secured party has the possession of property, a reasonable person should ask the reason for it. If there was no security interest, it would be in the debtor's possession.

Possession of the collateral is the only way to perfect a security interest in money or negotiable instruments. The giving of possession is called a "pledge," and it is a common practice in situations involving pawnbrokers and similar institutions.

▪ Gabriel is a musician who needs some money. He takes one of his trumpets to Pete's Pawnbrokers. He receives a loan of $50 which is payable in a month. Pete takes the trumpet as collateral on the loan. This is a pledge. ▪

▪ George Gotrocks has stock worth $50,000. He wants to borrow $100,000 to expand his business. Sam lends him the money and has George sign a security agreement. Sam takes possession of George's stock. This places other creditors on notice of the security interest. ▪

A second method of perfecting a security interest is to file a financing statement at the appropriate legal location. Filing a financing statement is the only way to perfect intangibles such as accounts receivable. It is also a practical way to perfect a security interest and allow the debtor to retain possession of the collateral.

The financing statement provides notice to the public of the security interest. It should contain the debtor's name and address, the name and address of the secured party, and a reasonable description of the collateral. It has become common practice for creditors to draft security agreements so that they also meet the requirements for a financing statement.

The financing statement should be filed at the location specified by state law. This is normally either the secretary of state's office or at the clerk's office in the county of the debtor's residence. A financing statement is valid for five years. However, the creditor may file a continuation statement for an additional five years.

People who want information about the status of a "debtor" may request it from the government office where financing statements are filed. This is a common practice among potential creditors looking for information about customers or borrowers. A financing statement is not a credit history, but it provides notice that a creditor has a security interest on the debtor's property.

The debtor may request information about the status of his debt from the creditor every six months. This provision is intended to help a consumer debtor understand the amount of his debt and to protect him from dishonest creditors. When the debt is paid, the debtor may ask the creditor to file a release statement to terminate the security interest.

Automatic Possession

The third method of perfecting a security interest is the attachment of the security interest to consumer goods. This is sometimes called "automatic perfection" because the secured party need not take any further actions after the security interest is created.

There is a practical reason for not requiring the secured party to do anything beyond having the security interest attached. One clearly cannot demand that the secured party take possession of the goods. That form of perfection would defeat the entire purpose of such transactions. The purchaser of consumer goods wants to use them in her home.

Filing of financing statements would also be impractical and undesirable when consumer goods are involved. Millions of consumer goods are sold on credit every year. If retailers were compelled to file financing statements to perfect their security interests in these goods, there would be a paperwork blizzard.

If the secured party lent money to the debtor to allow her to purchase the property subject to the security interest, automatic possession applies. If the secured party extended credit to allow the debtor to purchase the property, automatic possession applies. The role of the creditor in permitting the debtor to make this purchase is a reason that it is called a purchase-money security interest.

> Mary purchases a new sofa for $500. The sofa will be used in her home. Mary bought the sofa on credit from Hilda's Sofas. Because Hilda has extended credit for consumer goods, she now has a purchase-money security interest. The security interest has attached and is perfected automatically. ▪

> Dan wants to purchase a tool bench and set of tools. He goes to the Personal Finance Company and borrows $1,000. He signs an agreement that gives the finance company a security interest in the tools and tool bench. It also sets forth the terms related to repayment of the loan. Dan takes the check, goes to Tooley's Tools, and buys a tool bench with tools. ▪

The three elements related to the creation of a security interest have been satisfied. Because Personal Finance lent him the money to make the purchase, it has a purchase-money security interest in the tools. The elements required for attachment of a security interest have been satisfied, and it has been perfected automatically.

PRIORITIES OF CLAIMS

A person with a security interest has priority over creditors without a security interest (general creditors) in the property. This is a major reason for obtaining a security interest. If the debtor gets into financial difficulty, the secured creditor may take the collateral to satisfy its claim.

If more than one creditor has a security interest but none of them has perfected the interest, the creditor whose claim attached first has priority. If more than one creditor has perfected the security interest, the party that gave notice of the interest first will have priority.

> Tim wants to purchase a $50,000 automobile. He borrows $40,000 from the Ninth City Bank on June 1st. He rushes next door and borrows $10,000 from Tenth City Bank. He signs security agreements giving both banks a security interest in his new Hubmobile.

Ninth City files its financing statement on June 3rd. Tenth City files its financing statement on June 4th. Ninth City Bank will have priority over Tenth City Bank in the event Tim cannot pay the loans. ▪

BUYER IN DUE COURSE

The drafters of the UCC wanted to encourage the easy flow of commerce. This includes permitting a buyer of property to do so without being required to inquire into the claim of title or the existence of security interests.

Under the UCC, a buyer in due course who purchases items from a merchant takes these goods free from any security interest. This permits the buyer to retain ownership even if the merchant defaults on the security agreement. This is true although the buyer knows of the existence of the security interest.

A buyer of goods from a previous purchaser (second-hand consumer goods) will take the goods free of the security interest if she gave value for them. This will not be true if she had actual or constructive notice of the security interest. A financing statement filed in the proper location does provide notice to the buyer.

However, holders of security interests in consumer goods seldom file because they receive automatic perfection when the security interest attaches. In addition, the legal costs of pursuing claims against second-hand buyers would be high. As a result of these two factors, the risk to second-hand buyers is rather low.

CREDITORS' RIGHTS TO COLLATERAL

A secured creditor has the right to seize the collateral if the debtor defaults. The creditor may take the collateral without legal assistance if he can do so without disturbing the peace. It would be disturbing the peace to break into a building in order to take the property.

▪ Matthew buys a car from Rollies Used Car Lot. Rollie extends Matthew's credit so Matthew can purchase a used truck. Rollie takes a security interest in the truck. Matthew defaults on the loan. Rollie sends one of his men to Matthew's house where the truck is parked on the street in front of the dwelling. Rollie's agent may take the truck. ▪

▪ Matthew's truck is parked in his garage. Rollie's agent may not break into Matthew's garage in order to take the truck. ▪

If the secured party has possession of the collateral, she has a duty to take reasonable care of the property. A secured party who acts in a negligent manner will be liable to the debtor for any damage.

The secured party may sell the collateral in any commercially reasonable manner. This would include either a public or private sale. The secured party must give the debtor notice of the sale unless the debtor has given up this right.

After the collateral is sold, the secured party should use the proceeds to pay for expenses related to taking the property and preparing it for sale, and to pay off the remaining portion of the debt. If any proceeds remain, secondary security interests should then be paid.

Any remaining surplus belongs to the debtor. If there is a deficit, the debtor remains liable for the difference. The creditor may go to court to obtain a judgment for the deficiency.

The debtor has the right to redeem (take back) the collateral before the creditor disposes of it. In order to redeem the collateral, she must pay any obligations owed and expenses the creditor incurred to obtain it.

Definitions Reviewed

Debtor is the party who owes the debt and gives the security interest.

The **creditor** is the person or business to whom the debt is owed.

Security agreement is the agreement between the debtor and the secured party (creditor) which creates the security interest.

Security interest is the right of the creditor to seize the property of the debtor.

Secured creditor is the creditor who holds the security interest in the debtor's property.

Attachment is the process of creating the security interest.

Perfection is the process of providing legally adequate notice to other potential creditors of the creditor's security interest in the property.

Pledge is the giving up of possession of the secured property by the debtor. The possession of negotiable instruments is the only way to perfect a security interest in them.

A **floating lien** allows the creditor to take a security interest in after-acquired property.

Financing statement is the statement filed by the secured party to perfect the security interest in certain types of collateral. A financing statement is usually filed in the county seat where the property is located.

Core Concepts Reviewed

- A debt is an obligation owed by a debtor to a creditor. If the debt is meaningful, the terms of the ob-

ligation should be put into writing. The agreement should include the period for repayment, interest rate, procedures related to default by the debtor, and any other material terms related to the loan.

- A creditor who relies on the income and general assets of the debtor to be repaid is a general creditor. A creditor who takes a security interest in a specific piece of property is a secured creditor.

- The creation of a security interest is called an attachment. An attachment requires a security agreement between the debtor and the creditor, ownership rights in the property by the debtor, and the giving of value to the debtor by the creditor.

- The secured creditor must also give notice to other potential creditors in order to protect the security interest. This is called perfection. The three ways of perfecting a security interest are possession, filing a financing statement, and automatic possession.

- A perfected security interest is protected from other creditors and potential creditors of the debtor. It is also protected in a bankruptcy action.

- A secured creditor may obtain the collateral after the debtor's default either through self-help or through judicial process. The creditor has the obligation to act reasonably with respect to the disposition of the collateral.

Questions

1. What is a general creditor?
2. What is a secured creditor?

3. How is a security interest created?
4. Name two different types of property categories under the UCC.
5. What are "consumer goods"?
6. Name three different types of perfection.
7. Name a category of property to which each form of perfection applies.
8. What is a pledge?
9. What is automatic perfection?
10. How are security interests in negotiable instruments perfected?
11. What is a floating lien?
12. Does a perfected security interest prevail over a buyer in due course?
13. Who prevails in a contest between two creditors with perfected security interests?
14. Name some responsibilities a secured party has with respect to collateral.
15. How can a secured party obtain the collateral upon the debtor's default?

Problems

1. Fred borrows money from the Hampton Finance Company to purchase a large workbench. Fred signs a loan agreement, but he does not sign a security agreement.

   A year later, Fred gets into financial difficulty and is unable to pay Hampton or his other creditors. Hampton argues that it ought to have first priority in the workbench because Hampton lent Fred the money to purchase the workbench. Fred's other creditors argue that Hampton is simply a general creditor. Will Hampton prevail?

2. Walter wants to purchase 1,000 ashtrays from Al's Ashtrays to sell from his store. Many stores in the area have run into financial difficulty.

   Walter wants to make a partial payment to Al, and obtain the remainder of the ashtrays on credit. Al would like to sell Walter the ashtrays, but he is worried about being paid. Al has come to you for advice. What do you recommend?

3. Michael is an entertainer who wants to purchase the copyrights to the songs written by a singing group known as the Steelies. He asks Larry Largebucks for a $1,000,000 loan to buy the copyrights.

   Larry is concerned that the income from Michael's career may not be sufficient to pay the loan. He has come to you for advice as to how to advance the money in a manner that will increase the likelihood of his being repaid. He also wants to know how to gain priority over Michael's other creditors. What steps do you recommend that he take?

4. Eleanor wants to purchase new living room furniture. The furniture set will cost $1,500. She goes to Frieda's Finance Company and signs a security agreement with Frieda's on June 1st.

   Frieda's files a financing statement on June 3rd. On June 5th, Frieda's Finance Company gives Eleanor a check for $1,500. Eleanor purchases the furniture on June 5th. Did Frieda's perfect a security interest? On what date?

5. Marvin's Merchandise borrowed $10,000 to finance its business inventory. It gave a security interest on the inventory to Cathy's Credit Company. David is a businessperson in the area. He knows a great many details about other businesses in the region. He is aware of Cathy's security interest in Marvin's inventory. He purchases $500 worth of goods from Marvin's inventory in the ordinary course of business.

   A few weeks later, Marvin gets into financial difficulty, and Cathy's Credit Company forecloses on Marvin's inventory. Cathy's also attempts to obtain the goods purchased by David. Cathy argues that David was aware of the perfected security interest and that she has a greater claim to the goods. Is she correct?

6. Smith's Sundries borrowed $15,000 to finance its inventory of products from Ferdie's Finance Company. It gave Ferdie's a security interest in the inventory. Ferdie's does not perfect the interest.

   Suzie, in the ordinary course of business, buys a large table from Smith. She then sells it to Sally, who had no knowledge of Ferdie's security interest. When Smith defaults on its loan, Ferdie's Finance attempts to reclaim the property from Sally. It argues that its security interest has priority over Sally's interest. Who will prevail?

7. Jason goes to the Sixth National Bank and obtains a loan to buy a specially made ax. Jason signs a security agreement with the bank which gives it a security interest in the ax. The bank files a financing statement on June 2nd.

   Jason buys the ax on the same date. He goes to the First Finance Company and obtains a $1,000 loan. He signs a security agreement with First Finance and gives it a security interest in the ax. First Finance files its financing statement on June 3rd.

   Jason disappears into the countryside and defaults on both loans, but he leaves his ax behind. Both the bank and the finance company claim the ax. Which will prevail?

8. Bob defaults on his loan with Giant Credit Company. Bob had given Giant a security interest in his snowmobile. Giant takes the snowmobile, which is listed as being worth $2,500 in Stuffy's Snowmobile Report. It sells Bob's snowmobile to one of its best customers for $1,500. It then pursues a judgment for the $1,000 deficiency in Bob's loan. Does Bob have any remedy?

9. Vinnie buys a pool table for household use from Paul's Pool Tables. He puts $50 down. Paul's extends Vinnie credit for the remaining $950. Vinnie signs a security agreement that gives Paul's a security interest in the pool table.

Before the loan is paid, Vinnie gets into financial difficulty and cannot pay the loan or his other debts. At a meeting of Vinnie's creditors, one of them states that all of his assets should be liquidated and distributed among the creditors.

When Paul argues that he is entitled to the pool table, the other creditors argue that because Paul did not file a financing statement or take possession of the table, he has no greater right to it than the other creditors. Who will prevail?

Chapter 20

Bankruptcy

- Creditors have a number of legal rights if a debtor does not pay debts. Creditors' rights and remedies often depend on how the debt was created.

- Debts may result from extensions of credit or from loans. They may also result from work performed by people on behalf of the debtor.

- If the debtor defaults on the debt, the creditor may place a lien on the debtor's assets. The creditor may also obtain an order to seize the assets. In addition, creditors may also be able to obtain (garnish) a portion of the debtor's wages or salary.

- If a debtor is unable to pay his debts, the creditors may work out an alternative payment schedule to allow the debtor to pay off the debts over a longer period of time.

- The debtor may voluntarily enter into bankruptcy or be compelled to enter into bankruptcy by the creditors. Chapter 7 requires the debtor's assets be liquidated and distributed to the creditors. Chapter 11 allows a corporate debtor to reorganize its capital structure and to remain in business. Chapter 13 allows an individual debtor, with the help of a trustee, to reorganize her own financial structure and to pay off her debts over an extended time.

CREDITORS

A person or company may be a general creditor or a secured creditor. A general creditor must obtain payment from the income or general assets of the debtor. A secured creditor has a security interest in specific property of the debtor.

The creditor may grant a loan or extend credit to a debtor, or perform work on behalf of the debtor. People who perform work on behalf of another are entitled to a **lien** on that person's property. Some of these liens are derived from the common law and some are statutory in nature. If the debtor does not pay off the lien, the creditor may foreclose on the property by notifying the debtor and by publishing a notice of the sale in a paper of general circulation.

TYPES OF LIENS

One may obtain a lien on real property by lending another person the money to purchase the property. This is called a mortgage. A mortgage is usually recorded at the clerk's office of the county where the property is located. This record places other parties on notice of the mortgage holder's interest.

It is common for a person to have more than one mortgage on the property. When this is the case, both mortgage holders have a lien on the real property and both may record it.

Persons who perform work on land, such as contractors, may also obtain a lien on the real property. This is sometimes called a **mechanic's lien** because of the nature of the work performed. In order to secure the lien, the person must file a notice of the lien in the county seat where the property is located. The notice must indicate the amount of the claim and the name of the claimant, and it must describe the real property.

The notice must be filed within a certain time after the work is performed. Notice of the lien must also be given to the owner of the real property. The lien places the owner of the real property in the position of being unable to sell the land until the lien is paid. When the lien is paid, the owner of the property may request a release of the lien, which can then be used as evidence of payment.

Attachment

A person to whom a debt is owed may go to court and obtain a judgment against the debtor. But the creditor may also obtain some relief before the court judgment. A writ of **attachment** allows the creditor to take the debtor's property while the suit is pending.

In order to obtain the writ, the creditor must submit a bond that will cover the value of the property taken by the creditor. The bond will cover any losses to the debtor if the debtor prevails. The creditor may perfect the lien by filing a financing statement for personal property or a mortgage lien for real property in the appropriate location.

If the court approves, a writ of attachment will be issued. The property will be used to satisfy the claims of the creditor if she prevails. If the debtor wins, the property will be returned to the debtor. The debtor will also be entitled to any damages resulting from the action.

Garnishment

Garnishment is the taking of a portion of the debtor's wages by the creditor. Congress has enacted laws to prevent creditors from garnishing an excessive amount of a debtor's wages or salary. In essence, the law permits the debtor to retain 75 percent of his income after taxes. If the garnishment is related to support for children or a former spouse, the creditor may obtain a higher amount.

Composition of Creditors/Extension of Credit

The debtor and his creditors may agree to settle existing debts for a lesser amount or allow the debtor to pay the debts over an extended period of time. The agreement is called a **composition** of creditors or an extension of credit. An individual creditor may join the agreement or pursue her own remedies.

Although a composition of creditors reduces the amount of debt or, in the case of an extension of credit, allows the debtor to pay over a longer period, it does not need to be supported by additional consideration by the debtor. If the debtor does not pay, the creditors may pursue the debt in the composition agreement or the previous debt. If the debtor pays the amounts in the composition agreement, the debts are discharged.

Assignment for Creditors

Many states have a procedure that allows a debtor who is unable to pay debts, to **assign** property to a trustee. The trustee holds the property for the benefit of the creditors. Individual creditors may join in the assignment or pursue their own remedies. If a creditor joins the assignment, she will receive a pro rata share from the proceeds of the sale.

■ Bob gets into financial difficulty. He has only $3,000 in assets, but $15,000 in debts. Each creditor would be entitled to receive 20 percent of its amount due.

Bob owed Mary $500. If she joins the assignment on behalf of the creditors, she will be entitled to receive $100. ■

SURETY AND GUARANTY RELATIONSHIPS

A creditor may not be willing to extend credit to a person or business unless someone with better credit joins in the agreement. The debtor may be a minor, a person with little credit history, or someone with a poor credit history. In these cases, a creditor would want a third person to join the debtor.

The third person or organization is called a **surety** or **guarantor** and acts as an ensurer for the credit. If the debtor does not pay the debt, the surety or guarantor must pay. The surety's or guarantor's promise should be placed into writing because it is a promise to pay the debt of another and will fall within the statute of frauds.

There are business organizations, such as insurance companies, that earn profits by acting as a surety or guarantor. The difference between the two is that a surety is primarily liable for the debt and a guarantor is only secondarily liable. If the debtor defaults, the creditor may demand immediate payment from the surety, whereas the creditor must first attempt to collect from the debtor before demanding payment from the guarantor.

Both surety and guarantor relationships are based on the laws relating to contracts. When a business organization is involved, the debtor usually pays a fee to the surety or guarantor. This supplies the consideration for the promises of the surety or guarantor. Because of the nature of the relationship, the parties must strictly adhere to the provisions in the contract.

If the debtor defaults, the surety must step in and pay the debt. The surety now steps into the shoes of the creditor and acquires all the rights of the creditor against the debtor. This assumption of the creditor's rights is called subrogation. The surety may now move against the debtor and try to recover the amount the surety paid on the debtor's behalf.

The right of the surety to demand payment from others for amounts paid on the debtor's behalf is called the right of indemnity. The surety is entitled to be paid the proportionate shares from any other sureties. Although each surety is liable to the creditor, a surety may demand that the other sureties contribute their share.

■ XYZ Corporation borrows $1,000,000 from the Quick Money Financial Corporation. XYZ retains Safe Surety Company and Safer Surety Company as sureties on the loan. When XYZ defaults, Quick Money demands payment from Safe Surety Company. If Safe Surety makes the payment, it can then receive a proportionate share ($500,000) from Safer Surety Company, or one-half of the amount Safe paid to Quick Money. ■

Defenses of Surety

A surety may raise all the defenses normally associated with a contract. In addition, there are certain defenses that are especially relevant to the surety. The surety is bearing the risk of paying a large debt if the debtor defaults. Therefore, both the debtor and the creditor have a special obligation not to conceal material facts that may bear on this responsibility.

■ Big Bucks Finance Company would like to lend ZBT Company $1,000,000. However, ZBT has defaulted on two previous loans, and Big Bucks lost some money on each of them.

  Big Bucks believes that the management of ZBT has improved and the loan is worth the risk. A portion of the new loan will be used to help pay off the old loans. ZBT Company retains Behemoth Insurance Company as a surety for the loan. Neither Big Bucks nor ZBT inform the insurance company of the facts related to these previous loans. This would be a failure to disclose a material fact and would be a defense available to the surety (Behemoth). ■

Discharge of the Surety or Guarantor

The obligation of the surety or guarantor is to pay the debt if the debtor does not. Therefore, the obligation of the surety or guarantor is discharged if the debtor pays the creditor. It is also discharged if the creditor wrongfully rejects the debtor's payment, alters the obligation of the debtor without the surety's consent, or impairs the debtor's collateral.

✳ Bankruptcy

The term "bankruptcy" has an ominous sound for many people. However, bankruptcy now means a process in which the courts attempt to treat both the debtor and the creditor as fairly as possible. The creditors will receive some portion of the amount owed, and the debtor will receive a fresh start.

After the debtor satisfies the court that he has complied with the bankruptcy laws and regulations, the debtor will be relieved of his obligations. He may then start over financially. This process is called a discharge in bankruptcy. If the process is not abused, the debtor may receive a discharge of his debts or be able to extend them.

Another major advantage for debtors is that a bankruptcy proceeding stops all further actions of creditors while the proceeding continues. Creditors' actions may be very annoying, time consuming, and costly.

> Joan owes $30,000 to five different creditors. She has only $500 in assets and an income of $1,500 per month. Joan will find it difficult to pay these debts. She is likely to be the subject of calls from creditors, letters from bill collectors, and actions relating to attachment or garnishment.
>
> If Joan initiates a bankruptcy proceeding, these actions will be stopped. Depending on which chapter is selected, Joan may be able to retain certain assets, receive a discharge of her debts, and start over. ■

The Federal Bankruptcy Code has different chapters. Chapter 7 provides for the liquidation of the debtor's assets and distribution of the proceeds to the creditors. Chapter 11 allows a corporation to reorganize its debts and capital structure and to remain in business. Chaper 13 permits an individual to work with the trustee and the creditors to restructure debts.

Chapter 7 Actions

Chapter 7 provides for the liquidation of the debtor's assets by the trustee in bankruptcy. After the assets are converted to cash, the trustee distributes the proceeds to the creditors. The debtor is then discharged from his debts as permitted by law. Chapter 7 liquidation may be initiated by the debtor or by the creditors.

A voluntary bankruptcy case is initiated when the debtor files a petition with the bankruptcy court. The commencement of a voluntary bankruptcy case is a request for relief. It stops the creditors from pursuing individual remedies. In addition, if the debtor follows the laws, procedures, rules, and court orders, she will receive a discharge from debt. Individuals, partnerships, and all corporations *except* railroads, banks, insurance companies, savings and loan associations and credit unions may initiate voluntary proceedings. The organizations that cannot file for bankruptcy are regulated either by their states or by provisions that apply directly to their handling of financial difficulties.

An involuntary bankruptcy case may be initiated by the debtor's creditors. If there are 12 or more creditors, at least 3, whose unsecured claims total $5,000 or more, must sign the petition. If there are fewer than 12 creditors, the case may be initiated by any creditor whose unsecured claim is at least $5,000. Secured creditors are protected by the security interest they have in the property. They will be involved in the bankruptcy action only to the extent their claim is unsecured.

If the creditors file an involuntary petition, the debtor may contest it. If the debtor does not contest the petition, the court will grant an order for relief if the debtor is generally not paying his debts as they become due. It need not be shown that the debtor was committing acts of misconduct.

As noted, the filing of a voluntary or involuntary bankruptcy petition acts as an automatic stay against the debtor's creditors, preventing the creditors from initiating other actions. The stay does not end until the debtor receives a discharge or the proceedings are terminated.

Upon the filing of the petition, an independent trustee will be chosen. The role of the trustee is to carry out the terms of the laws relating to the bankruptcy.

The trustee becomes the "owner" of the debtor's property, except for property that is exempt.

Powers of the Trustee   The trustee faces a challenging task. She must protect the interests of the debtor while safeguarding the interests of the creditors. In order to accomplish her objectives, the trustee must cancel transfers of property that would allow a creditor to receive more than she would have received if the debtor's assets had been liquidated in bankruptcy.

Some debtors may try to transfer property before the bankruptcy proceeding in a manner that would prevent creditors from receiving their proper share. The trustee in bankruptcy can cancel such transfers made by the debtor within one year if the debtor's intent was to hinder or defraud the other creditors. Transfers to "insiders" such as relatives or partners would be presumed to fall into this category.

The trustee may also set aside transfers of property if their effect was to make the debtor insolvent or to reduce the assets to an unreasonably low amount. A debtor is considered insolvent when her debts exceed her assets. The trustee may also recover property transferred by the debtor if the transfer was to pay an earlier debt, was incurred when the debtor was insolvent, was made within 90 days before the filing of the bankruptcy petition and allowed the creditor to receive more than she would have received in a liquidation of the estate. These transactions, which may be set aside, are called preferential transfers.

The trustee may not set aside transfers that are contemporaneous in nature. Payments of routine bills or cash purchases would not be considered a preferential transfer. Debtors must be allowed to conduct these transactions in order to carry on day-to-day living.

Chapter 7 Administration   The debtor will submit a list of creditors to the bankruptcy court. Each creditor will receive a notice of the bankruptcy proceeding. A creditor wishing to participate must file a proof of claim, which should indicate the amount and the basis of the claim. The claim should set forth the reason for the debt. This might include the repayment of a loan, extension of credit, or other reason. The claim must be filed within 90 days of the first creditors' meeting.

After-Acquired Property   The purpose of a bankruptcy is to allow the debtor to share the bankruptcy estate with his creditors and then to receive a discharge from debts. Because each creditor is likely to receive less than the full debt owed, it is fair that the debtor should share all of his property. This includes certain property received after the bankruptcy began. The bankruptcy estate must include all property received by the debtor within 180 days after the filing of the petition and which was acquired by inheritance, from a life insurance policy, or as a result of a divorce.

Priorities   Claims include the costs of administration and general claims not secured by a security interest in specific property. The costs of administering the bankrupt's estate have first priority because otherwise it would be difficult to find people to do those administrative tasks. These costs would typically include fees from the trustee, accountants, attorneys, and other experts called on to settle the estate.

Claims arising in the ordinary course of the debtor's affairs after the proceedings began but before the appointment of the trustee have second priority. The next group of claims having priority include salaries and related amounts arising from the debtor's business. The amount of such claims is limited to $2,000 for each person.

Claims for contributions to employee benefit plans have fourth priority. Claims up to $900 by consumer creditors are next. Federal and state income taxes due within three years of the petition also have priority. Other general creditors must divide up what remains.

 Exemptions   The purpose of bankruptcy is to give the debtor a fresh start. Part of this new beginning is to permit the debtor to retain some assets. The Federal Bankruptcy Code permits certain exemptions from creditors' claims. These include:

1. A homestead exemption of up to $7,500.
2. A motor vehicle exemption up to $1200.
3. A per item exemption of $200 for household items.
4. Jewelry for personal use up to $500.
5. Interest in any property up to $400 plus some of the unused portion of the $7,500 homestead exemption.
6. An exemption for tools, professional books, or implements of up to $750.
7. A life insurance policy.
8. Health aids such as hearing aids.
9. Government benefits such as veteran's or public assistance benefits.
10. Certain rights to receive income such as alimony and child-support payments.
11. Interests in personal injury awards and other benefits reasonably necessary to support the debtor and his dependents.

Some of these exemptions are relatively minor and serve only to reduce the amount of cash available to the creditors.

The trustee should recover the voidable transfers, grant the exemptions, gather up and sell the assets, and then pay the creditors. If the appropriate procedures were followed and the debtor acted properly, the debtor will be granted a discharge from previous obligations.

There are certain debts that will not be discharged. These include the following:

1. Taxes accrued within three years before the filing.
2. Fines and penalties imposed by various levels of government.
3. Claims based on fraud or willful or malicious injury.

4. Claims resulting from breaches of one's fiduciary capacity.

5. Alimony, maintenance, and child support.

6. Debts that were not scheduled.

7. Certain claims relating to the purchase of luxury goods.

8. Certain claims relating to the use of a credit card or revolving credit.

9. In certain cases, student loans.

If the debtor commits certain acts, the debtor will not be discharged. Generally, these acts relate to conduct that is wrongful or fraudulent. They include the following actions:

1. Fraudulent acts committed to obtain credit or to conceal property from creditors.

2. Fraudulent acts committed with respect to his financial condition.

3. Failure to account for some assets.

4. Failure to obey an order of the bankruptcy court.

5. Failure to cooperate with creditors or the court.

6. Obtaining a discharge within the previous six years.

The prohibitions against discharges are designed to discourage wrongful conduct and to encourage a greater sense of financial responsibility in the future. Bankruptcy actions are a burden to society. Taxpayers are paying to operate the courts, and other consumers must help pay for the loss to the creditors.

In addition, there is an age-old policy not to reward a person who has engaged in wrongful conduct. Fraudulent actions have always been punished and failure to disclose assets or attempts to shift them to others cannot be tolerated.

Chapter 11 → reorganisation!

Chapter 11 is designed to allow the debtor to reorganize its financial affairs. It has become an important vehicle for corporations and permits the debtor to hold on to assets while reorganizing. Unlike Chapter 7, the assets of the debtor are not liquidated.

Keep in business
— things will turn around!
(Donald Trump)
— Put on budget
— Pay off over time

The purpose of a Chapter 11 proceeding is to permit the debtor to continue business while rearranging debt and capital structures. Unlike a Chapter 7 proceeding, a trustee is not appointed unless there is evidence of wrongful conduct such as fraud, dishonesty, or gross mismanagement.

A Chapter 11 may be filed voluntarily. The debtor need not allege insolvency, but must state only that it has debts. An involuntary filing need only state that the debtor is not paying debts on time.

The debtor in a Chapter 11 proceeding continues to operate the business. The debtor may enter into contracts, incur debts, and conduct activities that are related to running the business.

When a Chapter 11 proceeding has begun, the court will appoint a creditors' committee to represent the unsecured creditors. The court may also appoint a committee to represent secured creditors and holders of equity in the debtor. They have a duty to represent their entire group of creditors.

A Chapter 11 filing allows the debtor to file a reorganization plan within the first 120 days. The debtor has the right to obtain the creditors' approval within the first 180 days. After 180 days, any interested party may propose a reorganization plan.

The reorganization plan should set forth the proposed new capital structure of the debtor. The plan must propose changing the claims of both the debtors and the equity holders. The plan must state how the claims will be altered to permit the debtor to continue its business.

> ■ The debtor proposes a plan to reorganize its debts and capital structures. The plan states that general creditors will have their debts reduced by 50 percent, secured creditors will receive equity shares, and common stockholders will have their dividends eliminated until the company begins to earn a profit. The plan also provides for the sale of certain assets. ■

Confirmation of the Plan   The plan of reorganization must be approved by the court before it is effective. The plan may be confirmed by the acceptance of the members of the various classes of claims and interests. In order to be approved, the plan must be in the best interests of each class as determined either by the unanimous vote of the members of the class or the plan must stipulate that they would receive at least as much as they would in a liquidation action.

The plan must be feasible in that it will permit the debtor to continue as an ongoing business. The plan must be accepted by the vote of at least one class of claims. The plan is accepted if approved by at least 50 percent of the number of the class members representing two thirds of the dollar amount of the class interests.

Every class must have its claims and interests unimpaired by the bankruptcy proceeding. This requirement that the claims are unimpaired will be satisfied if the rights of the class members are not altered by the plan. If the rights are altered, the requirement will be satisfied if the members of the class vote to accept the plan.

"Cram-Down" Method   The "cram-down" method allows the court to force the parties to accept a reorganization plan even if the claims of a class are impaired. The plan must be fair and equitable to the impaired class. It will be fair and equitable to secured creditors if they are allowed to retain the lien on the collateral, place a lien on the proceeds, or receive a lien on equivalent property. It will be fair and equitable to general creditors if they receive cash or property equal to the discounted present value of the claim or if no class below them receives anything.

The holders of equity, such as common stock, will be treated fairly if they are paid the greater of the fixed redemption preference or the discounted present value of the equity interest. The plan will also be considered fair and equitable to this class if no class below it receives anything.

Chapter 13

Chapter 13 is a part of the bankruptcy code which allows an individual debtor to request an extended time in which to pay his debts. If the debtor has a regular income, he may go to court and submit a plan for paying his debts over a longer period of time. This permits him to avoid the problems associated with a liquidation. It also permits him to show good faith with respect to his creditors.

The Chapter 13 plan is similar to a budget that sets forth the income of the debtor and how she will pay off the debts. In some cases, a representative of the court will be appointed to assist the debtor in carrying out the plan.

The plan should treat every member of a class of claims in a similar manner. In addition, creditors entitled to priority under the bankruptcy code must be paid. If the plan was done in good faith and is in the best interests of those parties with claims, the court will approve it.

The debtor should pay the debts along the lines specified in the plan. After the plan has been completed and the debts paid, the debtor may apply for a discharge. The discharge will release the debtor from all debts except those that would not be released in a Chaper 7 discharge. These are primarily debts that indicate some wrongdoing or are related to tax or family obligations.

Definitions Reviewed

A **lien** is a claim that a creditor has placed either on real or personal property.

An **attachment** is the creditor's right to seize property.

Garnishment is a creditor's right to seize a debtor's salary or wages.

Composition is an agreement among the creditors to alter the terms of the debt.

Assignment is the right of the creditors to take property of the debtor.

Surety or **Guarantor** is a relationship where one party agrees to guarantee another's loan.

Questions

1. What is a composition agreement?
2. What is an extension agreement?
3. What is an attachment?
4. What is a garnishment?
5. What is an assignment for the benefit of creditors?
6. What is a Chaper 7 proceeding in bankruptcy?
7. What requirements exist for a voluntary filing in Chapter 7?
8. What requirements exist for an involuntary filing in Chapter 7?
9. What are the duties of the trustee in a Chapter 7 proceeding?
10. What are "voidable preferences"?
11. What are a trustee's powers with respect to voidable transfers?
12. What is "after-acquired property"?
13. What are the debtor's responsibilities with respect to after-acquired property?
14. What is the difference between a Chapter 7 bankruptcy and Chapter 11?
15. What is the purpose of a Chapter 11 reorganization?
16. How might a plan under Chapter 11 be "accepted"?
17. Which debts will not be discharged in a Chapter 7 proceeding? In a Chapter 11 proceeding?
18. What types of conduct by the debtor will prevent the debtor from receiving a discharge under Chapter 7? Under Chapter 11?
19. What is the purpose of a Chapter 13 bankruptcy?
20. What are the qualifications for a debtor to be admitted under Chapter 13?

Problems

1. Marcella has $1,000 in assets and $10,000 in debts. Her debts relate mostly to routine purchases, which seemed to snowball. There are no debts related to major luxury purchases. She has a regular income. Marcella has begun to receive calls and letters from creditors. She has become concerned and asks your advice. What do you suggest?

2. Sal is one of Frank's major creditors. Vince and Harold are the other two major creditors. The three of them are owed debts of $12,500. None of their debts are secured. They do not want to force Frank into bankruptcy, but will do so if they must. They have come to you for advice. What do you suggest to them?

3. Joan has gone into Chapter 7 bankruptcy. Nine months before she filed, she transferred furniture worth $10,000 to her sister, Jenny. The creditors discover this fact and want to put the furniture back into the bankrupt's estate.

   They contact Jenny and ask her to return the furniture voluntarily. Jenny tells them that the furniture was a gift and to "get lost." Do the creditors have any remedy?

4. "Tough Luck" Tony files for bankruptcy on April 1st. On May 1st he is notified that his uncle died and left him $1,000. He decides to go out and spend the money on a buying spree in memory of his uncle.

   Before he spends the money, he comes to you for advice. What do you tell him?

5. The ZXY Company has had some financial reversals and is unable to pay its debts. It does have an income flow and has some outstanding prospects for future contracts.

   But the owner of ZXY Company, Joe Knox, is being hassled by the company's creditors and does not believe that the company will be able to pay the debts. He believes that he has no choice except to close shop and go out of business. Before he does, he has come to you for advice. What do you tell him?

6. Edgar has been married three times. His alimony and child-support payments are $5,000 per month. He decides to go into bankruptcy in order to get a discharge from these obligations related to his marriages.

   Before he fills out his voluntary petition in bankruptcy he comes to you for advice. What do you tell him?

7. NBZ Corporation is in a Chapter 11 bankruptcy. Your friend, Alan Antcy, has been asked to do some accounting work for them. This is a big job and the hourly rate looks very profitable.

   But Alan is worried about being paid and has come to you for advice. What do you tell him?

8. OLZ Corporation is in a Chapter 11 bankruptcy. The president of the corporation, Zeke L. Olsom, has tried to put together a plan that will satisfy all of the parties with debts and the other shareholders.

   But the group of secured creditors is not satisfied with the plan and refuses to confirm it. They do not want to surrender their claim on corporate assets, but they want to continue receiving regular payments. Zeke would like to have a plan approved so that OLZ Corporation can continue doing business, but he is running out of ideas. He has come to you for advice. What do you suggest to him?

9. Wilson needs a loan to open a business. He approaches Jones about helping him in the business and assisting him with the loan.

   Jones is interested in joining the business, but she does not want to be primarily liable on the loan. Jones is aware that you know something about the law, and has come to you for advice. What do you tell her?

10. Watson had gotten into considerable financial difficulty. His debts exceeded his assets, and he was unable to make his regular payments. He discussed his problems with a friend who had just completed a business law course.

    With the help of his friend, Watson worked out a composition agreement with his creditors. Samuelson was one of the creditors who signed the agreement. Watson worked hard to pay off the debts. After a year, he paid all the debts in the agreement, including the one to Samuelson.

    Samuelson now claims that the composition agreement was not supported by consideration and that Watson still owes him the original debt. In a lawsuit between Watson and Samuelson, who will prevail?

11. ABC Corporation wants to buy a generator from Generation Generators on credit. Certain Surety Company agrees to act as surety on the loan.

    Three months after purchasing the generator, ABC Corporation discovers that the generator does not work as described in the contract and stops making payments. Generation Generators brings an action to enforce the surety of the Certain Surety Company. Does Certain Surety have to pay? If it does have to pay, does it have any remedies that it may pursue?

Chapter 21

Accidents, Liability, and Insurance

■ Accidents are a part of life. They may result in damage to property or in bodily injury. In a society of automobiles, heavy machinery, and dangerous materials, accidents can be serious matters. The amounts of money related to accidents can be enormous. The Exxon *Valdez* accident caused billions of dollars of damages. An important issue is who will be held responsible for losses from accidents.

■ Torts are acts that result in either property damage or bodily injury. Torts may be accidental or deliberate. A person will be held responsible for accidental torts if his conduct was negligent. The legal standard for negligence is the failure to use the degree of care as would have been used by a reasonably prudent person in the same circumstances.

■ The legal standard of care means that a person may be held liable for injuries related to automobile accidents, household accidents and accidents associated with recreational activities. This potential liability is a reason for having automobile, household, and medical insurance.

■ Damage may also result from natural or human causes like hurricanes, floods or fire. Insurance is also available to cover property damage caused by these hazards. One can also obtain insurance to cover one's life. Life insurance is useful because it can cover funeral expenses and the costs of a person's last illness.

■ In order to obtain insurance for either property loss or life, one must show an insurable interest in the property or life. An insurable interest is showing that one would suffer a financial loss if the property is destroyed or the life is lost.

■ An insurance policy is a contract and is subject to the same laws that govern contracts. The insurance contract will determine the scope and level of coverage by the insurance company.

ACCIDENTS AND TORTS

Accidents occur on a regular basis. Like successes and failures, they are a part of living. If no substantial loss results, the parties may ignore the accident. But if there is substantial property loss or bodily injury, the injured party may want the party responsible to pay for the loss.

Torts are acts that cause damage to property or to a person. Torts may be deliberate or accidental.

■ Joe goes to a bar, gets into a fight with Dennis, and punches him in the mouth. This would be a deliberate tort. Joe would be responsible for injuries to Dennis's mouth, lips, and teeth, and would have to pay him for the damages suffered. ■

■ Sally is driving her brand-new Hupmobile at 70 miles per hour when she runs a stop sign. She crashes into Sylvia, who was driving through the intersection.

Although Sally did not intentionally cause the accident, she will be liable for Sylvia's injuries. This was negligent (perhaps reckless) conduct on her part. ■

When the tort is deliberate, liability is normally clear. Most deliberate torts either are also criminal conduct or border on criminal activity. A punch to someone's face is not only a deliberate tort, it is also an assault for which one may be criminally prosecuted.

A person who injures someone while driving under the influence of alcohol or drugs will be liable for the cost of the injuries. The driver might also face criminal charges for causing injury or death to another while driving under the influence of intoxicants.

Improper disposal of hazardous materials can result not only in liability for subsequent injuries or property damage, but is also a criminal offense. The disposal of hazardous wastes is becoming a more important issue as society determines that chemicals previously regarded as safe are more dangerous than was believed.

When the tort results from actions that were not intended to injure, the issues become more complex. The person must establish certain facts relating to the conduct of the defendant. In addition, in most states, the plaintiff must also establish certain facts regarding his own conduct.

The Negligence Doctrine

The law has always recognized that the individual bears the responsibility for the consequences of his or her conduct. If a person's actions cause harm to another, one must pay for them. The law requires the person injured (the plaintiff) to show certain facts before she may recover damages.

The plaintiff must show that the defendant's conduct was in violation of her duty of care to the plaintiff. One must first show that there was a duty of care. While one normally has a duty of care to everyone, the level of that duty is higher to some people than to others.

A person who owns land has little duty to a trespasser who enters the land without permission. The owner's only duty is to not deliberately injure the trespasser. For example, the property owner cannot decide to shoot someone who is crossing the property.

One has a duty of reasonable care to people one "invites" on the property. These would include guests and people who perform routine services such as postal workers, meter readers, and other people who do repair work. Reasonable care is defined as the level of care which a reasonably prudent person would exercise in the same circumstances. Failure to exercise this degree of care is **negligence.**

■ Charles owns Blackacre and the house on the property. The sidewalk is slippery even when dry. After a snowfall, it becomes even more slippery. The town's ordinances require a homeowner to keep the walk clear and to shovel away the snow. Despite this, Charles does not shovel the snow and Howard slips and falls when walking in front of Blackacre. It was negligent of Charles to allow the snow to accumulate. He will be liable for Howard's injuries. ■

This duty of "reasonable care" extends to other areas and forms the basis of the laws relating to liability for one's actions. A person has a duty of reasonable care to others when driving an automobile or performing other activities. It is often difficult to determine what is reasonable care. At a minimum, the law provides a floor for determining reasonable care.

■ Edward has a hunting license. When he received the license, he also got a handbook of laws and rules. One of those laws prohibits the discharge of firearms within 1,000 feet of any residence.

Despite this, Edward fires a couple of rounds from his back porch. The bullets fly over his fence and injure his neighbor's pet cat. Edward's conduct is negligent as a matter of law, and he will be responsible for the injuries to the cat. ■

■ Orville is driving his car on a local road where the speed limit is 35 miles per hour. He is traveling 55 on a rainy day. When a car in front of him stops, Orville steps on the brakes, but he slides into the stopped car. Orville was negligent for driving fast on a slippery road. He will be responsible for the damage to the car in front of him. ■

Not only must the plaintiff show that the defendant's conduct was negligent, she must also show that the conduct was the **proximate cause** of the damage. Proximate cause means that the negligent conduct must have been the direct cause of the damage or injury. There must be a close link between the defendant's actions and the injuries.

■ Hawkins hits a car stopped in front of him. That car bumps into the car in front of it, and that car hits a bicyclist walking in the crosswalk. Normally, proximate cause is clear. In this case, it is not absolutely clear that Hawkins's conduct was the proximate cause of the damage to the bike rider. If Hawkins had hit the bicyclist, proximate cause would have clearly existed. ■

There are a number of situations when determining proximate cause may be difficult. But the courts have generally tended to try to find proximate cause if negligent conduct was a contributing cause to property damage or bodily injury.

Plaintiff's Negligence   In some states, any negligence on the part of the plaintiff will prevent recovery by him. This is known as the **contributory negligence** doctrine. It is based on the idea that a plaintiff must be free of blame if she is to recover.

■ Cusack stopped his automobile at an intersection. His vehicle is just across the stop line into the intersection. Baxter's vehicle runs a red light and crashes into Cusack's automobile. Baxter was clearly the more negligent of the two parties, although Cusack was also negligent for allowing his car to be in the intersection. His negligence could bar his recovery in some jurisdictions. ■

The doctrine of contributory negligence has been weakened, as it was seen as unfair to injured plaintiffs. A very small amount of negligent conduct by the plaintiff could bar any recovery and she would not receive anything from a defendant who may have been very negligent.

As a result, many states are enforcing **comparative negligence.** This doctrine states that the plaintiff's and defendant's respective negligence will be weighed, and the plaintiff's recovery will be allocated accordingly.

■ In the preceding example, the trier of fact finds that Cusack's negligence contributed 15 percent to the accident and Baxter's negligence contributed about 85 percent.

　　If Cusack suffered $200,000 in damages, he would receive 85 percent of that total or $170,000. ■

The concept of comparative negligence should result in a more balanced allocation of responsibility for losses resulting from accidents. However, the responsibility for these losses still must be resolved through the legal process, which can be very expensive and time-consuming.

"No-Fault" Insurance

As automobile use increased, the number of lawsuits related to motor vehicle accidents grew rapidly. The cost of these lawsuits also began to grow sharply. In addition, it was difficult for people to recover for their loss. In order to reduce the costs of these lawsuits and to increase the likelihood of recovery, many states adopted **no-fault** insurance. No-fault is based on the concept that motorists should pay for insurance that will cover their own losses.

In states with "no-fault," the owner of the automobile agrees not to bring legal action unless damages are over a certain amount or unless there are serious bodily injuries involved. Below these thresholds, the person's own insurance will cover the loss.

■ Bob and Ray collide at an intersection. Both of their cars suffer minor damage, but there are no serious bodily injuries. Under a no-fault system, Bob's auto insurance will pay for his loss and Ray's company will pay for his. Neither Bob nor Ray will be able to sue each other. ■

While no-fault insurance has probably reduced the costs of automobile insurance and probably increased the likelihood of recovery, it has been criticized on at least two grounds. First, it limits the "innocent" party's ability to recover from the negligent party. In addition, the system tends to make good drivers pay for bad drivers.

Product Liability

Another area that has become increasingly important is product liability. Accidents relating to products are quite common. They may result from product misuse or from some defect in the product itself.

Under traditional legal doctrines, a party injured in a product-related accident had to show some negligence by the person who made the product. The negligence could be found in the design or manufacture of the product. In addition, the plaintiff also had to demonstrate her negligence did not contribute to the damage or injury.

■ Pat is injured while using a lawnmower when the blade comes out of its housing guard and cuts his foot. Under traditional legal doctrine, Pat would be required to show some negligence on the part of the manufacturer. That is, Pat must show lack of reasonable care in some aspect of the manufacturer's conduct. The negligence could be in the design, manufacture, or instructions for using the lawnmower. Furthermore, Pat would have to demonstrate that he used the product correctly. ■

The doctrine of contributory negligence would still apply. In this example, if Pat had removed the guard or otherwise acted improperly, he could not recover. In addition, the concept of proximate cause also applies. Pat must demonstrate that there was a direct link between the defendant's negligence and his injuries.

Although one could recover under the theory of negligence, it was not always easy. An injured plaintiff might find it difficult to determine why the product did not work as expected. It was often difficult to gather information on product design or on matters relating to the product's manufacture.

More recently, the Uniform Commercial Code has allowed the plaintiff to recover under a *warranty* theory. The UCC provides that every merchant who regularly sells a product gives buyers a warranty that the product will work for the purposes intended. The courts have extended this warranty to anyone who might have been reasonably expected to be affected by a product defect.

The warranty theory makes it easier for plaintiffs to recover from defendants. They no longer need to show specific acts of negligence; if they can demonstrate that the defect caused the damage or injury, they will recover.

■ Murray buys a hedge clipper and uses it to trim the hedges in his yard. The blade slips and Murray is injured. He needs to show only that a defect in the product resulted in his injury. He does not need to show a specific act of negligence. ■

The defendant may still assert the defense of product misuse. In this above example, if Murray had used the hedge clipper to cut his hair or for some other unintended purpose, the defendant would prevail. The courts will not hold the defendant liable unless the use could have been reasonably anticipated.

Medical Malpractice and Other Liabilities

The issue of medical malpractice has assumed greater importance as the nation searches for answers to rising health-care costs. Many have argued that a major reason for these higher costs is the increased number of suits brought against physicians.

A medical malpractice suit is governed by the normal rules relating to negligence actions. The plaintiff must show that he was injured as a result of negligence by the physician. In these cases, the plaintiff must show that the physician did not perform her activities as a reasonable physician would have done.

It is not an easy matter to recover damages. Bringing forth evidence that demonstrates that the physician did not act in a competent manner usually requires that the plaintiff produce other physicians who will testify that the defendant performed his services improperly.

■ Mary's baby is delivered with multiple birth defects. She brings an action against the physician who delivered her child. During her portion of the case, her attorney introduces three physicians who testify that the defendant physician should have delivered the baby by C-section.

Dr. Quickbuck introduces two physicians who testify that Quickbuck did exactly what they would have done in the same circumstances. The jury must determine which of the witnesses is closest to acceptable medical standards. ■

In the preceding example, the plaintiff had to prove that the defendant was negligent. In other cases, the defendant must step forward to show that she was not negligent if the defendant's actions appear negligent.

■ Thelma Lou goes to a physician to examine the pain in her right leg. Instead of curing her right leg, Dr. Sawbones cuts off Thelma Lou's left leg. Dr. Sawbones must introduce evidence to show that he was not negligent, which will be difficult to do in this case. ■

The same standard of reasonable care also applies in other cases when injuries or property damage resulted from another person's negligence. Automobile accidents are among the most common, but other types of accidents occur regularly, which is one of the reasons that people have insurance.

INSURANCE

Insurance is a method of protecting oneself against the risks associated with various activities. In some cases, the law requires that people carry liability insurance. In other cases, it is advisable to obtain insurance. In still others, a financial institution or other organization will require a person to obtain it.

There are various types of insurance, but they share in common a contract, known as the policy, between the insurance company and the individual. The scope and amount of insurance as well as the other terms are outlined in the policy. In many states, the provisions are tightly regulated by the department or commissioner of insurance.

Homeowner's Insurance

A **homeowner's insurance policy** is designed to cover the most common types of losses and hazards associated with owning a house. A bank will not grant a loan unless the borrower also purchases homeowner's insurance. The policy covers risks associated with fire and liability to others.

While house fires are less frequent than in previous decades, they still occur. Without insurance, a fire could destroy a homeowner's equity in the house. In addition, a fire could eliminate the bank's security interest.

A fire insurance policy covers "hostile fires." This term means that the fire must have escaped its usual boundaries. Losses resulting from "friendly fires" are not covered. Friendly fires are those that are being used for the purposes intended.

■ Herb regularly makes baked beans for both lunch and dinner. He throws the can of beans into the same pot for every meal. After several years, the bottom of the pot has become black. Herb cannot recover for the damage to the pot. It is the result of friendly fire. ■

■ One day, Herb turns on the stove to cook his baked beans and walks away. The grease from the baked beans catches on fire. The fire leaps out of the stove and ignites the kitchen drapes. The house catches on fire and is severely damaged. When the fire escaped from the stove it became a hostile fire, and Herb may recover for this loss. ■

Generally, the same rules apply to smoke and water damage relating to the fires. If the smoke or water damage was related to a friendly fire, it will not be covered. However, if it resulted from a hostile fire, it will be covered.

After the hostile fire, the property owner has the obligation to reasonably protect the house from further damage. If he does not take these measures, the additional losses will not be covered.

■ After a house fire, Macklin's house has a hole in the roof. He takes no measures to cover the hole for more than one week. Several heavy rainstorms cause additional damage. Macklin would not be able to recover for these damages. ■

Most fire policies require a minimum level of coverage by the policyholder. The reason for this is that most fires result in less than total losses. If policyholders were allowed to obtain only a small amount of coverage, they would be able to cover most losses with small premium payments. If minimum coverage is required, a policyholder who does not hold the minimum level of coverage required must share some of the loss with the insurance company.

■ Bob has a $100,000 house. The minimum coverage required is 80 percent. Instead, Bob obtains insurance of only $60,000.

His house has a fire and sustains $10,000 worth of damage. If Bob had obtained $80,000 of total insurance, the company would have paid the full $10,000. In this case, the company will only pay $60,000 — $80,000 or 75 percent of the loss. This would equal $7,500. Bob must pay the remaining $2,500. ■

A second major form of homeowner's insurance relates to liability. A homeowner may be held liable for injuries that occur on the property. As noted, the homeowner may be held liable for deliberate or accidental torts.

■ Johnson owns a home on Blackacre. He permits the front steps to become loose. One of his guests walks on one of the loose steps, falls down, and injures his back.

He sues Johnson and recovers $50,000 in damages. If Johnson did not have liability insurance, the guest could attach Johnson's equity in his house. ■

Homeowners may also obtain insurance against a number of other hazards. In certain areas, it is critical to have insurance against natural disasters such as hurricanes, floods, or windstorms. The Midwestern United States is regularly flooded by the Mississippi River. The Gulf Coast regularly experiences the onslaught of hurricanes, which destroy businesses and homes.

A homeowner may obtain insurance against these hazards. However, the cost of this insurance is expensive and premiums may be high. Often, the government will help homeowners purchase this insurance.

Tenant's Insurance

Tenants have similar needs as homeowners. If there is a fire in a tenant's apartment, her possessions, including furniture, could be destroyed. If she has no insurance, she will have to bear the loss herself. **Tenant's insurance** can cover losses from fire.

Tenants may also be held liable for activities in their dwelling which cause injuries to others. The general rule relating to landlord/tenant relations is that while a landlord is liable for common areas, a tenant will be liable for torts within the tenant's premises.

■ Donna has an apartment in Seaview Apartments. She has a series of throw rugs in her living room. She invites David to her apartment for dinner.

David slips on one of the rugs and falls down, injuring his back. He brings a legal action against Donna and recovers $25,000 in damages. If Donna has no insurance, she must bear the loss herself. If she has insurance, her insurance company can pay David. ■

Like homeowners, tenants may also obtain insurance against other hazards such as floods, hurricanes, and earthquakes.

Automobile Insurance

Automobile insurance is necessary because of the large number of car accidents which occur. An accident often results in both property damage and bodily injury. Insurance can help cover these costs. The most important type of automobile insurance protects the policyholder from liability for personal injury.

■ Britt drives his car to work. One day, he is thinking about the day's activities and goes through a stop light. He slams his automobile into a van of senior citizens. The van is damaged and several of the passengers are injured. ■

Britt's negligence was the cause of the accident and it was also the cause of the damage to the van and its passengers. This is why states require drivers to have liability insurance. If Britt did not have this insurance, he would have to pay for these damages out of his own pocket. For most people, this would be very difficult.

One can also obtain insurance for damage to one's own car. This is known as collision insurance. Normally, there is a deductible clause associated with collision insurance. This clause provides that the insured must pay a certain amount of the damage before the insurance company begins to pay.

■ Harvey has a deductible clause in his automobile insurance which states that the insured will pay for the first $100. The policy provides that the insurance company will pay for the remaining damage.

Harvey's car is damaged in an accident. It cost $1,000 to have it repaired. He must pay the first $100 and the company will pay the remaining $900. ■

A car owner can also obtain insurance to cover the theft of one's automobile. (There has been a sharp increase in the number of automobile thefts in the United States.) This type of insurance also usually contains a deductible clause requiring the owner to contribute a certain amount to the loss.

Life Insurance

Many people obtain life insurance for a variety of purposes. If the insured is the principal earner for the family, **life insurance** provides a safety net if the insured should die. The insurance may be used to pay off the mortgage on the house or for family living expenses.

The insured usually names a beneficiary to receive the proceeds from the insurance. If the insured is married, the named beneficiary is usually the surviving spouse.

A person may obtain life insurance on another. However, one must have an "insurable interest" in that person's life in order to obtain such insurance. "Insurable interest" means that one must suffer a financial loss if that person dies. One may obtain insurance on a spouse, child, business partner, or key employee.

One may not obtain life insurance on a person in whom one has no insurable interest. Society does not want to encourage people to acquire life insurance on others in whom one has no interest in keeping alive.

■ Stu, who is a student in a business law class, takes out a life insurance policy on his professor. Stu may be encouraged to foster the business law professor's demise in order to collect the proceeds from the life insurance policy. ■

Life insurance helps families cover the expenses related to the last illness of the deceased. It is also useful to pay for the funeral expenses of the insured. For families of greater affluence, life insurance can be utilized to pay estate taxes or establish trusts.

Property Insurance

Both individuals and businesses may purchase insurance to cover damage to *property*. This may include damage from fire, storm, or vandalism. A person or organization must also have an insurable interest in the property.

A person must have an insurable interest in a life when the policy is acquired. However, the insurable interest must exist at the actual time of loss in the case of property insurance.

■ Bobby buys property insurance from Behemoth Insurance Company to cover the store that houses his business. The policy includes coverage against fire.
Bobby later sells the building to Betty. After the sale, the building catches on fire and is severely damaged. Bobby may not collect on the insurance policy. ■

Society's interests are served by requiring that a person have an insurable interest when the property is destroyed. If the insured did not have such an interest, he might be encouraged to destroy the property. In cases involving life insurance, the legal principle that the insurable interest need only exist when the policy was acquired allows someone who was divorced to retain the policy as part of divorce settlement.

Business Insurance

Businesses also obtain insurance to cover their risks. They own buildings for which they may obtain coverage against fires and other hazards. They have similar liability concerns as individuals.

Businesses may also obtain life insurance on partners and key employees. A business has an insurable interest in these individuals because it would suffer a loss if they were to die. They also allow a partnership to buy out the interests of a deceased partner's heirs. This allows the partnership to continue normal operations.

Banks, financial institutions, and retail operations often obtain theft or embezzlement insurance to cover larcenous activities by employees. This type of insurance usually requires that the business perform certain activities or lose their coverage.

■ Ralph's retail store has a policy to cover it against employee theft or embezzlement. The policy requires that Ralph's notify the insurer if an employee is discovered committing a theft.

Philip is caught stealing $100 from a store cash register. Ralph does not notify the insurer and decides to give Philip another chance. The next month, Philip is caught recruiting a series of accomplices and stealing $10,000. Ralph has violated a provision of his insurance contract and will not be able to recover for the $10,000. ■

These contracts also usually require audits of the insured's financial operations on a regular basis. Audits by accountants are likely to uncover major wrongdoing or negligence by business employees. In an age of transfers of substantial sums by computer, these audits assume greater importance.

■ The Forty-fifth National Bank conducts most of its major financial transfers by computer. These transactions generally provide for rounding off of cents to the nearest dollar.

Richard is an employee of the financial transfer section of the bank. He has programmed the computer to send the change from these transactions into his own account. No one audits this area for three years. During this time, Bob manages to place $471,543.79 in his account. ■

If the bank has a clause in its embezzlement insurance contract requiring regular audits, coverage of this loss will be denied. Audits are a good business practice regardless of whether one has embezzlement insurance.

Errors and Omissions Policy   People will make mistakes in business, problems will occur, and some ventures will go badly. A recent trend has been a sharp increase in the number of lawsuits brought against officers and directors based on allegations that they breached their fiduciary duty to the shareholders.

A director has the obligation to always act on behalf of the shareholders and not in his own interest. He also has the obligation to act as a reasonably prudent person would act under the same circumstances. These duties can lead to possibilities of error or other wrongdoing.

■ ZPA Corporation is a favorable target for merger because it has a number of patents in key high-technology areas, few debts, and a relatively low stock price. NLM Corporation makes a tender offer for ZPA Corporation. The offer provides that NLM will pay twice the market value per share of ZPA Corporation.

The officers and directors of ZPA know that NLM has a habit of replacing the officers and directors of acquired companies with their own. The officers and directors of ZPA recommend to its shareholders that they reject the tender offer. Shareholders of ZPA later bring a suit against the directors and officers and claim that they violated their fiduciary duty by opposing the shareholders' interest. ■

■ YXW Corporation has had poor earnings for years. Stock analysts reports and other outside observers argue that the company has too many senior managers and pays them salaries that are too high. This is said to be particularly true of the chief executive officer, who is paid over $1,000,000 per year.

Despite these reports, the directors take little action to correct the problems. The poor earnings become negative earnings and the directors still do very little to correct the problems. The shareholders bring a legal action against the directors. They claim that the directors did not exercise good business judgment by allowing the corporation's earnings to decline without trimming costs. ■

■ Harvey is a director of JIH Corporation. He regularly asks his fellow directors to approve loans to him at below market interest rates. His directors approve the loans.

The shareholders sue Harvey and claim that he violated his fiduciary duty to the corporation by accepting the loans. They also sue the other directors and claim that they should not have approved the loans. ■

These three situations indicate the legal hazards associated with being an officer or director of a corporation. Previously, a directorship was a coveted position of little responsibility. More recently, shareholder suits against directors have become quite common.

In order to protect themselves against such suits, directors may obtain liability insurance. This is called an errors and omissions policy. It will cover directors against certain forms of negligence. It will usually not cover them against gross negligence, violations of the law or deliberate breaches of their fiduciary duties.

Insurance Policies as Contracts

An insurance policy is a type of contract. As such, many of the same rules that apply to contracts will also apply to an insurance policy. However, because of the nature of insurance, certain modifications exist.

The major types of insurance are closely regulated by the states. The provisions of the policy may need to receive state approval before they may be offered to the public. The general rule of contracts that ambiguous clauses or terms will be construed against the party that drafted them is applicable to insurance policies.

A whole life insurance policy often accumulates cash surrender value and this value may generally be assigned to another. Term life policies do not accumulate cash surrender value, and there is nothing to assign.

An insurance policy also requires an offer and an acceptance. Usually, an agent for the insurance company will preliminarily accept the applicant as a policyholder. The agent must receive final approval from his company. The agent will issue a binder that covers the applicant from the period of the agent's acceptance until the company's final acceptance.

There is a special relationship between the insured and the insurer. This is especially important with respect to life or health insurance, which may require a physical exam or statements with respect to one's current state of health.

The insured has the absolute obligation to tell the truth to the insurance company. The insurance contract may be set aside if the insured lies on his application. This would be fraud by the applicant and would violate her duty to the company. The courts are reluctant to set aside such contracts, but will do so in cases of fraud.

Definitions Reviewed

Torts are acts that cause damage to property or to a person.

Negligence is the failure to use the degree of care that would have been used by a reasonable prudent person.

Proximate Cause is the direct cause of the damage.

Contributory negligence is the failure of the plaintiff to use reasonable care.

Comparative negligence is the doctrine that compares the negligence of the plaintiff and defendant to determine the amount of recovery.

No fault is insurance that allows the insured to recover regardless of which party was at fault.

A **warranty** is a guarantee.

Homeowner's insurance covers liability arising from ownership of a house.

Tenant's insurance covers liability arising from the renting of property.

Automobile insurance covers liability and damage arising from driving an automobile.

Life insurance covers a person's life.

Property insurance covers one for damage to property.

Business insurance covers a business for losses resulting from an embezzlement, mistakes, or other reasons.

Core Concepts Reviewed

- Torts are actions that cause damage to either a person or to a person's property. An individual who commits either a deliberate or accidental tort will be liable for the damage.

- Negligence is the failure to use that degree of care which a reasonable person would have used under the same circumstances. Proximate cause is the direct reason for the injury. If a person's negligence is the proximate cause of the injury, she will be liable to the person injured.

- A person may obtain insurance to cover herself against liability. Insurance may be obtained to cover one's liability for driving an automobile and one's liability as a homeowner.

- Damage may also result from natural hazards such as fire, flood, earthquake, or hurricane. One may obtain insurance against these problems. Homeowner's insurance may cover this type of damage. Businesses may also obtain similar types of insurance.

- One of the most common types of insurance covers a person's life. This is useful because the proceeds may be used to help provide for the insured's family, to pay the deceased's expenses related to the last illness, and to pay funeral costs.

■ In order to obtain life or property insurance, one must have an insurable interest in the life or the property. An insurable interest is a sufficient financial interest.

■ Businesses may obtain special types of insurance to cover specific risks associated with their business. Errors and omissions insurance covers certain errors made by business organizations.

Questions

1. What is a tort?
2. Define negligence.
3. What is proximate cause?
4. What is homeowner's liability insurance?
5. What is covered by automobile insurance?
6. What is contributory negligence?
7. What is comparative negligence?
8. In those jurisdictions that apply these doctrines, what is the effect of contributory or comparative negligence?
9. What is warranty liability?
10. What is collision insurance?
11. What is "no-fault" insurance?
12. What is an insurable interest?
13. What is an errors and omissions policy?
14. What types of risks does an errors and omissions policy cover?

Problems

1. Jim is driving his pickup truck on a secondary road. He is about to enter a highway when Joe's car hits him in the back. The jolt causes damage to Jim's truck and Joe's car. The two of them get out and start yelling at each other.

   Jim screams that Joe rear-ended him. Joe yells back that Jim stopped too quickly. The verbal argument escalates into a fistfight. Both Jim and Joe manage to hit each other several times before they are separated by a passing policeman.

   The two of them decide that the cop has become too involved and they both begin yelling at him. The police officer becomes enraged. He takes an

ice pick out of his squad car and stabs the tires of both Jim and Joe's vehicles. Discuss the possible torts involved in this incident.

2. Phil runs a company that disposes of hazardous waste. Phil is required by law to dispose of the hazardous waste at an approved waste site. Despite this, Phil dumps the hazardous waste materials into city park land.

   He is seen by a city inspector and receives a summons. Despite this, Phil leaves the waste materials on the land. The materials seep into the groundwater. The city rushes its maintenance workers to clean up the hazardous waste materials. Discuss Phil's possible liabilities.

3. Hank owns a home on Blackacre. One day, the mail carrier steps on his front walk to bring the mail to his house. Hank's pet pig rushes out of the house and knocks down the mail carrier. The carrier is injured. Discuss Hank's liability and the measures he could take to deal with it.

4. Bonzo is a clown who performs magic acts for children. One of his routines is to squirt water from a seltzer bottle at his assistant. Bonzo sprays his assistant and leaves puddles on the floor.

   One of the children slips on the puddle and falls on the floor. The child is injured and her parents sue Bonzo. What is his liability and could he protect himself from its consequences?

5. Donald is driving his car when he reaches a stoplight. State law permits making a right turn after coming to a stop. Donald stops the car, looks quickly to his left, and begins to turn right.

   Joan, who has the right of way, is entering the intersection at 40 miles per hour. The speed limit is 25. The two collide in the intersection. Both Donald and Joan are injured. The accident was in a comparative neligence state. Discuss the issues regarding the liability of both Donald and Joan.

6. Merkle is walking through the park near a baseball field when a ball is hit in his direction. The players call for him to throw the ball back into the game.

   Merkle throws the ball in the direction of the players. The ball hits a light pole nearby. The pole falls over and hits one of the players. The player brings a lawsuit against Merkle. Is he liable for the player's injuries?

7. Frank lends Wilson $100,000 to finance his new business. He wants to take out a policy on Wilson's life for $100,000. Does he have a sufficient insurable interest in order to acquire the life insurance policy?

8. Emily owns a house on Whiteacre. She obtains a fire insurance policy from the Large Insurance Company. She transfers ownership of her house to Marilyn on April 3rd. The fire insurance policy is still in effect until June 30th.

   The house burns down on April 16th. Can Emily collect any proceeds from the policy?

9. Mark owns a house on Greenacre. One day, he starts a fire in his fireplace but neglects to open the flue. The house catches fire and the fire spreads to the house next door to Greenacre. The fire burns much of both houses. Mark has a little fire insurance. Is he liable for his neighbor's loss? How could he have protected himself against any potential liability?

10. After the fire, neither Mark nor his neighbor do anything about covering the houses. A bad wind and rain storm does even more damage to the houses. Will either Mark's or his neighbor's insurance companies be liable for this additional damage?

11. Terry's TV Town has a large inventory of television sets which it sells to customers. Because TV sets are easy to sell in the marketplace, they are in constant danger of being stolen.

    Terry's takes out a policy against possible theft of the sets. The policy requires that Terry's take reasonable precautions to safeguard the inventory of $1,000,000 in television sets. One night a gang of burglars break into the store. They load the sets into a truck.

    Terry's had installed a burglar alarm that cost $39.95. The burglars cut the alarm within ten seconds. Terry's had no security guard on its premises. Will it be able to recover the loss from its insurance company?

Chapter 22

Professional Liability

- Every person is responsible for his own conduct. This includes professionals and businesspeople. If they engage in conduct that causes injuries to another, they will be held liable.

- Professionals are held to the standards of their profession. This is usually a very high standard, consistent with examinations, personal qualifications, and a license permitting them to be paid for performing certain tasks.

- Professional malpractice is defined as the failure to use that degree of care which another qualified professional would have used under similar circumstances. If that failure causes injury to another person, the professional will be liable for the injury.

- People in business are expected to utilize good business judgment when they carry out their duties. They may be held liable for failing to perform their activities in accord with this standard.

- The person injured by someone's negligent or deliberately wrongful conduct may bring an action under tort law in order to recover for their injuries. If the conduct related to a contract, the person injured may also bring an action for breach of the contract.

MALPRACTICE

Professionals occupy a special place in our society. People who are licensed to practice a profession are entrusted with many of society's most important tasks. Physicians take care of us when we are ill, lawyers help guide us through the mazes of the law, architects build our homes, and accountants keep track of our personal and business finances.

Because of their special roles, professionals are held to the standards of people in that profession. If their care does not meet that norm, they can be held liable for **malpractice.**

- Dr. Quickbuck is an eye doctor who does examinations and surgery. He charges $100 for the examination, but earns $2,000 for the surgery.

  As a result of his fee structure, he has an incentive to perform eye surgery. Dr. Quickbuck performs more eye surgeries than are necessary. He performs surgery on one in ten patients, whereas the typical average is one out of one hundred.

  One of his patients, Betty Trusting, believes that Dr. Quickbuck performed unnecessary surgery on her. She has her records reviewed by Dr. Eyeful, who agrees with her suspicions. She has both a legal remedy in tort and in contract against Dr. Quickbuck. She could recover the $2,000 surgery fee, and if her eye was injured by Quickbuck, she could recover additional amounts in tort. ■

- Dan Debit is an accountant who has not read any of the court decisions or revenue rulings relating to corporate taxes for years. Despite this, he continues to give opinions to clients on these matters. The average accountant reads the rulings or retains someone else to perform work outside of his specialty.

When one of his clients, Bob Bobbett, loses money as a result of Debit's tax opinion, Bob sues him and argues that Don has committed malpractice. Don argues that tax work is not his area of specialty and that he should not be held liable. Don is not correct. He owed his client the duty to keep his knowledge in the field up to date. ■

■ Larry Lawyer practices law in a one-person office. His practice primarily consists of performing real estate transactions, writing wills, and doing some defense work for people charged with motor vehicle violations.

One day a client asks Larry to do legal work related to a public offering of stock. Larry has never done this work before, and there are attorneys in the area who are acknowledged experts in the field. Nevertheless, Larry decides to take on this client. He makes several mistakes that cost his client a significant amount of money. Larry will be held to the standard of an attorney who practices in that field. He can be held liable for malpractice.

The client may pursue either a contract action or tort action against the professional. Third parties, such as investors, may also bring an action against the professional. Tort actions have several advantages because they may be brought for larger amounts, and there is a longer time limit in which to bring a legal action. ■

BUSINESS JUDGMENT

Professionals are also businesspersons and they advise businesspeople. They are expected to exercise "reasonable care" in their business activities. This does not mean that all business ventures must succeed or that people will not make mistakes. But professionals should exercise the degree of care which a prudent businessperson would have exercised under the same circumstances.

■ Harold decides to get into the business of building a shopping mall. He has never been involved in this activity before. He does no market research and makes no financial projections.

He hires Aaron to be his accountant. Neither of the two of them spend a great deal of time organizing the financial records, but they do begin seeking investors. They find five investors who each put up $100,000. Harold adds $250,000 of his own money and they begin to build the mall.

During the mall's construction, Aaron and Harold are rather sloppy about their record keeping. Money comes in and money goes out with few controls. Halfway through the project, the mall is in serious financial difficulty. Neither Harold nor Aaron exercised good business judgment and both could be held liable to the investors. ■

An accountant or attorney bears a special responsibility in this area. Businesspeople will see them as experts whose judgment they can trust. They should exercise appropriate judgment and err on the side of caution.

Activities that were tolerated in previous years may no longer be deemed acceptable. This is particularly true of activities that appear to be self-serving rather than in the interests of the organization.

■ Hodgkins is chairman of ZBN Corporation, which is publicly owned. Its shares are traded on one of the public exchanges. He wants to obtain a loan from the corporation to build a new home. The amount would be $1,000,000, which is far above any loan previously given to a corporate officer.

Hodgkins plans to ask the board of directors to approve the loan at their next meeting. He calls in the corporation's attorney and ask her to draw up the agreement. He calls the accountant and asks him to make certain that the financing will be available.

Both the accountant and attorney should advise Hodgkins that this is not a good idea. The Securities and Exchange Commission (SEC) and shareholders are increasingly concerned about this type of transaction. Even if an independent board of directors approves the loan, it has the appearance of being improper and of not reflecting good business judgment. ■

FIDUCIARY RESPONSBILITY

A **fiduciary** relationship is one of special trust between a person and another who acts on behalf of that person. A professional such as an accountant or attorney is likely to be named as a fiduciary or as an advisor to a fiduciary.

One type of fiduciary is an executor or administrator of an estate. This person has the responsibility to collect assets, pay debts, and distribute property in accord with the desires of the deceased. The executor is legally responsible for always acting on behalf of the estate and is accountable for his actions.

As a result, the executor often needs to obtain legal and accounting assistance. The attorney can provide advice with respect to the probate process, the provisions of the will, and other legal issues.

An accountant may help inventory the assets, analyze the financial records of the deceased, pay the estate's debts, and keep the estate's records. If the estate is large, the deceased may have provided for some of the assets to pour over into trust accounts. As the estate becomes more complex, the probate court is likely to require a detailed accounting of the executor's activities from the estate's inception to its termination.

Another fiduciary is a trustee. A person or organization may be a trustee for a corporate bond or debenture. The trustee is responsible for protecting the interests of the investors and ensuring that the debtor carries out the terms of the bond or debenture.

A person or an organization may also be the trustee of an individual trust account. Some organizations such as trust companies or banks are professional trustees. They manage large trusts for a fee. They regularly consult outside counsel or use accountants to help maintain the records. Because they hold themselves as professional trustees, they are held to a high standard.

■ Guy Gotrocks leaves $1,000,000 in trust, and names Trusts Company of the United States as trustee. He also names his daughter, Jean Gotrocks, as beneficiary.

Unfortunately, Trusts Company's investment staff does not handle the money well, and the $1,000,000 is soon down to $400,000. In addition, the account managers fail to check with either lawyers or accountants and thousands of dollars in dividends are lost. The trustee can be held liable for both the principal and income losses. If the trustee had been given poor advice by the professionals, they could also be held liable. ■

Trustees may also manage large corporate accounts such as pension funds. The Employee Retirement Income Security Act (ERISA) requires the pension fund manager to act as a fiduciary. This requires the manager to act in the best interests of the fund and to exercise reasonable care in managing the investments of the pension fund. The manager of a pension fund may require advice from other professionals.

■ Dartsthrow is the new pension fund manager for the Brakefast Corporation. The pension fund holds all of its assets in the stock of Brakefast. The previous fund manager believed that this gave the fund added leverage in the company.

Dartsthrow consults with the accounting firm of Edwards and James. Dan Dartsthrow asks Eddie Edwards about the advisability of keeping all of the fund assets in Brakefast stock. Eddie looks at Brakefast's income statements and balance sheet. Eddie decides that Brakefast is a profitable company with a promising future. He tells Dan that Dartsthrow may continue investing the fund in Brakefast stock.

This is not good advice. It would be better to diversify the portfolio into a number of different stocks. In today's turbulent and international economy, no company is safe from marketplace changes. As a result, placing a portfolio into several stocks reflects better business judgment. ■

A trustee in bankruptcy is yet another type of fiduciary. This trustee's job is to represent the interests of the creditors of the bankrupt's estate and to be fair to the debtor. A bankruptcy is a complex matter and requires the assistance of legal and accounting professionals.

Many professionals may be reluctant to take on bankruptcy work because of the debtor's precarious financial situation. However, they should recognize that fees for trustees, attorneys, and accountants are given first priority with respect to claims from the estate. Bankruptcy is a complicated area and people who specialize in the field can be very successful.

Attorneys can advise clients about the advisability of filing for bankruptcy, help them file, work with them during the filing process, and help them obtain a discharge that will free them from their debts. The attorney could also help them negotiate with and work out an agreement with the creditors.

Accountants can organize the records of the debtor's assets, debts, and creditors. They can maintain the records of the estate as it goes through the bankruptcy proceeding, and they can calculate the amounts that will be divided among the creditors after fees have been paid, expenses disbursed, and exemptions deducted.

Accountants, lawyers and other professionals may also take part in business planning discussions that could involve them in situations that might result in liability. Accountants are often asked to prepare financial records and other papers to help clients obtain loans. These documents will be given to a bank, which will rely on these documents when making their decision. If they are prepared incorrectly, the accountant may be liable to the bank.

■ Swanson and Company needs a business-expansion loan from Thirty-third National Bank. Swanson asks Agnes Accountant to prepare the financial papers related to the loan.

Unfortunately, Agnes prepares them incorrectly. The bank lends Swanson the money based on figures that have inflated the company's income. If the loan is not repaid, Agnes could be held liable to Thirty-third National for preparing the papers incorrectly. ■

LIABILITY TO OTHER PERSONS

A professional may become liable to other persons in a number of different ways. An accountant's first responsibility is to her client. If she commits an act of malpractice, she clearly will be liable to that client under the contract. She may or may not also be liable to other parties depending on who they are. The same rights exist against other professionals such as architects or attorneys.

■ An architect, under contract to a landowner, designs a house in a defective manner. If the owner sells the house, there would be some question as to whether the new owner would have the right to recover from the architect. Under traditional common law, the architect would not be liable to the new owner. There is a growing trend to allow owners to hold subsequent architects and builders liable for actions in the construction of the house. ■

For many years, the law required some "privity of contract" between a professional and the person bringing the action against him. Privity of contract meant that there had to be a direct relationship between the parties for the plaintiff to recover. As the law permitted third parties to recover for defective products made by a manufacturer or for other acts of negligence, it was natural that the right of third parties to recover from professionals would also be expanded.

The rule in most states is that a professional, such as an accountant, will be liable to third parties that were intended to benefit by the professional's actions. Some states have expanded this to include any third party that the accountant could have reasonably foreseen would be affected by his actions. This is particularly relevant as it relates to the sale of securities to the public.

SALE OF SECURITES

In the early part of this century, the standards for the sale of securities were more than just lax. People made fortunes by selling worthless securities or manipulating the markets. The collapse of the securities markets was one of the reasons for the Great Depression.

Congress, as part of the legislation passed during the New Deal, enacted the Securities Act of 1933. This act and subsequent regulations require issuers of securities to submit a registration statement to the SEC and to give potential investors a prospectus. Accountants are often employed to prepare these statements. The act imposes liability on accountants who misstate or omit material facts or who fail to discover such misstatements or omissions. Accountants may be held liable for negligence or fraud for such actions.

While the act's provisions can impose substantial liability, accountants may raise the defense of **due diligence.** But, the accountant must show that his actions were not negligent, and that he acted in a way to discover and disclose any improper actions on the part of the issuer.

■ Alan is an accountant who examines the books for Bonkers Betty, a store that sells electronic equipment like stereos, VCRs, and TV sets. Betty keeps fraudulent records that she uses to defraud investors and others associated with the company.

Betty's records are not fraudulent on their face, but a thorough accountant would be able to detect the fraud. Alan is pleased to have the work and the associated fee. He accepts the records at face value without examining them carefully. As a result, he does not detect the fraud. Bonkers Betty shareholders could hold Alan liable for negligence, and if Alan knew of the fraud, he could also be guilty of fraud. ■

■ Alice is the accountant for Slippery Sally. Sally maintains some accurate and some fraudulent records. The fraud is cleverly hidden. Slippery Sally's records have fooled other accountants with more experience than Alice.

Alice checks the records thoroughly, but is unable to detect the fraud. Slippery Sally sells her stock to investors. If they lose money as a result of Sally's actions, they may recover from her. If they bring an action against Alice, she can claim she acted diligently to detect the fraud and should not be held liable. ■

Attorneys, investment bankers, underwriters, company officers, and other professionals who knew or should have known of fraud or errors may also be held liable by investors who suffered losses as a result. Professionals should err on the side of caution and full disclosure when preparing and distributing financial statements. A good rule to follow is to place oneself in the position of the investor and to ask if an investor would be misled by the omission or by unclear information.

■ XYZ Corporation files a registration statement with the SEC and issues a prospectus. XYZ Corporation has a great deal of old inventory that it will have a difficult time selling. It would be misleading to investors not to disclose the inventory's low value, and if XYZ does not disclose this inventory, all the professionals who could have prevented the deception could be held liable for failure to do so. ■

The Securities Exchange Act of 1934 was designed to prevent many of the trading practices that were common during the early part of this century when insiders would manipulate the markets for their advantage. The act and subsequent regulations prohibit actions that would defraud investors and require regular reports and other information.

The 1934 Securities Exchange Act makes it unlawful for any person to commit an act in interstate commerce which would defraud another in the purchase or sale of securities. People who are injured by such conduct may bring an action to recover damages.

The 1934 act has often been used to bring an action against accountants and other professionals. The Supreme Court has ruled that mere negligence is not sufficient to hold a party liable under the 1934 act. Rather, the Supreme Court held that there must be some intentional misconduct. This holding helps limit the liability of professionals with respect to the 1934 act.

The plaintiff must show either deliberate or reckless misrepresentations in order to hold the defendant liable under this act. As noted previously, the 1934 Securities Exchange Act requires companies to continue submitting reports about their financial status. Accountants may be held liable for submitting misleading information in these reports.

CRIMINAL LIABILITY OF PROFESSIONALS

Professionals are given special privileges in our society. In addition, they bear special responsibilities. If they abuse these privileges and responsibilities, they may be held criminally liable for their actions.

- Attorneys are allowed to retain their clients' funds until the funds are distributed in accordance with the law. This practice has continued because the vast majority of attorneys act in an ethical manner. Alan Attorney receives $100,000 from the opposing party's attorney in a personal injury action. But instead of giving the money to his client, Alan spends it on himself. Alan is subject to being disbarred, and he has also committed theft, for which he faces criminal charges. ■

- Phil Physician performs internal surgery for his patients. Phil earns a good living, but has built up a considerable amount of debt because of his lavish lifestyle.

  In order to obtain more money, Phil begins to perform unnecessary operations. Not only has he committed malpractice, but Phil has also committed fraud, for which he may be held liable by his patients. ■

- Alex Architect is responsible for supervising the construction of his clients' building projects. One contractor wants to use lower-quality cement than required by the contract. Alex permits the contractor to use the lower-quality cement in exchange for the contractor's promise to name him the architect on the contractor's next job. As a result of their actions, the building is weakened. It collapses during the next major rainstorm, injuring ten people. This is a criminal act. Alex could be held liable for the injuries and he could be held criminally liable for his actions. ■

- Alexis Accountant is the accountant for XYZ Corporation. He agrees to prepare fraudulent financial records that will allow XYZ Corporation to issue stocks to the public. The president of XYZ wants to make some quick money and then leave the country. If Alexis deliberately prepares fraudulent statements, he may be held criminally liable for his actions. ■

The Securities Act of 1933 and the Securities Exchange Act of 1934 stipulates criminal penalties for those who violate its provisions. This is particularly true with respect to provisions relating to conduct that would deceive others. Professionals could also be held liable for violating other criminal provisions, including, among others, tax laws, election laws, consumer protection statutes, mail fraud regulations, and antitrust laws.

TAX LAW VIOLATIONS

Individuals and businesses pay a variety of taxes and governmental fees. Individuals pay local taxes, county taxes, school taxes, state taxes, and federal taxes. Businesses pay the same taxes and are also responsible for paying various taxes that relate to their employees. In addition, they are responsible for collecting certain taxes on behalf of the government.

Tax laws are complicated and the process of paying and collecting taxes can be fraught with pitfalls. Professionals such as accountants and attorneys are paid to help guide people through this process. Tax laws, however, can also prove to be traps for careless or dishonest professionals. Federal tax law penalizes those professionals who carelessly prepare tax returns or who help a taxpayer to prepare a fraudulent return. One of the penalties is to be barred from the practice of tax preparation.

State tax laws are often modeled on federal laws and may stipulate similar penalities. In addition, state laws usually stipulate personal liability and criminal exposure for not paying payroll and unemployment taxes. This liability often extends to every officer of a corporation. A professional such as an accountant or attorney who accepts a position as treasurer or secretary of a firm may find himself facing personal liability for its actions.

ELECTION LAW VIOLATIONS

Professionals are often asked to run for office or to serve as advisors for political campaigns. Attorneys are often candidates or legal counsel to political parties. Accountants may be asked to serve as treasurers of political or campaign committees. A word of caution is in order before one rushes out to perform one's civic duty.

Political campaigns have become similar to small-business operations. The concept of the office seeking the individual has been obliterated by the need to raise money to appeal to voters and to fend off the opposition's campaign.

Congress and state legislatures have passed numerous laws to regulate campaigns and campaign financing. These laws may provide for both civil and criminal penalties if they are violated. Typical of these laws are the limitations on campaign contributions by individuals or corporations. Attempts to circumvent these laws may result in significant punishment. Similarly, the filing of inaccurate or fraudulent reports may result in punishment and public embarrassment.

■ Amanda Attorney and Alice Accountant share offices in a downtown professional building. Amanda's practice consists of real estate closings, wills, and minor motor vehicle infractions. Amanda and Alice meet a young candidate for the state legislature and decide to work on his campaign. Amanda becomes the campaign counsel and Alice becomes the campaign treasurer. Unfortunately, neither is aware of how complex the election laws have become.

Within ten days of assuming her position, Alice begins to receive notices from the state Election Law Enforcement Commission reminding her to file campaign reports. Alice calls Amanda, who begins to wade through the 30-page document on campaign expenses.

Amanda has difficulty figuring out the various campaign limitations and reporting requirements. She notes that the campaign must establish a bank account in its name almost immediately. In addition, the first campaign financing report is due in ten days. She tells Alice that they need a list of each contributor's name, occupation, and employer.

Alice notes that a number of people have already contributed and that no one listed an occupation or employer. Amanda tells Alice that she will have to track down that information before the report is submitted. It takes Amanda a few extra days to compile the information.

Alice then discovers that several individual contributors seem to have the same last name as some of the corporate contributors. She wonders about that, but is worried about getting the report in on time. She files the report by sending it to the election commission. Another report is due in 30 days.

Three weeks later, Alice and the candidate receive notices that they are in violation of election laws. They face fines for being late with the filing, for exceeding the per-person contribution limit, and for not including the occupation and employer for each contributor. Alice immediately calls Amanda, who contacts the Election Commission. Amanda works out an agreement with its staff. They submit the required reports and also pay a fine of $50. The staff agrees to close the case. ■

MAIL FRAUD

It is against federal law to use the mails to defraud the public. This law affects advertisements sent through the mails which are designed to deceive the customer. Many companies advertise in a way that is either deceptive or is close to being fraudulent. An individual who allow his or her name to appear in such literature could be held liable for the conduct of these companies.

■ Taxes Unlimited mails out advertisements to prospective customers telling them that they employ "tax experts" who can reduce anyone's taxes. Anita Accountant allows her name and credentials to be placed at the bottom of the advertisement.

In fact, the "experts" have little tax experience and "save" taxpayers money by wrongfully calculating the amount of tax due. This is fraud and Anita may be held liable for allowing her name to be used if she knew Taxes Unlimited's fraudulent claims. ■

■ Dieters Delite regularly sends out advertisements describing how much weight Dieters Delite users have lost. Dr. John Blimp endorses the weight-loss claims in the advertisement. In fact, the people in the advertisement have always been thin, and the claims are false. Dr. Blimp may be held liable if he knew that the claims were false. ∎

Businesses should consult with legal counsel before mailing out advertisements with claims that cannot be completely supported. Federal law prohibits mail fraud and state laws prohibit deceptive advertisements. Professionals who advertise should also be careful that their claims are supported by facts.

SECURITIES LAW

Accountants bear special liability under the federal securities laws because they place their names on annual reports and indicate that the financial statements meet approved financial and accounting standards.

An accountant may be criminally liable under the 1933 Securities Act if the financial report is incorrect or omits important information, which an investor would want to know and would rely on to make an investment decision. It is also a criminal offense to deliberately violate any provision of the act, just as it is also a criminal act to knowingly violate any provision of the 1934 Securities and Exchange Act or SEC regulations that relate to the act. Because the 1934 act requires regular reports signed by accountants, they are in a position to be held liable for fraudulent or inaccurate reports. As previously noted, court rulings have required a showing of deliberate wrongdoing in order to sustain a violation.

OTHER CRIMINAL ACTS

The Racketeer Influenced and Corrupt Organizations Act (RICO) has been used by federal prosecutors to pursue a variety of organizations that may be influenced by corrupt elements or that may be committing unlawful acts. The act may be used to pursue crime in labor unions, businesses, or other organizations.

The use of RICO has been criticized because it is rather vague and very broad in its scope. It invites overzealous or incompetent prosecutors to bring actions without adequate knowledge of the workings of the organization. This is particularly true with respect to organizations that deal with complicated financial matters. As a result, the act can be dangerous for both guilty and innocent professionals.

∎ Aaron is an accountant for the Schemesters Union, which is influenced by criminal elements. Aaron does not know of the unsavory people who help run the union's affairs.

The local district attorney's office launches an investigation of the union and requests all its records. They believe the union's leadership is siphoning off union members' dues and giving the money to the mob. Aaron finds no entry entitled "mob money" when he audits the union's books. Nevertheless, he is interviewed by the prosecutors at length about his knowledge of "mob payouts."

Aaron hires Alacyn Attorney. She immediately advises him to cease talking with the district attorney's office. The union is later charged with participating in corrupt acts. Aaron is called as a witness. His attorney negotiates a grant of immunity and Aaron testifies regarding the union's financial records. No criminal charges are ever proved. ■

■ Alice is the accountant for Mayor Montgomery. The mayor has been buying parcels of land zoned residential and selling them after they have been zoned for commercial use.

The local prosecutor begins an action to determine if the mayor improperly influenced the local board of adjustment to change the zoning requirements. Alice is called to testify to discuss the mayor's financial records although she knows nothing about his activities.

If Alice had altered the records to hide the dates of these transactions, she could also be held criminally responsible. ■

SPECIAL PROBLEMS FOR ACCOUNTANTS

Accountants might perform an audit of a company. An audit should comply with generally accepted auditing standards (GAAS), which specify proper methods for conducting an audit. The auditor examines the financial records and statements of a company to ensure their accuracy. The auditor also samples the inventory, checks contracts, examines bank accounts, and performs other procedures. Failure to follow GAAS is negligence.

Auditors will issue an opinion about the company's financial status. The qualified opinion indicates the company has some problems, whereas an unqualified opinion indicates that the company's financial statements fairly represent its financial position.

A company wants to obtain an unqualified opinion. The company pays the auditor's fee and the auditor would like the company's business in the future. The company may try to pressure the auditor to change a qualified opinion to an unqualified one, putting the auditor in a difficult position. She must be mindful of her responsibility to the public. If she improperly issues an unqualified opinion, she may be held liable for negligence.

While communication between an accountant and the client is not subject to the same privilege under federal law as that between an attorney and her client, some states do recognize the privilege. In addition, some states also give the client a privilege that prevents the use of the accountant's work papers against him.

Definitions Reviewed

Malpractice is the failure of a professional to use the degree of care which a reasonable professional would have used under similar circumstances.

Fraud is the making of deliberately or recklessly false statements about a material fact with the intention of deceiving another person.

Fiduciary is a person who has the legal responsibility to act on behalf of another.

Due diligence is the use of due care by a professional.

Core Concepts Reviewed

■ Professionals, like others, are held liable for their conduct. If they fail to meet the standards of their profession, they may be held liable for negligence. This liability may extend to clients and to third parties.

■ Professional malpractice is defined as the failure to use that degree of care which another qualified professional would have used under similar circumstances. A professional who practices in a special area of expertise will be held to the same standard as other professionals in that area.

■ Businesspersons are expected to utilize sound business judgment in their affairs. Professionals are often retained to advise business people. They must also act with good judgment. Negligent persons may be held liable under theories of contract or tort.

■ Professionals may be named as fiduciaries, which will require them to act in the best interests of another person. This position demands an extremely high degree of loyalty and competence.

■ A professional may also be held liable for criminal conduct. The making of untrue statements or the deliberate omission of material facts is fraud and is sometimes found in matters related to the sale of securities. Professionals may also be held criminally liable for violations of mail fraud, election laws, and federal racketeering laws.

Questions

1. What is the legal standard for malpractice by a professional?
2. How does the standard of care for a professional differ from that for an ordinary person?
3. What is the legal standard of judgment required for businesspersons?
4. What is the purpose of the Securities Act of 1933? What role do accountants have with respect to the act?
5. What is a fiduciary?
6. What are a fiduciary's responsibilities?
7. Why would a professional want to work for a bankrupt's estate?
8. What responsibilities does a professional have to third parties? When may professionals be held liable to parties other than the client?
9. When may a professional be held liable under the Securities Exchange Act of 1934?
10. When may a professional be held liable under federal tax law?
11. What is RICO?

Problems

1. Dr. Fasthands examines little Tommy's appendix and decides to take it out after noticing some tenderness in the area. Tommy also complains of pain in the area.

   The average physician would have asked for X rays before performing the operation. Dr. Fasthands does not request the X rays because he prefers to rely on his own judgment. If Tommy's appendix is later discovered to have been healthy, will Dr. Fasthands be liable?

2. Alex Accountant does an audit for the Joe Jones Company. The audit discovers some minor problems with the financial reporting of the company. Alex tells Jones that he intends to issue a qualified opinion.

   Jones informs him that he is seeking a bank loan and needs an unqualified opinion. He pleads with Alex to change his mind. Alex examines the situation and issues an unqualified opinion. If Jones defaults on the loan, what is Alex's liability?

3. Harry is a veterinarian who examines Mrs. Gotbuck's little Chinese pug. Harry conducts a thorough examination and finds nothing wrong. Despite this, Mrs. Gotbuck's insists that her pug does not look right and is not eating well. Harry conducts another examination, but still can find nothing wrong.

   A few weeks later, the Chinese pug becomes sick, vomits excessively, and dies. Mrs. Gotbuck's sues Harry for the loss of her dog and for emotional distress. Harry introduces the testimony of three other vets who state that Harry's examination was proper. May Mrs. Gotbucks recover?

4. Suzie is the administrator of her mother's estate. She wants to buy one of her mother's necklaces from the estate. She has it appraised at $5,000.

   Before she makes the transfer, she seeks the opinion of Ada, who is the estate's accountant. Ada tells her that she may buy the necklace as long as she is paying fair market value. Is Ada's opinion correct?

5. Bob Builder constructs houses and apartment buildings. He is in the process of building High-Rise Heaven. Despite building-code requirements that a certain quality pipe be used, Bob uses a lesser quality pipe.

   Later, the building's plumbing springs leaks throughout the building. One of the tenants slips on some of the water and is injured. The tenant sues the building's owner, manager, and Bob. Is Bob liable?

6. Stuart is an accountant who is preparing financial statements for T. B. Bennet and Company. Bennet hands Stuart some papers relating to the amount and value of the company's inventory. The company has overstated the value of the inventory because it wants to issue some new securities.

   Stuart has a large number of job assignments and does not bother to check the inventory figures. Bennet issues the stock and a number of investors lose money because of the overvaluation of the inventory. If they bring an action against Stuart, will he be held liable?

7. Charles is an attorney with a small firm specializing in personal injury cases. Charlie usually wins about 50 percent of the cases and settles many others.

   Charles sends out a mail advertisement that reads "We always win!" He obtains a number of new clients. He takes a new client's case to court and loses. The client brings an action for malpractice against Charles and contacts the postal authorities. What are Charles's potential liabilities?

8. Ricky is the accountant and auditor for Hawkins and Company. Ricky's investigation discloses that Hawkins has been submitting false expense vouchers and that he has received about $15,000.

   Hawkins begs Ricky not to disclose this fact to the company's board of directors. He swears that he will repay the money to the company. Ricky decides not to disclose this fact to the board. Hawkins later steals $500,000 from the company and skips town. Does Ricky have any liability to the company's shareholders?

9. Alicia Attorney and Azure Accountant decide to become involved in the campaign of Ron Pegit, who is running for the state legislature. They agree to let him use their names in Pegit's literature.

   Ron, unbeknownst to them, has been sending out fraudulent literature through the mails with their name on it. They suddenly get calls from the local prosecutor and the U.S. Attorney's office inviting them to help their offices investigate the matter. What should they do? What is their liability? Do you have any advice for them with respect to future campaigns?

PART VII

AGENCY AND EMPLOYMENT

Chapter 23

Agency

■ An agency agreement provides that one person will work on behalf of another. The person who performs the work is the agent and the person on whose behalf the work is performed is the principal.

■ An agency is a fiduciary relationship that requires a high degree of trust between the agent and the principal. The agent must always work in the best interests of the principal and account for all money spent and all activities on her behalf. The principal's obligation is to pay the agent and to comply with the other terms of the agreement.

■ A principal will be liable for contracts entered into on his behalf if the agent had received some "authority" from the principal to agree to such contracts. Authority is either actual, implied, or apparent.

■ An agent is someone who works on behalf of the principal and is subject to a high degree of control. An independent contractor is someone who does a particular job and is not subject to the same high degree of control.

CREATION/TYPES OF AGENCY

☆ power of attorney ☆

Agency forms the basis of most work relationships, including employer-employee agreements. It is a consensual arrangement between the parties built on trust, which allows one party to work on behalf of another. The person who retains the other party is the principal and the person being hired is the agent.

An agency is a fiduciary relationship built on trust because the agent must always work on behalf on the principal and the principal has certain responsibilities to the agent. The agency may be for broad, general purposes or for very narrow purposes.

Although it is usually better to put agency agreements in writing, an agency may be either written or oral. An agency agreement to sell or buy land, and an agency for more than one year must be in writing.

A general agent has broad powers to act on behalf of the principal. A manager, executive, or professional is an agent who falls into this category. A special agent is someone who is appointed to carry out specific tasks in accordance with the principal's instructions, and is likely to have little discretion in terms of carrying out her duties. Workers such as waiters and gas station attendants are examples of special agents.

A power of attorney is a document that gives an agent the power to do activities on behalf of the principal. The agent may be given either broad or specific powers. This agent is known as an **attorney-in-fact**. She should not be confused with an attorney-at-law who has been admitted to the bar and is licensed to practice law.

A real estate agent is someone who is retained by an owner of a house for the specific purpose of finding a buyer. While the agent is supposed to be primarily representing the owner, a real estate agent actually acts as an intermediary between the buyer and seller. The agent shows houses to prospective buyers, and then helps the buyer and seller work out the price and other contractual details.

An **agency coupled with an interest** allows an agent to perform a particular act, and permits the agent to protect his interest in the property subject to the agency.

> XYZ Bank lends money to Jones so that he can buy a 1993 Smashmobile car. Jones buys the car and gives XYZ Bank an interest in the car, which will allow the bank to sell the Smashmobile if Jones does not repay the loan. Jones also gives the bank an agency agreement permitting it to sell Jones's car. Because Jones is the owner of the car, the bank must have an agency in order to sell it. This is an example of an "agency coupled with an interest." It may not be terminated without the bank's consent. ■

Independent Contractors

Specific functions!

pays himself!

Can only are the independent contractor!

An **independent contractor** is someone who performs activities in a way similar to an agent, but is regarded differently for purposes of the law. The key difference is one of high control by the principal over an agent, as opposed to the low degree of control over an independent contractor. A principal can exercise a high degree of control over an agent. She can direct the hours to be worked, the tools to be used, and the way the work is performed.

An independent contractor often does the job in the way he believes to be appropriate. He sets his own hours and uses his own tools. In distinguishing between an agent and an independent contractor, one should look at how much control the principal exercises over the other party. If the amount of control is high, the person is likely to be regarded as an agent. If it is low, the person is an independent contractor.

> Shaney hires Peter to paint his house. Peter paints when he wants, buys his own paint, and is paid by the job. Peter would be an independent contractor. ■

> Shaney hires Sam to help paint houses and he asks Sam to paint his house. Shaney tells him how to do it, and supplies the paint and brushes. Sam would be regarded as Shaney's agent. ■

While a principal is liable for many of the acts of an agent, she is less liable for the acts of an independent contractor.

Duties of Agent and Principal

An agency is a fiduciary relationship that must be characterized by special trust on the part of both parties. An agent has the duty of utmost loyalty to the principal. An agent must act only on behalf of the principal and not for his own benefit. This is a duty so strict that an agent will always be held liable to the principal for acting in a way that might benefit himself rather than the principal.

> Peter Principal instructs Alan Agent to buy a particular vase for his collection for no more than $5,000. Unknown to Peter, Alan owns such a vase. Alan brings the vase to Peter and states it can be purchased from the owner for $4,500. Peter

Agent is not allowed to keep secret from principal.

purchases the vase. He later discovers what Alan did. He has the right to discharge Alan and bring an action for damages. ■

Can't sell outside principal

■ Alice Agent works for Polly Principal as a dress designer. She develops a dress pattern that she begins to sell to a few selected customers. This is a breach of her duty to Polly. ■

■ Aaron Agent works for Paul Principal finding locations for shopping centers. One day, he finds a location he thinks would be ideal for apartments. He purchases this land for himself and builds the apartments. This is a breach of his duty to report business opportunities to the principal, and Paul can hold him liable for failing to do so. He may also recover lost profits. ■

The agent must also account for all his activities and for any of the principal's money spent on business-related activities. The agent must also render his best efforts on the principal's behalf. An agent may not compete with the principal or engage in other activities that would harm the principal's business. This would include disclosing confidential information to competitors, customers, or suppliers.

An agent who receives notice or information that could affect the principal's business should notify the principal immediately. An agent's knowledge of a notice or other information may be attributed to the principal.

An employee is a particular type of agent and is subject to a very high degree of control by the employer. The employee also owes the employer a very high degree of loyalty. Often, employers ask employees to agree to convenants not to compete and not to disclose certain information. Covenants not to compete are enforceable by the courts as long as they are reasonable in terms of time and geographical scope.

TYPES OF AUTHORITY

Authority is the authorization by the principal which allows the agent to engage in certain activities. The authority could be broad or narrow. The concept of authority is important because it is the principal's granting of authority which gives an agent the right to bind the principal to contracts. If the agent has the authority to engage in an activity, the principal will be liable for the agent's conduct.

Explicit authority is express authorization by the principal that an agent may engage in certain activities. It forms the basis for other types of authority.

■ The principal informs the agent that she may "sell" his property. This normally gives the agent the right to engage in activities such as advertising the property, soliciting buyers, and showing the property. Authorization to sell property normally does not give the agent the right to actually convey the property. ■

Any specific authority to perform certain activities would be regarded as express authority. Another example of express authority would be if Peter Principal hires Albert Agent to paint the house and fix the plumbing. It would also be express authority to allow an agent to drive a cab from the owner's fleet.

Closely related to the concept of express authority is the granting of **implied authority.** This authority stems from those activities that are related to the express authority.

Peter Principal gives Anna Agent the authority to manage his store. Anna has the implied authority to engage in those activities necessary to manage the store. She has the authority to hire and fire employees, and to buy and sell inventory. As a result, if Anna enters into a contract to buy inventory, Peter Principal will be bound by that contract. He will also be obligated to honor a contract with respect to rent, employment, or any other matter reasonably related to the management of the store. ▦

Implied authority is an extremely important concept because it significantly expands the liability of a principal for the acts of an agent. The principal will be liable for any acts of agents which could be seen as reasonably implied by their job's responsibilities.

▦ Swanson is a salesperson for Boothe's Books. He decides to give free samples of the textbooks he sells to every teacher he knows. Boothe cannot recover these books even if he did not approve of Swanson's actions. ▦

A third type of authority is **apparent authority.** It results from the impression the principal gives to a third party. If a principal engaged in conduct that led a reasonable third party to believe that the agent had certain authority, the principal will not be permitted to deny that the agent had such authority.

▦ Mike tells Ike that Luke is the best restaurant manager he has ever had. He also says that he has utmost confidence in Luke's ability to handle any matter relating to the restaurant and to deal with anyone.

   Mike has instructed Luke to have no dealings with Ike. Luke ignores these instructions and deals with Ike. Mike would be liable for giving Ike the impression that Luke could deal with him. This is called apparent authority. Mike would not be able to disclaim a contract that Ike had agreed to with Luke. ▦

When one combines actual, implied, and apparent authority, it is apparent that a principal should give special care to the selection of an agent. These three types of authority give the agent significant opportunities to bind the principal through his conduct. This is particularly true with respect to contracts. Given the potential liability attached to contracts, agents should also receive adequate training and supervision.

Principal's Responsibilities

The principal's major duty is to compensate the agent in accordance with their agency agreement. If nothing has been specified in the agreement regarding the agent's compensation, the agent should receive reasonable compensation. The agent should also receive reimbursement for reasonable expenses incurred while performing the principal's business.

▦ Eva works as a seamstress for Gloria. In the first week of her agency she works 40 hours. Nothing was said about her compensation. Eva also had to purchase some needles and spools of thread related to her work.

One can go to the marketplace to determine the prevailing hourly wages of a seamstress. Large stores and other institutions employ seamstresses. Gloria and Eva can determine an hourly rate and multiply it by 40. Eva should have kept receipts for her purchases, as she is entitled to reimbursement for the needles and thread. ■

An employee is a special type of agent because he is under the direct control of the principal and works for the employer on a regular and continuous basis. Both the federal and state goverments have passed numerous laws that govern the principal's responsibilities in the workplace with respect to employees.

Minimum-wage laws now establish floors for wages that an employer must pay an employee. State and federal laws also set norms with respect to standard workdays and workweeks as well as for overtime pay. Employers also have the responsibility to pay various taxes associated with having employees. These include their share of Social Security taxes, state unemployment taxes, and contributions to workers' compensation funds. Employers will be held personally liable for failing to pay these levies.

Increasingly, employers are being required to ensure that employees have safe working conditions. The Occupational Safety and Health Act (OSHA) has toughened safety standards in the workplace. The act also provides for inspections of the workplace to ensure that its standards are being met. Courts have also held employers liable for negligence and allowed employees to recover damages because of the failure of the employer to provide safe working conditions. Furthermore, the definition of safe working conditions seems to be expanding to include a variety of environmental factors not previously considered.

■ Peter works for XYZ Corporation as a drill press operator. On Tuesday, Peter notices a large crack in the press, and reports it to his supervisor. Nothing is done and Peter is told to continue working on the same press. On Friday, the press flies apart and injures Peter. XYZ could be held for negligence and for failing to provide safe machinery. ■

■ Frank works in a large hospital as a maintenance worker. The pipes and other structures where he works are covered by loose asbestos. If Frank inhales some of the asbestos particles and becomes ill, XYZ can be held liable. ■

As a result of federal and state civil rights laws, the employer also has a responsibility not to discriminate on the basis of race, gender, creed, or age.

■ ABC corporation needs to lay off people in order to reduce costs. The senior executives decide to dismiss every middle-level manager over the age of 50. ABC could be held liable for age discrimination under federal law. ■

Sexual harassment has become an increasingly important area in recent years. Employers have a responsibility to provide a workplace free from sexual harassment. Courts have also begun to define sexual harassment from the point of view of the person who is being harassed. The standard is whether a reasonable person would feel harassed.

■ Greg is constantly approached for dates by Mary, his supervisor at Pat's Pools. He refuses, but she persists. Greg gets married, but Mary continues to ask for dates and to touch Greg. On one day, Mary has Greg's office destroyed and cuts back on his duties at Pat's Pools. Pat's Pools could be held liable for allowing an environment of sexual harassment to occur. This would be true even on these facts, but would gain added weight if Greg had told Mary's supervisor about the situation. ■

■ Judy works as a taxicab driver. Her co-workers, all of whom are men, regularly make off-color and suggestive remarks. They also have pictures of scantily clad women on the walls. When Judy complains to her male supervisor, she is told to forget it. This situation at Tom's Taxi continues for several years. Finally, Judy feels so uncomfortable that she quits. Tom's Taxi could be held liable for allowing the environment of sexual harassment to continue. ■

At common law, the principal could discharge an employee at will. This doctrine has been changed to prevent a firing or other disciplinary action based on race, religion, creed, or age. More recently, courts have stated that an employer must follow its own internal procedures for discharge or be held liable for not doing so.

■ Max works for LMN Corporation. Its employee manual states that no employee may be disciplined or fired unless the action has been reviewed by a committee composed of the immediate supervisor's supervisor, a union representative, and an officer from the human resources department. Max is fired without such a review being conducted. LMN can be held liable for not following its own procedures. Max could recover damages for back pay and other losses. ■

Just as an agent is required to be loyal to her principal, a principal has the equal duty of loyalty to the agent. The principal must not act in a way that would interfere with the agent's accomplishing the purposes of the agency.

■ Anita is Polly's agent for the purpose of selling Polly's emerald collection. Polly tells Anita that she has an exclusive agency for this purpose. Despite this, Polly also retains Agnes as an agent to sell the collection. Polly would be liable to Anita for interfering with Anita's agency. ■

Definitions Reviewed

Attorney in fact is an agent who has specific powers.

Agency coupled with an interest gives an agent the authority to sell property in which the agent has an interest.

An **independent contractor** is a person who performs a particular job for another.

Express authority is specific authority given to an agent by the principal. It is also known as actual or explicit authority.

Implied authority is the powers an agent has to carry out her express authority.

Apparent authority is derived from what a reasonable third party believes based on words or conduct of the principal.

Core Concepts Reviewed

■ An agency is a consensual, fiduciary relationship between a principal and an agent.

■ The agent has various duties to the principal. These include the duty of loyalty, the duty of good faith, and the duty to account.

■ The agent can bind the principal to contracts if given authority to do so.

■ The major types of authority are explicit, implied, and apparent. These types of authority give the agent the power to bind the principal to contracts.

- The principal has responsibilities to the agent. These include the duty to pay the agent and to maintain safe and secure working conditions. Protection of an employee's job and freedom from sexual harassment have become increasingly important in recent years.

Questions

1. What are the agent's duties to her principal?
2. What is an "agency coupled with an interest"?
3. What is explicit authority?
4. What is implied authority?
5. What is apparent authority?
6. Why is the concept of authority important?
7. What are the principal's major responsibilities to an agent?
8. What is an independent contractor? What is the major difference between an agent and an independent contractor?
9. What is the key legal test in determing whether a person is an agent or an independent contractor?

Problems

1. Arlene is Peter's agent. She has been given authority to run his restaurant. Despite Peter's instructions to spend money cautiously, Arlene decides to reduce the cost of obtaining meat by ordering a very large quantity at discount from Bob's Butchers. Peter refuses to honor the contract. Will he be liable? Why?
2. Nancy is Sally's agent. She is told to buy a certain type of Chippendale table for no more than $2,000. Nancy's mother owns such a table and wants to sell it. Nancy buys the table from her mother for $1,900 and gives it to Sally. Sally later discovers what has happened and demands that the sale be rescinded and that Nancy's mother return the money. Is she correct? Why?
3. Morton owns a clothes cleaning business. He hires his son and names him head of supply. Morton brings his son around to meet all the suppliers and introduces him as vice president of supply.

   Morton's son, Martin, orders 1,000,000 plastic clothes hangers from one of the suppliers at a cost of $25,000. Morton is furious when he learns of the contract and tells the supplier that he will not honor it. The supplier seeks to enforce the contract. Will he prevail? Why?
4. Hanson is Smather's agent for finding new sources of fruit for Smather's jellies and jams. Hanson finds a grove of fruit trees near two major highways. He buys the grove for himself and opens a fruit stand. Does Smather's have any remedy?
5. Irving buys a hot dog franchise from Hot Dog Heaven. Irving is paid from the profits earned by his franchise, but he is required to buy the hot dogs from Hot Dog Heaven (HDH). He is also required to buy napkins and all condiments, such as mustard, ketchup, relish, and sauerkraut, from HDH. He also must attend HDH University to undergo regular training in HDH methods of running a franchise. Is Irving an agent of HDH or an independent contractor? Explain why.
6. Morris runs a pet store in which he sells dogs and cats. He does not keep the cages as clean as they should be. Nor does he vaccinate the pets in accordance with the law. This leads to an outbreak of diseases that can also be transmitted to humans. George works in the store and he is often ill. He believes that his illnesses can be traced to the unsanitary conditions in the store. Does he have any remedy?
7. Michael works for Donna as a truck driver. Donna promises to pay him $300 per week. Michael drives the truck for four weeks, but Donna pays him only $600. She states that she needs to cut costs and that she must let him go. Does Michael have any remedy?

Chapter 24

Liability of Parties

CORE CONCEPTS

- An agent will be liable on contracts she signs unless it is clear that she has agreed to the contract on behalf of the principal.

- A principal will be liable for contracts his agent agreed to on his behalf as long as the agent had the authority to agree to the contract.

- A principal will be liable for actions on her behalf by an agent as long as the agent was within the scope of his employment. This is the doctrine of respondeat superior (let the superior answer for the actions of subordinates).

- The most serious form of liability for the principal is tort liability for the injuries to third parties caused by the actions of the agent.

- Because an agency is a consensual arrangement, it may be terminated by the mutual consent of the parties. It may also be terminated by certain actions of either the principal or agent. In addition, certain circumstances will terminate the agency as a matter of law.

LIABILITY OF AGENT

An agent is liable to the principal for failing to be loyal to the principal, for failing to act in good faith, or for failing to give an adequate accounting to the principal. The agent can also be held liable to a third party for agreeing to a contract in his own name rather than the name of his principal.

The agent should always agree to a contract in the name of the principal rather than in his or her own name.

- Alice is an agent for Paula. She enters into a contract on Paula's behalf. If she signs the contract "Alice, agent for Paula," she will not be liable under the contract. Assuming that Alice has proper authority, only Paula will be liable under the contract.

  But, if Alice had simply signed the contract as "Alice," she would be personally liable to complete the contractual provisions. If the third party discovers that Alice had meant to agree to the contract as an agent for Paula, the third party could also hold Paula, as principal, liable for performance of the contract, assuming Alice had proper authority. ■

An agent has implied authority to act reasonably on behalf of the principal in an emergency even if the agent did not have explicit authority.

- Zeke is the caretaker at Chauncy's estate. Zeke normally performs only routine tasks and Chauncy handles all the major functions. When Chauncy is abroad on vacation, a major hurricane hits the area and the house is damaged. There are also reports of looters in the area. Zeke quickly hires a carpentry firm to repair the damage to the house. He also hires a security firm to protect the home. Both of these actions are reasonable given the emergency conditions, and Chauncy will be bound by Zeke's agreements with the carpenters and the security firm. ■

Of course, an agent will be liable to the principal for any actions outside of his authority. For example, a manager has wide authority to run a store. This would include the implied authority to buy and sell inventory and to hire and fire employees. A store manager, however, does not have any authority to "sell" the store to a third party. If he does so, he would be liable for damages to both the principal and the third party.

An agent might agree to contracts for a fully disclosed principal, a partially disclosed principal, or an undisclosed principal. A **fully disclosed principal** is someone who is known to the agent and the third party. The agent normally signs the contract as agent on behalf of the principal. A **partially disclosed principal** is someone whose exact identity may not be known to the third party, but the third party may know that the agent is acting on someone's behalf. An **undisclosed principal** is someone whose identity is not known by the third party. Principals may be undisclosed because the principal does not want her identity known to the other party for financial reasons.

> Hudson is a very wealthy man who wishes to purchase some real estate. He knows the price will go up if his identity is known. He enters an agreement with Aaron to buy the house as his agent. The contract provides for Aaron to purchase the real estate and then sell it to Hudson. Aaron will receive $3,000 for his efforts.
>
> Aaron signs a contract to purchase the property from Wilkins. Aaron is personally liable on the contract to Wilkins. Aaron will be able to recover from Hudson if Hudson does not perform the contract. ■

CONTRACTUAL LIABILITY OF PRINCIPAL

As noted in the previous chapter, principals are liable for contracts agreed to by agents who have explicit, implied, or apparent authority. A third party is expected either to know the reasonable limits of the agent's authority or to inquire about the agent's limits. If she does not, she will have no remedy against the principal of an agent acting outside the scope of her authority.

> Maggie is an assistant vice president of Last National Bank. She has no authority to sell one of the bank's buildings. Nevertheless, she enters a contract with Newhouse to do so.
>
> Newhouse should have known that assistant vice presidents do not normally have such authority. If he did not know, he should have checked. The bank will have no liability to Newhouse. Of course, Margaret will be liable to both Newhouse and Last National for any losses they may have incurred as a result of her actions. ■

TORT LIABILITY

A principal will be held liable for torts of an agent committed during the scope of an agent's employment. A tort is an act that causes an injury to a person or a person's property. If the agent was not acting within the scope of employment, the principal will not be liable. The legal reasoning for this doctrine is that a principal should have to answer for the acts of her agents or employees. This is called the doctrine of **respondeat superior.**

■ Bob drives a limousine for Larry's Limos. One day, while driving for Larry, Bob runs a stop sign and injures Tiny Tommy, who was riding in another car. Both Bob and Larry's Limos are liable for the negligent act that caused Tiny Tommy's injuries. ■

In the majority of cases it is clear if the agent was within the scope of employment. If the agent was working at the principal's business, she is within scope of employment. If the agent was at home or conducting his own business, he was not within the scope of employment. In the preceding example, had Bob been on vacation and driving his own car, he would not have been within the scope of employment and the principal would not be liable.

Sometimes, it is not clear if the agent was within the scope of employment or not. Normally, an agent commuting to and from work is not considered to be within the scope of employment. But if the agent is on the principal's business during the commute, the agent is probably within the scope of employment.

■ Aardvaark works as Polly's agent. Before leaving for home, Aardvaark is asked by Polly to deliver a package to Smithers. Aardvaark stops working at 5 P.M. Smithers' place of business is between work and Aardvaark's home.

While on his way to Smithers' place of business, Aardvaark runs a stop sign and injures Molly. Because Aardvaark was working for Polly at the time of the accident, both he and Polly will be liable for Molly's injuries. ■

The major advantage for the injured person if the agent is within the scope of employment is that she can hold both the agent and principal liable for the injury. This gives the injured party two sources of assets from which to seek recovery.

■ Same facts as preceding except that Aardvaark had already dropped off the package at Smithers' and was on his way home. In this case, Aardvaark was no longer within the scope of employment and Polly would not be liable. ■

Other questions are raised when the agent has a regular route to drive and departs from that route to go on a mission of her own.

■ Herb drives a truck for Norma. His regular route is Route 1 from Florida to Maine. Normally, he stops at a diner along Route 1, as instructed, and buys his lunch. One day he departs from his route to visit a new diner his friends have told him about. The diner is about 30 miles off Route 1. On his way to the diner Herb gets into an accident. Not only is this a violation of his instructions from Norma, it is beyond what Norma should have expected. Only Herb will be liable for the accident. ■

■ Frank drives a truck in Montana for Mike. In this state, there are very few places to eat along the major highways. Mike is aware of this fact. Frank drives his truck 20 miles off the highway in order to find a place to eat. On his way back to the highway, he gets into an accident. Frank would probably be regarded as being within the scope of employment and Mike would also be liable for the accident. ■

Some courts have decided this issue based on the "reasonable expectation" test, or to what extent could the principal have expected the agent to make this departure. If the departure could have been reasonably expected by the principal, the principal will be held liable. If it was not reasonable to expect this departure from employment, the principal will not be liable.

Other courts have adopted the "working for the principal" test. If the agent was still working for the principal when the negligence occurred, the principal will be held liable. If the agent was not working for the principal, but was clearly on a frolic of his own, the principal will not be liable.

The previous examples discussed the liability of the principal for the negligence of the agent. The next section focuses on the liability of the principal for the intentional torts of the agent.

Intentional Torts

While the general rule has been that a principal will not be held liable for the intentional torts of the agent, the rule has been modified in certain important respects. If use of force is an inherent part of the job, the principal will be liable for deliberate torts.

■ Jake works as a bouncer in Big Bob's Bar. One night he takes an unruly customer, Randy, and throws him down three flights of stairs, and then punches him in the ribs for good measure. In this case, use of physical force is an inherent part of the job. Big Bob will be liable for Jake's excessive use of force on Randy. ■

If the principal has negligently hired or failed to adequately train the agent, the principal can be held liable.

■ Jerry has twice been convicted of aggravated assault. After leaving prison, he gets a job with Chuck's Chicken as a counterman. On his first night, he shoves a customer. The manager persuades the customer to forget the incident by giving him an extra bucket of chicken. He tells Jerry to "cool it" but says nothing more.

The next night, Jerry punches a customer in the mouth because he asked for extra biscuits. Although this was a deliberate tort, Chuck's Chicken is probably liable because, given Jerry's past record and behavior, they failed to properly monitor him. ■

A third exception relates to an agent's attempt to promote the principal's business.

■ Joe and Sam both drive trucks for DFG Corporation. They know that if they can get to the loading dock quickly, they can get out with an extra load before their shift ends. They begin racing each other down the highway. They begin knocking into each other. They near the loading dock, where a competitor's truck is in their way. They bump into it and push it off the highway. The driver of the other truck is severely injured and brings legal action against DFG.

In this case, the drivers believed that they were promoting the principal's business. DFG is likely to be held liable for their deliberate torts. ■

PROXIMATE CAUSE

As previously noted, a principal will be liable for the negligence of his agents. This does not mean that a principal will be liable for whatever the agent does that might cause an injury. As discussed, a principal may or may not be liable for the deliberate acts of an agent which cause an injury. Similarly, the principal will not be liable unless the agent's act was negligent and actually caused the injury. This means that the agent must have acted without that degree of care which a reasonable person would have used under the same circumstances. In addition, the act must have been the **proximate cause** of the injury. That is, the cause of the injury must have been directly related to the actions of the agent.

■ Stanley drives his principal's car up on the sidewalk. The car hits and injures Little Larry. This would be a lack of due care indicating negligence. The negligence was also the proximate cause of the injury. Clearly, the injury was the direct result of Stanley's failure to use due care. ■

■ Herb is driving his car when it hits a large stone in the road. The stone kicks up over the curb and hits a board balanced on a windowsill. The board falls off and hits Sharon on the head.

In this case, there is a problem with both the concepts of negligence and proximate cause. It is difficult to find any lack of due care on Herb's part. Even if one argues he should have avoided the stone, it is difficult to find that it was the direct cause of any injury. ■

INDEPENDENT CONTRACTOR

In the previous chapter, the distinction between an agent and independent contractor was discussed. The key difference between the two is the level of control exercised by the principal. The principal exercises a high degree of control over an agent, but less control over an independent contractor.

While a principal is liable for the negligence of an agent, she is not normally liable for the negligence of an independent contractor.

■ Peter hires Alan's Plumbers to do some plumbing in the Peter building. Alan's Plumbing fails to connect a line properly and water damages the building.

Alan's Plumbing was paid on a per job basis and uses its own tools and sets its own hours. Alan's Plumbing is an independent contractor and Peter has no liability for its negligence. ■

One may be liable for an independent contractor's conduct under some circumstances. First, one may not escape liability for engaging in ultrahazardous conduct by retaining an independent contractor.

■ Nelson needs some blasting done on his property. He hires Kaboom Blasting Company, an independent contractor, to dynamite a rocky area in order to lay a foundation on his property.

Kaboom sets too much dynamite and blows one of the rocks through a neighbor's building. This is an ultrahazardous activity and Nelson may not escape liability for the consequences simply because it was done by an independent contractor. Nelson owed the public close and adequate supervision of the ultrahazardous activity. ■

A second area of liability is when an independent contractor performs an activity required as a matter of law.

> Most towns and cities require home and business owners to clean the sidewalk in front of a home or business after a snowstorm. Smith hires Bobby, from next door, to shovel the walk. Bobby does a fair job for a 13-year-old, but leaves several patches of ice on the walk. Aunt Blabby slips and falls on the ice and breaks her hip. Blabby can recover from Smith because he cannot avoid his legal liability for cleaning the sidewalks adequately. ■

RATIFICATION OF AGENTS ACTS

An agent might enter a contract without authority to do so from the principal. When the principal learns of the agent's actions, she may disavow them, in which case there is no binding contract. The principal may also **ratify** the agent's actions. She may do so by explicitly notifying the other party that she is confirming the agent's actions. She can also ratify the agent's actions by waiting beyond a reasonable time to disavow them.

> Harold is a janitor for Suzie's supply store. A salesman for writing paper talks Harold into buying a substantial amount of stationery for a reduced price. Harold has no authority to engage in such a transaction.
>
> Suzie disavowed this transaction, it would be void. She could also ratify the contract by agreeing to the contract with the salesman, or she could simply accept the stationery, which would also be a form of ratification. ■

TERMINATION OF AGENCY

An agency may be terminated by the mutual agreement of the parties, a revocation of the agent's authority, operation of law, unfulfilled conditions, or by the fulfillment of the agency's purpose.

Completion of an Agency's Purpose

The most common reason for terminating an agency is the fulfillment of the agency's purpose. An agency is a consensual agreement. If it is for long-range and broad purposes, the agency may last for a considerable period of time. If it is for a specific purpose, the agency will terminate when the purpose is fulfilled.

> Agnes is retained as Pepe's real estate agent to help sell Pepe's house. Agnes brings numerous people to Pepe's house. These prospective buyers look through the various rooms on weekends and at nights. When Pepe sells the house, the agency is terminated. It would serve no purpose to continue to have Agnes bring people through Pepe's house between the date of sale and the date of closing. ■

if died, insign

Unfulfilled Conditions

A condition is a clause in the contract which relates to some event. The condition may state that the contract will take effect only if a certain event occurs.

> Agnes and Pepe sign a contract to permit Agnes to sell Pepe's house. There is a clause in the contract stating that the contract will take effect only if the purchase price of the house is at $250,000 or higher. If the purchase price is not $250,000 or higher, the condition is unfulfilled, and the agency terminates. ■

Operation of Law

An agency will terminate as a matter of law upon certain events. If either the agent or the principal die or are declared insane, the agency will terminate. If the agency was related to a specific subject matter, the agency will be terminated if that subject matter is destroyed.

If the agency was created to handle financial matters, the agency will terminate upon the bankruptcy of the agent or principal.

> Andy is Paul's financial advisor and has the authority to sign checks and conduct other business on his behalf. Paul would have a legitimate concern if Andy were to become bankrupt. Someone who is bankrupt may be tempted to take advantage of the easy access to the principal's finances. ■

REVOCATION OF AUTHORITY

Because the agent works for the principal, the principal may revoke the agent's authority at any time. If there is a contract that is associated with the agency, the principal will be liable on the contract.

> Al and Pal have an agency agreement that has been placed into a written employment contract. It provides that Al will manage Pal's store for three years at a salary of $40,000 per year. It further provides that Al will have all the authority normally associated with the position of store manager.
>
> One year into the contract, Pal decides he is not satisfied with Al's performance and revokes the agency. Pal may do this, but he will still be liable for paying Al for the remaining two years on the contract. ■

 ## Mutual Agreement

Because an agency is a consensual agreement, it may be terminated by the parties at any time. As long as this is done by mutual consent there is no liability associated with the termination. As noted previously, if one of the parties terminates the agency, she can be held liable for any underlying breach of contract.

NOTIFYING THIRD PARTIES

When an agency is terminated, third parties who may have dealt or might deal with an agent should be notified by the principal. An agent may agree to contracts on the principal's behalf and it is important to notify third persons that the agency is over.

It is legally sufficient to notify the general public by placing a notice in a paper of general circulation. The notice should list all names under which the principal or agent has conducted business, and the names of the principal and agent as well as a statement that the agency has been terminated.

The principal should give actual notice to any party with whom the agent has previously conducted business. If he does not, he can be held liable if the agent later takes advantage of his previous agency relationship.

■ Amanda was Priscilla's agent. She left Priscilla's employment after working with several dress designers, including Clara of Cleveland. While she was employed by Priscilla, she used to have dresses delivered to various locations around the country.

When Amanda left, Priscilla put a notice in the paper but neglected to specifically notify each of the designers with whom Amanda had worked. One month after leaving, Amanda ordered 500 dresses from Clara, a normal order, and had them delivered to her house.

Because Priscilla had failed to notify Clara, she will be liable if Amanda takes the dresses, sells them, and keeps the money. If she had notified Clara, she would not be liable. ■

■ Albert works as a purchasing agent for Porter. When Albert leaves his employment, Porter puts a notice in a paper of general circulation. His notice outlines the names of the parties, the name of Porter's company, the nature of the agency, and the fact that Albert's agency has been terminated.

Albert goes to a furniture supplier and orders several items of furniture and has it sent to a warehouse he owns. He sells the furniture and disappears with the money. If Albert had previously not dealt with the supplier, Porter would not liable. If Albert had dealt with the supplier, Porter would be liable for the purchase price. Of course, Albert would be liable to the furniture supplier and to Porter if he had to pay for the furniture. ■

AGENCY COUPLED WITH AN INTEREST

As noted in the previous chapter, an agency coupled with an interest is subject to different rules than other agencies. An agency coupled with an interest is primarily for the benefit of the agent rather than the principal. In this case, the agency may be terminated only with the agent's consent and may not be revoked by the principal.

■ Angeline lends Paula $3,000. To secure payment she has Paula sign an agreement allowing Angeline to sell Paula's car if she does repay the loan. It would not make sense to allow Paula to revoke the agency. If she could do so, Angeline's protection would disappear. ■

Definitions Reviewed

A **fully disclosed principal** is one who is known to the agent and the third party.

A **partially disclosed principal** is one whose exact identity is not known to the third party, but the third party knows the agent is working on someone else's behalf.

Undisclosed principal is one whose identity is not known to the third party.

Respondent superior is the legal doctrine that a principal will be liable for the torts of his agent.

Proximate cause is a direct cause of the injury.

To **ratify** is to approve an agent's acts after they occur.

Core Concepts Reviewed

■ Principals will be liable for all contracts agreed to on their behalf if the agent had explicit, implied, or apparent authority to enter into the contract.

■ A principal will be liable for the negligent acts of an agent committed within the scope of the agent's employment. The principal may also be liable for the deliberate torts of the agent.

■ A person is usually not liable for the negligent acts of an independent contractor unless they are of an ultrahazardous nature.

■ Agencies may be terminated by mutual agreement, revocation by the principal, change of circumstances, unfulfilled conditions, or the fulfillment of the agency's purpose.

■ An agency is a consensual agreement and may normally be terminated by the parties without liability unless there is an underlying contract that has been breached.

Questions

1. When is a principal liable for the deliberate torts of an agent?
2. What is an agency coupled with an interest?
3. Outline some ways an agency may be terminated.
4. What are some circumstances under which an agent may be liable under a contract?

5. What is an undisclosed principal?
6. When would it be useful for an undisclosed principal to employ an agent?
7. An agent agrees to a contract with a third party on behalf of an undisclosed principal. If one of the parties refuses to perform the contract, what are some of the legal remedies available to each of the parties?
8. What are the obligations of a principal to third parties if an agency is terminated?
9. What are the possible liabilities of a principal to a third party after an agency is terminated?
10. When is a principal liable for the negligent acts of an agent?

Problems

1. Amanda is Perry's agent. She works in his restaurant as a waitress and is responsible for carrying plates from the kitchen to the patrons' tables. One day she drops one on the floor.

   Before she can pick it up, a patron who was walking to the cashier steps on the plate and falls. The patron hits her head on the edge of a counter and opens a deep gash over her eyebrow. What is the liability of both Amanda and Perry?

2. Alan is Peter's agent. Alan drives a truck that hauls cargo between Boston and New York. One day he leaves his route to visit his girlfriend, who lives ten miles away. After his visit, he is driving back to his route when he runs a stop sign and flattens Petite Polly. Can Petite Polly recover from Peter?

3. Alice works as a trainer for the Trale Harmony Company. She teaches a class on improving interpersonal relationships. One day a student makes her angry and she punches him in the face.

   Alice had a prior conviction for aggravated bodily assault stemming from a previous classroom incident. Will the company be liable for the student's injured face?

4. Dr. Sawbones is a physician who works for Brains Unlimited, Medical Corporation. One day, Dr. Sawbones is performing brain surgery and is having trouble working the brain saw.

   Sawbones brings in Gomer, a salesman for the Brain Saw and Plumbing Company, who sold Sawbones the drill. He asks Gomer to show him again how to work the drill. This time, Gomer drills a hole into the patient's head. Unfortunately, he drills the hole just a little too deep and the patient's brain is critically injured. Discuss the possible remedies that the patient may have against Dr. Sawbones, Brains Unlimited, Gomer, and the Brain Saw and Plumbing Company.

5. Alyce is Patty's agent. She works at Patty's Pet Palace, which grooms cats and dogs. Alyce makes repeated sexual comments to Bill, one of the professional groomers at the Palace.

   Bill resists her advances but Alyce persists. Bill reports her advances to Patty, but she laughs and does nothing about his complaints. Does Bill have any remedy against Patty?

6. Tracy was Larry's agent. In her capacity as agent, she would hire bands and other talent for Larry's nightclub. One of the bands, White Bread, was so terrible that Larry fired Tracy.

   Larry did not say anything to White Bread, but left town for a week instead. To get even, Tracy signed them to a one-year contract. Is Larry liable?

7. The town of Dry Gulch is responsible for repaving the roads within its jurisdiction. It hires Dave's Paving to repave one of its major thoroughfares. Dave leaves a large hole in the road during the job and covers it with plywood. The wood is weakened by the traffic. Tom drives over the plywood, but it breaks and his car crashes into the hole. Tom suffers serious injuries and brings an action against Dry Gulch. The town claims it is not liable because the work was performed by an independent contractor. Is the town correct?

Chapter 25

Employment Law

CORE CONCEPTS

■ Historically, relationships between employees and employers were characterized by the hands-off attitude of society and government. Employers were able to fire employees for any reason or no reason. This was called the "employment-at-will" doctrine. In addition, all terms of employment were considered subject to negotiation between employer and employee. If the employee did not like the terms, she was free to go elsewhere.

■ After the turn of the century, government assumed a more active role as it recognized that the bargaining positions of employer and employee had become less equal. Industrial giants had replaced individual employers and senior management had become more remote from individual employees.

■ The legislative and judicial branches have modified the employment-at-will doctrine to permit exceptions based on contracts, statutes, and public policy.

■ Congress also passed legislation to strengthen the position of employees with respect to bargaining power, wages, hours worked, and child labor. Other legislation, which legitimized and strengthened the power of unions, recognized the right of employees to engage in collective bargaining.

EMPLOYER/EMPLOYEE RELATIONS

Until the early part of this century, relations between employers and employees had been regarded as private matters relating to contracts between a principal and an agent. But, the growth of industrial giants and the corresponding growth of labor unions often led to violent clashes between workers and management. The hands-off attitude on the part of the government needed to change if only to restore order in American society.

The Fair Labor Standards Act established the minimum wage, which is periodically changed by Congress, and overtime pay requirements. It also outlawed child labor except under certain conditions. The act applies to employers engaged in interstate commerce. It exempts certain managerial, administrative, and professional employees. There are also exemptions for employees who are provided food and lodging, and for students and apprentices. These provisions are designed to ensure that every worker at least has a living wage.

Under the act, employers may not require employees to work for more than forty hours per week unless they are paid 1.5 times their regular pay for overtime hours.

■ Bob is paid $6 per hour for working as a mechanic for Gabang Corporation. One week, the company has a special order and Bob must work 60 hours. He should be paid as follows:

Regular Time:	40 × $6 =	$240
Overtime Pay:	20 × $9 =	$180
Total		$420 ■

Children were regarded as requiring protection from exploitive labor practices. This was particularly true in hazardous industries such as mining where the plight of child workers gained nationwide publicity. Under the act, children may not work as anything other than newspaper carriers until age 14. Children between 14 and 15 may work some hours in nonhazardous jobs. Children ages 16 and 17 may work unlimited hours in nonhazardous jobs.

Employees' Unions

As companies grew, the individual employee had less ability to negotiate fairly with the employer. In order to increase their power, employees organized into unions to bargain collectively with employers.

Many courts saw unions as interfering with the individual rights of an individual employer and employee to reach a contract between themselves. Businesses and some government administrations were also hostile to unions. As a result, Congress passed legislation allowing employees to organize into unions, to strike, to picket, and to bargain collectively with their employer.

As unions began to prosper, many people believed that they had gained too much power. As a result, there was a backlash against many union activities. This was particularly true with respect to certain unions that had ties to organized crime.

The history of labor legislation has been to find the proper balance between the rights of workers and the rights of management to represent the corporation. Perhaps the most important development in federal labor law was the creation of the National Labor Relations Board (NLRB), which helps mediate this balance between the interests of workers and those of employers.

Workers may form a union by establishing an appropriate bargaining unit. The unit must reflect similar job functions and interests so that it may effectively bargain with management. It may be all workers in a particular facility or all workers with similar tasks. Management may not be part of the union. Unions controlled by the company are illegal.

If the workers can show that 50 percent of them are interested in joining a union, they may petition the NLRB for elections to form a union. The NLRB can supervise the election. There are rules relating to the rights of employees to campaign on the employer's property and what actions the company may take with respect to the election.

After the union is formed, the company and the union must **bargain in "good faith."** This does not mean that they must reach agreement on all issues. It does mean that they must make a reasonable effort to reach agreement on issues that are suitable for collective bargaining. Attempts to stall or refusal to meet would be indications of bad faith bargaining. Good faith would include having regular discussions, listening to the other side's position, and making some progress toward reaching an agreement.

Wages, hours, and other conditions of employment are suitable topics for collective bargaining. It would not be permissible to agree to discriminate against certain employees because they did not join the union or for other reasons. Historically, corporations have been unwilling to negotiate matters considered exclusively within the realm of management. More recently, some corporations have seen value in including workers in management decisions and have placed union representatives on their board of directors.

Unions have the right to strike if an agreement is not reached. A strike is simply the lawful right not to work without a contract. Strikes are normally recommended by the union leadership if talks with management seem stalled. But, the union may call a strike only if a strike vote has been ratified by a majority of its members. Individual employees may honor the strike, continue working, or return to work after a period of time.

> ■ Tom is a member of the local ironworkers' union. It votes to strike at the local Iron City plant when it is unable to reach an agreement with the corporation's management.
>
> Tom joins the picket line with the other strikers. After three weeks, he returns to work. It was permissible for him to strike and it is permissible for him to return to work after a period of time. ■

Strikes that promote violence, encourage workers to simply stop working while being paid, or are without union authorization are unlawful. Strikes in violation of a contractual provision prohibiting strikes or strikes which are in violation of a court order are also unlawful.

Because of the large number of destructive labor-management conflicts that occurred during the middle of this century, Congress passed the Taft-Hartley Act, which gave the president the power to order both the unions and management to keep bargaining. This is referred to as a **cooling-off period.** Presidents have utilized this provision to compel workers in vital industries to stay on the job. The "cooling-off" period permits workers and management to keep talking until they reach an agreement. The Taft-Hartley Act also gave workers greater rights to participate in union management.

Modifying Employment-at-Will

The traditional doctrine between employer and employee has been referred to as **employment-at-will.** The worker had the right to work elsewhere when she wanted, and the employer had the right to terminate the worker's employment when she wanted. This doctrine has been modified to reflect public policy and contract exceptions. For example, it is not permissible to discharge someone on the basis of race, religion, gender, age, or handicap, and doing so would be grounds for charge of discrimination.

It is also not permissible to discharge an employee for failing to carry out an order to perform an illegal act or an act that will endanger the public safety.

> ■ Don Dogood is told by his manager, Bill Badd, to dump hazardous waste products into a lake that supplies the city with drinking water. He refuses to do so and Mr. Badd seeks to have him fired. This would be a wrongful discharge and Don would be able to bring a court action to recover his job. It is in the public interest not to permit someone to fire a person who is attempting to protect the public safety. ■

Recent rulings have also held that a tort could be an exception to the employment-at-will doctrine. If an employer defrauded the employee or inflicted emotional distress, a court could find these acts caused a wrongful discharge. In addition, the issue of sexual harassment has assumed greater importance in recent years. Courts have held that an employer will be liable if it permits an environment of sexual harassment to exist and does nothing about it.

■ Maria works as a secretary for Charlie's Callous Cabs. The office is adorned with pictures of nude women, and her co-workers regularly make obscene comments to her.

When she complains to Charlie, he tells her "tough." This has created an environment of sexual harassment, and if she leaves Charlie's employment because of this, she will be able to recover damages. ■

Employment Contracts

Most employees have "at-will" contracts. Except for the exceptions noted, employees may leave or be fired at the discretion of the employer. But, some employees are able to obtain employment contracts. This is often the case for senior level executives who have long-term written contracts.

■ Bob Bigwig becomes the new vice president for marketing at GIG Corporation. He agrees to a three-year contract with the corporation. Because the contract's terms will take more than one year, they are put into writing. The employer may not terminate Bob's employment at-will. If it terminates Bob's employment, it must pay Bob for the remainder of the contract. ■

Recent court rulings have found some implied contracts between employers and employees. These are based on handbooks or other information that an employer may give to an employee. This information might outline specific procedures that are to be followed before an employee can be terminated. Courts have ruled that these procedures create an implied contract that may not be violated.

■ Mary works for NBT Corporation. When she started working at NBT, she was given an employee manual that stated that no employee would be terminated unless the supervisor's superior approved the decision. This provision creates an implied contract between the employee and the corporation. Mary cannot be fired unless NBT Corporation complies with this provision. ■

Injuries on the Job

Before the legislation of **workers' compensation,** when employees were injured on the job, they had no recourse except to bring a legal action against their employer. They had to demonstrate that the employer was negligent in a way that injured the employee.

This could be a difficult case for the employee to prove. She first had to show negligence by the employer. She also had to show that the employer's negligence was the proximate cause of the injury. In addition, she had to show that she was not negligent in a way that contributed to the injury.

Furthermore, there was a doctrine known as the "fellow servant" rule. If a fellow employee caused the injury, the employee could not recover. In addition, some courts ruled that an employee assumed the risks associated with the hazards of employment when the employee took the job. This prevented the employee from recovering. This was called the assumption of risk doctrine.

> ■ Frank goes to work in a mine. One of his fellow workers runs over his foot with an ore cart. Under the old law, the fellow servant doctrine and the assumption of the risk doctrine would have barred Frank from recovery. ■

These results seemed unfair and led to a large number of workers being unable to recover for their injuries. As a result, the states established workers' compensation funds in order to pay people for injuries suffered on the job.

Employers must participate in these funds either by paying into the system or by arranging to have their own funds available to pay for the injuries of their workers. Employers may not decide to ignore the situation and wait to be sued by injured workers.

Workers' compensation is based on **strict liability.** It does not matter whether a person's negligence contributed to the worker's injury. It does not even matter if the worker was negligent. If the worker can show that she was injured as a result of her employment, she can recover. A worker cannot recover if he deliberately injured himself or engaged in some conduct that indicates a wrongful intent.

The state normally has a schedule of recovery amounts based on the type of injury and the seriousness of the injury. For example, loss of a limb might entitle a worker to a certain amount, whereas a worker's death might permit the worker's heirs to receive a greater level of recovery.

Normally, access to the workers' compensation fund is the injured worker's exclusive remedy. The worker may not bring suit against the employer or a fellow worker. An exception would be if the employer deliberately injured the worker. In this case, the employee could bring an action against the employer.

An emerging area of workers' compensation law relates to stress-related illnesses such as depression. Similarly, some workers have claimed they suffered a disease resulting from activities on the job. In some cases, workers were allowed to recover for these difficulties. These types of cases will probably receive greater attention in the future.

Pensions

Congress became increasingly concerned about the safety of workers' pensions. Some workers who were fired immediately before retirement reported the loss of their pension benefits. Furthermore, some pension funds had been inadequately funded, causing additional losses.

As a result, Congress passed the Employee Retirement Income Security Act (ERISA). The act requires a company to name a pension fund manager who must act as a fiduciary on behalf of the pension fund. A fiduciary must always act on behalf of its principal. In this case, the fiduciary must exercise reasonable business judgment regarding the funds, meaning careful investment of the money in a diversified portfolio. A prudent fiduciary would also prevent raids on the fund by insiders or improper loans to corporate officers or directors.

The act also establishes rules with respect to the rights of employees to receive pension benefits. The act requires that employee contributions to a pension plan vest when made. It also establishes rules for shorter vesting of employer contributions which better protect the interests of the employee. "Vesting" means the right of the employee to receive pension benefits.

ERISA does not require that a company establish a pension plan. If it does have a plan, the plan must conform to the requirements of the act. This is a way of better protecting the rights of the worker and makes a pension plan a contract between the worker and the employer.

Social Security and Unemployment

In the 1930s, the federal goverment set up the Social Security system. It was primarily designed to help older people who had few retirement benefits. Since that time, it has grown to include providing benefits to many other individuals who are disabled or hospitalized.

Employers and employees must make contributions to the Social Security fund. It is the employer's responsibility to deduct the payments. If it does not do so, it can be subject to various civil and criminal penalties.

There is also a federal unemployment compensation program that the state governments carry out. An employer must pay unemployment taxes to the state government. Employees do not pay unemployment benefits. Again, an employer may be held criminally liable for failing to pay these taxes.

■ Frank's business gets into difficulty. In order to cut down on the outflow of cash, he stops paying state unemployment taxes. This is a criminal offense for which Frank could be punished. ■

Definitions Reviewed

Bargain in good faith is the obligation of both labor and management to negotiate in good faith when working out an agreement.

"Cooling-off" period is the authority of the president to order the parties of a labor agreement to continue negotiating.

Employment-at-will is the traditional common-law doctrine that an employer could fire an employee at any time, for any reason.

Workers' compensation is the federal system that allows workers to collect for injuries suffered on the job.

Strict liability means that under the system of workers' compensation, the employer will be held liable for worker's injuries suffered on the job without regard to fault.

Core Concepts Reviewed

■ The old laissez-faire philosophy of allowing business and labor to negotiate without government interference has disappeared. Federal and state governments regulate hours worked, wages, and child labor.

■ The employment-at-will doctrine that allowed employers to fire employees for no reason at any time has been eroded by contractual, public policy, and statutory exceptions.

- The National Labor Relations Board sets rules and procedures for the election of unions and for collective bargaining with management. The Taft-Hartley Act allows for a cooling-off period if a labor strike or a management lockout would hurt the economy.

- Workers' compensation systems allow employees injured on the job to recover for their injuries without regard to fault.

Questions

1. What were the purposes of the Fair Labor Standard Act?
2. Explain how overtime provisions work.
3. What is the National Labor Relations Board?
4. What are the obligations of labor and management with respect to collective bargaining?
5. What is the employment-at-will doctrine?
6. What are some exceptions to the employment-at-will doctrine? What is the purpose of these exceptions?
7. Discuss the law surrounding sexual harassment.
8. Discuss workers' compensation systems. What is their purpose? When is a worker eligible to recover?
9. What is the Employee Retirement Income Security Act? How does it protect workers' pensions?
10. What is a pension administrator's obligation with respect to investing the fund?

Problems

1. Jones works for ABC Corporation for $400 per week. One week he works an additional 20 hours of overtime. Calculate his wages for that week.
2. Sam works for QLZ Corporation as a truck driver. One day he is riding with his boss. They stop at a diner where they get into an argument with another truck driver from a different company.

   Suddenly, Sam's boss grabs the driver's arms and pins them behind his back. He yells at Sam to "sock him one for good old QLZ." Sam walks away instead. Later, Sam's boss fires him and tells Sam, "We don't want any sissies in this outfit." Does Sam have a remedy?

3. Joan works for Smetdown Corporation, which makes chemicals for industrial use. Because she was hired as a senior-level executive, she was able to obtain a three-year written contract.

   After she had been working at Smetdown for six months, she had observed that the company was polluting the air with its chemicals. She talked to Smetdown's president and he said he would look into the matter.

   One month later, Joan observes the same level of pollution and talks to the president. He tells her that there is no problem. When she persists, he tells her to shut up and mind her own business.

   Joan continues to protest and the president fires her. When Joan reminds him that she has a three-year contract, he tells her that its his company and he can fire whomever he wants. Does Joan have any remedy?

4. Sarah works at Grandmom's Diner as a new chef. After two weeks, she observes large rats running around the kitchen. Sarah says nothing for about a week. During the third week Sarah notices that the stew has a funny rodent-like taste. She talks to Grandmom, who tells her to keep cooking and to leave the recipes to her.

   Sarah reports the diner to the local board of health. When Grandmom finds out, she fires Sarah and tells her, "we don't want a little snitcher working here." Does Sarah have a remedy?

5. Smits works for NMN Corporation as a deliverer of packages. His route takes him north and south on Route 1. He regularly stops at local diners in order to eat lunch and dinner.

   One day he leaves a diner and trips on some loose pavement in the parking lot. Smits falls down and breaks his arm. When he files for a workers' compensation claim, he is told that the injury was not job-related and he cannot recover. The state examiner tells him that when he left Route 1 he was no longer delivering packages, but was on his own time. Does Smits have any remedy?

6. Henry works for Niblit Corporation as a forklift operator. One day he is unloading some products from a truck. He places them on a forklift and then starts it up. Unfortunately, he backs the lift over his foot. He brings a claim under workers' compensation. He is told that because the accident was his fault, he may not collect any money. Does he have any remedy?

7. Jones is named pension manager of ZBT Corporation. He is thinking of placing all of the assets of the pension in ZBT stock. He has come to you for advice. What do you tell him?

8. Michael is a construction worker for the Handyman Company. In Michael's spare time he lifts weights and he has won several body-building titles. One day his female boss, Mary calls him into her office and asks Michael to pose for some pictures. He refuses, but she persists. This practice goes on for several weeks. When Michael continues to refuse to pose for the pictures, Mary fires him. Does he have any remedy?

PART VIII

BUSINESS ORGANIZATIONS

Chapter 26

Proprietorships and Partnerships

- The three major types of business organizations are proprietorships, partnerships, and corporations. A proprietorship is owned by one person. A partnership is owned by two or more persons. A corporation is an artificial entity owned by its shareholders. Corporations will be discussed in Chapter 27.

- A proprietor is individually liable for the debts and actions of the business. All partners are individually liable for the debts and actions of the partnership.

- A partnership is a fiduciary relationship in which the parties owe certain duties to one another to always act in the best interest of the partnership

- A partnership may be dissolved on the death of one or more of the partners, by agreement, and when certain acts occur. The partner who is responsible for dissolving the partnership and the individual partners have specific responsibilities to each other and to the parties with whom the partnership may have dealt during the dissolution stage.

- A limited partnership is a special type of partnership that allows people to make investments while limiting their role in the organization.

SOLE PROPRIETORSHIPS

A **proprietorship** is the most simple form of business organization. It is also the easiest to form because it requires only one person to organize it. A disadvantage is that only one person brings her abilities and resources to the business.

Another drawback to a sole proprietorship is that the sole proprietor is responsible for all the debts to creditors generated by the business. She is also responsible for all torts that she or the proprietorship may generate. The sole proprietor is also responsible for all fees and taxes that a business is responsible for paying.

- George operates a grocery store on the corner of Maple and Elm. The store has some difficult times and George owes a significant amount of debt. He also owes $3,000 from a lawsuit brought by a customer who slipped on a banana in the store. George's creditors and the customer may both file claims against George's business and his personal assets, including his house and car. ■

The main advantages of a sole proprietorship include ease of formation, ease of management, unrestricted use of profits, and relative freedom from governmental regulations. The disadvantages include lack of resources and personal liability.

PARTNERSHIPS

A **partnership** is an association of two or more persons acting together as partners in a trade, profession, or business in which the partners share profits and losses. But not every association is a partnership: various nonprofit associations and charitable groups do not make profits.

In some cases, there may be doubts about whether a partnership exists. A key test is whether the parties intended to create a partnership. Another test is whether the parties are dividing the profits and losses. A third test is whether the parties are actually conducting a business.

■ Dorothy, Sylvia, and Marilyn pool their resources as part of an investment club. They buy various stocks and bonds.

Although they divide their profits, they are not a partnership. There was no intent to create a partnership. In addition, pooling investment resources is not a business for profit. ■

A partnership is a fiduciary relationship in which each partner owes a duty of loyalty and trust to each other and to the partnership. The partners are agents of the partnership and of one another. Absent an agreement to the contrary, the partners will share profits and losses equally regardless of their contributions in terms of capital or work.

While a partnership agreement often accompanies the formation of a partnership, there need not be a specific contract. If there is an agreement, the usual rules relating to contracts will apply. The partnership contract must be for a lawful purpose, it must be supported by consideration, the parties must have capacity, and the contract must reflect a definite agreement about every material term.

The partnership and every one of the individual partners are liable for debts incurred by the partnership. In addition, because every partner is an agent of the partnership and of each of the other partners, every partner is liable for the authorized contracts and torts of one another.

■ Bob and Rob form a trucking partnership. Both Bob and Rob drive the trucks. If one of them should negligently injure someone while driving a truck, the partnership and the other partner would be personally liable. ■

A partnership may exist for a limited or an unlimited time. The length of the partnership ought to be spelled out in the partnership agreement. Similarly, the agreement may state the nature of the activities of the partnership.

A partnership should be distinguished from a **joint venture.** This latter type of business organization has become very popular in an international economy with rapidly changing technology and markets. Joint ventures can be formed for limited purposes and for limited periods of time. In addition, some corporations have been forming joint ventures that allow them to take advantage of each other's special skills without all the liabilities associated with being a partner.

Partners' Duties and Rights

A partner normally makes a capital contribution when entering the partnership. Often, the partners' share of the partnership's profits will depend on the amount of the capital contribution. The partnership capital contribution may be in the form of property, services, or money.

Partnership property that is bought with partnership funds is generally held in the name of the partnership. It is presumed that property held in the partnership's name or used in the business belongs to the partnership.

But it is quite common for a partner to use personal property in the partnership business. If it is unclear whether the property belongs to the individual or to the partnership, the intent of the parties controls. This intent can be determined from the funds used to purchase the property, the name in which it was held, how it was used, and any other factors that may show intent.

Partnership property may be used by any of the partners in the business. Each partner has an equal share in partnership property although this does not mean that a partner may take away his share.

When a partner dies, his share of partnership property belongs to the partnership and not to his heirs. But the heirs must be paid the value of the deceased partner's accrued profits and share of future profits. This is a reason to make provisions for dealing with these issues in the partnership agreement.

A common way of coping with this problem is to obtain life insurance on each of the partners. When the partner dies, the insurance policy's proceeds may be used to pay the heirs of the partner.

Management of Partnership

The articles of partnership will normally outline the rights and responsibilities of each of the partners with respect to the management of the partnership. If nothing is said, each of the partners has an equal right to participate and vote regarding the management of the partnership.

In many partnerships, an executive or management committee is responsible for the day-to-day management of the partnership. Some partnerships will have a senior or managing partner who is responsible for managing the partnership's financial affairs. The executive committee may have significantly more power than the majority of individual partners, which may be permissible if it is permitted by the articles of partnership or the bylaws.

■ Douglas is the managing partner for a major law firm. He and the senior partner form the executive committee. The bylaws give him the power to fire any partner he thinks is violating the partnership agreement. Douglas believes that one of the partners, Michael, is preparing to leave the firm and take some clients with him. Douglas discharges Michael and has him removed from the building until he can schedule a hearing in front of all the partners. Douglas has the power to do this if he complies with the provisions of the partnership agreement and bylaws. ■

The partnership agreement should also establish how major decisions are reached. The articles and bylaws may provide for a two-thirds majority or any other method they want. If no method is stated, each of the partners will have a vote and decisions will be made by majority vote.

The partnership agreement should be in writing if the partnership is going to buy and sell real estate or securities. The agreement should also state who has the authority to agree to contracts on behalf of the partnership. If nothing is said, every partner is presumed to have the authority to agree to contracts that are in the normal course of the partnership's business.

> ■ Pete and Jim form a partnership for the purpose of selling tennis equipment. Unless there is a different agreement, both Pete and Jim will have the authority to buy and sell inventory and to hire and fire partnership employees. ■

This does not mean that a partner has the authority to do everything on behalf of the partnership. For example, a partner does not usually have the authority to sell real estate owned by the partnership without the consent of the other partners, unless the partnership is in the business of buying and selling real estate.

In addition, a partner may not forgive large debts owed to the partnership, sell partnership property, or settle major litigation without the consent of the other partners. A partner may also not take any action that would interfere with the partnership business. This would include attempts to dissolve the partnership. While a third party can assume a partner has authority to perform routine transactions, she should check into the partner's authority to engage in major transactions that affect the partnership.

> ■ Mike is a partner with M and H partnership. He deals on a regular basis with Joan. She can presume that Mike has the authority to sell her inventory from the partnership. She should not presume that Mike has the authority to sell the building that houses the partnership. ■

Profits and Losses

The partnership agreement should state how the partnership profits will be shared. If nothing is said in the agreement, the partners will share profits and losses equally. If the agreement states how profits will be shared but says nothing about losses, the losses should be shared on the same basis as profits.

To avoid bad feelings later, the partnership agreement should state how profits are shared. The agreement could split up profits based on capital contributions or on the services that the partners provide to the partnership. The partners could also agree to pay salaries or other compensation for work performed on behalf of the partnership.

Some partnerships are divided into senior and junior partners. Partnerships can also employ associates who normally earn salaries or wages. A partner's compensation usually depends on the level of profits, although each partner might take income payments throughout the year.

A partner may not assign his share of partnership property, but may assign the **interest in partnership profits.** In addition, while a partner may not bequeath his share of partnership **property** to his heirs, he may bequeath his share of partnership **profits** to heirs. This also means that creditors can attach a partner's share of partnership profits.

> ■ B, D, and G partnership has three partners, Barbara, Dinah, and George. Barbara has contributed $100,000. Dinah has contributed $50,000 and George has contributed $50,000. The partnership agreement provides that each partner will share profits in accordance with the amount of her capital contributions.

The partnership earned net profits of $400,000 in 1994. Barbara would be entitled to $200,000. Dinah and George would be entitled to $100,000 each. George had managed to acquire debts of over $100,000 during the year. His creditors would be able to attach his share of profits, but not his proportionate share of partnership property. ■

Partners' Fiduciary Duties

Each partner is an agent of every other partner and of the partnership. As an agent, a partner has the duty to always act on behalf of the partnership and to avoid self-dealing. This includes the duty to refer all business opportunities to the partnership and not to use the knowledge for his own benefit. The duties of loyalty and good faith include the duty not to compete.

■ Hillary and Julie form a partnership to make and sell wines. One of Julie's duties is to find land suitable for growing grapes. During one of her trips, Julie finds a valuable piece of land and buys it for herself. ■

This is a violation of her duties of loyalty and good faith. The partnership would be able to recover any lost profits because of the breach of the duty not to compete.

A partner must exercise reasonable business judgment on behalf of the partnership. This does not mean that she can never make a mistake or have a business venture fail. It does mean that she should not act recklessly or in disregard of the interests of the partnership.

■ Joe is a partner at H and F partnership. Despite the instructions of Frank, the senior partner, not to buy any products from Nelson, Joe orders a substantial number of items from him at a significant cost.
    As usual, Nelson's products are defective and this costs the partnership a large amount of money. Joe did not exercise sound business judgment and could be held liable by the partnership. ■

While a partner normally has the implied authority to engage in certain activities on behalf of the partnership, including entering into contracts, this does not mean the partner can do whatever she wants. If the partner exceeds her authority, she can be held liable by the partners and the partnership.

Liability

Partners can be held personally liable for the actions of other partners as well as the partnership generally. This liability extends to responsibility for both contracts and torts. This is one reason that it is important to screen partners carefully for judgment and maturity.

■ Jeff has been a long-term associate of Pipes Unlimited. During this time, he primarily had responsibility for ordering limited quantities of pipes and tobacco. After seven years of employment, he is named a partner by Beth and Bob, the two existing partners. The new title goes to Jeff's head and he soon contracted with Oliver, a supplier with whom Jeff had previously dealt, for $2,000,000 in pipes and tobacco. This was an excessive amount of inventory for a relatively small store. Despite this, the partnership, Beth, Bob, and Jeff are all liable on the contract.

If the partners breach the contract, each of them can be held liable for the full amount. If Pipes has only a small amount of assets, Bob, Beth, and Jeff will have to reach into their personal assets to pay any money damages owed to Oliver. ■

If one of the partners commits a tort, the plaintiff should name the partnership and each of the partners in the complaint and summons. This permits the plaintiff to hold the partnership and every partner liable for any injuries.

■ Clark is a partner with BO & Associates. The other partners are Bill and Ollie. One day, Clark is driving a partnership car. He runs a stop light and crashes into Wilson's vehicle. Both Wilson and his wife are severely injured.

The Wilsons' attorney names the partnership, and Bill, Ollie, and Clark in the complaint. If the partnership does not have adequate assets to pay for the Wilsons' injuries, he may reach the personal assets of each of the partners. In cases of severe personal injuries, this means that the partnership's assets may be drastically reduced or eliminated by a substantial lawsuit. In addition, the partners might lose a meaningful amount of their own personal assets if the partnership assets are insufficient. ■

This example also illustrates the importance of the partnership carrying adequate insurance to protect the business and the partners from these types of lawsuits. In addition, the partners should insure that they are personally covered by partnership insurance or have their own individual policies.

Changes in Partnership

It is common for a partnership to have changes in partners. The addition of new partners or the deletion of existing partners should be provided for in the partnership agreement. In most law and accounting partnerships, decisions regarding the admission of a new partner is one of great significance for both the incoming partner and for the firm itself.

The new partner usually makes a capital contribution to the firm. While the new partner is not personally liable for actions of the firm before she became a partner, her capital contribution is part of the partnership assets. She also will be subject to future partnership debts.

■ Joan has worked at the law firm of Sueman and Slicer for eight years when she is offered a partnership. The firm has an outstanding claim of $100,000 as the result of a settlement with a client who tripped over a box of files carelessly left near one of the office doors.

Joan contributes $25,000 to partnership capital. While Joan's personal assets are not subject to the $100,000 debt, her fellow partners could use her contribution to help pay it. ■

A partner may also leave the partnership. She may decide to retire or to move on to other avenues of employment. While a partner who has left is liable for debts incurred while she was a partner, she will not be liable for future debts.

Because the partner is an agent for the partnership, the partnership should notify persons with whom the partner had previously dealt that she is leaving. The partnership should also place a notice in a paper of general circulation that the partner is leaving. The notice will put people with whom the partner has not dealt on notice that the partner will not be responsible for future debts, and that the partner may no longer act on behalf of the partnership.

The partnership will be protected from unauthorized actions of former partners if it complies with these notice requirements. If will be subject to liability for improper actions by a retiring partner if the partnership does not comply.

■ Allen is a partner with ZT partnership. Allen was responsible for arranging travel for partners, customers, suppliers, and other employees for ZT. Allen leaves the partnership on bad terms after some disagreements with the other partners.

The partnership does *not* notify the travel agents with whom Allen dealt when he leaves. He arranges trips for himself and several friends to Hawaii and bills the trips to ZT. ZT will be liable for these trips because it did not comply with the notice requirements. ■

■ Linda worked for ZBT partnership. As a partner, she was responsible for purchasing steel plates. When she leaves, Linda orders ten steel plates for her own use from Sam's Steel, which has received notice of her departure.

ZBT will not be responsible for her order because it provided notice to Sam. If it placed a notice in the paper, it will not be responsible for orders Linda may place with new customers or suppliers. ■

Ending the Partnership

A partnership may end because of the mutual agreement of the partners. Because a partnership is a consensual agreement, the partners may end it at any time. There will be no liability unless there has been a violation of the partnership agreement to the detriment of one or more of the partners.

If a partner dies, the partnership will terminate unless the partnership agreement provides to the contrary. This is a major reason to have an agreement. Major law and accounting firms would not be able to operate if they had to rearrange the partnership whenever a partner passed away or retired.

■ Sincere and Old have 40 senior partners, 70 junior partners, 100 associates, and 200 other employees. The partnership agreement is regularly updated. The partnership takes out insurance on all the senior partners. If one of them dies, the insurance goes to the family and the agreement provides that this will be the sole compensation for the deceased partner's family. ■

Bankruptcy of a partner does not necessarily end the partnership, although a bankrupt partner's ability to obtain or guarantee credit is reduced. This may affect the partnership's ability to obtain credit because its credit standing is bolstered by the personal liability of each partner. In addition, the bankruptcy of one or more partners may significantly impact the partnership's ability to conduct its business. If the bankruptcy adversely affects the essential purpose of the partnership, it may dissolve the partnership as a matter of law.

■ Lender and Ketchum offer financial advice and specialized loan services for their clients. In order to lend money they must be able to borrow it from other sources. The banks and other financial institutions rely on the partnership's and individual partners' credit in order to be repaid.

If Ketchum goes bankrupt, it will severely affect the credit of the partnership as well as its essential business purpose. The partnership should be dissolved. ■

Because a partnership is a contract, it would be dissolved by the intervening illegality of the subject matter or lack of capacity on the part of the partners.

■ Sam and Dave have a partnership with the specific purpose of selling alcoholic beverages to 21 to 25-year-olds. They do research, conduct a variety of tests and develop new products to reach this market. The entire partnership business is built around this market niche.

Because of a series of fatal car crashes related to drunken driving, the state legislature decides to raise the legal drinking age from 21 to 25 in order to prevent people in their early twenties from driving drunk. Because of the intervening illegality, the partnership should be dissolved unless the parties can restructure the partnership with a different purpose. ■

Unless the parties had sufficient mental capacity when they entered into the partnership agreement, the agreement is voidable. If the parties had capacity at the time of the agreement, but one of them lost capacity, the agreement should be dissolved.

■ Sam and Sarah have a partnership to sell glass bowls. The partnership continues for several years until Sam becomes insane.

The partnership should be dissolved. If Sam is insane, he will no longer be capable of performing his duties as a partner. ■

Winding up the Partnership

Dissolution is the moment in time when the purpose of the partnership changes from conducting partnership business to that of ending the partnership. The partnership may reorganize itself into a new partnership. If it does not, it should begin the process of winding up its affairs.

The first step would be to cease conducting new business other than routine activities that are necessary to ending the partnership. A "winding-up" partner should be named to perform these activities. Her responsibility is to perform those duties necessary to winding up the partnership and beginning to liquidate partnership assets.

As the "winding-up" partner liquidates partnership assets and collects outstanding bills, she will have a pool of cash to distribute. She should first pay creditors of the partnership. Her next distribution should be to creditors of the individual partners. She should then pay individual partners who made loans to the partnership.

The winding-up partner's next distribution should be to refund the capital contributions made by the individual partners. If a sufficient amount is not available, the partners should be paid in amounts proportionate to the amounts contributed. Finally, if any assets remain, they should be distributed in accordance with the partnership's provisions with respect to the sharing of profits.

■ Barbara has finished liquidating the assets and collecting the debts of the BAD partnership. She has $500,000 in cash available.

The partnership has $100,000 in outstanding debts. Each of the three individual partners have outstanding debts of $50,000. Charles, a partner, made a loan to the partnership of $50,000. Each partner made a capital contribution of $50,000. The partners have agreed to split profits equally. This distribution would be as follows:

Amount available for distributions: $500,000,

Less:

Partnership debts	$100,000
Partners' debts	$150,000
Repay loan to Charles	$ 50,000
Repay capital contribution	$150,000
Subtotal	$450,000
Remaining profits for distribution:	$ 50,000

Each partner should receive $16,666.66. ■

■ Alex is the winding-up partner for ABC partnership. After collecting debts and liquidating assets, he has $600,000 in cash. Partnership debts amount to $500,000. Alex made a capital contribution of $100,000 and Beth and Charlie both made contributions of $50,000 each. There are no loans. Each partner has agreed to share the profits equally. Alex should divide up the cash as follows:

Amount to be distributed:	$600,000
Less: Partnership debts	$500,000
Subtotal	$100,000

Total contributions are $200,000
Amount available equals $100,000
Proportionate share equals $100,000–$200,000 = 50%
Alex should receive $50,000 and Beth and Charlie should receive $25,000 each. There are no profits available for distribution. ■

■ Harriet is the winding-up partner for HIJ partnership. She has cash of $800,000. There are partnership debts of $500,000 and the creditors of individual partners have claims of $250,000. Harriet loaned the partnership $50,000. The three partners made capital contributions of $100,000 each.

In this case, the partnership and individual partner's creditors will be paid. Harriet will be repaid her loan ($500,000 + $250,000 + $50,000 = $800,000). The partners will not recover their capital contributions or receive any profits. ■

Limited Partnership

A **limited partnership** gives a person the right to make an investment in the partnership without becoming a general partner. A limited partner has no right to take part in management and does not share in profits to the same extent as a general partner.

Conversely, a limited partner does not have unlimited liability for the debts of the partnership. This frees the limited partner from much of the liability associated with partnership contracts or partnership torts. This is one of the major advantages of being a limited partner. One can invest in the partnership and share in profits while avoiding the unlimited liability of general partners.

A limited partnership should file a certificate with the state. This puts creditors on notice of the existence of the partnership and also protects the limited partners from being identified as general partners.

The limited partners should not allow their names to be in the partnership name. In addition, they should stay away from the day-to-day management of the partnership or from becoming involved in relationships with creditors. A limited partner who leads a creditor to believe that she is a general partner or who has put her credit on the line will be held liable for any credit extended to the partnership.

> ■ Bombastic Bert is a limited partner in ZBT. He owns about 100 units out of the 1,000 limited partnership units outstanding. He has no general partnership interest or rights. However, he regularly tells creditors, customers, and suppliers that he is actually running the partnership and that he calls all the shots. This would lead a reasonable third party to believe Bombastic Bert has placed his personal credit in support of partnership debts. ■

Limited partners may buy and sell their interests in accord with the partnership agreement. Limited partnerships have proven to be extremely valuable tools for high-risk ventures such as oil exploration. They allow people to make investments and earn a profit while reducing risk to an acceptable level.

Definitions Reviewed

Proprietorship is a business run by one person.

Partnership is an association of two or more persons to run a business for profit.

Joint venture is a short-term partnership.

Interest in partnership profits is a partner's right to share in partnership profits that are assignable to another person.

Dissolution purpose of partnership changes from earning a profit to winding down the business.

Limited partnership allows people to invest in the partnership without becoming general partners.

Core Concepts Reviewed

■ A partnership is an association of two or more persons who carry on a business for profit. The partners have a fiduciary relationship with each other and the partnership. They must be loyal, act in good faith, and always act in the best interests of the partnership.

■ Partners are also agents of each other. As agents, they have the authority to bind one another to contracts, and will be liable for each other's torts. This liability extends to partnership assets and the personal assets of each partner.

■ A partner may enter into contracts on behalf of the partnership. Normally, every partner may bind the partnership on normal business matters. Extraordinary matters require the approval of the partnership in accordance with the partnership agreement, by laws or other rules of procedure.

■ A partnership may be terminated by the mutual agreement of the partners. It may also be terminated by the withdrawal of a partner and by operation of law.

■ Dissolution of the partnership is that moment in time when the pupose of the partnership changes from pursuing the original business purposes to winding up the partnership business. At that moment, the partnership should cease performing activities that will extend the partnership, and start collecting debts and liquidating partnership assets.

■ Upon dissolution, the winding-up partner should first pay the partnership's creditors and then the creditors of the individual partners. After the creditors are paid, loans to partners should be refunded. Capital contributions may then be repaid. The distribution of what remains may then be paid out as partnership profits.

■ Limited partnerships have at least one general partner who operates the partnership and has unlimited personal liability. It has limited partners who generally are not personally liable for partnership actions.

Questions

1. Define partnership.
2. What are some key tests in determining if a partnership exists?
3. What is a joint venture?
4. What are the partners' duties to the partnership?
5. What is a partner's liability with respect to the torts of an agent of the partnership?
6. Name some reasons why a partnership may be dissolved as a matter of law.
7. What is the priority of claims when a partnership is dissolved?
8. Explain how a limited partnership differs from a general partnership.
9. How should a limited partner minimize her liability?

Problems

1. Nan is a partner with the LMN partnership. Her two partners are Lucy and Mabel. The partnership has three vases in its reception area. Nan decides that one of the vases would look better in her living room. When her partners object, she tells them that there are three partners, three vases, and one of them belongs to her. Do Lucy and Mabel have a remedy?

2. Stu is partner with Harold and Tom in the SHT partnership. Stuart has become angry with Harold and Tom and has begun to disclose partnership information to some of the competition with a view to joining a competitor when he leaves the partnership. Harold and Tom protest, but Stuart states that he is a partner and there is nothing that they can do about it. Do Harold and Tom have a remedy?

3. Catherine is a partner with CDE partnership. She signs a contract with Fred to supply $400,000 of inventory to the partnership. This is far more than the usual order size and above what partners are expected to order without the consent of the other partners.

   Later, there is a dispute about the contract and the partnership does not pay the $400,000. Fred brings suit against CDE — Catherine, Davita, and Erica. Davita and Erica ask that the suit be dismissed on the grounds that they had not authorized the contract and should not be held responsible. Will they prevail?

4. Bob is a partner with Albert and Daniel in the BAD partnership. BAD sells clothing products for infants and children. One day, Bob is driving a BAD truck and the brakes fail.

   Bob crashes the truck into a school bus, strewing cargo across the road. One child is injured in the collision. Who should the child's attorney name in the lawsuit?

5. Lucretia is a partner with Ursula and Violet in the LUV partnership, which provides potions to the young couples' market. Lucretia is responsible for mixing the potions. One day, she adds too much bat blood and the potion comes out wrong. When applied, it tends to stain any part of the body to which it is applied. LUV, Lucretia, Ursula, and Violet are sued by Whitey, whose back is now a bright red. Ursula and Violet argue that mixing the potion is Lucretia's sole responsibility and that they should not be held liable. Will they prevail?

6. The CAT partnership is the process of dissolution. After collecting its debts and liquidating its assets, it has $600,000 in cash. The partnership owes debts of $300,000 and the individual partners have creditors to whom they owe $150,000.

   Charles, one of the partners, made a loan of $50,000 to the partnership. Charles, Ariel, and Tom all made capital contributions of $50,000 each. The partners had agreed to split profits equally. How should the $600,000 be distributed?

7. The LOS partnership had ageed to share profits, with Les receiving 40 percent and Oliver and Sam splitting the remaining 60 percent. Unfortunately, the LOS partnership had losses in the first year of operating of $20,000. How should they be split between the three?

8. Chauncy Uppercrust is a limited partner of the Goblotz and Gablotz partnership. The two general partners ask for permission to use his name, well known in the area, in exchange for an additional 100 limited partnership units.

   A plaintiff injured by one of Uppercrust, Goblotz and Gablotz drivers sues the partnership and names Uppercrust as well as Goblotz and Gablotz. Uppercrust argues that he is a limited partner and can not be held liable. Will he prevail?

Chapter 27

Corporations

■ A corporation is an "artificial person" with the same rights to conduct business as a natural person upon the granting of a charter of incorporation by the state in which it is incorporated.

■ A corporation is made up of shareholders, a board of directors, and corporate officers. Each of these groups has separate powers and responsibilities. Ultimately, the individual shareholders are the owners of the corporation. They delegate their ownership powers to a board of directors which has general responsibility for running the corporation. The corporate officers have specific responsibility for corporate activities.

■ One major advantage of the corporate form of organization is the limited liability it affords corporate shareholders. They can invest in the corporation by buying shares without incurring liability beyond the value of the shares.

■ There are private corporations whose purpose is to earn a profit on behalf of their shareholders. These are the corporations found in the business world. Not-for-profit corporations are those formed for some specific purpose other than to earn a profit. Hospitals, schools, and churches are often in this category. Public corporations are those established for governmental purposes.

■ Because corporations are chartered by the state, they are subject to many regulations designed to protect the public and the shareholders.

■ Officers and directors are fiduciaries of the corporation and must always act in the best interests of the shareholders. As agents of the corporation, they are subject to the requirements of good faith, loyalty, and reasonable business judgment. These issues have assumed greater importance in an increasingly turbulent business climate and litigious society.

CORPORATIONS

The development of the corporate form was a major advancement for the world of business. One could argue it was essential to permit the growth of the economy during the shift from a rural, farm-based economy into the urban industrial and postindustrial ages.

A corporation is an artificial person established by a charter granted to it by the state in which it was incorporated. A corporation may sue and be sued in its own name. It may enter into contracts and is protected by most of the constitutional rights that are afforded to a natural person.

A corporation's major advantage is its ability to raise resources by encouraging people to invest in the corporation in the expectation that it will earn profits. This will allow the corporation to distribute dividends and to achieve capital growth. Investors may buy stock without incurring the same liability associated with a sole proprietorship or partnership. The most an investor may lose is the amount she invested. Her personal assets are not at risk.

Another major advantage of the corporate form is that it permits perpetual life. Sole proprietors and partners will die, but a corporation can live forever. If it continues to adapt to the changing environment and to grow, a corporation can continue to survive.

Stockholders are not fiduciaries or agents of the corporation. They may not bind the corporation to contracts and the corporation is not responsible for their torts. The only right of the shareholders is to receive dividends declared by the board of directors and to share in any distribution of assets by the corporation.

The shareholders elect a board of directors which has responsibility for the management and financial well-being of the corporation. For many years, being a director was regarded as little more than an honorary position with not much responsibility. As many American industries and companies have declined and lost market share to foreign competitors, shareholders and other groups have begun to question the judgments of boards and to hold them responsible.

Among the duties of the board of directors is to select officers who will actually operate the corporation. The president has ultimate responsibility for running the corporation. The treasurer has responsibility for the financial affairs and keeping the financial records of the corporation. The board usually also names a secretary and one or more vice presidents.

Forming a Corporation

A corporation is formed by a **promoter** who encourages people to invest in it by purchasing stock subscriptions. A subscription is a contract to buy shares when the corporation is legally formed. The promoter may put together a prospectus that discusses the nature of the corporation's business and usually contains some financial information. If the promoter sells either shares or subscriptions to the general public, she must comply with federal and state securities laws that are designed to protect unsophisticated investors.

The **certificate of incorporation** sets forth the types of business activities in which the corporation will engage. The usual practice is to state these areas rather broadly so as not to restrict corporate activities in the future. The certificate also lists the name of the corporation. The organizers must select a name that will not be confused with a corporation of a similar name. It must be cleared by an official in the secretary of state's office.

The certificate must also indicate the location of the corporate offices. It must state where the corporation could be served legal process and could be reached by the secretary of state's office. The certificate must also state the number of shares and classes of stock the corporation may issue.

The most issued classes of stock are common and preferred. Common stock allows an investor to share in the profits of the corporation in the form of dividends. Investors hope that dividends will continue to grow, and that the stock's price will rise. Preferred stock is more similar to a bond. A shareholder will receive a regular dividend of a certain amount. The advantage for the preferred stockholder is that she can rely on the dividend, but, the dividend will stay the same and she will not share in the growth of the corporation.

The certificate should include any restrictions on the transfer of stock. Normally, stocks may be freely bought and sold in the marketplace. However, a corporation may want to restrict this right in order to control who is a shareholder. A closely held corporation is one in which the shares are owned by only a limited number of people. Most family-owned corporations are closely held corporations; the family wants to prevent outsiders from owning stock and interfering with corporate management. They may accomplish this objective by placing provisions in the certificate of incorporation and by putting a notice on the shareholder certificates that the corporation has a right to purchase the shares before they may be sold to anyone else.

This "right of first refusal" will be permitted because it serves a useful function. However, the notice must be placed in the certificate of incorporation to protect the public, and on the shareholder's certificate to protect the prospective buyer.

Other information may be included in the certificate of incorporation depending on the requirements of state law. These could include the names of directors, the original shareholders, information about dividends, and the accounting period. The objective is to give needed information to people who may deal with the corporation.

Promoter's Activities and Liabilities

The **promoter** is the person who organizes the corporation. She arranges to find buyers of stock subscriptions and shares of stock. She also finds an attorney who will do the legal work on behalf on the newly formed corporation. She will also hire an accountant who will begin organizing the new corporation's financial affairs and records.

The promoter may also begin to perform preliminary activities on behalf of the corporation. These could include ordering supplies or arranging for future services on behalf of the corporation. This raises issues about the extent of the promoter's personal liability for contracts primarily for the benefit of the corporation.

The promoter will be personally liable for contracts he has signed unless the corporation relieves him of liability by agreeing to accept liability for the contract.

■ Jones is the promoter for XYZ corporation. He agrees to a contract to obtain $500,000 worth of leather that XYZ will make into shoes for sale. Jones signed the contract with his own name and did not mention XYZ corporation.

If XYZ corporation is not formed, he will be liable on the contract. If XYZ is formed, he will remain liable on the contract unless its board of directors agrees to accept liability for the contract. ■

This example highlights a challenge for promoters. They must engage in activities to get the corporation started, activities for which they can be held liable. It is important for the promoter to ensure that the directors will ratify his contracts. The usual practice is to have close friends or relatives serve as directors of the new corporation.

The promoter will not be liable to the other party if he made it clear that he was agreeing to the contract on behalf of the corporation.

■ Smith is the promoter of the RMN corporation. He agrees to a contract with Hanson to supply $600,000 worth of materials to be used in RMN's manufacturing process. He signs the contract as follows: "William Smith, promoter on behalf of the RMN corporation, a soon-to-be-formed corporation under the laws of New Jersey."

This signature clearly places Hanson on notice that Smith has agreed to this contract only on behalf of RMN. Hanson should know that Smith is not assuming liability in the event that RMN is not formed. ■

Board of Directors

After the certificate of incorporation has been filed and approved, the directors should meet and begin the process of organizing the corporation. The directors have the fiduciary duty of managing the corporation and safeguarding the interests of the shareholders.

At the first meeting, the board of directors should select a chairman of the board, choose the major officers of the corporation, approve any contracts on behalf of the corporation agreed to by the promoter, approve the issuance of stock and the stock certificate, adopt bylaws, the minutes book, and the corporation's other documents. The board should also select an accountant, legal counsel, and the corporation's bank accounts.

Although it may delegate the daily activities of the corporation to corporate officers, the board of directors remains responsible for the management of the corporation. The members of the board must act in the interests of the shareholders rather than their own.

■ Frank is a member of the board of directors of XYZ corporation. He learned at a board meeting that the corporation is going to build a major new plant on the corner of Peachtree and Magnolia streets.

Frank buys up a significant amount of land in the area surrounding that corner. These actions are in violation of Frank's fiduciary duty to the corporation. He will be liable for any loss to the corporation resulting from his actions. ■

■ Sam is a member of the board of directors of EDC corporation. He convinces the other directors to grant him a loan of corporate funds at an annual interest rate substantially below that of market rates.

Sam has violated his fiduciary responsibility to the shareholders. The other directors may also have violated their obligations to the corporation. ■

■ Sharpie is a member of the FAT corporation board of directors. He learns that FAT is negotiating with a number of vendors regarding the purchase of a major portion of the annual inventory.

Sharpie calls one of the vendors and reveals some of the information he learned at the directors meeting. This would be in violation of his fiduciary duty to FAT. ■

The corporate officers have similar responsibilities to the corporation. Although they are employees, they are also agents. As agents they must always act in the corporation's best interests.

■ ZBT corporation receives a merger offer from MNO corporation. Tom, president of ZBT, worries that he will lose his position if ZBT is merged with MNO. He recommends to his board of directors that the merger be disapproved. This would be in violation of his fiduciary duty to do what is in ZBT corporation's best interests. ■

If either the directors or the officers violate their duties to the corporation's shareholders, the shareholders may ask the board to take action to correct the situation. The board of directors has a responsibility to prevent violations of the fiduciary duty of corporate directors and officers.

If the board fails to act, the shareholders may bring a **derivative suit** to require the board to act. The courts have required that shareholders first exhaust all possible remedies within the corporation before asking the courts to intervene.

■ Gary is the President of ZXY Corp. He regularly arranges to have corporate property sold to him at reduced prices. Because the board is controlled by Gary and his friends, it does nothing to stop the practice.

Several shareholders go to Gary and request that he stop these actions. He tells them he is doing nothing wrong. The shareholders then speak against the practice at a meeting of the board of directors. The board chairman states that the directors will look into the matter.

One year passes and despite additional written requests from the shareholders, Gary continues to sell himself corporate property and the directors still do nothing. It would now be appropriate for the shareholders to bring suit and ask a court to stop these practices. ■

Restrictions on Limited Liability

One of the advantages of the corporate form is that shareholders normally have their liability limited to the amount of money they have invested. However, in corporations in which there is only one or a few shareholders, this limited liability will not apply if it is used to commit a fraud or to promote an injustice. The courts will disregard the corporate form and hold the shareholder individually liable. This is called **piercing the corporate veil.**

■ Jack is sole shareholder of Jak, Inc. He regularly mingles his personal assets with corporate assets. In addition, Jack drives the corporation car on both personal and Jak business nearly every day. One day, he runs into Sally's car and injures her severely. Jack quickly shifts many of his personal assets into the corporation.

In this case, the court will not permit the corporate form to shield Jack from personal liability for his negligence. The court will pierce the corporate veil and allow Sally to recover from both Jack and Jak assets. ■

Generally, the corporate veil will be pierced when personal and corporate conduct seem to merge. If personal and corporate assets are commingled, the courts are more likely to pierce the corporate veil. Courts are also more likely to disregard the corporate form if someone is attempting to use the form to prevent enforcement of an existing judgment.

> ■ Lou is the sole owner of HMR, Inc. He has a substantial number of personal debts and owes a significant amount of money to a Ms. Baby Boothe.
>
> Ms. Boothe brings an action to collect, and is awarded a substantial judgment. Lou immediately shifts personal assets into HMR, Inc. If Ms. Boothe later brings an action to enforce the judgment against Lou and HMR, Inc., the court will pierce the corporate veil in order to allow Ms. Boothe to collect. Lou's actions verge on fraud, and it would be an injustice not to allow Ms. Boothe to collect. ■

This does not mean that the corporate structure will be disregarded simply because the corporation has a sole owner. The law encourages the use of the corporate form to limit personal liability because it serves a useful social function. If there is no evidence of fraud or attempts to commit an injustice, the corporate shield will be preserved.

> ■ Frank constructs new buildings and shopping malls. He has accumulated a substantial amount of wealth. He decides to build a new shopping area near his home. He forms a new corporation called Berry Hill, Inc. He uses the corporation to raise money and build the shopping center. Frank constructs a beautiful shopping center, but the economy falls into a recession and the shopping center does poorly.
>
> Berry Hill, Inc., has a substantial number of debts and creditors. Berry Hill, Inc., does not have enough money to pay off the creditors, who seek to attach Frank's personal assets. In this case, there is no evidence of fraud or improper conduct. The corporate form will protect Frank's personal assets. ■

Private Corporations

Private corporations are those found in the business world. They range from giants such as AT&T, Exxon, McDonald's, and IBM to small, locally based businesses like printing shops, dry cleaners, and auto repair stores.

The larger corporations are publicly held and are subject to rules and regulations regarding the sale of securities and the reporting of profits. Smaller corporations are usually called closely held corporations because their shares are held by a small number of people.

As noted earlier, closely held corporations normally place restrictions on the sale of shares in the certificate of incorporation as well as on each share of stock. Normally, the restriction gives the corporation the right to purchase shares from a holder before they can be sold to any other party.

> ■ CSM, Inc., is a small corporation that is entirely held by the C. S. Manson family. The corporation placed restrictions on the sale for shares in the certificate of incorporation and on each share of stock.
>
> Mabel Manson becomes angry with the other family members and attempts to sell her shares to Bert Bombastic. CSM, Inc., can prevent the sale by invoking their right of first refusal. ■

Other Types of Corporations

Public corporations are those that serve some governmental function. These may include school districts, towns, villages, cities, and townships. These corporations are also given their charters by the state. They are instruments of the state and may be abolished or changed by the state government at any time. Many people believe their town or school district has some inherent or constitutional right to exist, but this is not true.

■ Students from the Dokes City schools have consistently failed the state's high-school proficiency test. The schools have become so bad that their nickname is "Flunk City."

The governor of the state has the authority to order a state takeover of Dokes City's schools in order to make sure that students receive an adequate education. The governor takes this action. The school district has no remedy. ■

■ The town of New Regency discovers that its police chief and half of the police department were selling drugs to the young athletes in the Police Athletic League. The state government has the authority to step in and take over either the town or its police department. ■

Public corporations may also include special-purpose organizations such as the U.S. Post Office, the Federal Deposit Insurance Corporation, state and local authorities, and other organizations. Special-purpose public corporations are likely to become more important in the future to cope with needs like waste cleanup, recycling, and garbage removal.

These special-purpose public corporations also offer opportunities to do some creative governmental financing. They can issue bonds and raise revenues that are not a part of regular governmental operations. These bonds can result in tax-exempt income for investors and the completion of necessary projects for governmental units.

Subchapter S corporations allow the corporation to be treated as a partnership for income tax purposes. Normally, corporations must pay taxes on corporate net income, and then the shareholders must pay individual taxes on the dividends they receive. This results in a double taxation on income for corporate investors. The federal subchapter S provisions allow investors to avoid this burden while still retaining the limited liability associated with corporations. This is particularly helpful to small businesspeople.

Professional corporations allow individuals who practice professions such as law, medicine, or accounting to incorporate. This permits them to achieve income tax advantages beyond those in a partnership. They also allow professionals to defer earnings and place them into favorable retirement accounts. Normally, the corporate form does not shield them from liability for malpractice.

Nonprofit and not-for-profit corporations are those organized for charitable or community purposes, such as colleges, hospitals, and churches. The income cannot be distributed to participants, but must be reinvested in the corporation or put back into the community.

STATE OF INCORPORATION

There is no inherent right to incorporate a business. The privilege of incorporation is one granted by the state. A charter allowing incorporation will be approved only if the incorporators comply with all state laws. The charter may also be revoked if the corporation does not comply with state rules and regulations, pay taxes, or commit other improper acts.

If an organization incorporates in a particular state, it is called a domestic corporation. If it does business in a particular state but is incorporated in another state, it is called a foreign corporation. This does not mean that it is a corporation from another country.

■ WNO, Inc., is incorporated in Delaware but also does business in New Jersey. WNO would be a domestic corporation in Delaware, but a foreign corporation to New Jersey. ■

A corporation from another country is called an international corporation. Like an American corporation in a foreign country, it may be subject to a variety of requirements of the state in which it wishes to do business.

States may not impose undue burdens on foreign corporations in a way that would interfere with interstate commerce. However, the states may impose requirements necessary to protect the health, safety, and welfare of its citizens. While the federal constitution's interstate commerce clause prevents unreasonable restrictions on out-of-state businesses, each state is a sovereign and may exercise reasonable powers to protect the community. Such activities as fraud, deceptive business practices, or antitrust violations could result in the revocation of the corporate charter.

FRANCHISES

One of the fastest growing businesses is that of franchising. A franchise allows a person to have his or her own business and earn profits while taking advantage of the national reputation and resources of a larger entity.

The organization that grants franchise rights to another is called the **franchisor**. McDonald's is a franchise operation whose business is built on this premise. Similar franchises have been able to take advantage of this desire to be one's own boss.

The person who acquires the franchise rights is called the **franchisee**. This person usually pays a certain amount of money and is granted the right to own a franchise. She also normally receives exclusive rights within a particular area. The franchisor also supports the franchisee with training, marketing activities, and other support services.

An interesting legal question is often raised with respect to franchisor and franchisee relationships. The issue is whether this relationship is an agency or if it is more similar to the legal concept of an independent contractor. The courts have decided this issue based on the amount of control the franchisor has over the franchisee.

■ Zeke owns a Rattle Prince franchise, which gives him the right to sell rattlesnake meat at a Rattle Prince stand in the town of Dry Gulch. Rattle Prince made Zeke attend Rattle University where he learned how to cook rattlesnake meat, how to mix a rattlesnake cooler, and how to make rattlesnake pie. They also taught him general operations and specific techniques of running a Rattle Prince franchise.

Rattle Prince also requires Zeke to purchase all of his meat from the franchisor. In addition, Zeke must also purchase every cup, napkin, and plate from Rattle Prince. Furthermore, Rattle Prince regularly sends an inspector to check on Zeke's stand in Dry Gulch where every phase of his operation is monitored. Every Rattle Prince has similar, although not identical, prices for its products.

In this case, Zeke does look like an agent because of the high degree of control Rattle Prince exercises over him. As a result, Rattle Prince would be liable for torts that Zeke might commit. ■

This does not mean that every franchise will be held to be an agent of the franchisor. In this example, nearly every phase of the franchisee's business is controlled by the franchisor. If fewer elements are controlled, the franchisee will not be an agent.

The franchise agreement is a contract and is subject to the usual requirements of contract law. The agreement must reflect a definite meeting of the minds and should include the price of the license which the franchisor is granting to the franchisee. It should also include the territory the franchise covers as well as the length of time being granted.

It might also include information about the number and types of products and services the franchisee must purchase from the franchisor. In addition, it should list the services the franchisor will provide to the franchisee.

Although franchisors want to maintain a degree of uniformity throughout their franchises, they should be careful to avoid requiring franchises to set certain prices for products or services. It is permissible to suggest certain prices, but it is a violation of antitrust laws to require those prices.

■ Burpee Gas Company offers franchises to sell its gas and other fuel-related products throughout the United States. If it requires the Burpee Stations to sell its gas, oil, fuel filters, and other products at the same price, it is probably in violation of antitrust laws. If it merely suggests, but allows each station to set its own prices, it is probably safe. ■

Ultra Vires Actions

A corporation may perform only those activities stated in the certificate of incorporation. Actions that are not stated in the certificate are regarded as improper or **ultra vires**. At common law, a contract that was made by the corporation and was not within the certificate's provisions, could be set aside either by the corporation or the other party. The premise was that since the corporate actions were ultra vires, the contract was void.

Later decisions recognized that this gave the other party an unfair advantage. If that party believed the contract was to its advantage, it could proceed to enforce it. If it did not, it could claim the contract was ultra vires and argue it was void. Later decisions have rejected many of these previous rulings.

The concept of ultra vires acts still has legal relevance. The shareholders may request the directors to have the corporation stop performing ultra vires acts. They may also ask the court to order the corporation to stop these acts if the directors will not do so.

> ■ The ABC Corporation was chartered to manufacture sports equipment. It begins to get into oil exploration. The shareholders believe this is too risky and ask the directors to stop. They may bring a court action that would order the directors to stop if the board refuses. ■

The state is also an interested party to ultra vires actions. If a corporation is performing activities outside the scope of its charter, the state's attorney general's office may order the corporation to stop, or it might go to court and obtain an injunction ordering them to cease such activities.

The ultra vires doctrine has less significance than in previous years. Attorneys for corporations attempt to ensure that the language in the certificate is as broad as possible. In addition, the suggestion of state action is usually all that is necessary for the directors to stop these activities.

Definitions Reviewed

Certificate of incorporation is the document that forms the corporation.

The **Promoter** is the person responsible for forming a corporation.

Derivative suit allows the shareholders to sue the board of directors on behalf of the corporation.

Piercing the corporate veil is when a court will look past the corporate form and hold the individual shareholder(s) personally liable.

Public corporations are governmental units.

Subchapter S corporations allow shareholders to be treated as partners for tax purposes.

Franchisor is the person granting a franchise.

Franchisee is the person receiving a franchise.

Ultra vires is an act outside of the corporate activities permitted by the articles of incorporation.

Core Concepts Reviewed

■ Corporations are "artificial persons" composed of investors who are granted a certificate of incorporation by a state in order to perform the activities outlined in the certificate. A corporation may enter into contracts in its own name, sue, and be sued in its own name.

■ The major advantages of the corporate form are its access to individual resources, limited liability for shareholders, and a potentially unlimited life.

■ The officials responsible for the management of a corporation are the board of directors. They must exercise reasonable business judgment on its behalf, and they have a fiduciary duty to the corporation, each other, and to the shareholders to act with loyalty to the shareholders' interests.

■ The daily operation of the corporation is delegated to the management, which is normally headed by a president who is the chief operating officer and a treasurer who is responsible for the corporation's financial affairs and records.

■ Types of corporations include private corporations (which predominate in the world of business), not-for-profit corporations, and public corporations.

■ Ultra vires acts are outside the scope of the corporate charter. Shareholders and the state may bring an action to stop such acts.

■ Franchises are growing in importance in the business community. A franchisor grants the franchisee the right to use its trade name.

Questions

1. What are some advantages and disadvantages of the corporate form of organization?

2. What is a public corporation?
3. What is a franchise?
4. What is a shareholder's derivative action? When is it appropriate?
5. What are the main duties of a promoter?
6. When will a promoter be held liable under a contract? When will a promoter not be held liable?
7. What is an ultra vires act? Why has the ultra vires docttine diminished in importance in recent years?
8. What is the doctrine of piercing the corporate veil? When will it be applied?
9. Discuss the reasonable business judgment rule.
10. What is a subchapter S corporation?

Problems

1. Sam is a director of ZBT company. He learns at a board meeting that ZBT will be building a major furniture construction plant in the town of Blatz. Sam quickly buys the lumber mill down the street at a reduced price. Does ZBT have any remedy?

2. Hartwick is a director for NOP, Inc. He demands that the president put his girlfriend on the payroll even though she has no qualifications. The president does as he is told. Do the shareholders have any remedies? Against whom do they have remedies?

3. Paul is the promoter for the soon-to-be-formed HIJ Corporation. He signs a contract with Jane to have 1,000 bales of polyester to be delivered to his home. The contract is for the benefit of HIJ, but he signs it just "Paul." The directors decide the contract is not in the interests of HIJ and refuse to approve it. What is Paul's liability?

4. Pamela is the promoter for KLM Corporation. She enters into a contract with Max to supply 10,000 flanges to the KLM headquarters. She signs the contract "Pamela, agent for KLM Corp." Max argues that because KLM has not yet been formed, Pamela cannot be its agent and is personally liable on the contract. Is he correct?

5. Joe is a member of the POR Corporation board of directors. Unfortunately, his own business activities require him to be frequently absent. POR gets into severe financial difficulty because of the mismanagement of corporate funds by its treasurer.

   When the shareholders bring an action against Joe and the other directors for negligence, Joe claims he could not be held liable because he missed many meetings while he was out of town. Is he correct?

6. Jones is the president and majority owner of Jones, Inc. His mother owns the remaining shares. Jones pays himself $200,000 per year as president, has a company car, a company condo, and a company cabana.

   Unfortunately for Joe's mom, the company showed no net income for the year, and paid no dividend's on her stock. Does Mom have any remedies?

7. Pater's Taters is a large company that sells licenses to franchisees who open Pater's Taters shops throughout the country. Pater's Taters sells french fries, fried potatoes, and fried hash browns to the public.

   One day, Peter eats a fried potato at Pater's Taters store in Palmerville. Peter picks up the potato and pulls out a large piece of glass. He notices the glass has bite marks on it. He begins to gag and coughs up blood. He is taken to Palmersville Hospital where a large piece of glass is removed from his throat. When he tries to collect the cost of his medical bills from Pater's Taters, they tell him that he can recover only from the Palmersville franchise because it is an independent contractor. Pater's Taters tells Peter not to call them later because their decision is final.

   Peter's attorney finds evidence that Pater's Taters requires all franchises to purchase all potatoes from them. Pater's Taters also supplies napkins, plates, and other supplies to the Palmersville franchise. Can Peter recover from Pater's Taters?

8. Geraldo, who owns stock in the NZT Corporation, believes that the company is engaging in various activities outside of its corporate charter. He would like them to stop.

   He knows that you have taken a course in business law and he has come to you for advice. What do you tell him?

9. Allan Accountant is a member of an accounting partnership that has no retirement plan. The partners would like to reduce their tax burden and establish such a plan. Allen has come to you for advice because he has heard that corporations are allowed to set up beneficial retirement plans. What do you suggest to him?

PART IX

BUSINESS IN RELATION TO THE GOVERNMENT AND THE INTERNATIONAL ENVIRONMENT

Chapter 28

Regulation of Business

■ Corporations, especially those engaged in interstate commerce, are subject to many laws and regulations. Among these are tax laws and regulations. Corporations pay a form of double federal income tax because corporate earnings are subject to taxes and then dividends paid to shareholders are taxed again. Corporations are also subject to state and local taxation.

■ Large corporations are also subject to federal and state antitrust laws. These laws are designed to keep corporations from monopoly or near monopoly and stifling competition.

■ The Sherman and Clayton Antitrust Acts prohibit actions that may substantially lessen competition. These could include price fixing, allocation of markets and other actions designed to reduce competition.

■ Corporations, whose stock is bought and sold by the general public, also must comply with federal and state securities laws that are designed to protect the unsophisticated investor. They prevent manipulation of the markets and require full financial disclosure. In addition, they mandate the filing of various reports and financial statements.

■ Corporations are also subject to laws designed to protect the air, land, and water from pollution. In addition, the federal and state governments require corporations that generate chemical and other waste to clean up these wastes on site. Liability for not complying with these laws can be substantial.

CORPORATE TAXATION

Corporations are subject to federal, state, and local taxation. Because corporations do not vote, they often become easy targets for governmental taxation. The federal corporate income tax has fluctuated during the second half of the twentieth century.

One major complaint of corporate shareholders is that their income is subject to double taxation. The corporate income is taxed when the corporation earns it, and corporate dividends are taxed again when they are distributed to the shareholders (personal income tax). This discourages investment in corporations and reduces resources available for corporate activities.

Smaller companies receive some relief from this problem through subchapter S federal tax provisions that allow corporate shareholders to be taxed as partners. In this way, corporate income is not taxed, but is simply passed through to the shareholders who pay personal income tax.

Corporations are also subject to state corporate income taxation. Usually, this means that the state in which the company is incorporated will impose taxes in addition to the federal income tax. This further eats into corporate profits and resources.

A corporation may also be taxed by states in which it is doing business, a practice that has raised consitutional issues about the ability of states to levy these taxes. The courts have ruled that there must be a sufficient link between corporate business activities and the state in order for the tax to be levied.

■ ABC Corporation has a mail-order catalog business. It sometimes mails products to customers in the state of New Taxes. It has no other business operations in the state.

New Taxes imposes a tax on all of ABC Corporation's income, and cites its mail-order business as the reason for the tax. If ABC Corporation brings a court action, the tax will be declared invalid because there is not a sufficient link between the tax and the level of business in the state. ■

States often also require corporations to collect sales taxes on the sale of their products and they may also mandate the payment of workers' compensation assessments and other payroll-related taxes. Corporate officers can be held liable for failure to ensure payment of these taxes and assessments.

■ The state of More Tax requires DEF Corporation to pay unemployment taxes based on the number of people on its payroll. DEF fails to make these payments. The president of DEF, Sam Tonto, can be held personally liable for the failure to make these payments. The usual sanctions are to require payment of back taxes, interest, and penalties. ■

Local governments also impose property taxes on corporate-owned real estate within the town's boundaries. These taxes are normally determined after the property has been evaluated by a tax appraiser and its market value assessed. The town's tax rate is then applied to the value of the property to determine the amount of tax due.

■ PRS Corporation has a large factory in the town of Bunion. The tax appraiser assesses the factory at $1,000,000. The local tax rate is 3.40, which equals 3.4 percent. PRS Corporation will owe $34,000 in local property taxes to Bunion.

If PRS Corporation does not pay its property taxes, the local tax collector may obtain an order to place a lien on the property. If taxes continue to accumulate, the local tax collector may obtain an order to sell the property. ■

ANTITRUST LAWS

As the United States evolved from an agrarian to an industrial society, some large corporations had established a monopoly position in certain industries. Some of these were in sectors critical to the economy. In addition, some of these corporations began to abuse their dominant position. As a result, Congress passed legislation to reestablish more competition by reducing or eliminating monopolistic control.

The Sherman Antitrust Act, passed in 1890, stated that business combinations that restricted trade were unlawful. As a result of this legislation, courts have broken up such corporate giants as Standard Oil and AT&T. The act has been utilized by the government to help establish more competition in the economy. More recently, some have argued that certain governmental actions, while legally defensible, make little economic sense. This position will be discussed later.

The Clayton Act and the Robinson-Patman Act further bolstered the antitrust laws. The Wagner, Clayton, and Robinson-Patman acts give the Justice Department and the Federal Trade Commission, an adminstrative agency established by Congress to help administer antitrust laws, wide-ranging authority to eliminate practices that are deceptive or reduce competition. Some of these activities are discussed in the following sections.

Perhaps the most critical area of antitrust enforcement relates to price discrimination. Corporations may not charge different prices to different buyers if the effect may be to create a monopoly or to substantially lessen competition. It is permissible to charge different prices based on legitimate reasons such as differences in quality or quantity.

- ZBT and TBZ are the two largest corporations in their markets and they supply each other with a variety of products. They work out an arrangement to supply each other with various products at prices significantly lower than they would charge other people.

   This gives each of them an unfair advantage over their competitors and may tend to substantially lessen competition. This would be a violation of federal antitrust laws. ■

- NYZ Corporation gives regular quantity discounts to every customer who orders at least 100 units of its product. The discount is 3 percent off the usual price if the order is 100 units. The discount is 6 percent if the order is over 500 units. These discounts would not violate federal antitrust laws because they are based on legitimate reasons. ■

- KLM makes a widget specifically designed to fit with a special type of flange. It is the largest supplier of these widgets in the country.

   A competitor opens a widget factory and begins to contact actual and potential customers within the state of New Jacket. The quality of its widgets is similar to the quality of KLM's.

   KLM quickly contacts all its actual and potential customers within New Jacket and offers them widgets at prices substantially less than those it offers to customers in other states. By taking these actions, KLM hopes to make it difficult for its new competitor to get a start in New Jacket. This would be using prices for the purpose of reducing competition and would be impermissible. ■

The antitrust laws do not prohibit a corporation from lowering prices to meet the competition's prices. This is permissible if prices are lowered in a general competitive area. Antitrust laws do prohibit treating individual customers differently or using prices to gain a monopoly or to eliminate competitors.

Another practice that violates federal antitrust laws is that of price-fixing. If two or more corporations agree not to sell below a certain price, the law has been violated. In addition, a wholesaler may not require a retailer to sell at a specific price. This is called a resale price maintenance agreement. The first of these prohibited practices is called horizontal price-fixing. The second is referred to as vertical price-fixing.

A wholesaler should only suggest retail prices and would be permissible as a way of working with retailers. However, competitors should never discuss an agreement to set prices. Any attempt to reach an accommodation on prices is likely to be regarded as unlawful.

■ John and Joan work as quality control vice presidents for competitive corporations. They meet at a bar and discuss the quality of one of their products.

They mention that their customers would be better served if one product was of higher quality. They note that the higher level of quality could be achieved if they could maintain a certain price. But if they agree to set a certain price, they will be violating antitrust laws. ■

Competitors may not agree to set prices, although government officials may decide that regulation of prices serves a useful function. For example, it has been commonplace for governments to regulate the prices of certain products such as alcohol. Governments may require businesses not to sell products below a certain price. This is permissible even if it tends to lessen competition because of the need to protect the public from cheap, unhealthy products.

Governments may also establish monopolies for certain types of industries. Public utilities tend to fall into this category. In some areas, competition could actually be against the public interest. For example, it would make little sense to allow such fierce competition among utilities that there were power lines crowding against each other. In addition, it could become highly unprofitable for them to compete in such a manner.

Size of Corporation

It is not against the law to be a large corporation or to have a dominant position in the marketplace. It is against the law to attempt to create a monopoly or to use one's position to monopolize a market. It is often not easy to determine which corporate actions could result in a monopoly.

If the laws were read too strictly, nearly every corporate action could be viewed as violating some antitrust provision. As a result, the courts have applied a rule of reason which states that only unreasonable restraints of trade will violate antitrust law.

One factor the courts will examine is the competitive effect of the action—that is, to what degree will the corporation's specific action promote or diminish competition in that field. The court will look at the current competitive nature of the industry, because some industries are very competitive and have a significant number of large companies. Other industries have a few large corporations with dominant positions. A merger among two or more of these companies would violate antitrust laws.

Another practice that violates antitrust laws is for competing corporations to divide up markets among themselves.

■ ZDT Corporation and TGF are competitors in the outdoor furniture market. They decide that competing throughout the country is unproductive and unprofitable. They meet and divide up the country so that ZDT will sell furniture in the South and East while TGF will sell in the North and the West. This would violate federal antitrust laws regardless of the reasons for which it was done. ■

Price-fixing and the dividing of markets are considered per se illegal if done by corporations because they lessen competition. This does not mean that governments will prohibit all corporate actions. It will depend on their positions in the market. Mergers of corporations might lessen competition.

The firm's position in the industry is perhaps the most important factor. Some corporations have enormous power within their industry. Even minor actions can have a substantial impact on the level of competition.

> KLM Corporation has a 50 percent share of the market in the nimrod industry. In some areas it has less than 50 percent and in some areas it has more than 50 percent. In one of the latter areas, if it buys a competitor, its market share would jump from 60 percent to 75 percent. This would be a major change and would reduce competition significantly. ■

Another factor would be the history and duration of the proposed action. For example, a large corporation purchasing one of its industry's major suppliers could be viewed as a significant restraint on trade. However, a short-lived joint venture is less likely to be seen to be as anticompetitive. This would be especially true if it did not involve giving the corporation an advantage when obtaining supplies.

Refusing to purchase products from someone else unless they agree to purchase products from you is a **tying agreement** and is not permitted. Using one's position as an important customer to gain an unfair advantage in the purchase of products or services is also improper because it reduces competition. This is particularly true if one firm is very large because that firm would have a substantial advantage over its competitors.

A corporation will be liable for violating antitrust laws if it has monopoly power and it willfully acquired or maintains that monopoly power. The monopoly position need not be throughout the country. It is legally sufficient that the monopoly exist in a particular product and geographical market. Defining the exact parameters of product and geographical markets is often difficult.

> Cones, Inc., has a very substantial share of the ice-cream cone market and wants to acquire another competitor in the ice-cream cone business. It argues that its size of the cone market is not relevant. Instead, it contends that the relevant market must also include ice-cream cups, of which it has a very small market share. It argues that both cones and cups hold ice cream and that is what counts. ■

> NPT has a very large share of the market in New Jersey but very little in New York or Pennsylvania. It argues that the market should be measured by the tristate area. ■

Determining if a monopoly exists can be very complicated and can require the testimony of experts in economics, finance, marketing, and mathematics. There are people who specialize in each of these areas and can assist the courts in making these decisions.

The subject of mergers assumed special importance during the 1980s when mergers were rampant. The Clayton Act prohibits mergers when the effect of such an acquisition "may be to substantially lessen competition." The Justice Department now requires large-scale enterprises to notify its Antitrust Division before a take over. The company must then wait for a specified time for the government to object to the proposed merger.

Because much of the burden for antitrust actions falls on the federal government, the attitude of enforcement officials will have a major impact on the effect of these laws on corporations. The Reagan administration was sympathetic to the idea that American corporations needed to become larger in order to effectively compete against their larger international counterparts. Other presidential administrations have not been as sympathetic.

Antitrust decisions will take on even greater importance for large corporations in the rapidly changing and highly competitive global economy. It will be necessary and difficult for corporations to balance the need to grow without running afoul of antitrust laws. The attitudes of American lawmakers is also likely to undergo changes as they recognize that what may lessen competition domestically may increase the ability of American corporations to compete globally.

Remedies

Both criminal and civil penalties can be applied to violations of federal antitrust laws. Corporations may incur substantial fines and the court may issue an injunction to stop the wrongful conduct. Individuals may be imprisoned for willful violations of federal antitrust law.

Individuals can also bring private actions under federal law. Remedies include the recovery of triple the damages for a violation that causes injury to another.

> NYZ Corporation is damaged when FGH Corporation, a competitor, engages in tying arrangements with various suppliers. This makes it more difficult for NYZ to buy supplies at a competitive price. As a result, NYZ loses sales of $1,000,000 and profits of $100,000. NYZ could recover $300,000 in damages from FGH. ■

The state's attorney general's office can also bring actions under state antitrust laws on behalf of the state's citizens. Convictions for violating antitrust laws can be grounds for revoking the corporation's charter to do business in that state.

Another business practice prohibited by law, and by Federal Trade Commission rulings, is deceptive advertising. Coercing by refusing to sell, boycotting, disparaging a competitor's product, enforcing payments wrongfully, spying on one's competitors, stealing confidential information, encouraging breach of contracts, and simulating corporate names, trademarks, or a competitor's goods have also been declared to be unlawful.

FEDERAL SECURITIES LAW

In the early portion of this century, legal standards for the sale of securities were rather loose. Unscrupulous individuals were able to sell worthless securities to unsuspecting individuals. Many promises were made which could not be kept. Financial statements had little meaning or were deceptive.

Another common practice was to sell worthless securities and then to manipulate the markets. Securities manipulators were able to buy and sell securities and artificially boost the price of stock. They would sell more shares of worthless companies, then walk away, leaving their investors with meaningless pieces of paper. Their promises were said to be full of "blue sky" and little else.

Manipulation of the securities markets was a major reason for the crash of 1929 and the Great Depression that followed. Many people lost their investments while others became rich through deceptive practices. As a result, confidence in the stock markets and the free-enterprise system was severely weakened.

When the Great Depression continued into the 1930s, it became apparent that the federal government needed to regulate the securities markets in order to reduce the level of deceptive practices and to reestablish public confidence. The Securities Act of 1933 and the Securities Exchange Act of 1934 prohibited certain activities and set up the Securities and Exchange Commission to regulate the issuance of stock and the stock markets.

Securities that are sold in interstate commerce are regulated by the 1933 act. All newly issued securities must be accompanied by a **prospectus** approved by the SEC. This does not mean that the commission has endorsed the sale or recommended the securities. It only means that the prospectus conforms to SEC format provisions, and that the financial information is disclosed in accord with SEC requirements.

At the bottom of the prospectus, the issuing corporation must note that the SEC is not recommending the purchase of the securities.

> OMN Corporation issues new shares of stock and complies with all of the SEC rules and regulations. A bold-type statement at the bottom of the OMN prospectus informs potential buyers that the SEC does not approve or disapprove the purchase of these securities. ∎

Securities include common or preferred stock, bonds, notes, or other investments involving risk to the investor. Unless the issuer falls within one of the exemptions related to the sale of investments to sophisticated investors (not the general public), the issuer must comply with all laws and regulations promulgated by the SEC.

The first requirement is to file a registration statement, which contains an outline of the nature of the issuer's business, a description of the securities, information about management, and the compensation of senior managers. It also includes other information that would assist investors in making an informed decision.

The entire issue of senior management compensation has assumed added importance in recent years and may become even more significant in the future. The public, investors, shareholders, and the government are all asking whether senior management deserves the level of compensation granted. Future stock issuers should reflect on the consequences of disclosing this information to the public.

The second requirement is to issue the prospectus. Much of the same information is found in both documents. The prospectus is a sales tool for attracting potential investors. This is one reason that the SEC must review the prospectus before it is shown to the public.

Because federal legislation applies to interstate commerce, there is an exemption for offerings that are sold only in one state. However, the phrase interstate commerce has been construed broadly, and the issuer should be cautious about relying on this exception. In addition, most states have their own securities laws that are usually patterned on the federal law.

Individuals may be held criminally and civilly liable for violations of the 1933 act and the regulations promulgated by the SEC. This is particularly significant for corporate officers and the professionals, such as attorneys and accountants, who provide advice in particular areas requiring special expertise to corporations issuing securities.

The Securities Exchange Act of 1934 was designed to regulate the subsequent trading of securities after their issuance. The SEC required periodic financial reports and for civil and criminal penalties for violating its provisions for the submission of these reports.

Publicly traded companies must file periodic reports called forms 10-K with the SEC. These provide additional information to the public and to investors. They help maintain the pattern of full disclosure begun when the stocks were issued.

The act also prohibits the use of manipulative or deceptive practices in violation of the rules and regulations of the SEC. These rules are intended to prevent some of the fraudulent practices in which people engaged in previous years. They prohibit schemes to defraud the public by the making of untrue statements or other conduct intended to gain an unfair advantage through deception. The courts have interpreted the rules as meaning that there must have been some intent to deceive. Acting in a negligent manner will not be sufficient to constitute a criminal violation under the rules.

Insider Trading

A problem that has existed since the establishment of the markets is the trading in stocks by people with **insider information**. The opportunity to use information unknown to the public and to make a quick killing has proven too tempting for many people. In fact, for many years, using one's position as an insider to make some quick money was seen as one of the advantages of holding certain positions.

One of the purposes of the rules of the SEC was to protect the public by prohibiting insider trading. Insiders are defined as directors, officers and certain employees of private corporations. Insiders also include attorneys, accountants, consultants, and anyone else who has access to information not known to the general investing public.

Insiders who have material information unknown to the general public should either abstain from trading altogether or, at the minimum, abstain from trading in the stock until the information becomes known to the general public.

It is both a criminal and civil offense to trade on "material" inside information. This is significant information not generally known. It would not include relatively minor information or speculations about the future success of the organization.

- Tim is a director of the GTM Mining Corporation. He learns that the company has just discovered a major vein of gold. Tim runs out and buys 10,000 shares of stock of GTM Mining. This is a clear violation of insider trading provisions. This was material insider information and, because the information was not known to the general public, Tim's purchase was improper. ■

- Sally is an employee with FRN Corporation. She meets the new head of marketing and sales for the corporation. She decides that Frank is a very dynamic individual and will help the company grow through new policies and practices.

  Sally buys 100 shares of FRN Corporation stock. This would not be a trade based on material inside information. Her judgment of Frank's ability to develop the company is not the type of knowledge which should prevent her from trading. ■

- Marcia works for RST Corporation. Every year she evaluates the financial reports of RST. When the report comes out for the current year, she again examines it carefully and decides that RST looks promising.

  She buys 500 shares of RST stock based on her evaluation of its future. This would not be trading on material inside information. Marcia acted on knowledge that had been released to the general public. ■

Although an investor may feel secure that she is not trading on material insider information, the rules on this subject have become rather strict. A person who is found to have traded on insider information will be required to disgorge any profits and may have to pay additional penalties. A trader could be subject to substantial legal fees and adverse publicity even if found innocent of insider trading. As a general rule, the potential investor can resolve any doubts by not trading.

A more recent development are the **tippee** rulings. A tippee is someone, either inside or outside of the company, who receives knowledge of material inside information from another (tipper). Previously, the communication of these "tips" was common in the securities industry. Under current law, a "tippee," even though not an insider, may be held liable for acting on such information.

- Tinkers gives Evers some material insider information about a large, new, very profitable contract just signed by the Chicom Corporation. Evers buys 1,000 shares of Chicom at $5 per share. A few weeks later he sells the shares for $10,000. He will be liable to the Chicom shareholders for $5,000, which represents the profits gained by using this information.

  If Evers had passed along this "tip" to Chance and he had acted on this information, Chance would also be liable for profits made. The tippers could also be held liable to the corporate shareholders for profits made by the tippees. ■

Individuals who are guilty of insider trading may be subject to SEC consent orders in which they agree to stop such conduct. The SEC could also obtain an injunction from a federal court which would compel the defendant to stop such activity. A person guilty of insider trading could also be imprisoned and fined, while a corporation would be subject to heavy fines. Courts have ruled that private parties injured by this conduct, such as other shareholders, may bring their own actions to recover damages for their losses.

Rule 16(a) of the Securities Exchange Act requires that certain insiders—officers, directors, and 10 percent stock owners—submit reports to the SEC on their trading activities. This helps the SEC determine if there has been insider training. Rule 16(b) states that all short-swing profits made within six months by insiders belong to the corporation.

> ■ Dickinson is a director of NML Corporation. On April 1st he buys 1,000 shares of NML at $30 per share. He sells the shares on June 1st for $40 per share. Because the purchase and sale occurred within six months, the $10,000 profit will belong to the corporation. ■

Market Manipulation and Other Wrongful Conduct

The securities laws now also prohibit the types of market manipulation which were prevalent during the twenties. It violates the law to artificially conspire to raise the price of stock by buying and selling shares, or by using other deceptive techniques to defraud investors. It would also be unlawful to attempt to hide trades or to hide the identity of the person making the trade by using fictitious accounts or some other practice.

The Penny Stock Reform Act of 1990 recognizes that the low-price, or penny stock, market has been characterized by a high degree of fraud. It gives the SEC increased enforcement powers and requires greater disclosure than previously from those engaging in the sale of penny stock.

> ■ Kelly sells stocks that have a price of less of than $1. He arranges with an employee of a large brokerage house to buy some of these stocks just before he sells them to the general public.
>   This causes the price of the stock to rise from 50 cents to $1. This would be an attempt to defraud other investors and to manipulate the markets. Kelly would be guilty of securities fraud. ■

PROTECTING THE ENVIRONMENT

Corporations are also subject to a variety of laws designed to protect the nation's air, land, and water. This is particularly true of corporations that engage in the manufacture of chemicals or other hazardous materials. The federal and state Superfunds have required payments by chemical and other corporations to help clean up hazardous waste sites.

The disaster caused by the Exxon *Valdez* highlighted the damage that could be caused by corporate negligence. Federal and state legislation has placed increased burdens on corporations to deal with environmental matters.

While many chemicals have helped improve the productivity of our agricultural sector, they can also present hazards to the nation's land and water. As a result, Congress has given the Environmental Protection Agency broad powers to regulate the manufacture and use of such chemicals. Corporations must register pesticides with the EPA before they may be used, and the EPA can deny registration and use if it deems the chemicals to be a hazard.

The EPA also has the power to test toxic substances and to ban their use if they are deemed to be a hazard to human life or health. Congress has also enacted laws giving the EPA the power to regulate the manufacture, sale, use, and disposal of hazardous waste materials.

Corporations now have "cradle-to-grave" responsibility for these hazardous wastes and must dispose of them in a manner approved by the EPA. Materials such as asbestos, which were once seen to be mankind's protection against the ravages of fire, have now been determined to be highly hazardous. Asbestos must be removed from schools and other public buildings so that airborne particles do not create health problems for those exposed to them.

The Superfund legislation gave the EPA the authority to begin identifying and classifying the most serious hazardous waste sites in the country. The EPA may order those corporations that created the sites to clean them up. If the corporation does not, the EPA has the authority to clean up the site and require the corporation to pay for its cost. With over 25,000 such sites identified, the private and governmental sectors have barely scratched the surface of this problem.

The EPA imposes strict liabilities on the parties involved. It does not matter who was at fault. The EPA may impose liability on the transporter of the waste, the owner of the site at the time of disposal, the current owner of the site, and the corporation that generated the waste. All of these parties together and each of them as individuals can be held liable.

The Federal Clean Air Act established national clean air standards and it permits the EPA to enforce these standards if the states, which have primary enforcement authority, fail to do so.

The Federal Clean Water Act defines national clean water standards and gives the states primary authority for enforcing these standards, but again, the EPA may enforce them if the states do not. The act expressly forbids the discharge of heated waters into the nation's waterways because the heat may upset the ecological balance.

States have also enacted a variety of laws designed to protect the environment. In addition, localities have planning and zoning ordinances that pertain to development by corporations. Many of the states now require an **environmental impact statement** prior to the construction of a major development. These statements must indicate, in considerable detail, the effect the development will have on the surrounding land, air, and water. In addition, particular attention is being given to the protection of local wetlands because of their critical role in the overall environment.

Some states have also begun to require that both buyers and sellers clean up lands that have been used for certain environmentally sensitive purposes before state environmental agencies will approve the sale. These regulations can add to the length of time required for the completion of real estate transactions, and can also significantly add to the costs associated with the sale. Normally, there are certain industrial use codes states can utilize to help identify specific industries that may make or use environmentally sensitive materials. The states can then pass rules requiring that lands that have been subject to environmentally sensitive uses must be cleaned up as a condition of the sale.

Definitions Reviewed

Tying arrangement is the unlawful refusal to purchase products from another unless they purchase products from you.

A **prospectus** is a document required by the Securities and Exchange Commission when stock is issued. It is given to the investor.

Insider Information is information not available to the general public. It is not permissible to trade on this information.

A **tippee** is someone who receives insider information.

An **environmental impact statement** is a statement required of a developer which analyzes a proposed development's impact on the environment.

Core Concepts Reviewed

■ Large corporations are subject to antitrust laws that help foster economic competition by prohibiting monopolies.

■ Corporations that issue securities must comply with the Securities Act of 1933 and the Securities Exchange Act of 1934. These acts require submission of financial information and prohibit actions that would defraud investors.

■ Recently, the federal and state governments have passed laws requiring businesses to take actions to protect the environment. Businesses that work with chemicals and other hazardous substances must comply with numerous laws and regulations.

Questions

1. What is meant by double taxation of corporate income?

2. What is a subchapter S corporation?
3. How are local property taxes calculated?
4. What are the purposes of antitrust laws?
5. What are resale price maintenance agreements?
6. What is the difference between horizontal and vertical price-fixing?
7. What is insider trading?
8. What are "short-swing" profits?
9. What is the requirement with respect to short-swing profits?
10. Who is subject to the short-swing profits requirement?
11. What is a tipper? What is a tippee?
12. How have the laws with respect to tipping changed?
13. What is the liability of a tipper? What is the liability of a tippee?

Problems

1. JRT Corporation has a factory where the property tax rate is 3.60 percent. The factory is assessed at $2,000,000. JRT is attempting to have its assessment reduced to $1,500,000. If successful, how much will JRT save in taxes?
2. OTP Corporation has pretax earnings of $200,000. It is subject to a corporate federal tax rate of 36 percent. How much will it have to pay in federal taxes? Miss Maples receives a dividend check of $1,000. She has a personal tax rate of 15 percent. How much will she pay in taxes?
3. The president of XZY Corporation, which controls 60 percent of the shoe market in the state of Lost Hope, wants to reduce the price of its shoes by 5 percent in order to undercut one of its competitors. The president knows that you have taken a course

in business law and asks for your advice. What do you tell him?

4. The president of ZBC Corporation wants a uniform pricing policy in his stores. He shows you a memorandum that would require all of his stores to charge exactly the same price for the same product. He asks for your advice. What do you say?

5. You work for Kbang Cola. One of the directors for Kbang tells you that the company has just signed a contract to supply Kbang Cola to every one of a large restaurant chain's stores in America. He suggests that you buy as many shares of Kbang Cola stocks as possible. What do you do?

6. Zippy Zippers is about to issue some new stock. The president of Zippy suggests at a meeting that every employee buy 100 shares as soon as the stock is issued because the price will go up and the corporation will bring in more money. What do you say to her?

7. MLT Corporation plans to issue stock. It has been keeping two sets of records. One set was designed for public consumption, and the other reflected lower profits and was for internal use.

Aardvaack and Company, an accounting firm, looked at the records and then issued a report that approved the records of MLT. Later, when the stocks proved worthless, Aardvaack and Company claimed that it should not be held liable because it had only approved the public records, and was not responsible for the fraud of MLT. Is Aardvaack and Company correct?

Chapter 29

Consumer Protection

■ Businesses may conduct their affairs if they conform to laws designed to protect consumers from dishonest business practices and unsafe products.

■ Businesses making products that are put on the human body or are for internal consumption are strictly regulated by the federal and state governments. The Federal Drug Administration regulates these products.

■ Because of complaints about discrimination with respect to the granting of credit, the Equal Credit Opportunity Act was passed by Congress. It prohibits discrimination based on criteria such as race, religion, gender, creed or location.

■ When debt collections practices became the subject of complaints, Congress passed legislation that put limits on the practices of debt collectors.

■ The Federal Trade Commission regulates the sale of goods by prohibiting deceptive sales practices and monitoring the safety of products that are sold in interstate commerce.

CONSUMER PROTECTION

When purchasers bought items from small merchants, they were better able to protect themselves from shoddy or unsafe items. As manufacturers grew larger, it became more difficult to determine which merchandise was safe and to enforce a remedy if there was a defect.

The latter part of the nineteenth century and the early part of the twentieth century were marked by a large number of books and newspaper stories about unsafe products made by various industries. Congress became especially concerned with products that were placed on the body or taken internally by the consumer.

The federal Food, Drug, and Cosmetic Act sets standards regarding the wholesomeness of drugs, food and cosmetics. The act established the Federal Drug Administration (FDA), which administers laws and regulations to prevent the sale of food and drugs that are not pure or are improperly labeled. The FDA also has the power to approve all drugs before they can be sold. The FDA's review process protects the public, but also tends to delay the introduction of new drugs that might prevent or diminish the effects of disease.

■ Harry has a fatal disease for which there is no cure. There are a number of experimental drugs that might help retard the disease and that are available in other countries.

The FDA requires drug manufacturers to carry out a significant number of tests before it will approve the drug for sale. Until the tests are completed, Harry will not be able to obtain a drug that might save his life. ■

EQUAL CREDIT

Obtaining credit to purchase homes or other costly items such as automobiles or large household items has often been a problem for women and certain groups who have traditionally suffered discrimination. The 1975 Equal Credit Opportunity Act attempts to prohibit discrimination in the granting of credit by applying its provisions to all businesses that regularly grant credit to customers.

■ Joan, an unmarried woman, wishes to obtain a loan from Twelfth National Bank. She is denied the loan and told to go get married first. This would be an illegal denial of credit under the act. ■

■ Bill lives in an area of town in which Twelfth National Bank has decided no one will be granted credit. This is known as redlining and is not a permissible practice under the act. ■

The act allows the injured party to bring a civil action and to recover damages as well as reasonable attorney's fees. Nothing in the act would prevent a lending institution from setting different rates based on credit experience, assets, or income.

■ It would be permissible to charge Bert Bigbucks a lower rate of interest than Bart Badcredit who has a history of unpaid loans and little income. ■

The Fair Credit Reporting Act is designed to protect people who are seeking relief from incorrect information in a credit report. It is a common practice for a lending institution to request an outside credit report on a prospective borrower. If the report contains incorrect information, it may be a reason that the institution denies credit to a prospective borrower.

■ Mary C. Richards applies for a car loan at Thirteenth National Bank. They run a credit check on her which shows that a Mary G. Richards had gone into bankruptcy a few years before.
  There is some confusion about the names and Mary is denied the loan she requested. Under the act, she would be able to request a copy of the report. This will enable her to correct the information and receive her loan. ■

A person injured by negligence or a willful violation may bring an action to recover monetary damages. The Fair Credit Reporting Act is designed to protect consumers and not businesses who seek loans. Businesses are better able to protect themselves.

The Truth in Lending Act is another federal law designed to protect the borrower. This law states the methods by which the lender must inform the borrower about the terms of the loan. It gives particular emphasis to full disclosure of the actual **annual percentage rate** (interest rate) being charged to the borrower.

The methods of calculating and collecting the principal and interest due can be quite different. They can also be rather confusing to the average borrower. This can give unscrupulous lenders an enormous advantage over individual borrowers. The act was designed to help protect these consumers by requiring the lender to state the actual interest rate.

■ Jones borrows $1,000 at 10 percent interest for one year from Nineteenth National Bank. The loan is to be repaid at the year's end with interest charged at that time of $100. This is simple interest, and the annual percentage rate charged is exactly 10 percent. ◼

◼ Jones borrows $1,000 from the Twenty-first National Bank for one year. The bank subtracts the $100 interest payment at the time it gives the principal to Jones. Even though the bank states that the interest rate is 10 percent, it is actually higher.

Jones must still repay the $1,000, which is the full amount of the principal due, at the end of the year. In the first example, Jones has use of the full $1,000 for the entire year. In the second example, he only has use of $900 and is still charged $100 interest. In this case, the annual interest rate was actually $100 divided by $900 = 11.11%. ◼

There are many ways to calculate interest payments, and financial institutions must now advise the borrower of the actual rate. The law requires the inclusion of all penalties, late charges, and other fees in the calculation of the annual percentage rate. The lender must also include information about the taking of any collateral and the methods for disposing of it.

The act also has a number of other provisions relating to points, appraisal charges, and insurance. The act also states that a credit card holder is liable for only $50 on unauthorized charges if the card is stolen.

The act further provides that consumers have a three-day "cooling-off" period in which to cancel a loan that uses their home as security on the loan. The act also provides for consumers to bring class-action suits if the act is violated.

While the act does not set forth maximum interest rates, states do set rates above which interest may not be charged. These are called usury rates and were designed to protect borrowers from unscrupulous lenders. Some people have argued that what they actually accomplish is to drive borrowers into the hands of even more dishonest lenders.

◼ Smith needs $1,000 to pay off some current bills. He goes to a bank to get a loan. However, his credit is so bad that the bank would have to charge above the usury rate in order to justify the risk of lending Smith the $1,000. They refuse to give him the loan.

Smith then goes to a "street lender" and borrows the $1,000 for 100 percent interest and a promise to have his legs broken if he does not repay. ◼

DEBT COLLECTION

Some people get into severe debt difficulties. This is not unusual in a consumption and debt-driven society. If the creditor has a security interest that allows the creditor to take some property, the creditor can seize the property or obtain it through legal action.

But there may be no property to seize from the debtor. The only recourse may be to try to collect the money from the debtor. While the creditor may bring a court action to collect, legal suits are expensive and may take a substantial length of time. As a result, some creditors employ debt collectors to assist them.

While the majority of debt collectors are honest and ethical, the abusive practices of a few led Congress to enact legislation to curb some of their overly agressive techniques.

It is now impermissible to call a debtor at inconvenient times. These are presumed to be after 9 P.M. or before 8 A.M. It is illegal to call the debtor's employer if the employer objects. It is not permissible to threaten physical harm, to pretend that a debt collector is an attorney, or to engage in other deceitful or abusive practices.

> ▪ Jones owes Henple's Department store $500 for items he purchased on credit. He receives frequent calls from a debt collector working on behalf of Henple's, but he refuses to pay his debts.
>
> The debt collector puts Jones's name in the paper and circulates flyers with the amount of Jones's debt throughout his neighborhood. This would be regarded as abusive and improper harassment. ▪

It is now against the law for a debt collector to make a second call if the debtor requests him by letter not to do so. States may pass laws that are even more protective of the debtor. Debtors may bring actions against creditors or debt collectors who violate the act. Violators may face fines for each violation.

REGULATION OF SALES

For many years, the general rule in the marketplace was caveat emptor or "let the buyer beware." This placed the burden on the buyer to carefully examine merchandise and the surrounding aspects of the transaction before making a purchase.

Recently, the federal and state governments have passed a variety of laws outlawing the sale of shoddy or unsafe merchandise. The new slogan should be "let the seller be careful." Violations of these laws may subject businesses to fines and very substantial product liability suits.

Perhaps the most dramatic change in the relationship between the buyer and seller has occurred as a result of the passage of the Uniform Commercial Code. Adopted by the vast majority of states, the law provides that a merchant who regularly deals in goods gives every buyer a **warranty of merchantability**. This warranty guarantees that a product will be safe for the normal purposes for which it is used. If it is not safe and a person is injured, that person has a remedy against the manufacturer of the goods. This warranty is discussed in greater detail in Part IV.

However, because this warranty has caused such a revolution in the business world, it needs to be discussed again. This warranty has caused an explosion of lawsuits against manufacturers of unsafe products. It is no longer necessary for plaintiffs to show negligence (lack of reasonable care) in order to recover. They need only to show that the warranty was violated. Many businesspeople have complained that this explosion of lawsuits has raised the costs of doing business. But, it has allowed more people to be compensated for their injuries and it has also promoted a higher degree of product safety.

■ Sergeant Motors Corporation makes and sells automobiles. Maggie buys one of its cars. One day she is driving her car and the brakes fail. She is injured and brings a legal action against Sergeant. She need only show that the brakes failed, that the warranty was breached, and that she was injured as a result of the breach. While this will cost Sergeant some money, it will encourage it to make safer cars. ■

The state legislatures have also passed laws prohibiting a variety of sales practices that deceive the customer or that pressure them into buying products they do not want. For example, door-to-door salespeople have regularly sold a variety of products to homeowners. The need to make sales caused some salespersons to adopt high-pressure tactics to convince people to purchase products they did not need. Most states have now adopted laws that give consumers cooling-off periods in which the purchaser may cancel the sale.

■ Stu sells tableware door-to-door. He meets with Suzie and tells her that she will never get married unless she has a complete set of tableware.
    Suzie buys a set of tableware. After talking to her mother the next day, she decides she does not need the tableware. Suzie may call Stu and cancel the sale despite his attempts to change her mind. ■

Under common law, it was not considered illegal for a business to run a newspaper advertisement in which it offered low-priced items for sale while having only a few in stock. Buyers would go to the store, and then find that they could not make a purchase. When a customer could not make a purchase, a salesperson would attempt to convince the person to buy a more expensive substitute. This became known as the "bait-and-switch" technique. Not only was this annoying to customers, but it bordered on fraud.

This technique has now been outlawed in the majority of states. Businesses can still advertise low-cost products, but, if a customer cannot find the advertised product, the business must give the prospective buyer a "rain check" so that she will be able to buy the item at the same price in the future.

The Federal Trade Commission and state departments of consumer affairs have been vigilant in searching out practices they believe deceive the average consumer. For example, these authorities have been rigorous in their pursuit of manufacturers and sellers of toys that may be dangerous to children.

Although the danger from a product may appear remote, both federal and state authorities have the authority to have it withdrawn. While the seller has the right to appeal, the costs and the adverse publicity may make it unwise to do so.

Other deceptive practices may include exaggerated claims or hidden fees. Products that promote health or fitness, financial services, and food products commonly fall under the scrutiny of these agencies.

■ Big Butt, Inc., operates fitness centers throughout the state of Rigorous Regulation. Big Butt shows a TV advertisement in which it demonstrates a large number of exercise machines and equipment being used by customers.

The equipment shown in the TV ads is not available at all of Big Butt's facilities. This is likely to be regarded as a deceptive advertisement in the state of Rigorous Regulation. ■

■ Go-Go Mutual Funds advertises its funds throughout the state of New Busybodies. Its advertisements stress that there are no charges or fees related to buying any of their funds.

While it is true that there are no sales charges related to buying the funds, Go-Go does charge a management fee based on the amount of assets in the funds. The director of consumer affairs in New Busybodies is likely to bring an action for deceptive advertising. ■

■ Sally's Salads, Inc., sells a variety of salad dressings. One of the dressings is called Sally's Lite Dressing and is sold in the state of South Governmental.

Sally's Lite contains less calories than Sally's Regular Dressing, but the same level of calories as many other regular dressings. The director of consumer affairs seeks a court order compelling Sally to stop using the word "Lite" on the dressing bottle. The director will probably prevail. ■

These three examples demonstrate how strict the standards have become. Practices that might have been regarded as mere puffery in prior years are now often regarded as unlawful.

Over the years, legislatures became concerned about the quality of products. Automobiles were a continual source of complaint. People would purchase cars only to discover that the vehicle had on-going mechanical problems and could not be driven. As a result, many legislatures passed **lemon laws** that state that an automobile dealer can make a limited number of attempts at repairing an automobile. If the dealer cannot repair it, she must either refund the purchase price or supply the buyer with a new car.

The statutes provide for arbitration procedures to resolve disputes between buyers and sellers. These laws seem to have worked fairly well. The number of complaints and controversies regarding defective automobiles seems to have dropped sharply. In addition, the quality of new automobiles seems to have improved.

■ Dotson buys a new crashmobile from Franklin Motors. He is unable to shift gears from second to third when he takes the car on the road. Franklin Motors service manager informs him that there is a problem with the transmission, but it will be repaired.

The tranmission works well for about a week, but then breaks down. Dotson brings the car to Franklin again. They "fix" the transmission but it falls out of the car when Dotson leaves the parking lot. His crashmobile is towed back into the shop. If this continues to occur, Dotson may ask for his money to be refunded or for a new crashmobile. If there is a dispute about the law or the contract, it may be submitted to an arbitrator who can make a decision about the car. ■

REGULATION OF UTILITIES AND OTHER BUSINESSES

Certain types of businesses have always been tightly regulated by the federal and state governments. Those businesses that offer essential services to the public fall within this category. These would include utilities providing electricity, gas, or phone service. These utilities must receive permission to construct their facilities. The appropriate state agency would also divide up territories and make decisions regarding rates.

■ Elster Electric was granted authority to construct electric lines in the northwest area of the state of Old Providence. It built these lines under the supervision of the board of electric utilities. The board dictated precisely the manner in which the facilities were to be constructed.

In 1994, Elster wants to raise its rates. It must appear before the board and submit a lengthy proposal. At the hearing, the attorney for Elster presents the proposal. Also appearing on behalf of Elster is its president and senior financial officer. In addition, Elster offers the testimony of an industry consultant who performed a survey of the rates of other utilities in the state and throughout that area of the country. The survey supports Elster's rate request.

Also appearing before the board is an attorney for the group Citizens against Electrical Oppression. She introduces evidence that Elster's power lines might be a contributing cause of the high cancer rate in the area. The representative of Consumer Watch argues that rates are too high already and that the request should be denied.

Several consumers testify that they have had problems with their electricity during bad weather. Another states that he has had some problems with his bills and believes the increase should be denied until these difficulties are cured.

The board of electric utilities listens to all of this testimony, which is transcribed by a court stenographer and made into a written transcript. The board asks their staff to review the record and to make recommendations for the board members to consider at their next hearing. After reviewing all of the evidence, the board grants half of the rate request of Elster Electric. ■

Other highly regulated industries include those involving alcohol, tobacco, and firearms. In recent years all three have suffered from negative publicity and have become even more tightly regulated by the government.

■ The state of New Interference has had a rash of drunken driving fatalities. It raises its drinking age from 18 to 21. In addition, it stiffens the penalties for drunken driving. As a result, the revenues of Bob's Bar drop off sharply. In addition, the amount of revenue derived from sales taxes related to alcohol also drops off sharply. ■

■ The state of New Busybodies has passed a number of statutes which restrict smoking in public. This reduces the sale of tobacco related products at Terry's Tobacco Store. In addition, the overall sales tax revenues from tobacco-related products also drop. ■

Minors are forbidden to buy tobacco in the state. In addition, the state has substantially increased the sales tax on tobacco.

■ Frank's Firearms sells guns and ammunition to the general public. Recent state handgun legislation has made it more difficult to sell these items. While there was a sharp increase in sales following passage of the legislation, Frank remains concerned that his sales may be negatively affected. ■

Ultrahazardous activities such as construction are also highly regulated. More recently, various levels of government have begun to regulate businesses that make or sell products affecting the environment. Certain service industries, such as garbage collection, are also closely regulated by various levels of government.

■ Gary's Garbage has been granted a franchise from the state to collect garbage in the city of Lost Hope. The state approves the territory of each garbage hauler.

The state regulates all of the haulers by assigning them to territories. It also establishes the rates and the level of service. If Gary wants a rate increase, he must apply to the board of regulators and submit materials that justify the increase. Gary must retain an attorney and an accountant to help him with these applications. ■

■ Sam runs a service station in the town of Hampton Heights. Sam is required to submit regular reports to the Department of Environmental Protection regarding disposal of oil and gas products. Sam must bring them to approved disposal sites and dispose of them in ways that meet the state's standards. ■

Definitions Reviewed

Annual percentage rate is the total amount of interest a lender charges a borrower. This rate must be disclosed to the borrower.

Warranty of merchantability is the guarantee merchants give to consumers that goods purchased will be fit for normal purposes.

Lemon laws are laws regulating the number of times an automobile dealer can attempt to repair a car before either refunding the purchaser or supplying a new car.

Core Concepts Reviewed

■ Because of past abuses, governments now regulate business products and practices more closely than previously.

■ The extension of credit is now governed by federal law, which prohibits discrimination and requires full disclosure of the terms of the law.

■ Debt collection practices are also more tightly regulated. Abusive practices such as late-night or excessively frequent calls are now prohibited.

■ The Federal Trade Commission and state departments of consumer affairs regularly monitor the safety of products and sales practices of businesses. These governmental agencies may order a business

to remove unsafe products and to stop deceptive business practices.

Questions

1. What is an annual percentage rate?
2. What is the warranty of merchantability?
3. Name some deceptive sales practices that are prohibited.
4. What is a "cooling-off" period with respect to door-to-door sales?
5. What are the functions of the Federal Drug Administration?
6. Name some improper debt collection practices.
7. What are "lemon laws"?
8. How do lemon laws protect the consumer?
9. How are utilities regulated by the government?
10. Why are utilities regulated by the government?
11. Why should products that may injure the environment be subject to additional regulations?

Problems

1. Molly believes that her family's relish, which has been handed down from generation to generation, also cures pimples, skin rashes, and other blem-

ishes. She has used it on herself and a few friends and she believes the results have been good. She now wants to market the relish as a skin cure throughout the country. She has come to you for advice. What do tell her?

2. Hanson applies at the Thirteenth National Bank for a home mortgage to purchase a house in the Old Mill section of town. Although Hanson is gainfully employed, the loan officer tells him that the bank will not grant mortgages to buy houses in Old Mill to anyone. Does Hanson have any remedy?

3. Jones also applies for a loan at Thirteenth National Bank. He is told that the bank will not give him a loan because it has stopped granting loans to anyone. Jones checks around, and discovers that while his friends named Smith, Brown, and Green have been granted loans, no one named Jones has been granted loans. Do the Jones's have any remedy?

4. Scott owes Larry $1,000. Larry hires a debt collection agency to obtain the $1,000. The agency calls Scott in the middle of the night for two consecutive weeks.

When Scott complains, he is told "to pay up or shut up." Does Scott have a remedy?

5. Sally owes the Pay or Else Finance Company $5,000. When she is late with her payments, the company places an advertisement in the local paper which lists her debt amount and Sally's home phone number. Does Sally have any remedy?

6. Fred is the director of consumer affairs for the state of South Government. He walks into Pop's Diner in order to have a piece of "homemade pie" as advertised in the window of the diner. While eating lunch, Fred notices three boxes of pies brought into Pop's. What should Fred do?

7. Tony decides he is unhappy with the local electric service. He gets a group of investors to put up some money and begins to contact some potential customers. Before he puts up lines he comes to you for advice. What do you tell him?

8. Hilton goes to the Twenty-fourth National Bank for a loan. The bank officer sets out the terms of the loan in a manner which Hilton can not understand. Does he have any legal remedy?

Chapter 30

International Business Transactions

■ Because every nation is a sovereign, each country may establish its own laws. In addition, entities within a nation may have their own laws and customs. In the United States, each state has its own laws, rules, and regulations.

■ As a result, there is no "true" international law. There are treaties, conventions, and agreements, but one must conduct international business with an understanding of the potential complexity of such transactions.

■ Some of the hazards associated with international business include the possibility of not being paid, different legal standards, changes in currency rates, potential expropriation of property by a foreign government, "creeping" expropriation, requirements for domestic ownership, governmental changes, and changes in popular attitudes toward foreign businesses.

■ Foreign businesses may partially protect themselves through their contract with the other party. They may stipulate the location, which will determine the applicable law, the currency to be utilized, the method of payment, and other factors relating to the transaction.

■ The General Agreement on Tariffs and Trade (GATT) was created shortly after World War II in order to promote the goals of economic development and free trade. GATT permits each country that is a party to the agreement to be treated by the other parties as a most favored nation. There are exceptions relating to a country's national security, economic development, or the protection of its agricultural economy which permit it to impose tariffs on another country's exports.

SOVEREIGNTY

Many people discuss the concept of international law or international lawyers without understanding that there is no one place where one can find international law. Each nation has **sovereignty,** which means that it may promulgate its own laws without regard to the international community.

The United States and most English-speaking countries throughout the world base their law on a combination of statutes and judges' decisions. They have a long tradition of private ownership of property and freedom of contracts.

As a result, these countries have a sufficient legal infrastructure to support a free-enterprise economy. Businesspersons can conduct their transactions with reasonable assurance as to the laws that undergird their transactions. While they may complain about excessive taxation or governmental regulation, they know that their property will not be seized without due process and that contracts will be enforced.

The culture that American businesspeople take for granted may not exist in other countries. For example, earning money in business is highly valued in the United States. It is less valued in other nations. In England, money is valued if it is inherited. It is less valued if it is earned in business.

The tradition of common law and free enterprise do not exist in many countries. When the Communist regime in Eastern Europe collapsed, many people believed there would be a flourishing of private enterprise in these lands. But these nations lack legal infrastructure to support free enterprise. As a result, the common experiences and laws that guide Western businesspeople are not yet available in these countries.

Management training and other skills are needed in Eastern Europe. New legal concepts, forms, and contracts are also needed. In the United States, free enterprise is supported by highly structured systems to provide capital for new and existing companies.

A firm's officers can seek out this capital from a variety of financial institutions, which might include a bank, savings and loan association, or credit union. If they want to obtain capital from the public, they can issue stocks or bonds within well-regulated financial markets. Similar institutions do not exist within the Eastern European countries. In addition, facilitators of these transactions, such as legal, accounting, and financial experts, are not common in these nations.

Similarly, there are no comparable legal or financial structures in the Middle East. The cultures of many of these societies are based on the principles of Islam. These may not be consistent with the concepts of a free-market society and private wealth. They often regard Western society as decadent, with values that are contrary to a belief in Allah. This makes it difficult to conduct many transactions that we take for granted in the United States and other Western countries.

Societies in the Pacific Rim are often quite different than our own. While Japan is a thriving society based on principles of free enterprise and democracy, mainland China remains a communist-controlled country with a rapidly growing free-enterprise sector. Other Pacific Rim countries have surging economies that are producing businesses highly competitive with those in the United States.

But, these countries often have traditions of philosophies that are quite different from those found in the West. Teachings of Eastern philosophies emphasize harmony, "saving face," and trust. This is often quite different than the American "let's get the job done now" approach. While American businesspeople often want to sign contracts during the first meeting, Far Eastern businesspeople want to spend considerable time getting to know their Western counterparts. Only after a period of assessing their trading partners' "trustworthiness" will they feel comfortable conducting business together.

Because customs, religious teachings, and philosophies tend to form the basis for a nation's laws, these other countries have developed different laws than those in the United States. There is no international agency that can override a nation's internal laws. The sovereignty of a nation is complete. Differences in laws are a difficulty when doing business in other countries.

Because the laws are different in foreign countries, an American businessperson might believe that she would not receive a fair hearing in the courts of another country. One way of dealing with this problem is to place a clause in the contract stating the forum for resolving disputes relating to the transaction.

> Mike wants to sell his product to Max, who is in another country. But, he is worried about the differences in the laws and how the courts might resolve any disputes.
>
> Mike inserts a clause in the contract stating that all matters relating to the contract will be resolved according to the laws of the State of New Jersey. The contract further provides that all disputes will be presented to a commercial arbitrator named by the American Arbitration Association. ▪

In addition to differences in laws, there may also be other differences connected with doing business internationally. Culture differences make international business both rewarding and challenging. In addition to the differences in culture and law, there are other hazards associated with international business. A successful businessperson must know how to cope with these problems.

HAZARDS OF INTERNATIONAL BUSINESS

A major problem in conducting business internationally is getting paid. When one sells goods in another country, one may not know the buyer. One may also have difficulties bringing legal actions and obtaining a remedy.

One way of dealing with the problem of getting paid is to ask the buyer to obtain a **letter of credit**. A letter of credit is an agreement that allows the seller to be paid by a bank. In this way, the bank's credit substitutes for the buyer's, and the seller will be paid. While letters of credit may also be used domestically, they have gained prominence in the area of international transactions. Many large banks have a significant number of people who work with letters of credit.

> Swanson wants to sell 100 crates of widgets to Ada Imi in the country of New Zapland. Swanson has not had any previous dealings with Ada.
>
> He is not certain that Imi will pay him. He asks Ada to obtain a letter of credit. Ada Imi goes to the First Bank of New Zapland and obtains a letter of credit. The letter provides that the bank will pay Swanson upon the delivery of the crates. When the crates arrive, the bank will make the payment. It will then debit Ada Imi's account for the amount paid to Swanson. ▪

Banks charge a fee to issue a letter of credit, which can prove very profitable for them. Letters of credit can present complicated questions in terms of payments. The bank issuing the document has a fiduciary responsibility to carefully check the documents associated with the transaction. The bank may be held liable for an improper payment to a seller.

Another risk of doing business internationally is the differences in currency. One issue may be which currency will apply. The applicable currency should be placed in the contract. For example, the contract might specifically state that the purchase price will be paid in U.S. dollars.

Another issue is whether the seller will receive the proper purchase price if the value of either the domestic or foreign currency should fluctuate. The seller could specify in the contract payment in a particular currency. She could also arrange to buy currency futures that act as a hedge against currency fluctations. This process is known as **arbitrage.**

Another risk is that relating to a foreign country's government taking all or a portion of a business. This is known as **expropriation** or **"creeping" expropriation**.

■ ABC Corporation owns a foreign subsidiary in the country of Mulaberg. After seven years of operation, a new government takes control of Mulaberg. The government demands that ABC Corporation sell 30 percent of its subsidiary to domestic nationals (residents of Mulaberg) and give another 30 percent to the government. ■

■ Same facts except that the government demands ABC Corporation sell 50 percent to domestic nationals. ■

■ Same facts except that the new government seizes the entire subsidiary. This is called nationalizing the company. ■

One can obtain insurance against foreign expropriation, but it is quite expensive. There are other methods of doing business in other countries that are less risky. Two of these would be to license a product or to engage in a joint venture.

A license allows another person or company to use, make, or sell a product depending on how the license is worded. One can grant a company a license to sell a product in a particular country. The license may be exclusive or nonexclusive. This permits one to do business in another country with limited risk.

■ NZY Corporation has a product it would like to sell in the country of Hackswood. NZY Corporation is worried about the political stability in Hackswood. It decides to grant a license to Hackyhut to sell its foot-long hot dogs. In this way, it does not need to open any operations in Hackswood.

   NZY Corporation may grant a license to Hackyhut to sell the hot dogs. The license can be exclusive or nonexclusive. An exclusive license would give Hackyhut the sole right to sell foot-long hot dogs in Hackswood. A nonexclusive license would allow NZY Corporation to grant licenses to other sellers as well. NZY Corporation may want to grant licenses that carve up Hackswood into different regions. ■

The granting of licenses allows the company to earn profits while minimizing risk. The granting of a license does not require the building of a plant or the establishment of a subsidiary. There are no up-front expenditures or threats of having one's assets seized by a foreign government.

Another method of reducing risks is to establish a joint venture with another entity. A joint venture is similar to a partnership except it is for a shorter period of time and for a limited purpose. It permits one to do business while involving another party in the sales of the product.

■ LBD Corporation wants to sell its umbrellas in the country of Hotsun. It establishes a joint venture with Shade Incorporated. LBD Corporation will supply the parts and Shade will assemble the parts and sell the umbrellas.

The agreement further provides that the two parties will split the profits equally. In addition, the agreement also provides that both parties will conduct a review of the contract after one year and that either party may withdraw from the joint venture at that time. ■

A joint venture permits the parties to share skills and resources. In addition, the junior partner is usually a domestic company of that nation. This reduces problems associated with potential expropriation or nationalization of a company's resources.

Another risk relates to different languages and customs. One can buy in any language, but one has to learn to sell in the language of the buyer. This means that one should probably be prepared to place the contract in the buyer's language. Many countries teach their students languages other than English. Few Americans know a language other than their native tongue.

These differences can lead to changes in attitude toward foreign businesses in certain countries. American companies may view their activities as filling consumer needs, creating jobs, and building needed capital. Domestic residents may view the same activities as foreign exploitation of their labor and resources.

One way of overcoming negative attitudes would be to involve domestic residents in the business activities as much as possible. Licensing activities and joint ventures are ways to accomplish this objective. This permits residents of the country to share in the profits and to participate in the business. It also promotes greater sensitivity to the needs, concerns, and attitudes of the local residents.

International Business Law

Although each country is a sovereign and has its own rules and laws, there are a series of laws and regulations that make up international law. International law has become a mix of domestic law, the law of foreign countries, treaties, agreements, and the rules of international organizations.

Treaties with another country or countries are a major source of international law for citizens of the United States. A treaty is negotiated by the country's executive branch, and approved by Congress. The president proposes treaties, but they must be approved by two-thirds of the Senate. A treaty becomes part of the law of the United States and supersedes all other U.S. law except the U.S. Constitution. While American history has been filled with conflicts between the president and Congress about treaties with foreign policy implications, many treaties relate to international trade and commerce.

Executive agreements between the president and other heads of state are another source of law. Often these agreements establish guidelines for international trading among countries and businesspersons. These agreements do not need to be approved by Congress.

A third source of "law" is the practices, customs, and traditions that develop in commerce. Courts may discuss in their decisions principles of fairness and justice which have developed in civilized nations. In the United States, every contract has an implied warranty to act in good faith. Many other western countries have similar concepts of fairness and equity which become part of the "law."

■ Jones and Smith have a contract under which Smith has an "exclusive right" to sell chocolate-covered eggs on the East Coast of the United States. The eggs will be made by Jones.

Despite the contract, Jones supplies a very large number of chocolate eggs to a company in Canada which sells the eggs to customers on the U.S. East Coast. This would be a breach of the implied covenant of good faith between Jones and Smith, and would be a breach of contract. ■

Similar principles exist in other countries. This is particularly true in countries that were influenced by the U.S. presence after World War II. The widespread adoption of the Uniform Commercial Code (UCC) in the United States provided a model law for many other countries.

Sale of Goods

Goods are tangible, movable items. They are commonly sold in interstate and international commerce. Merchants are individuals and organizations who regularly deal in goods of that kind. In the vast majority of states, the sale of goods is governed by the UCC.

Unlike the common law of contracts which developed over the centuries on a case-by-case basis, the UCC is a series of statutory provisions designed to create a contract and to maintain it. The UCC provides for a series of gap-filling provisions that will provide the major terms of the contract if the parties do not reach agreement on these terms.

The UCC is similar to the civil law codes found in many countries. For example, in Germany, the principles relating to the formation of contracts are set forth in statutes rather than court decisions. Many of the major concepts are the same, and an American businessperson would feel comfortable with the German code. German civil codes also state principles of good faith and fair dealing. This would prohibit unethical business practices, and is similar to the American tradition of prohibiting unconscionable contracts. It is also similar to the implied covenants of good faith.

Under the UCC, a party is excused from performance if circumstances have changed such that the performance has become commercially impractical. This contemplates excusing performance if circumstances have been changed by external causes in a way that was reasonably unforeseeable.

■ Symms has a contract to supply Gottfried with 100 crates of widgets on October 10th. On October 9th, the first earthquake ever recorded hits the area and destroys all the roads between Symms and Gottfried. This would be an example of a change in circumstances that would make performance commercially impracticable. ■

The German Civil Code has similar provisions that would excuse performance under circumstances that would make it impractible. Other countries with civil codes have provisions that are more similar to the older American common law standard of impossibility. This required an even higher standard of difficulty in order to excuse performance.

At both common law and under the UCC, the purpose of legal remedies was to place a party injured by a breach of contract in the same position he would have been if the contract had been performed. This allowed both monetary and equitable relief.

■ Haroldson agrees to buy a guitar owned by Jones. If Jones does not perform the contract, Haroldson will be entitled to money damages from Jones.

If Haroldson purchases another guitar of similar quality after the breach, she will be entitled to money damages equal to the difference between the price of the purchased guitar minus the contract price.

If the guitar was unique because it was once owned by Elvis Presley, Haroldson may obtain a decree of specific performance which will compel Jones to sell her the guitar. ■

The same remedies exist in the German Civil Code. In addition, it allows greater use of the remedy of specific performance. Under American law, this equitable decree will be granted only in cases of unique or specially manufactured goods. Under German law, it will be granted to enforce contracts for routine goods.

Other cultures have concepts relating to contracts similar to those found in the United States. For example, most legal systems prefer contracts to be placed in writing. In addition, the quantity involved is the most critical term in the writing. The writing provides the necessary evidence that a contract actually existed.

Dispute resolutions exist in all countries but they are often handled differently. In the United States, parties to a contract may call for their attorneys to resolve the dispute. In the Middle East, the parties may wish to ensure that their actions are in accord with the laws of Islam. In Japan, the parties will try to work out matters amicably with a view to maintaining their business relationship in the future.

International Contract Law

The Convention on Contracts for the International Sale of Goods (CISG) treaty was an attempt to blend the laws relating to contracts from a variety of differing legal systems into a standardized international sales contract. It became part of the U.S. federal law in 1988. It applies to the sale of goods, but not to services or other contracts.

The CISG leaves some areas of contracts to the law of the individual nation. For example, the validity of the contract and the extent of product liability is left to national law. The CISG does create rules for the formation of the contract and for the obligations of the parties. These rules are similar although somewhat different from the provisions of UCC which govern the sale of goods in the vast majority of American states.

Under the UCC, the seller has the obligation to deliver goods that conform to the contract. Under the CISG, the seller also has the obligation to deliver any necessary documentation. This reflects the special importance of documents of title with respect to international sales transactions.

The CISG and the UCC have similar warranties extending from the seller of the goods to the buyer. These include a warranty of merchantability which guarantees that the goods will be fit for the purposes for which they were purchased. The CISG also provides for warranties of fitness for a particular purpose and for other specific warranties.

Both the UCC and CISG provide for monetary damages to be awarded in the event of a breach of contract. In addition, both the UCC and the CISG provide for the remedy of specific performance. The UCC permits the remedy to be granted only in cases involving "unique goods," whereas the CISG is more liberal in granting the remedy.

Resolving Disagreements

In any contract, there are bound to be disagreements between the parties. The issue for international lawyers, businesspersons, or managers is how to resolve them while maintaining the business relationship. While these issues exist in domestic disputes, there are some additional issues which relate to international business.

Among these include questions regarding choices of law and the forum for resolving these disputes.

> American Amanda sells 1,000 crates of widgets to French Frankie. There is a dispute about the contract's provisions. This immediately raises questions about which law will be used to resolve the dispute. The parties could utilize American law, French law, or some other law. Both parties will be concerned about receiving a fair trial, the production of witnesses, travel, and other factors. ∎

In this example, parties could try to choose a specific legal forum for hearing the case. However, they are likely to have significant disagreements about which forum will be chosen. In addition, courts will not render advisory opinions or take cases unless there is a specific dispute. As a result, it may not be satisfactory to select a specific legal forum.

Furthermore, using the court system can be very expensive. In addition, many courts are not comfortable deciding cases with complications relating to the application of international law. Because of these problems, many parties have begun to search for alternative methods for resolving disputes.

Two of the most common are **mediation** and **arbitration**. Both of these dispute-resolution methods require the two parties to agree to submit contract disputes to a third party. Usually the parties agree to do so in their initial agreement. When a dispute occurs, the parties can submit it to either a mediator or an arbitrator.

Mediation is a process in which the mediator attempts to work out disagreements between the parties. The mediator studies the documents and any claims of the parties, and then suggests possible solutions. Mediation may take an extended period of time and still reach no conclusion. Often, a mediator can only suggest solutions. If the parties do not want to accept them, the dispute continues.

Arbitration is different. It recognizes that the parties may need help in reaching closure with respect to disputes. Arbitration may allow the arbitrator to impose a solution on the parties.

> Harry and Mary have a dispute about the quality of the goods subject to an international sales contract. The dispute also goes to the proper amount of the sales price. They choose Arty Aaronson to act as arbitrator.
> Both Mary and Harry submit proposals to Arty. Under binding arbitration, Arty could select one of these proposals or develop one of his own. The decision of the arbitrator would bind the parties. ■

The parties could insert an arbitration clause in the contract which would compel them to submit disputes to an arbitrator. Arbitrators should have some legal or business training. While many are lawyers, they could also be businesspersons or professionals with a particular area of expertise.

Arbitration has the advantage of being faster than court proceedings. In addition, there is less publicity associated with arbitration. Court cases are open to the public, and could lead to the disclosure of embarrassing or secret information.

The American Arbitration Association provides alternative dispute resolution within the United States. The International Chamber of Commerce located in Paris provides arbitration services for International disputes. Other organizations that supply similar services include the London Court of International Arbitration, the Stockholm Chamber of Commerce, and the International Center for the Settlement of Investment Disputes.

Some parties to a contract have begun to employ "private" judges to resolve disputes. This is part of the "privitization" trend which has swept much of the world. Rather than waiting for years to have the case heard in a government court, the parties are hiring "judges" to resolve their cases. Usually, these judges are older attorneys who have either been judges or have practiced extensively in that field.

None of these alternate dispute-resolution techniques will have much practical value unless the judgments are capable of being enforced. Only courts sanctioned by the government can compel enforcement. In order to make these techniques effective, the parties must agree to comply with the decision. Another alternative is to provide that the decision is immediately enforceable in the courts if not carried out by the parties. This is less satisfactory because many advantages of the alternative dispute-resolution techniques will be lost.

GENERAL AGREEMENT ON TARIFFS AND TRADE

The General Agreement on Tariffs and Trade (GATT) was signed shortly after World War II. Its purpose was to promote free trade among the various signatories to the agreement. This was based on the widely held belief that the various tariffs that had emerged following World War I were one underlying cause of the war. If a country was unable to sell its goods in other markets, they might be tempted to seize the markets through military conquest.

The various signatories established an agreement whereby each country would treat the others as a most-favored nation. This means that it will be exempt from many tariffs that would be imposed on the goods of other nations.

The major exemptions to this prohibition on tariffs include the ability to protect a country's national defense capability, to promote a country's economic development, or to protect a country's agricultural economy. These exceptions have allowed certain countries to take advantage of the agreement. The production of steel can usually be cited as essential to an economy's growth and its national security. The acquisition of natural resources could also fit into this category.

A country's agricultural products are also exempt from the restrictions against tariffs. This was intended to permit a country to avoid having its food supply become dependent on foreign exports. This would place a country at a severe disadvantage in times of war and of peace. Other countries would be in a position to blackmail the dependent country. It is difficult to bargain when one does not have have enough to eat.

Many people have argued that Japan has used this exemption to protect itself from the import of American farm products. This is a serious point of contention because American farmers would like to be able to export products, such as beef, to Japan. This would be a profitable venture for U.S. farmers and would help reduce the U.S. trade deficit with Japan.

One of the principles of GATT is to prohibit dumping, which is the practice of exporting large amounts of goods to another country at extremely low prices. This is done in order to unfairly capture a larger share of a country's market in certain goods.

A second principle is to prevent unfair subsidies from being given to businesses that engage in substantial exporting. These subsidies could take the form of payments, loans, tax deferrals, or other subsidies that would give a business an unfair advantage over other firms.

In the United States, neither federal nor state governments have been willing to subsidize businesses. However, this is a common practice in countries that urge closer cooperation between government and business. The lack of subsidization has led to complaints from American companies that foreign firms are competing unfairly. The Department of Commerce may assess countervailing duties if unfair practices such as dumping are discovered.

International Business Rights

Copyrights represent ownership rights in cultural or artistic works. In the United States, a copyright will extend for the life of the author plus 50 years. Given the rapid growth of worldwide communications and technology, these property rights will assume greater importance in future years. For example, a song recorded in a small village in one country may be an international success within 24 hours.

Business in Relation to the Government and the International Environment

There is no international copyright, although the Berne Convention for the Protection of Literary and Artistic Works provides some degree of protection for holders of copyrights. Signatory nations agree to give holders of copyrights the same national protection for authors in any member country. For example, a foreign author publishing a copyrighted work in one country will have the same degree of protection as a domestic author.

Patents give someone who has created an invention or a scientific process the exclusive right to manufacture or use it for a certain period of time. In the United States, a patent will last for 17 years. Again, patents are national property rights. A person holding a patent in one country does not have the automatic right to assert it in another nation.

The laws relating to patents differ from country to country. This reflects the rapid growth of high technology in certain areas. Some nations will grant patents for new scientific processes, but others will not.

The Paris Convention for the Protection of Industrial Property provides international protection for holders of patents. The holder of a patent in one signatory nation will be treated the same as a domestic holder.

A trademark is a word, symbol, or mark that designates a product. A legally protected trademark gives the holder the exclusive right to use the mark to sell the specific product covered. Trademark protection is a matter of the law of each country. Some nations will protect certain types of marks while others will not. Trademark holders must still rely on the law of each country. However, the Vienna Trademark Registration Treaty and the Madrid Agreement allow for simplified filings for trademark protection. The applicant may receive protection in the countries he or she designates.

NORTH AMERICAN FREE TRADE AGREEMENT

Congress has recently approved the North American Free Trade Agreement (NAFTA), which will create a free trade zone from Canada through the United States to Mexico. It should be a competitive counterforce to the European Community and the Asian nations.

The passage of NAFTA presents both problems and opportunities for businesspersons. Some industries will suffer dislocations while others should prosper. High-technology and information-driven businesses ought to be able to expand their operations across national boundaries. Other businesses which rely heavily on unskilled labor may find it more difficult to compete in a rapidly changing and fluid economy.

Definitions Reviewed

Sovereignty is the ability of a nation to promulgate its own laws.

A **letter of credit** is an agreement under which a bank agrees to pay the purchase price.

Arbitrage is the use of currency futures as a hedge against fluctuations in the value of currency.

Expropriation is a government's taking of all or a portion of a business.

Mediation is the use of a third party to help resolve disputes between parties.

Arbitration is a procedure that allows an arbitrator to rule on a dispute between parties. A decision may be binding or nonbinding.

Core Concepts Reviewed

- Each country is a sovereign entity and has the power to establish its own laws and regulations. There is no international law to which all nations adhere.

- International law is derived from treaties, conventions, agreements, and national customs.

- Some of the hazards associated with doing business internationally include not being paid, expropriation of assets, changing attitudes toward foreign businesses, and demands that the local government or residents help run the business or establish rules with respect to its operation.

- International businesspeople have developed some mechanisms for dealing with these risks. A letter of credit is a guarantee by a bank that a seller will be paid upon the shipment of the appropriate goods and documents. People conducting business internationally may also obtain insurance that helps protect against expropriation or creeping expropriation of assets.

- People conducting business internationally can also reduce their risk by licensing their products for sale in other countries or by engaging in joint ventures with people in foreign countries.

- The General Agreement on Tariffs and Trade (GATT) is an agreement that attempts to reduce the level of tariffs and stimulate trade among signatory nations. The exceptions to the agreement have allowed some countries to build certain segments of their foreign export business at the expense of other nations.

Questions

1. What does the concept of "sovereignty" mean to "international law"?

2. What is a letter of credit?
3. What purpose does a letter of credit serve?
4. What is expropriation? What impact does it have on a person doing business internationally?
5. What protection can an international business person obtain against expropriation?
6. What is a licensing agreement?
7. Name some different types of licensing agreements.
8. What are some advantages for the parties involved in a licensing agreement?
9. What is a joint venture?
10. What is the difference between a joint venture and a partnership?
11. What are some advantages of an international joint venture?
12. What is a copyright? What are some problems associated with its use internationally?
13. What is a patent? Name some problems associated with its use internationally.
14. What is a trademark?
15. What is GATT?
16. What are its purposes?
17. What are some exceptions to the "free trade" purposes of GATT?
18. What is arbitration?
19. What is mediation?
20. What are the differences between the two?
21. How can mediation and arbitration be used in international transactions?
22. What is a decree of specific performance?
23. How does it relate to an international sale of goods?

Problems

1. Watson has a new product that he would like to sell overseas. He would like to market the product in a country that would be a brand-new source of business for him. He has a couple of potential customers in this new country. But, Watson is worried about getting paid, and has come to you for advice. What advice do you give him?

2. Watson was very pleased with your advice. He is now attracting new customers and is concerned about possible disputes that might develop between him and his new customers. Again, he has come to you for advice. He mentions that he would like to have any disputes resolved in accordance with the

laws of the United States.

He would also like to resolve any disputes with a minimum of legal fees. He suggests that lawyers merely tend to make disputes harder to resolve amicably. What advice do you give him?

3. Despite your best efforts, Watson has still managed to get into legal disputes with some customers in other countries who refuse to perform their part of the contract.

   He mentions that he does not want money for breach of contract. Rather, he wants his customers to perform their part of the contract. He mentions that he has some idea as to how this works in the United States, but has no idea about how these remedies work in other countries. He asks you for advice. What do you tell him?

4. Maureen would like to sell her products overseas, but she does not want to begin manufacturing operations in a foreign country. She does know a company that makes and sells similar products.

   She has come to you for advice about how she might proceed. What alternatives do you suggest to her?

5. Maureen grants a license to sell her new chair and sofa deodorizer to Overseas, Inc. However, Overseas, Inc., buys another deodorizer and sells it instead. Maureen's contract provides that disputes may be resolved by the appointment of a mediator.

   You have been appointed as the mediator. Do you have any suggestions for Maureen and Overseas, Inc.?

6. Harold conducts business in a number of foreign countries. He regularly buys goods from foreign merchants. Because of the nature of his own business, he must ensure that the goods are of a certain quality. In some cases, he needs goods for special uses. Harold has come to you for advice about warranties available with respect to the sale of goods internationally. What do you say to him?

7. Jones conducts business in a number of foreign countries. His business runs on a close profit margin because he markets his products based on being the low-cost provider. As a result, the imposition of tariffs by another country would make it difficult for him to maintain his position as a low-cost provider.

   He has heard about the General Agreement on Tariffs and Trade. He wonders if studying its provisions could help him with his business. He has come to you for advice. What do you tell him?

8. Donaldson is a businessperson with operations in both the United States and other countries. He wonders about how the North American Free Trade Agreement will affect his business and the general economic climate in North America.

   Donaldson knows that you have taken some courses which discuss this issue. He would like you to discuss the positives and negatives of the agreement. What do you tell him?

Index